THIS box is 116 years old and literally full of history. It contains a careful account of every transaction on behalf of the Palladium Life Assurance Society—one of the many tributaries that eventually joined the mainstream of the Eagle Star Insurance Company. Between the faded lines of copper-plate handwriting on these musty, yellow documents, we read the mellow story of the Victorian era—age of prosperity, complacency and peace.

The 'Eagle' has many such links with the past. Its roots are sunk deep in history. And it is this rich maturity, coupled with a youthful spirit, that has gained for the 'Eagle' an enviable reputation for helpfulness and friendly efficiency.

EAGLE STAR

INSURANCE COMPANY LTD.

Life, Motor, Accident, Fire, 'All-in', Marine

I THREADNEEDLE STREET · LONDON · EC2

GOING AWAY ?

First check up . . .

Bought my ticket

Bought my seat

Insured myself and my baggage

 you've forgotten to insure
ring up and tell

THE
LIVERPOOL
AND
LONDON
AND
GLOBE

INSURANCE CO., LTD.,

and they will help to ensure
a perfect holiday.

Founded almost 2,000 years ago by the Romans as the headquarters of one of the three legions guarding Britain Chester can justly claim to be " Unique."

The UNIQUE city of

CHESTER

It really has something to suit all tastes both young and old. A beautiful Cathedral, Ancient Buildings, the famous Rows, a complete circuit of mediaeval defensive walls and Roman remains of great historic interest. Boating on the lovely River Dee, Fishing, a large Zoo, Cricket, Tennis, Bowls, Swimming, Theatre, Modern Cinemas and delightful shops, are but a few of the many items of interest and pleasure available.

Annual events include
Race Meeting in May. Regatta (Whitsuntide)
Cheshire Agricultural Show, June.

Write now to the Town Clerk's Department, Dept. 5, Town Hall, Chester, for copy of Official Illustrated Guide. Price 1/6.

*   *   *

FIRST LOCOMOTIVE NAMED PHŒNIX, this picturesque engine was driven by Robert Stephenson Jnr., in the
opening procession of the Liverpool and Manchester Railway
in 1830. By this time, the "Phœnix" had gained nearly a half-
century of experience in the business of giving protection by
insurance.

*Railway spotters should keep a look-out for the present-day
British Railways locomotive No. 45736.*

*   *   *

PHŒNIX ASSURANCE
COMPANY LIMITED
PHŒNIX HOUSE KING WILLIAM ST.
LONDON E·C·4

1782   PROTECTION

8

GUIDE TO LONDON

MINGLE
WITH
THE
MIGHTY
AT
MADAME
TUSSAUD'S
EXHIBITION
(Adjoining Baker Street Station)

OPEN
   WEEKDAYS: NOV. - APRIL   10 A.M. - 6 P.M.
                  MAY - OCT.   10 A.M. - 7 P.M.
   EVERY SATURDAY & SUNDAY 10 A.M. - 7 P.M.

●

ADMISSION 3/-   CHILDREN UNDER 14 1/-
   CHAMBER OF HORRORS 9d. EXTRA.

GUIDE

TO

LONDON

With Large Section Plans of Central London; Map
of London and Twelve Miles Round; Railway
Maps; Main Roads out of London; Hyde
Park and Kensington Gardens, and
Sixteen other Maps and Plans.
Numerous Illustrations.

Fifty-Ninth Edition ('952)

WARD, LOCK & CO., LIMITED
LONDON AND MELBOURNE

MAPS AND PLANS

Printed in Great Britain by
Wyman & Sons, Ltd., London, Fakenham and Reading

CONTENTS

THE WEST END

THE CITY

SOUTH LONDON

THE ENVIRONS OF LONDON

ILLUSTRATIONS

INTRODUCTION

"When a man is tired of London he is tired of life: for there is in London all that life can afford."—DR. JOHNSON.

D R. JOHNSON'S words are, if anything, more true now than when first written; for the centuries-old enlargement of London has continued, and it is continuing at such speed that even those intimately acquainted with the trends and movements of the Metropolis can hardly keep pace with its manifold developments. In this Guide we can attempt only to direct the stranger's footsteps so that in a given period he sees all that is most worth seeing of its streets and buildings, and to allude to just a few of the habits and customs which play so important a part in the life of what Sidney Smith aptly called "The Great Wen." Certainly in no city of ancient or modern days has there been such "fullness of life" as that which crowds the streets of the Metropolis at this period of our history; and if Dr. Johnson were alive to-day we can well believe that he would enjoy the traditional walk down Fleet Street with even more than his accustomed relish.

The Sightseer's London

Although the Metropolis is so vast that it would take the best part of a lifetime to traverse its 10,000 streets, and another lifetime to know intimately every part of the suburbs, the features of interest appealing especially to sightseers are, with few exceptions, confined to a central area, for the most part north of the Thames, measuring roughly some five miles from west to east, and three from north to south. We are far indeed from saying that there is not anything of interest outside this area; but we do say that the visitor, however hardy and determined, who has methodically and conscientiously "done" the orthodox sights, and taken a trip or two by way of relaxation to places like Windsor and Hampton Court, will have little heart or shoe-leather left for Islington and Kilburn, and other places in the "Middle Ring," unless the calls of business or of friendship lure him thither. We have accordingly dealt fully with

9

the West End and the City, and outlined all the principal excursions from London; but the reader who is in search of detailed information respecting suburban dormitories and nurseries must, we fear, be referred to volumes of greater capacity. We have done our best to squeeze a quart—ought we not rather to say a hogshead?—into a pint pot, but something has perforce been spilt in the process.

" From the top of a Bus, Gentlemen "

"The way to see London," said W. E. Gladstone in an oft-quoted remark to some American tourists, "is from the top of a bus—the top of a bus, gentlemen." The advice is no less sound to-day. A shilling or two judiciously invested in bus fares will enable all the main thoroughfares to be seen, with a much wider range of view than is afforded by taxi or car, and there are few better ways of appreciating London's very real traffic problems or of viewing the "tide of faces" which fascinated Heine as it fascinates all.

Local Characteristics

Limitations of space forbid anything like a general survey of London and its various quarters, but the interest of the provincial visitor will certainly be stimulated by remarking that the special aspects of many of the other great towns are reflected here. Thus, the observant will readily discover a commercial Manchester between the General Post Office and the Guildhall, and there is another Liverpool eastward of the Tower; the cathedral towns, with cloisters and closes, deans, canons and choirs, are superbly represented in the City of Westminster; while the Inns of Court, with their "quads" and lawns and stately chapels, are strongly reminiscent of Universities like Oxford and Cambridge.

Certain trades and manufactures are localized, and have been so for many years. The Spitalfields silk-weavers are known all the world over. Clerkenwell is as famous for watch-making as Geneva itself, and the manufacture of jewellery and optical, musical and electrical instruments is almost equally a speciality of that neighbourhood. Lambeth is a rival to North Staffordshire in producing artistic pottery. Southwark is the metropolis of the hop trade; and adjoining Bermondsey tans hides and makes leather for a great part of England. The cabinet-making, French-polishing and upholstering trades have a predilection for Shoreditch, Bethnal Green, and St. Pancras. About Aldgate is clustered the Jewish quarter. In Stepney and Whitechapel

large numbers of men and women are engaged in the tailoring
and dressmaking trades. Marylebone is another important
centre of the same industries. Bootmakers favour Bethnal
Green. A considerable settlement of foreigners, chiefly French
and Italian, is established about Soho, though they seem to be
leaving it for the Charlotte Street quarter, to the north of Oxford
Street. Between Farringdon Road and Gray's Inn Road, to the
north of the wider part of Holborn, is a large Italian community.
The chief markets for tea, corn, wine, and colonial produce are
in Mark and Mincing Lanes. The wholesale fruit trade has its
headquarters at Covent Garden. The wholesale fish merchants
have a natural liking for Billingsgate and its neighbourhood, a
liking which other members of the community do not share.

Dealers in diamonds collect in the neighbourhood of Hatton
Garden and Houndsditch, and carry on a quiet and mysterious
trade. Paternoster Row and the British book trade were nearly
synonymous terms, until the former's destruction in World War
II, and most of the larger publishing houses are now established
in other parts of London, notably in the streets adjoining Covent
Garden. Fleet Street—"the Street of Ink"—is the centre of
newspaper activity, and the adjoining streets and courts are
studded with printing-offices. Upper Thames Street is the centre
of the paper trade. The financial world of London—bankers,
stock and share brokers—for obvious reasons of convenience,
finds its centre round the Bank of England and the Stock
Exchange, Lombard Street, Prince's Street, Lothbury, and the
adjacent thoroughfares being almost literally lined by the headquarters of banks and insurance companies. Other great
mercantile and insurance companies and commercial firms are
represented in Cornhill, Old Broad Street, Moorgate, King
William Street, and other well-known thoroughfares. Shipowners and agents abound near Fenchurch and Leadenhall
Streets, with West End agencies at Cockspur Street, Trafalgar
Square. Just as naturally, barristers and solicitors congregate
in the neighbourhood of the Inns of Court, as we shall see when
we come to Lincoln's Inn, Gray's Inn, and the Temple. The
Strand, Leicester Square, Shaftesbury Avenue, Covent Garden
and St. Martin's Lane are eminently theatrical neighbourhoods;
Wardour Street is the centre of the cinema industry; Pall Mall,
St. James's Street and Piccadilly are "clubland"; painters,
musicians, authors and actors have a liking for St. John's Wood,
Bayswater, Kensington, and Chelsea; consulting physicians
favour Harley Street, Wimpole Street and Devonshire Street;

Great Portland Street, Bond Street and Long Acre are centres of the motor-car trade; and architects and civil engineers must generally be sought in Westminster, especially Victoria Street.

HOTELS AND TARIFFS

There are many hotels in London catering for visitors. Some are immense, having upwards of 1,000 bedrooms, and there are a considerable number of smaller establishments. Even so, at all times, available accommodation is taxed to the utmost. Bomb-damage and requisitioning have made serious inroads on accommodation and visitors, wherever possible, should make all necessary arrangements and reservations well in advance. It must be understood that the tariffs stated in the following pages are inserted rather as an indication of the grade of the various establishments than as a means of making even an approximate estimate of the cost of a visit. As a further indication of the grade of hotel we give immediately after the name the number of bedrooms. *In all cases inquiry should be made beforehand as to terms*. The list makes no pretence of being exhaustive.

In the following list Private and Temperance Hotels are distinguished by an asterisk (*). *Boarding Houses* are principally to be found in the Bloomsbury quarter, but there are many others in the attractive outer suburbs, such as Hampstead, Bayswater, Dulwich, etc. Advertisements of furnished apartments will be found in the daily newspapers.

Hotels, etc., in the Bloomsbury Quarter

(Plan I, I. K. L. 6 and 7)

[ABBREVIATIONS: *R.,* bedroom; *b.,* breakfast; *l.,* luncheon; *t.,* tea; *d.,* dinner; *g.,* garage; *fr.,* from; *temp.,* temperance.]

*Alexandra, 22, Bedford Place, W.C.1.

Ambassadors (100 rooms), 10, Upper Woburn Place, W.C.1: *R.* and *b.,* 18/6 single; 37/- double; *l.,* 4/6; *t.,* 2/-; *d.,* 6/9.

Bedford (248 rooms), 83-95, Southampton Row, W.C.1.

Bedford Corner (38 rooms), 11, Bayley St., W.C.1.: *R.* and *b.,* 22/6.

Bonnington (230 rooms), Southampton Row.

Connaught, Carlos Place, W.1.

Cosmo (130 rooms), Southampton Row.

County (175 rooms), 5-9, Upper Woburn Place, W.C.1. *R.* and *b.,* 17/6 single; 35/- double; *l.,* 4/-; *d.,* 6/6.

*Cranston's Ivanhoe (300 rooms), Bloomsbury Street, W.C.1: *R.* and *b.,* 19/6 single; 36/- double; *l.,* fr. 3/6; *t.,* 2/-; *d.,* fr. 5/-.

*Cranston's Kenilworth (200 rooms), Great Russel Street, W.C.

*Cranston's Waverley (112 rooms), 132, Southampton Row, W.C.1.

Endsleigh (200 rooms), 15, Endsleigh Gardens, W.C.1, near Euston Station.

Euston (140 rooms) (British Railways): *R.* and *b.,* fr. 27/6 single; fr. 47/6 double; *l.,* 8/-; *t.,* 3/-; *d.,* 10/6.

Gower (90 rooms), Euston Sq., N.W.1.

Grafton (150 rooms), Tottenham Court Road, W.1.

[ABBREVIATIONS: *R.*, bedroom; *b.*, breakfast; *l.*, luncheon; *t.*, tea; *d.*, dinner; *g.*, garage; *fr.*, from; *temp.*, temperance.]

Great Northern (British Railways), (68 rooms), King's Cross, N.1.

***Harley House**, 15, Bernard St., W.C.1

Imperial (650 rooms), Russell Square, W.C.: *R.* and *b.*, 21/– single; 38/– double; *l.*, 5/–; *t.*, 1/6; *d.*, 7/6.

Kingsley (180) rooms, 36 and 38, Bloomsbury Way, W.C.1.

Montague, 42, Montague Street, Russell Square, W.C.1.

Mostyn, Portman Street, W.1.

National (465 rooms), 38–51, Bedford Way, W.C.1.

Palace (250 rooms), Bloomsbury Street, W.C.1.

***Premier** (114 rooms), Russell Square.

Red Court, Bedford Place, Russell Square, W.C.1: *R.* and *b.*, 21/–; *l.*, 4/6; *t.*, 1/6; *d.*, 6/6.

Royal (777 rooms), Woburn Place, W.C.: *R.* and *b.*, 16/6 single; 33/– double; *l.*, 4/–; *t.*, 1/6; *d.*, 6/6.

Russell (350 rooms), Russell Square, W.C.: *R.* and *b.*, 25/– single; 49/– double; *l.*, 7/6; *t.*, 3/–; *d.*, 7/6.

***St. Donat's** (14 rooms), 9, Taviton Street, W.C.1: *R.* and *b.*, 14/6 single; 29/– double. (*private*).

Shaftesbury, Monmouth Street.

Tavistock, Tavistock Square, W.C.1.

***Thackeray** (200 rooms), 52–57, Gt. Russell Street, W.C.

***Warwick House**, Great Russell Street, W.C.1.

***West Central** (64 rooms), 101, Southampton Row, W.C.: (*temp.*).

***White Hall**, Guilford Street, W.C.1; Bloomsbury Square, W.C.1.

Hotels in the West End

(Piccadilly, Oxford Street, Kensington, Bayswater, etc.)

Alexander (75 rooms), 35–39, Queen's Gardens Court, W.2.

Almond's, Clifford Street, Bond Street.

Bailey's (200 rooms), 140, Gloucester Road, S.W.7: *R.* and *b.*, fr. 25/– single; fr. 50/– double; *l.*, 6/–; *t.*, 2/6; *d.*, 8/6·

***Balmoral** (120 rooms), 37, Queen's Gate Gardens, S.W.7.

Berkeley, 77, Piccadilly, W.1.

Berners (220 rooms), Berners Street, W.1.

Bolton Mansions (80 rooms), South Kensington.

Burlington, 27, Palace Court, W.2.

Cadogan (80 rooms), 75, Sloane Street.

Cadogan Court, 34–9 Queen's Gate Gardens, S.W.7: *R.* and *b.*, 22/6; *l.*, 5/–; *t.*, 2/–; *d.*, 6/–.

    Boarding terms: 35/– per day; 63/– per week-end.

Cavendish (80 rooms), 81, Jermyn Street, Piccadilly.

Claridge's (200 rooms), Brook Street, W.

Connaught (92 rooms), Carlos Place, Grosvenor Square, W.

Cumberland (1,000 rooms), Marble Arch, W.

De Vere (100 rooms), 48–50, Hyde Park Gate, and De Vere Gardens, W. *R.* and *b.*, 30/– single; 60/– double; *l.*, 8/6; *t.*, 3/–; *d.*, 10/6. Plus 10 per cent surcharge.

    Boarding terms: 45/– per day.

Dorchester (304 rooms), Park Lane, W.1;

Durrant's (80 rooms), 26–32, George Street, Manchester Square, W.1.

Fischer's, 11, Clifford Street, W.

Fleming's (47 rooms), 9–10, Half-Moon Street, and 41, Clarges Street, Piccadilly, W.: *R.* fr. 30/– single, fr. 45/– double; *l.*, 12/6; *t.*, 3/–; *d.*, 21/–.

Ford's (70 rooms), 13–16, Manchester Street, W.: *R.* and *b.*, fr. 21/– single; fr. 42/– double; *l.*, 7/6; *t.*, 2/–; *d.*, 7/6.

Garland's (50 rooms), 15–17, Suffolk Street, Pall Mall.

Garrick, 3–5, Charing Cross Road.

Great Western Royal (179 rooms) (British Railways), Paddington Station, W.

Grosvenor House (475 rooms): *R.* and *b.*, tariff on application; *l.*, 11/6; *t.*, 3/6, (4/6 week-ends); *d.*, 14/6; *g.*, fr. 3/6.

Hans Crescent (120 rooms), 1, Hans Crescent, Sloane Street, S.W.

[ABBREVIATIONS: *R.*, bedroom; *b.*, breakfast; *l.*, luncheon; *t.*, tea; *d.*, dinner; *g.*, garage; *fr.*, from; *temp.*, temperance.]

Hyde Park (172 rooms), 66, Knightsbridge, S.W.

Kensington, 1, Russell Gardens, Kensington, W.14.

*Lexham Gardens**, 112, Lexham Gardens, W.8.

*Linden Hall** (70 rooms), 131, Cromwell Road, S.W.

Mapleton (100 rooms), 39, Coventry Street, W.1: *R.* and *b.*, 20/– single; 36/– double.

May Fair (340 rooms), Berkeley Square, W.

New Norfolk (60 rooms), 25, London Street, and 2, Norfolk Square, Paddington.

Oddenino's (100 rooms), Regent Street, W.1: *R.* and *b.*, 35/– single; 55/– double; *l.*, fr. 7/6; *t.*, 3/–; *d.*, fr. 10/6.

*Orchard** (72 rooms), Portman Street, W.1: *R.* and *b.*, 19/– single; 38/– double; *l.*, 5/–; *t.*, 2/–; *d.*, 6/–.
   Boarding terms: 27/– per day.

Park Gate (over Lancaster Gate Tube Station), 57, Bayswater Road, W.2.

Park Lane (400 rooms), Piccadilly, W.

Park View (45 rooms), Hyde Park Corner, S.W.1

*Pembridge Gardens**, Notting Hill, W.2.

Phoenix, 19, Prince s Street, Cavendish Square. W.

Piccadilly (300 rooms), Piccadilly and Regent Street.

Prince of Wales, 16–18. De Vere Gardens, W.8 (120 rooms).

*Quebec** (100 rooms), Bryanston Street, W.1.

Regent Palace (1,119 rooms), close to Piccadilly Circus.

Ritz, Piccadilly, W.1.

Rodney Hotel (80 rooms), 28, De Vere Gardens, W.8.

Royal Court (100 rooms), 8–10, Sloane Square, S.W.: *R.* and *b.*, 25/– single; 47/6 double; *l.*, 6/6; *t.*, 2/6; *d.*, 8/6.

Royal Palace, Kensington High Street.

South Kensington (120 rooms), Queen's Gate Terrace, S.W.: *R.* and *b.*, fr. 22/6 single; fr. 45/– double; *l.*, 5/6; *t.*, 2/–; *d.*, 7/6.
   Boarding terms: fr. 32/6 per day; 227/6 per week.

*Tudor Court** (100 rooms), Cromwell Road, S.W.7.

*Vanderbilt** (120 rooms), 76–86, Cromwell Road, S.W.7.

Vandyke, Cromwell Road. S.W.

Washington, 6, Curzon Street, W.1: *R.* fr. 45/–; double fr. 60/–; *l.*, 12/6; *t.*, 3/6; *d*, à la carte.

*Westbourne**, Westbourne Terrace, W.2.

White's (70 rooms), 90–92, Lancaster Gate, W.1.

York, Berners Street, W.1.

Hotels in and about the Strand

(Plan II, K. and L. 8.)

Charing Cross (British Railways) (250 rooms).

Craven (64 rooms), 43–46, Craven Street, Strand.

Howard (200 rooms), Norfolk Street: *R.*, fr. 22/6 single; fr. 45/– double; *l.*, 8/6 or à la Carte; *t.*, 3/–; *d.*, 10/6, or à la Carte.

Norfolk (70 rooms), 30–32. Surrey Street, Strand: *R.* and *b.*, 21/– single; 42/– double; *l.*, 6/–; *t.*, 1/9; *d.*, 6/–.

*Opera** (33 rooms), Bow Street, Strand.

Savoy, Strand.

Strand Palace (900 rooms), Strand.

Waldorf (400 rooms), Aldwych, Strand.

York, 80–82, Waterloo Road, S.E.1.

Victoria and Westminster

(Plan II, H. I. and K. 10 and 11.)

(ABBREVIATIONS: *R.*, bedroom; *b.*, breakfast; *l.*, luncheon; *t.*, tea; *d.*, dinner; *g.*, garage; *fr.*, from; *temp.*, temperance.)

Belgravia (30 rooms), 84 & 86, Belgrave Road, S.W.1: *R.* and *b.*, fr. 18/6 single; fr. 37/6 double; *l.*, 5/6; *t.*, 2/-; *d.*, 6/6.
  Boarding terms: fr. 30/- per day; 57/6 per week-end; fr. 189/- per week.

Goring (100 rooms), Grosvenor Gardens, S.W.1: *R.* and *bath*, 27/6 single; 50/- double; *l.*, 6/6; *t.*, 2/6; *d.*, 9/6.

Grosvenor (300 rooms), Buckingham Palace Road, S.W.: *R.*, 23/6 single; 44/6 double; *l.*, fr. 7/6; *t.*, 2/6; *d.*, fr. 9/6.

Rubens (150 rooms), Buckingham Palace Road, S.W.1: *R.* and *b.*, 32/6 single; 60/- double; *l.*, 6/6; *t.*, 2/6; *d.*, 8/6.
  Boarding terms: 42/- per day; 294/- per week.

St. James's Court (250 suites), Buckingham Gate, S.W.1: *R.*, *bath*, *sitting-room* and *b.*, 73/6, single; 105/- double; *l.*, 6/6; *t.*, 2/6; *d.*, 8/6.

＊Victoria, 46, Buckingham Palace Road.

Wilton (88 rooms), Victoria (opposite Southern Region Station): *R.* and *b.*, fr. 21/6 single; fr. 42/- double; *l.*, 4/6; *t.*, 2/-; *d.*, 6/-.

City Hotels

(Plans I and II, M. N. O. 7 and 8.)

Brooke House, 19 & 20, Brooke Street, E.C.1.

Great Eastern (190 rooms), Liverpool Street Station, E.C.: *R.* and *b.*, fr. 25/- single; fr. 47/6 double; *l.*, 7/6; *t.*, 3/-; *d.*, 9/6.

Horn Tavern, 31 & 33, Knightrider St. E.C.4.

Victoria, Charterhouse Street, E.C.1.

Three Nuns (70 rooms), adjoining Aldgate Station.

Ye Olde Cock Tavern, 29, Fleet Street, E.C.4.

RESTAURANTS

It may be said of some of the first-class restaurants that they are not so expensive as they look, and humble mortals who are content with a "grill," or other simple dish, will pay little more than they would have to do elsewhere. The numerous establishments of J. Lyons & Co., Ltd., Slaters, Ltd., Aerated Bread Co., Ltd., Express Dairies Co., Ltd., Messrs. Fuller's, and other similar companies supply good and inexpensive meals. The luncheons and dinners served at some of the restaurants in the neighbourhood of Soho are astonishingly good and reasonable in price. A number of restaurants catering specially for their own "nationals"—the Indian, Spanish, Chinese, etc.—are increasingly patronized by British people accustomed to foreign travel or attracted by novel dishes.

In addition to the following, there are the restaurants and grill-rooms attached to the principal hotels, which are generally available to the public, and those provided for the convenience of customers at the large stores and drapery establishments.

A l'Ecu de France, 111, Jermyn Street, S.W.1.
Bagatelle, 1, Mayfair Place.
Boulestin's, 25 Southampton Street, W.C.2.
Café Monico, Piccadilly Circus.
Café Royal, 68, Regent Street.
Carr's, 264, Strand.
Cheshire Cheese, Wine Office Court, Fleet Street.
Comedy, Panton Street, Haymarket.
Corner House, Coventry Street, Piccadilly Circus.
Coventry, 7 and 8, Rupert Street, and 13 and 15, Wardour Street, W.
Criterion, Piccadilly Circus.
Cumberland, Marble Arch, W.
Fischer's, 18, New Bond Street.
Fleming's, 307, Oxford Street.
Frascati, 26–32, Oxford Street.
Hatchett's, Piccadilly.
Holborn, 218, High Holborn.
Hungaria, 14, Regent Street.
Kempinskis, 99, Regent Street.
Kettner's, Romilly Street.
Le Coq d'Or, Stratton Street.

Maison Lyons, Marble Arch, W.1.
Monseigneur, 16, Jermyn Street.
Oddenino's, Regent Street.
Oxford Corner House, Oxford Street.
Pagani's, Gt. Portland Street, W.C.
Pantheon, 83, Wigmore Street, W.1.
Pimms, 3–5, Poultry, E.C.2, etc.
Pinoli's, 17, Wardour Street, and 18 Rupert Street, W.1.
Potomac, 40, Jermyn Street, W.
Prince's, Piccadilly.
Quaglino's, 16, Bury Street, S.W.1.
Regent Palace, Piccadilly Circus.
Reggiori's, opposite King's Cross Station, and 25, Chapel Street, Edgware Road, N.W.1.
Rendezvous, 44, Dean Street, W.
Romano Santi, 50, Greek Street, W.1.
Rule's, 35, Maiden Lane, Strand.
Scotts, 18–20, Coventry Street, W.1.
Simpson's, Strand.
Slater's, various branches.
Strand Corner House.
Trocadero, Shaftesbury Avenue.
Veeraswamys, 99, Regent Street.

The City is noted for old-fashioned taverns, and others with old names but new-fashioned styles. In some a speciality is made of particular dishes on certain days. Luncheon is the speciality of these establishments, which are patronized for the most part by business men.

GRATUITIES.—On the question of the "tip," no hard and fast rules can be laid down, but in Hotels of medium standing, 2s. 6d. per person to the waiter or waitress and about half that sum to the chambermaid is sufficient for a stay of a day or two. The "boots" or hall porter, whose friendly counsel is often of the greatest service to strangers, will also expect to be "remembered." Most experienced travellers calculate tips at about ten to fifteen per cent of the hotel bill.

At **Restaurants** reckon about 1d. in the 1s. on the bill, with perhaps twice that sum in high-class West End establishments. Gratuities are not normally given in the cheaper tea shops, though a "staff-box" is often to be found near the cash desk.

Railway porters expect from 6d. to 1s. for carrying a hand-bag or rugs, and more for heavy luggage.

PRELIMINARY INFORMATION

AIRPORTS.—The main airport serving the Metropolis is the London Airport, situated at Feltham, Middlesex, some twelve miles west of Charing Cross. Services to the Commonwealth, North and South America, the Middle East, Far East and some European services operate from here. The main airport for European services is at Northolt, Middlesex. Other airports serving London are Croydon, Surrey; Blackbushe, Surrey; Bovingdon, Hertfordshire; and Gatwick, Surrey.

Details of current British overseas air services can be obtained from Airways Terminal, Buckingham Palace Road, S.W.1 (near Victoria Station, Telephone No. Victoria 2323): for British European services from Dorland Hall, Lower Regent Street, S.W.1 (Gerrard 9833). A number of air line operators, however, have their own offices in various parts of the West End.

The London Airport.—Underground railway to Hounslow West, thence by bus or Green Line Coach direct. Passengers by air services arriving or departing from the airport are conveyed to and from the West End by special motor coaches.

The London Airport is the main terminal in Britain for the principal scheduled air services to and from North and South America and the Commonwealth, Egypt, and for some scheduled services to and from European countries. The majority of European scheduled services, however, use Northolt (see p. 18). The London Airport is at present under construction and development, and passengers and services are necessarily accommodated in temporary buildings. When completed the airport will have an attractive grouping of permanent buildings and will be one of the largest, busiest and best equipped in the world. A temporary public enclosure has been provided to which spectators are admitted (6*d.*) during the summer and car-parking facilities (1*s.* 6*d.*) are available. Pleasure flights and conducted tours of the airport may be made from the enclosure, where refreshments are available.

Croydon Airport, Purley Way, Croydon.—Train to East Croydon or Waddon (Southern Region) and thence by bus; or by bus direct.

Its proximity to London makes Croydon Airport an important terminal for Charter Companies to whose use it is now confined. These Companies have offices in the Terminal Building and can offer ready facilities for transport of passengers and freight to all parts of the United Kingdom and abroad. Due to the limited size of the aerodrome, only the smaller aircraft can operate from here. There is a special enclosure for sightseers with facilities for refreshments. A car park is also provided and pleasure flights can be made.

Gatwick Airport, Horley, Surrey.—Train by Southern Region from Victoria and London Bridge.

This airport is used mainly by Air Taxi and Charter Companies, but British European Airways operate seasonal services from Gatwick to the Channel Islands.

As at Croydon, however, the larger aircraft are unable to operate and the services are usually confined to operations within the United Kingdom and European Continent.

Northolt Airport, Western Avenue, Ruislip.—Piccadilly Line to Ruislip, also train to Ruislip Gardens or South Ruislip (both on Central Line tube); thence by bus.

This is the main terminal for British European Airways Services. Aer Lingus also operates from here, and the Airport has a limited use for charter operations, and by companies operating services in association with British European Airways. Passengers are conveyed to and from the West End by special buses, as from London Airport.

Blackbushe Airport.—Train (Southern Region) from Waterloo to Camberley, thence by bus (2½ miles).

Blackbushe is used in bad weather conditions as a diversionary airport for the London Airport and Northolt. It is also used for charter operations (both passenger and freight) by the heavier type aircraft.

Bovingdon Airport.—Train (London Midland Region) to Hemel Hempstead, Hertfordshire, and thence by bus (3 miles).

Bovingdon is used in bad weather conditions as a diversionary airport for the London Airport and Northolt. This aerodrome is used for charter operations by the heavier four-engined aircraft as compared with smaller charter operations at Croydon and Gatwick.

AREA AND POPULATION.—The **City,** the London of history and tradition, occupies only a small part of the great Metropolis, 677 acres, to be exact. (For boundaries, see map "London at a Glance.") The night population is small (approx. 5,000), with a tendency to dwindle still further, but it has been found by actual count that considerably over a million people enter the City in twenty-four hours. The day population has been estimated at about 436,000, "all at work." The administrative **County of London,** the area under the jurisdiction of the London County Council (see p. 25), comprises, exclusive of tidal water and foreshore, 74,850 acres, or over 117 square miles, with a population of 3,348,366. The area recognized as Greater London includes the City, the whole of the counties of London and Middlesex, and parts of the counties of Kent, Surrey, Essex, and Herts. It is made up of all parishes of which any part is within twelve miles of Charing Cross, or of which the whole is within fifteen miles of Charing Cross. It is 693 square miles in extent, and comprises about 7,000 miles of streets, three-quarters of a million of separate dwellings occupied by over a million families, and has a total population of over 8 millions. Thanks to the suburban railway services and the facilities afforded by trams and buses, the population in this "Outer Ring" has for years been growing at a rapid rate. Within twenty-five miles' radius of Charing Cross there is a population almost equal to one-quarter of the total population of England and Wales, and about as many as inhabit the whole of Scotland and Ireland. The extent of the built-over area within a radius of twelve miles from Charing Cross may be appreciated from the fact that it exceeds the combined areas of Liverpool, Manchester, Bristol, Leeds, Cardiff, and Swansea, with their suburbs and open spaces. In 1631, when a census was taken by the Lord Mayor at the instigation of the Privy Council, the entire population of London, including the wards without the walls and the old borough of Southwark, was only 130,268.

The rateable value of the County of London is about £52,000,000;

that of the City only is just over 6 millions.* The latter figures give a rateable value of nearly twelve times as much per acre for the City as for the County of London generally.

The healthiness of Greater London is attested by its remarkably low **Death Rate**, which in a recent year was 11.1 per thousand inhabitants a record no other capital city can surpass.

BATHS AND BATHING.—Swimming and private baths, maintained by the local authorities, are to be found in nearly every quarter. An open-air swim can be had in the Serpentine, Hyde Park (see p. 137), at the Ponds on Hampstead Heath, and in most of the Parks. The L.C.C. have *Lidos* at Parliament Hill, Victoria Park and Brockwell Park. The great Empire Pool (indoor) at Wembley (see p. 155) is the largest of its kind in the world, but is normally only available from May to September, being used for ice hockey during winter. There is another huge swimming pool at Earls Court (p. 181).

Turkish Baths are situated at 92 Jermyn Street S.W. 1; 12 York Street, S.W. 1; 16 Harrow Road, W. 2; Bishopsgate Churchyard, E.C. 2; 7 and 8 Railway Approach, London Bridge, S.E. 1; Imperial, 66 Russell Square; Ironmonger Row, E.C.1.

BOROUGH COUNCILS.—These bodies, constituted in 1900, regulate matters of purely local concern, such as street maintenance, lighting, public health, etc. There are twenty-eight Boroughs and the City, which was but little affected by the Act. Westminster, by virtue of its ancient privileges, was also constituted a city. Each Borough has its Mayor, annually elected, with Aldermen and Councillors varying in numbers according to population. Kensington shares only with Windsor and Kingston the honour of being a Royal Borough. The following is a list of the Boroughs, with particulars of their area and population.

	Area. Acres.	Population.		Area. Acres.	Population.
Battersea	2,163	117,130	Lewisham	7,015	227,551
Bermondsey	1,503	60,661	Paddington	1,357	125,281
Bethnal Green	760	58,374	Poplar	2,331	73,544
Camberwell	4,480	179,729	St. Marylebone	1,473	75,764
Chelsea	660	50,912	St. Pancras	2,694	138,364
Deptford	1,564	75,694	Shoreditch	658	44,885
Finsbury	587	35,347	Southwark	1,132	97,191
Fulham	1,706	122,047	Stepney	1,766	98,581
Greenwich	3,858	91,492	Stoke Newington	864	49,137
Hackney	3,287	171,337	Wandsworth	9,107	330,328
Hammersmith	2,287	119,317	Westminster, City of	2,503	98,895
Hampstead	2,265	95,073	Woolwich	8,282	147,824
Holborn	406	24,806	City	677	5,268
Islington	3,092	235,645			(night)
Kensington	2,290	168,054			
Lambeth	4,083	230,105			

Beyond these Boroughs there are districts equally populous and equally entitled to be considered parts of London, which come within the areas of the Middlesex, Surrey, Kent and Essex County Councils. It is in these suburbs that the rate of growth is most rapid, some of them having doubled their population in a single decade. From time to time the more densely populated extra-London districts obtain

* The rateable value of the City of Westminster is still larger—over £10,000,000.

charters of incorporation, and there are now three county boroughs and thirty-eight municipal boroughs in this area.

BUSES.—*See p. 47.*   **CABS.**—*See p. 45.*

CHURCHES AND CHAPELS.—In addition to the churches in the City proper, there were, before the war, about fifty Metropolitan parish churches, and from five to six hundred ecclesiastical parish and district churches and chapels belonging to the Church of England. Of Nonconformist places of worship of every denomination there were upwards of eight hundred. Much destruction took place during the war and many of the fine buildings are now no more than a shell. Where it is not possible on the original site, services are held in neighbouring churches or in temporary premises. Owing to the de-population of the City, several of the churches there are closed on Sundays. The midday services during the week are generally well attended, however, and a point of interest is the tendency for a church to be associated more or less particularly with a neighbouring large bank, or office, from the staff of which choirs and other officials may be recruited.

The principal churches are described in other parts of this book, while the following list indicates the places of worship most likely to appeal to the visitor whose time is limited. Some of the Saturday daily and evening newspapers give a list of the principal preachers for the following day, with particulars of the music to be rendered, and similar information appears in some of the Sunday papers.

Note.—To meet prevailing conditions, hours of services are liable to change and should therefore be verified by current announcements.

CHURCH OF ENGLAND

St. Paul's Cathedral.—Sundays 7.50, 8, 10.30, 3.15 and 6.30; daily, 8, 10, and 4.

Westminster Abbey.—*See* p. 104.

Southwark Cathedral.—Sundays, 7.30, 8, 11, and 6.30; daily, 7.30, 8 and 5.

Temple Church.

Chapel Royal: St. James'—Sundays, 8.30 and 11.15.

Royal Military Chapel, Wellington Barracks—Sunday Parade Service, open to general public, 11. Open hours for visitors, see p. 121.

Chapel of the Savoy, Strand—11.15.

All Hallows, Barking, Great Tower Street, E.C.—8.30, 11 and 6.30.

All Saints', Margaret Street, Cavendish Square—Sundays, 7, 8, 9, 9.15, 10.30, 11.15, 3 and 6; week-days, 7, 7.30, 8 and 5.30; Wednesdays and Fridays, 11.45; Wednesdays, 8.30 p.m.

All Souls', Langham Place—8, 11 and 6.30.

Tower of London, St. Peter ad Vincula—Sundays, 8.30, 11 a.m. and 6.30 p.m.

Holy Trinity, Sloane Street—7.30, 8.30, 10, 11.15, 6.30.

St. Alban's, Brooke Street, Holborn—11 and 6.

St. Bartholomew-the-Great, West Smithfield—Sundays, 8.45, 11, and 6.30.

St. Dunstan's, Fleet Street—11 and 6.30.

St. George's, Hanover Square—8.15, 10, and 6; week-days, 8 and 6.30.

St. Giles's, Cripplegate.

St. James's, Piccadilly—8.15, 11 and 6. H.C. 1st Sunday also at 12 noon, 3rd Sunday also at 9.15 a.m.

St. Margaret's, Westminster—8.15 (also 1st and 3rd Sundays at 12.15), 11 and 6.

St. Martin's-in-the-Fields, Trafalgar Square—8.30, 9.30, 10.15, 11.30, 3.30 and 6.15; week-days, daily at 10.15.

St. Marylebone, High Street, Marylebone—8, 11, 12.15 and 7.

St. Mary-le-Bow (Bow Church), Cheapside.

Festival Church, St. John's, Waterloo Road.

BAPTIST

Metropolitan Tabernacle, Newington Butts—11, 3 and 6.30; Thursdays, 7.30 p.m.

Westbourne Grove, Bayswater—11 and 6.30; Wednesdays, 7.30 p.m.

Bloomsbury Central Church—11 and 7.

CATHOLIC APOSTOLIC

Gordon Square—10 and 5; week-days, 6 a.m. (Tuesdays and Saturdays), 10.30 (Wednesdays and Fridays), 5 daily.

CONGREGATIONAL

City Temple Services (at Marylebone, George St.)—11 and 6.30.
Lyndhurst Road. Hampstead—11 and 7.
King's Weighhouse Church, Duke Street, W.—8, 11 and 7.
Westminster, Buckingham Gate. S.W.—11 and 6.30.
Whitefield Central Mission and Youth Centre.
Whitefield Tabernacle, Tottenham Court Rd.—11 and 7; Tuesdays, 8 p.m.

METHODIST

Central Hall, Westminster—11, 3.30 and 6.30.
Wesley's Chapel, City Road—11 and 6.30.
Kingsway Hall—11 and 6.30.

PRESBYTERIAN

Regent Square, Gray's Inn Road—11 and 6.30; Wednesdays, 8 p.m.
Hampstead, High Street, Hampstead, N.W.—11 and 6.30.
Marylebone, Upper George Street, W.—11 and 7; Thursdays, 8.15 p.m.
St. Columba (Church of Scotland), Pont Street, S.W. (at Imperial Institute, S.W.)—11 and 6.30.
Scottish National Church, Russell Street, Covent Garden—11.15 and 6.30.

QUAKERS

The Friends' House, Euston Road—11 and 6.30.

UNITARIAN

Rosslyn Hill Chapel, near Hampstead Tube Station—11 and 6.30.
Essex Church, The Mall, Notting Hill Gate—11 and 6.30.

ROMAN CATHOLIC

Westminster Cathedral, Ashley Gardens, Victoria Street, S.W. *See* p. 115.
Oratory, South Kensington, W.—*See* p. 170.
St. George's Cathedral, St. George's Road, Southwark—7, 8, 9.30, 10.30, 12 and 6.30; week-days, 7, 6.30, 8, 10 a.m. and 8.15 p.m.
St. Anselm and St. Cecilia, Kingsway—8, 9, 10, 11.30, 6 Sundays; 8 week-days.
St. Etheldreda, Ely Place, Holborn—8, 10, 11.15, 4, 7; week-days, 7.15 a.m., except Mondays, daily 8 a.m.; Tuesdays, 8 p.m.; Wednesdays, 1.15; Fridays, 1.15 and 8.
Church of the Immaculate Conception, Farm Street, Berkeley Square, W.—12 and 4; Wednesdays, 6.30 p.m.; Fridays and Saturdays, 3.30 p.m.

St. James's, George Street—7, 8, 9, 10, 11, 12, 4 and 6: week-days 7, 8, 10.

CHRISTIAN SCIENCE

First Church of Christ, Scientist, near Sloane Square Station—11.30 and 7.

JEWISH

Central Synagogue, 129, Great Portland Street—Saturdays, 9.40 a.m.; week-days, 7.30 p.m.
Great Synagogue, Duke Place, Aldgate—Saturdays, 8.30, 2 and sunset; other days, 7.15 a.m.

WELSH

St. Benet's, Queen Victoria Street—11 and 6.30.
Welsh Presbyterian, Charing Cross Road, W.C. 2.

FOREIGN CHURCHES

Armenian (St. Sarleis), Iverna Gardens, W.8—11 a.m.
Danish (Lutheran), Marlborough House Chapel—4 p.m., and Ming Street, Poplar—11 a.m.
Dutch, St. Mary's, Bourden Street, W.1.
Finnish, Branch Road, Poplar—7 p.m.
French Catholic, Nôtre Dame de France, Leicester Place, W.C.—8, 9, 10, 11, 7. Daily 7 and 8 a.m.
French Protestant, 8, Soho Square—11 and 6.30.
French Reformed Evangelical, Monmouth Road, W.—11 and 6.30.
German (Roman Catholic), 47, Adler Street, Whitechapel—11 a.m.. 7 p.m. *Evangelische Christus Kirche,* Brompton Road—1st, 6.30; others, 11. *Hamburger Lutherische Kirche,* Ritson Road, E. 8.—1st, 4; others, 11. *Deutsche Wesleyanische,* 30, Drayton Park, N. 5—4 p.m.
Greek (St. Sophia's), Moscow Road, W. 2.
Italian (Roman Catholic), St. Peter's, Clerkenwell Road—7, 8, 9, 10, 11.15 and 7. Daily, 7, 8, 10 and 8.15.
Norwegian (St. Olavs), Rotherhithe—11 a.m.; 6.30 1st Sun. in month.
Russian (St. Philip), Buckingham Palace Road, S.W.1.
Swedish (Lutheran), Harcourt Street, Marylebone, 11 a.m., and 120a, Lower Road, Rotherhithe—7 p.m.
Swiss (Protestant):
French-speaking, 79, Endell Street, W.C. 2—11 and (except in August) 6.30 p.m.
German-speaking, at the Kingsway Hall, W.C. 2—11, and (2nd and 4th Sundays) 6.30 at Endell Street.

CINEMAS.—See p. 65.

CITY CORPORATION.—This ancient and dignified body has juris-diction over the City proper, and maintains an independent police force of 982 officers and men. It can claim an antiquity greatly exceeding that of the "Mother of Parliaments," for a charter granted by William I, still preserved in the City archives, runs "William king greets William bishop and Gosfrith portreeve, and all the burghers within London, French and English, friendly; and I do you to wit that I will that ye be all those laws worthy (i.e. possessed of privileges) that ye were in King Edward's day" (the Confessor). Soon after the Norman Conquest the title of Sheriff was substituted for that of Port-reeve. In 1191 Henry FitzAylwin, the first "Mayor," was appointed. He held office for twenty-four years, but on his death, in 1215, a new charter was granted by King John, which directed that the Mayor should be chosen annually. This practice is still followed, though it has happened that the same individual has held office more than once, the most notable instance being that of "Whittington, thrice Lord Mayor of London," who was in fact Mayor on four occasions. The earliest known reference to the chief magistrate as "my Lord Mayor" is dated 1414. The explanation of the title is probably to be found in a misinterpretation of the Latin title *dominus Maior*, which originally meant nothing more than Sir Mayor. In course of time it came to be translated into "the lord the Mayor," whence it was but a step to "the lord Mayor." It was a century later before the title "Lord Mayor" came to be generally used. The Lord Mayor of London is one of the five holders of similar offices entitled to be styled "Right Honourable," a title that came into use in the sixteenth century.

In early days the Mayor was elected by a general assembly of the citizens held in St. Paul's Churchyard. Now the Liverymen in Common Hall nominate two aldermen for the office, from whom the Court of Aldermen selects one, usually the senior. The **Lord Mayor** marks his assumption of office by proceeding in state on November 9th to the Royal Courts of Justice, to make his declaration of office before the Lord Chief Justice and other judges, and to invite them to the Banquet customarily held at the Guildhall that evening. The procession con-stitutes the famous **Lord Mayor's Show,** a pageant more highly esteemed by "country cousins" than by Londoners themselves. The cost of the "Show" and the Banquet usually amounts to about £4,000, which the Lord Mayor and Sheriffs have the privilege of paying. The Lord Mayor receives an allowance of £12,500, but invariably spends far more from his private means. In the City, he takes precedence of every subject of the Crown, including princes of the blood royal.

The two **Sheriffs** are appointed annually on Midsummer Day by the Liverymen, in pursuance of a privilege first conferred by Henry I in 1132. The **Aldermen,** of whom there are twenty-six, one for each of the wards into which the City is divided, are elected for life or until resignation. The **Court of Common Council** consists of the aldermen and 206 members, elected annually by the ratepayers. The legal and official title of the Corporation is "The Mayor and Commonalty and Citizens of the City of London."

The City revenues in the aggregate are about £3,500,000 pounds a year of which two-thirds is paid to other authorities, such as the L.C.C. The Corporation extends, when occasion arises, a sumptuous hospitality to foreign potentates and statesmen. It also does much solid and useful work for London, especially as regards education, the purchase of open spaces, maintainance of bridges, etc., without expense to the ratepayers. On occasions of national disaster it is usual for the Lord Mayor to open a Mansion House Fund, and by this means also large sums are frequently raised for charity.

CITY GUILDS.—Closely connected with the government of the City are the Livery Companies, or Guilds. There are seventy-nine of these Companies (of which twelve are considered "great"), each with its Master, Wardens and Clerk, and prior to the war many possessed handsome and commodious Halls. Some of the Companies are very wealthy, and have devoted large sums to educational and charitable purposes. The origin of the term "livery" in this connection is to be found in the feudal custom of barons and other great lords "delivering" to their retainers badges and liveries known as "Livery of Company."

CLUBS of all kinds—social, political, professional, athletic—abound in London. Admission to the exclusive and luxurious institutions in and around Pall Mall and Piccadilly is almost entirely a matter of social status. In most clubs, however, strangers will find a welcome.

Albany, 3, Savile Row, W. 1	Social.
Albemarle, 21, Curzon Street, W. 1.	Ladies and Gentlemen.
Aldwych, 18 Exeter Street, W.C. 2	Social; non-political.
Alpine, 74, South Audley Street, W. 1	Alpine Climbers.
American, 95, Piccadilly, W. 1	Americans.
Argentine, 1, Hamilton Place, W. 1	
Army and Navy, 36, Pall Mall, S.W. 1	Service Officers.
Arts, 40, Dover Street, W. 1	Artists, Authors, etc.
Athenaeum, 107, Pall Mall, S.W. 1	Politicians, Authors, etc.
Authors', 2, Whitehall Court, S.W. 1	Authors and Journalists.
Automobile Association, Fanum House, Coventry Street, W.	Motoring.
Bachelors', 106, Piccadilly, W.1.	Ladies admitted as guests.
Bath, 41–3, Brook Street, W. 1	Social, Swimming, etc.
Beefsteak, 9, Irving Street, W.C. 2	Social.
Boodle's, 28, St. James's Street, S.W. 1	Country Gentlemen.
Brooks's, 60, St. James's Street, S.W. 1	Liberal.
Buck's, 18, Clifford Street, W. 1	Social.
Caledonian, 9, Halkin Street, S.W. 1	Scots.
Carlton, 69, St. James's Street, S.W. 1	Leading Conservative Club.
Cavalry, 127, Piccadilly, W. 1	Mounted Forces.
Church Imperial, 212, Ashley Gardens, S.W. 1	Social, Church of England.
City Livery, Sion College, E.C. 4	City Liverymen.
City of London, 19, Old Broad Street, E.C. 2.	Merchants, Bankers, etc.
City University, 50, Cornhill, E.C. 3	
Connaught, 5. Norfolk Square, W. 2	Social
Conservative, 74, St. James's Street, S.W. 1 .	Political.
Constitutional, Northumberland Avenue, W.C. 2	Conservative.
Cruising Association, Chiltern Court, N.W. 1	Yachting, etc.
Devonshire, 50, St. James's Street, S.W. 1	Liberal.
East India and Sports', 16, St. James's Square, S.W. 1	Officers and Indian Civil Service.
Eccentric, 9, Ryder Street, St. James's, S.W. 1	Social, Drama and the Arts.
Farmers', 2, Whitehall Court, S.W. 1	Agricultural and Social.
Flyfishers', 23, Whitehall Court, S.W. 1	Fly-fishing and Social.
Garrick, 15, Garrick Street, W.C. 2	Actors, Authors, etc.
Golfers', 2A, Whitehall Court, S.W. 1	Social for Golfers.
Green Room, 62, Whitcomb Street, W.C. 2	Dramatic Literary and Artistic
Gresham, 15. Abchurch Lane, E.C. 4	Merchants, Bankers, etc.
Grosvenor, Grosvenor Hall, Semley Place, S.W. 1.	Social, and at Henley.
Guards' 16, Charles Street, W. 1	Guards Officers, Past and Present.
International Sportsmen's, Upper Grosvenor Street, W.1.	

Junior Army and Navy, Horse Guards Avenue . Officers, Past and Present.
Junior Carlton, 30, Pall Mall, S.W. 1 . . . Conservative.
Junior United Service, 11, Charles II Street, S.W. 1 Officers of Army and Navy.
Kennel, 84, Piccadilly, W. 1 . . . . Dog Fanciers, etc.
Linguist, 20, Grosvenor Place, S.W. 1 .
M.C.C., St. John's Wood Road, N.W. 8 . . Headquarters of Cricket
Marlborough-Windham, Orleans House, 52, Pall
    Mall, S.W. 1 . . . . Social.
National, 12, Queen Anne's Gate, S.W. 1 . . Protestant.
National Liberal, Whitehall Place, S.W. 1 . Liberal.
Naval and Military, 94, Piccadilly, W. 1 . . Army, Navy and Marines.
Nurses', 194, Queen's Gate, S.W. 7 .
Northern Counties, 3, Whitehall Court, S.W. 1 . Social.
Oriental, 18, Hanover Square, W. 1 . . . Social.
Orleans, 28, St. James's Street, S.W. 1 . . Ladies admitted as guests.
Overseas League, St. James's, S.W. 1 . . Non-party; Empire.
Oxford and Cambridge, 71, Pall Mall, S.W. 1 . Oxford and Cambridge Men.
Portland, 18B, Charles Street, W. 1 . . . Non-political.
Pratt's, 14, Park Place, S.W. 1 . . . . Social.
Press, St. Bride's House, Salisbury Square, E.C. 4 Journalistic.
Public Schools, 100, Piccadilly, W. 1 . . Public School Men.
Publicity, 2, Bucknall Street, W.C. 2 . . .
Queen's, Palliser Road, W.14 . . . . Tennis, etc.
Reform, 104, Pall Mall, S.W. 1 . . . . Liberal.
Rotary, 2, Clements Inn, W.C. 2 .
Royal Aero, 119, Piccadilly, W. 1 . . . Aviation.
Royal Air Force, 128, Piccadilly, W. 1 .
Royal Automobile, 89, Pall Mall, S.W. 1 . . Motorists.
Royal Societies, 100, Piccadilly, W. 1 . . Members of Learned Societies.
Royal Thames Yacht, 60, Knightsbridge, S.W. 1 .
St. James's, 106, Piccadilly, W. 1 . . . Diplomatic Services.
St. Stephen's, 1, Bridge Street, Westminster, S.W. 1 Conservative.
Savage, 1, Carlton House Terrace, S.W. 1 . Authors, Artists, etc.
Savile, 69, Brook Street, W. 1 . . . . Social.
Sesame, 49, Grosvenor Street, W. 1 . . . Ladies and Gentlemen.
Thatched House, 86, St. James's Street, S.W. 1 . Non-political.
Three Arts, 35, Gt. Cumberland Place,, W. 1 . Music, Art, Drama.
Travellers', 106, Pall Mall, S.W. 1 . . . Travellers.
Turf, 85, Piccadilly, W. 1 . . . . . Social.
Union, 10, Carlton House Terrace, S.W. 1 . Social, non-political.
United Service, 116, Pall Mall, S.W. 1 . . Combatant Officers.
United Sports, 4, Whitehall Court, S.W. 1 . Social.
United University, 1, Suffolk Street, S.W. 1 . Oxford and Cambridge Men.
University of London, 21, Gower Street, W.C. 1 .
White's, 37, St. James's Street. S.W. 1 . . Social, non-political.

LADIES' CLUBS

American Women's, 49, Upper Brook Street, W. 1
Bath, 41, Brook Street, W.1.
Church Imperial, 212, Ashley Gardens, S.W. 1. . Social, Church of England.
Cowdray, 20, Cavendish Square, W. 1.
Empress, 35, Dover Street, W.1.
Forum, 6, Grosvenor Place, S.W.1.
King George and Queen Elizabeth, 56, Sloane
    Street, S.W. 1 . . . . Service Women.
Ladies' Alpine, c/o Williams Deacon's Bank, Marylebone, N.W. 1.
Ladies' Carlton, 5, Grosvenor Place, S.W.1.
Ladies' Empire 69, Grosvenor Street, W. 1
Ladies' Park, 67, Eaton Square, S.W.1.
Three Arts, 35, Gt. Cumberland Place, W. 1. . Music, Drama, Painting.
United Nursing Services, 34, Cavendish Square, W. 1.
University Women's, 2, Audley Square, W. 1.
Victoria, 18, Wellington Street, W.C. 2.

CONCERTS. etc.—In the season the music-lover may make his choice any afternoon or evening from half a dozen first-class performances. The most important take place in the Royal Albert Hall, concerts for the most part sponsored by the British Broadcasting Corporation, in the Royal Festival Hall, and the Wigmore Hall in Wigmore Street. Concerts and orchestral performances are also broadcast by wireless every afternoon and evening.

In many of the City churches midday organ recitals are given for the benefit of workers, and in nearly all the parks, both in central London and the suburbs, there are regular band performances during summer.

COUNTY COUNCIL.—The London County Council was established by the Local Government Act, 1888, supplanting the old Metropolitan Board of Works. It has jurisdiction over 117 square miles, with a population of 3,348,366. The Council consists of 129 councillors, elected by adult suffrage every three years between 31st March and 19th April, and 21 aldermen elected by the councillors for six years, 10 (or 11) retiring every third year. Its deliberations are presided over by a chairman, vice-chairman and deputy-chairman, elected annually by the Council. The Council's headquarters are at the County Hall, Westminster Bridge, across the river from the Houses of Parliament. (See page 78.) Its annual expenditure is over 60 million pounds. Since 1889, the Council's powers and functions have been varied by a number of Acts of Parliament; at present its more important activities include education, personal health services, housing, town planning, fire service, parks and open spaces, care of children, of the aged and of the physically handicapped, civic restaurants, main drainage, major civil engineering works, licensing of places of public entertainment. The Council meets in public normally on alternate Tuesdays at 2.30 p.m., except during recesses.

DOMINION AGENCIES.—The Agencies of the Overseas Dominions, etc., are mostly in or near the Strand:

Australian Commonwealth, Australia House, Strand. W.C. 2.

British Columbia, 1, Regent Street, S.W. 1.

Canada, Trafalgar Square, S.W. 1.

Colonies, Crown Agents, 4, Millbank, S.W. 1.

Republic of Ireland, 33, Regent Street, S.W.1.

Malay States, 57, Trafalgar Square, W.C. 2.

New South Wales, 56/57, Strand, W.C.2.

New Zealand, 415, Strand, W.C.2.

Northern Ireland, 13, Lower Regent Street, S.W. 1.

Queensland, 409, Strand, W.C. 2.

Southern Rhodesia, Rhodesia House, 429, Strand, W.C.

South Africa, Union of, Trafalgar Square, W.C. 2.

South Australia, 499, Oxford Street, W. 1.

Tasmania, Golden Cross House, Duncannon Street, W.C. 2.

Victoria, Melbourne Place, Strand, W.C. 2.

Western Australia, 115, Strand, W.C.

EMBASSIES and CONSULATES

America, United States	Embassy, Consulate and Commercial Attaché, 1 Grosvenor Square, W.1.
Argentine	Embassy, 9, Wilton Crescent, S.W. 1.
Austria	Embassy, 18 Belgrave Square, S.W.1.
	Consular Section, 18, Belgrave Mews West, S.W.1.
Belgium	Embassy and Consulate, 103, Eaton Square, W.1.

EMBASSIES and CONSULATES—*continued*.

Brazil	Embassy and Consulate, 32, Green Street, W.1.
Bulgaria	Legation, 12 and 24, Queen's Gate Gardens, S.W.7.
Chile	Embassy and Consulate, 9, North Audley Street, W.1.
China	Embassy, 49, Portland Place, W.1.
	Consulate, 25, Weymouth Street, W.1.
Czechoslovakia	Embassy, 9, Grosvenor Place, S.W.1.
Denmark	Legation, 29, Pont Street, S.W.1.
Ecuador	Embassy and Consulate, 3, Hans Crescent, S.W.1.
Egypt	Embassy, 75, South Audley Street, W.1.
	Consulate, 26, South Street, W.1.
Finland	Legation, 65, Chester Square, S.W.1.
France	Embassy, 58, Knightsbridge, S.W.1.
	Consulate, 51, Bedford Square, W.C.1.
Greece	Legation, 51, Upper Brook Street, W.1.
	Consulate, 34, Hyde Park Square, W.2.
Hungary	Legation, 46, Eaton Place, S.W.1.
Iceland	Legation, 17, Buckingham Gate, S.W.1.
India	Embassy, India House, Aldwych, W.C.2.
Iraq	Embassy, 22, Queen's Gate, S.W.7
Israel	Legation, 18, Manchester Square, W.1.
Italy	Embassy, 14, Three Kings' Yard, Davies Street, W.1.
Latvia	Legation, 87, Eaton Place, S.W.1.
Mexico	Legation, 48, Belgrave Square, S.W.1.
Netherlands	Embassy, 117, Park Street. W.1.
	Consulate, 33, Weymouth Street. W.1.
Norway	Embassy, 25, Belgrave Square, S.W.1.
	Consulate, 26, King Street, E.C.2.
Pakistan	Embassy, 34, Lowndes Square, S.W.1 and 2, Palace Gate, W.8.
Peru	Embassy and Consulate, 52, Sloane Street, S.W.1.
Poland	Embassy, 47, Portland Place, W.1.
	Consulate, 52, Queen Anne Street, W.1.
Portugal	Embassy, 103, Sloane Street, S.W.1.
	Consulate, 8, Strathearn Place, W.2.
Spain	Embassy, 24, Belgrave Square, S.W.1.
	Consulate, 21, Cavendish Square, W.1.
Sweden	Embassy, 29, Portland Place, W.1.
	Consulate, 14, Trinity Square, E.C.3.
Switzerland	Legation, 18, Montague Place, W.1.
Turkey	Embassy, 69, Portland Place, W.1.
	Consulate, 18, Cadogan Gardens, S.W.3.
Uruguay	Embassy, 48, Lennox Gardens, S.W.1.
	Consulate, 66, Pont Street, S.W.1.

FIRE SERVICE.—The fire protection of the County of London is in the hands of the London Fire Brigade which traces its origin back through the Metropolitan Fire Brigade and the London Fire Engine Establishment to the insurance companies' fire brigades of the eighteenth century. For a while after August, 1941, the London Fire Brigade lost its identity and became part of the National Fire Service, but on April 1st, 1948, it again emerged as the London Fire Brigade when, under the Fire Services Act of 1947, county councils and county borough councils became fire authorities. The London Fire Brigade Headquarters are on the Albert Embankment.

The establishment of nearly 2,500 officers and men is posted to 58 land and 3 river stations situated in all parts of London. The Brigade has 175 appliances including pump escapes, pumps, turntable ladders, emergency tenders, fire boats, etc. Many of which are equipped with radio-telephony.

FREEDOM OF THE CITY.—This privilege—greatly prized—may be obtained by one of four methods: (a) By servitude (having been bound apprentice to a Freeman); (b) By patrimony (as the son of daughter of a Freeman); (c) By redemption or purchase; (d) By gift (honorary freedom).

HOTELS and tariffs.—*See* Introduction, pp. 12-15.

HOSPITALS.—The following are among the principal London Hospitals:

Charing Cross, Agar Street, Strand, W.C. 2.
Children's, Great Ormond Street, W.C. 1.
Elizabeth Garrett-Anderson (Women), 144, Euston Road, N.W. 1.
Guy's, St. Thomas's Street, S.E. 1.
King's College, Denmark Hill, S.E. 5.
London, Whitechapel Road, E. 1.
Middlesex, Mortimer Street, W. 1.
Moorfields Eye, City Road, E.C. 1.
Royal Eye, St. George's Circus, S.E. 1.
Royal Free, 256, Gray's Inn Road, W.C.1.
Royal Masonic, Ravenscourt Park, W.6.
Homœopathic, Great Ormond Street, W.C. 1.
St. Bartholomew's, Smithfield, E.C. 1.
St. George's, Hyde Park Corner, S.W. 1.
St. Mark's, City Road, E.C. 1.
St. Mary's, Praed Street, Paddington.
St. Thomas's, Lambeth Palace Road.
University College, Gower Street, W.C.1.
Westminster, Horseferry Road, S.W.1.

The Public Health Department of the L.C.C. also maintain a large number of Hospitals, both general and for the treatment of specific ailments.

HOUSES, MEMORABLE.—The following are among the numerous houses associated with bygone celebrities and distinguished by memorial tablets erected by the London County Council, the City Corporation, the Royal Society of Arts, the Incorporated Society of Musicians, or private individuals like the Duke of Bedford and the Duke of Westminster. Many of the houses are more particularly referred to in our descriptive rambles (*see* Index). In some cases the tablets have been affixed to houses not in themselves noteworthy, but occupying the sites of old houses that have had distinguished occupants.

The City Corporation have also affixed a number of plaques, denoting the sites of historic buildings, gates, etc., within their area.

This list does not profess to be exhaustive or complete.

"I ask anybody who is in the habit of taking long walks in London or in other cities, whether it is not an immense relief to come on some tablet which suggests a new train of thought, which recalls to the mind the career of some distinguished person, and which takes off the intolerable pressure of the monotony of endless streets."—*Lord Rosebery.*

Balfe, M. W., 12, Seymour Street, Portman Square.
Banks, Sir Joseph, 32, Soho Square.
Barry, James, 36, Castle Street, Oxford Street.
Beaconsfield Earl of, 29, Park Lane, and 19, Curzon Street, Mayfair (at death).
Blake, William, 28, Broadwick Street, Golden Square; South Molton Street, W.
Borrow, George, 22, Hereford Square, Brompton.
Browning, Elizabeth Barrett, 50, Wimpole Street.
Browning, Robert, 19, Warwick Crescent, Paddington.
Burke, Edmund, 37, Gerrard Street, Soho.
Byron, Lord, 24, Holles Street, Cavendish Square (bronze relief bust on modern premises). There is also a bust on 8, St. James's Street, S.W.1.
Carlyle, Thomas, 24 (formerly 5) Cheyne Row, Chelsea, and 33, Ampton Street, Gray's Inn Road.
Chamberlain, Joseph, 40, Princes Gardens, S.W.; 25, Highbury Place, N.
Chatham, William Pitt, Earl of, Pitt House, North End, Hampstead.
Chesterfield (2nd, 3rd and 4th Earls), 45, Bloomsbury Square.
Cobden, Richard, 23, Suffolk Street, Pall Mall.

Coleridge, Samuel T., 7, Addison Bridge Place Fulham.
Constable, John, 76, Charlotte Street, Fitzroy Square.
Cook, Captain, 88, Mile End Road.
Cruikshank, George, 263, Hampstead Road.
D'Arblay, Madame (Fanny Burney), 11, Bolton Street, Piccadilly.
Dickens, Charles, 48, Doughty Street, Mecklenburg Sq. (now *Dickens Museum*).
Dickens, Charles, 1 Devonshire Terrace, Portland Place (1839-51).
D'Israeli, Isaac, 6, Bloomsbury Square.
Dryden, John, 43, Gerrard Street, Soho.
Du Maurier, G., New Grove House, The Grove, Hampstead.
Eliot, George, Holly Lodge, 31, Wimbledon Park Road, Wandsworth.
Faraday, Michael, 48, Blandford Street, Portman Square.
Flaxman, John, 7, Buckingham Street, Fitzroy Square.
Franklin, Benjamin, 36, Craven Street, W.C.
Fox, Chas. J., 9, Arlington Street, Piccadilly, and 46, Clarges Street.
Gainsborough, Thomas, Schomberg House, 80, Pall Mall.
Gaskell, Mrs., 93, Cheyne Walk, S.W.
Gladstone, W. E., 73, Harley Street, and 10, St. James's Square.
Goldsmith, Oliver, 2, Brick Court, Temple.
Gray, Thomas, 41, Cornhill, E.C.
Handel, George Frederick, 25, Brook Street.
Hazlitt, William, 6, Frith Street, Soho.
Hallam, Henry, 67, Wimpole Street, Marylebone.
Hogarth, William, 30, Leicester Square; 119, Fenchurch Street.
Hood, Thos., 28, Finchley Road.
Hunt, Leigh, 10 (now 22), Upper Cheyne Row, Chelsea.
Hunter, John, 31, Golden Square.
Huxley, T. H., 4, Marlborough Place, St. John's Wood.
Irving, Sir Henry, 87, Newgate Street, E.C., and 15A, Grafton Street, W. 1.
Johnson, Samuel, 17, Gough Square, Fleet Street.
Kean, Edmund, 12, Clarges Street, Piccadilly.
Keats, John (birthplace), 85, Moorgate; (residence) Lawnbank, Hampstead.
Lamb, Charles, 64, Duncan Terrace, Islington.
Leighton, Lord, Leighton House, Holland Park Road, W.
Lind, Jenny (Mme. Goldschmidt), 1, Moreton Gardens, Kensington, S.W.
Lister, Lord, 12, Park Crescent, Portland Place.
Macaulay, Lord, Holly Lodge, Campden Hill, Kensington.
Mazzini, Guiseppe, 183, Gower Street.
Mill, J. S., 39, Rodney Street, Pentonville, and 18, Kensington Square.
Millais, Sir John Everett, 7, Cromwell Place, South Kensington.
Milton, John, 125, Bunhill Row.
Morris, William, 26, Upper Mall, Hammersmith, W.
Morris, Wm., D. G. Rossetti, and Sir E. Burne-Jones, 17, Red Lion Sq., W.C.
Mozart, W., 182, Ebury Street.
Napoleon III, 1c, King Street, St. James's.
Nelson, Lord, 147, New Bond Street.
Nightingale, Florence, 10, South Street, Park Lane, W.
Page, Walter Hines, 6, Grosvenor Square.
Pepys, Samuel (birthplace), 13, Salisbury Court, Fleet Street; (residence) 4
　　Buckingham Street, Strand.
Reynolds, Sir Joshua, 47, Leicester Square.
Romney, Geo., Holly Bush Hill, Hampstead.
Rossetti D.G., 17, Red LionSquare (with Wm. Morris and Sir E. C. Burne-Jones).
Ruskin, John, 54, Hunter Street, Brunswick Square.
Russell, Lord John, 37, Chesham Place, Belgravia.
Scott, Sir Gilbert, The Grove, Hampstead.
Scott, Captain, 56, Oakley Street, Chelsea.
Shakespeare, William, 13, Silver Street, Wood Street.
Sheridan, Richard Brinsley, 14, Savile Row.
Siddons, Mrs., 27, Upper Baker Street, and 54, Great Marlborough Street.
Smith, Sydney, 14, Doughty Street, Mecklenburg Square.
Stephenson, Robert, 34, Gloucester Square, Hyde Park.
Swinburne, A. C., 11, Putney Hill.
Thackeray, W. M., 16, Young Street, Kensington; 2, Kensington Palace Green
　　28, Clerkenwell Road; 36, Onslow Square W.

Turner, J. M. W., 23, Queen Anne Street, and 118, Cheyne Walk, Chelsea.
Walpole, Sir Robert, 5, Arlington Street.
Wolseley, Viscount Garnet, Ranger's House, Blackheath.
Young, Thomas, 48, Welbeck Street, St. Marylebone.

LIBRARIES, READING-ROOMS, etc.—Nearly all the London boroughs maintain **Public Libraries**, where newspapers, magazines and books of reference may be consulted without charge, though only local ratepayers and residents can, as a rule, borrow books. Among public libraries in the central part of London mention may be made of the **Guildhall Library**, Guildhall, E.C.; **Holborn**, High Holborn; the **St. Bride Foundation Institute**, Bride Lane, near Ludgate Circus; the **Bishopsgate Institute**, Bishopsgate Street, E.C., and the **Cripplegate Institute**, Golden Lane, E.C. The **Westminster Public Library** is in St. Martin's Street, Leicester Square.

Visitors who are interested in the history and associations of London should see especially the fine collection of books and prints at the Guildhall, the County Hall, and the Bishopsgate Institute. Here, too, may be seen the principal Directories (local and trade) of the world.

At the County Hall (p. 78) is also a valuable **Educational Library.**

Technical newspapers and journals are best seen at the Patent Office Library (p. 195), which comprises also a valuable collection of technical books and is open, without formality, to all.

A good selection of foreign newspapers can be seen at the Bishopsgate Institute and the Guildhall Library.

Circulating Libraries.—"**The Times**" **Book Club**, 42, Wigmore Street, **W. H. Smith and Son**, Kingsway, W.C., with branches in nearly all suburbs, and others. Boots's **Book-Lovers'** Library has branches throughout London and suburbs. **London Library**, 14, St. James's Square, W. (p. 126). The librarians will gladly give particulars as to subscriptions.

> **British Museum,** ticket necessary (*see* p. 163).
>
> **Guildhall,** on signing visitors' book (*see* p. 208).
>
> **Dr. Williams's,** University Hall, Gordon Square, W.C. On introduction of a minister. Chiefly theological.
>
> **Sion College,** Thames Embankment, Blackfriars. On introduction. Theological.
>
> **Patent Office,** Southampton Buildings, Chancery Lane. On signing visitors' book. Technical and scientific.
>
> **Lambeth Palace.** Valuable episcopal books and MSS.
>
> **Science Museum Library,** South Kensington. Scientific volumes and periodicals.
>
> **Victoria and Albert Museum,** South Kensington. Books on art, prints, drawings, photographs, etc. (*see* p. 171).
>
> **Imperial War Library,** Imperial War Museum (*see* p. 257).
>
> **Royal Empire Society Library,** daily (Sundays and public holidays excepted) from 10 a.m. to 8 p.m. Non-Fellows may use Library on presentation of a letter of introduction from a Fellow of the Society, or from an educational or other recognized authority.

LITTLE-KNOWN LONDON SIGHTS.—Lovers of the quaint and curious may be glad to have a list of a few London sights and reminders of Old London that frequently escape the attention of visitors who content themselves with the orthodox round of the great show-places. Many others could be named: the following are merely given to indicate the wealth of interest that lies off the beaten track. For descriptions consult Index.

Staple Inn, Holborn, opposite Gray's Inn Road.

17, *Fleet Street*, opposite Chancery Lane.

Panyer Alley, Newgate Street.

Roman Bath, 5 Strand Lane.

St. Etheldreda's Church, Ely Place, Hatton Garden.

Shepherd Market, between Curzon Street and Piccadilly.

York Gate, Embankment Gardens, near Charing Cross.

Standards of British Lineal Measures, Trafalgar Square and Guildhall.

Chapel of the Ascension and St. John's Burial-Ground, between Marble Arch and Lancaster Gate.

Royal Academy Diploma Galleries, Burlington House, Piccadilly.

Soane Museum, Lincoln's Inn Fields (north side).

London Stone, St. Swithin's Church, Cannon Street.

London Wall (fragments of), in thoroughfare of same name, and near Tower, and elsewhere in the City (*see* p. 69).

LOST PROPERTY.—In case of loss of articles in Underground trains, buses, or other vehicles of the London Transport Executive, inquire at the Lost Property Office, London Transport Executive, 200, Baker Street, N. W 1 (Mondays to Fridays 10–6; Saturdays 10–1); for articles lost elsewhere apply at Police Lost Property Office, Lambeth Road (close to Lambeth Palace; Plan II. L. 10), hours 10 to 4. A charge of 15 per cent of the value is usually levied on lost property restored by the police. If luggage is lost in a train or at a station belonging to one of the railways not under the control of the London Transport Executive inform the stationmaster, or if at a terminus, inquire at the "Lost Property Office" there. *Always remove old labels from luggage.* Much loss and inconvenience would be avoided by the observance of this simple rule.

MARKETS.—The great Markets of London, though not so popular a show as the Halles Centrales of Paris, are full of interest to the visitor. The wholesale part of the business, when shopkeepers from all over London come to provide for their customers, is mostly conducted early in the morning, but a considerable retail trade is done all through the day. The following are the principal markets:

Covent Garden (p. 188) is the principal fruit, flower and vegetable market. Tuesdays, Wednesdays, Thursdays and Saturdays are the principal market days.

Smithfield (p. 229). These extensive buildings comprise the London Central Meat Market and the poultry, fish, vegetable and hay markets. They are under the control of the City Corporation. Mondays and Thursdays are the busy days; the market is all but closed on Saturdays.

Leadenhall Market, Leadenhall Street, is an interesting sight.

Billingsgate, Lower Thames Street, London Bridge. This is the great fish market, but it cannot be described as attractive.

Spitalfields Market, for fruit, vegetables and flowers is among the largest and most modern markets of its kind in the world.

Shadwell and Columbia Markets also serve the East of London and the Borough Market the South.

MILITARY.—The only troops usually quartered in London are the Household Cavalry at Knightsbridge Barracks; a Royal Horse Artillery Battery at St. John's Wood and other artillery at Woolwich; the R.A.S.C. at Woolwich and Hounslow, and battalions of the Guards at Wellington Barracks (St. James's Park), Chelsea Barracks, and the Tower of London.

An interesting military spectacle each morning at eleven o'clock is the **Changing of the Guard** at St. James's Palace, or at Buckingham Palace (*see* p. 122). Troopers are on sentry duty daily at the Horse Guards (*see* p. 81), and are rarely without a circle of admirers, young and old, particularly at a little before 11 a.m. (Sundays 10) when the Guard is mounted, and at 4 p.m. when it is dismounted. Each afternoon a detachment of Guards proceeds from Wellington Barracks to the Bank of England, where it is on guard until the following day. The most imposing military pageant in London is that of **Trooping of the Colour**, on, or about, June 5th, the "official" birthday of the Sovereign (*see* p. 81). The **Royal Tournament** (Navy, Army and Air Force), held at Olympia during May or June, enjoys great popularity.

MONEY, BRITISH.—Since the 1914 War *gold* coins (sovereigns and half-sovereigns) have disappeared, being replaced by **Bank Notes** of the face value of twenty shillings and ten shillings. The silver coins are the crown (5s.), now very rare; half-crown (2s. 6d.); florin (2s.); shilling; sixpence (half a shilling); and "threepenny bits." Be careful to distinguish between half-crowns and florins; the former are larger. *Bronze*, or copper: twelve-sided threepenny piece (3d.); penny (1d.); halfpenny (½d.); farthing (¼d.). Farthings are but little used except at drapers' establishments. Silver coins are now being withdrawn and being replaced with coins to the same face value made of cupro-nickel.

Notes are also issued by the Bank of England for the sum of £5 (*see* p. 205). Former issues of higher denomination are, however, honoured on production.

MONEY-CHANGERS.—Foreign money can be exchanged for English at any Bank in the West End or City, at *Messrs Cook's Tourist Offices* and at authorized dealers.

MOTOR TOURS.—An agreeable interlude to sight-seeing may be had by taking advantage of the public coach trips from London. These are advertised in the daily papers, and seats can be secured at any of the tourist agencies. It is impossible here to give precise details, but among the runs are those to Buckinghamshire (Milton and Penn Country), and the Thames Valley, Brighton, Margate, Oxford, the Surrey Hills, etc.

Facing King's Cross Railway Station and in Buckingham Palace Road, beside Victoria Station, are important **Coach Stations,** whence vehicles set out not only for the trips round London but for journeys to all parts of England, and to Scotland and Wales. There are similar stations in the vicinity of Tavistock Square and elsewhere, but these details are subject to alteration

MOTORING IN LONDON.—*See* p. 46.

NEWSPAPERS.—Of the many hundreds of newspapers and period-icals published in London, the ordinary visitor is likely only to make acquaintance with the principal morning and evening and the illustrated weekly papers.

Morning Papers.—*The Times, Daily Telegraph and Morning Post, News Chronicle, Daily Mail, Daily Express, Daily Herald, Daily Graphic* (illustrated) *Daily Mirror* (illustrated), *Financial News, Financial Times, Sporting Life.*

Evening Papers.—*Evening News, Evening Standard, Star.*

Sunday Papers.—*Observer, Sunday Times, The People, Sunday Dispatch, News of the World, Sunday Referee* (sporting and theatrical), *Reynolds News, Sunday Express, Sunday Pictorial* (illustrated), *Sunday Graphic* (illustrated), etc.

Weekly Illustrated Papers.—*Illustrated London News, Sphere, Sketch, Tatler, Illus-trated Sporting and Dramatic News, The Field* (sporting), *Country Life, The Bystander, The Queen* (for ladies), *The Lady, Picture Post, Illustrated,* etc.

Punch is the leading humorous paper, and makes a speciality of political cartoons.

Weekly Reviews, etc.—*Spectator, Time and Tide, The New Statesman and Nation, Truth, John O'London, Public Opinion, Times Weekly,* etc.

Many **Overseas Papers** have offices in London, at which copies of recent issues can be obtained.

PARLIAMENTARY REPRESENTATION.—The metropolis was for-merly divided into fifty-eight constituencies, each electing one member, with the exception of the City, which had two members. Under the Representation of the People Act (1918), which extended the franchise to large numbers of women, seats were redistributed, and the County of London was divided into sixty-one parliamentary constituencies, each returning one member (except the City of London, which returned two). Under the provisions of the 1948 Act the number has been reduced to forty-three. Greater London has upwards of a hundred members.

PARKS AND OPEN SPACES.—No other metropolis possesses so many parks and breathing places as does this huge, overgrown city of ours. But it must be admitted that Londoners require as many "lungs" as they can get. Besides the great parks under the control of the Crown, like Hyde Park, Kensington Gardens, St. James's, Regent's and Greenwich Parks, amounting in the aggregate to nearly 2,000 acres, there are under the management of the County Council in this Administrative County, gardens and open spaces totalling 4,800 acres, to say nothing of the numerous small spaces controlled by the Borough Councils, which constitute an acreage of over 600. Alto-gether, therefore, leaving out of account the numerous semi-private gardens, like those owned by the Inns of Court, and the great Squares, we have in the County of London alone nearly 8,000 acres of parks and open spaces. If the survey is extended to Outer London, we get into touch with such magnificent expanses as Richmond Park, with its 2,358 acres; Hainault Forest, 1,108 acres; Bushy Park, with 1,100; Putney and Wimbledon Commons, covering over 1,000 acres; Mitcham Common, boasting an area of nearly 500 acres; Hounslow Heath, embracing about 281 acres. Nor does this exhaust the list of London's pleasure grounds, for in this connection we must take into account Epping Forest, whose 5,560 acres have been preserved to the public by the City Corporation; and Burnham Beeches, 492 acres in extent, which was another of the Corporation's gifts to the people of London.

The largest of the public parks in London proper is, of course, Hyde Park, which, with Kensington Gardens, covers 636 acres. If we take as one area (as we fairly may) the chain of open spaces formed by the Horse Guards' Parade, St. James's Park (93 acres), the Green Park

[Central Press

Buckingham Palace, the London residence of H.M. the King. The Palace derives its name from a mansion erected by the Duke of Buckingham in 1703.

London (b).

Lambeth Bridge and the Houses of Parliament. In the middle distance is Westminster Bridge and, beyond, the Charing Cross Railway Bridge carrying the railway from the great London terminal.

(53 acres), Hyde Park, and Kensington Gardens, we have an area of about 750 acres. It is, in fact, possible by just crossing the road at Hyde Park Corner to walk from the Westminster corner of St. James's Park in an almost direct line for nearly three miles through parks and gardens abounding in magnificent timber and wild bird life.

Of the 106 open spaces controlled by the London County Council, the finest is Hampstead Heath (288 acres), with Ken Wood (195 acres), Parliament Hill (271 acres), Golder's Hill (36 acres) and Waterlow Park (26 acres) adjoining. Blackheath (267), Battersea Park (199), Clapham Common (205), Tooting Common (218), Wandsworth Common and Park (195), Peckham Rye and Park (113), Beckenham Place Park (213), Bostall Heath and Woods and Lesnes Abbey Woods (349), are all large spaces south of the Thames. Bands play in many of the parks throughout the summer on certain evenings and on Sundays, and facilities are provided for bathing, boating, cricket, tennis, bowls, putting, etc. Refreshments can be obtained at moderate prices in most of the parks.

PICTURE GALLERIES.—In the case of public galleries the fees (if any) and hours of admission are given in our descriptive notes (*see* Index). On certain days of the week a charge of about 6*d.* is made for admission to some of these (*see* later pages); on other days admission is free. For private exhibitions in the galleries of well-known picture-dealers in Bond Street and elsewhere, see advertisements in daily newspapers. The general charge for admission to these is about 1*s.*

Dulwich Gallery, Gallery Road, S.E.

Guildhall Art Gallery, Basinghall Street, E.C.2.

Hampton Court Palace.

Imperial War Museum.

Leighton House, 12, Holland Park Road.

National Gallery, Trafalgar Square.

National Portrait Gallery, ditto.

Royal Academy, Piccadilly. Summer Exhibition, May to August.

Royal Institute of Painters in Water Colours, 195, Piccadilly.

Royal Institute of Oil Painters, 195, Piccadilly.

Royal Society of British Artists, Suffolk Street, Pall Mall East, S.W.1.

Sir John Soane's Museum, 13, Lincoln's Inn Fields.

Tate Gallery, Millbank.

Victoria and Albert Museum, South Kensington.

Wallace Collection, Hertford House, Manchester Square.

Whitechapel Art Gallery, 81-2, Whitechapel High Street.

POLICE.—Although a large number of offences are committed within the borders of London, a comparatively small number of police-men is found sufficient to protect its inhabitants from the Ishmaelites whose hands are against every man. The **City Police Force,** to whom is committed the protection of that London the evident wealth of which caused Blücher to exclaim, "What a city this would be to plunder!" numbers only about eleven hundred good men and true; while the establishment of the **Metropolitan Police,** who take care of Greater London, extending for a radius of 15 miles from Charing Cross, consists of about twenty thousand men of all ranks. There are also about 350 women police. The City Police Force is under the control of the City Fathers, and has its headquarters in Old Jewry; the Com-missioner of the Metropolitan Police is responsible to the Secretary of State for the Home Department, no local body having any authority over the force. The chief offices of the Metropolitan Police are at New Scotland Yard, on the Embankment. The City Police may be distinguished from the Metropolitan Police by the fact that their armlets are red and white instead of blue and white. Their helmets, moreover, are crested.

London (*b*)

The police of London, by their courtesy and readiness to assist strangers, have won a world-wide renown. When in doubt "ask a policeman" is a very good rule in London thoroughfares.

POSTAL.—To facilitate delivery and collection of letters, the metropolis is divided into postal districts, each with its local headquarters, and much prompter delivery of London letters is assured by adding to the address not only the initials of the district in which the receiver resides, but a number indicating the proper office of delivery. The districts are known as E.C., E., S.E., S.W., W., W.C., N.W. and N. Thus the principal Government Departments are addressed "Whitehall, S.W. 1," while this Guide is published from "W.C. 2." The greater part of the City is E.C. A subtle social superiority is supposed to cling to the letters W. and S.W. The principal delivery is made between 7 and 9 a.m., and there are others during the day.

Larger Post Offices are generally open from 8.30 a.m. to 6.30 p.m., and smaller ones from 9 a.m. to 5.30 p.m. or 6 p.m. On Sundays and Bank Holidays certain offices are open from 9 a.m. to 1 p.m. The latest time of posting in the Central Districts for the Provincial Night Mails to places in England and Wales is 6 p.m., but later postings, up to 8 p.m. may be made at certain offices. Letters prepaid with a late fee of $\frac{1}{2}d.$ in addition to the ordinary postage may also be posted in the boxes provided on mail trains to which sorting carriages are attached, up to the time of departure of the trains.

Air Mails.—Full information regarding Overseas Air Mail services is given in the current Air Mail Leaflet, obtainable free of charge at any Post Office.

On **Sundays** there is no general delivery of letters, but both in London itself and in the suburbs there is an afternoon collection about 4.15 p.m.

Poste Restante.—Strangers without a permanent address in London can have their letters sent to the General Post Office, King Edward Street, London, E.C.1, or to any branch office, marked "to be called for" or "Poste Restante." Proof of identity must be given. Letters from abroad not called for are kept one month; letters from provincial towns a fortnight: at the end of that time they are treated as undeliverable and returned to senders or destroyed.

Express Letters.—Letters and parcels may be sent (week-days only) from nearly 550 Post Offices to any part of London and suburbs at a charge of $6d.$ a mile or part of a mile.

Inland Telegrams are accepted during counter business hours at any post office or railway station at which telegraph business is transacted; the following offices are always open. London Chief Office, E.C. 1; Leicester Square Branch Office, 39, Charing Cross Road, W.C. 2. They may also be tendered by telephone at any hour of the day or night. Ordinary telegram charges: Except Irish Republic, 1s. 6d. for 12 words or less; $1\frac{1}{2}d.$ each for additional words. To Irish Republic, 2s. for 12 words or less; $1\frac{1}{2}d.$ for each additional word. Telegrams handed in on Sundays, Good Friday and Christmas Day are charged 9d. extra.

Telegrams other than Greetings telegrams may be addressed to a telephonic address for delivery by telephone.

Overseas Telegrams may be handed in at any Cable & Wireless or postal telegraph office or they may be telephoned. The principal overseas Telegraph Station at Electra House, Victoria Embankment, W.C.2, is always open (Tel. TEMple Bar 1214 and 8494).

Postal Underground Railway.—*See* p. 212.

Telephones.—Telephones are under the control of the General Post Office. Public telephone call office facilities are provided at many post offices, railway stations and shops; and in kiosks. The minimum charge for the use of a call office is 3*d.* Normally, the charge is based upon the radial distance between the exchanges concerned. Trunk (and toll) calls may be effected from all public call offices: a call office charge of 3*l.* is payable in addition to the appropriate trunk, etc., charge. Reduced rates are charged for trunk and toll calls made between 6 p.m. and 10.30 p.m. A message may be dictated from a call office to any post office in the United Kingdom which is a telephone express delivery office for delivery by express messenger, on payment of the appropriate telephone fee for the call (including a call office fee of 3*d.*) plus a writing-down fee of 3*d.* for the first 30 words and 1*d.* for each 10 words or part thereof in excess of 30: plus the express delivery charge of 6*d.* a mile, or part of a mile, from the office of delivery to the addressee.

(For detailed information concerning postal services, see the Post Office Guide, at any post office; for the Telephone services (home and foreign) see the Telephone Directory.)

RAINFALL.—The annual average is between 24 and 25 inches.

RESTAURANTS.—*See* Introduction, pp. 15-16

ROMAN LONDON.—There are more remains of the Roman occupation (1st to 5th century A.D.) than is generally understood. For sections of the Wall see p. 69. In Strand Lane is a portion of a Roman bath, and many other relics are preserved in the Guildhall, the London and the British Museums. The most extensive recent discoveries have been made at St. Albans (*see* p. 273).

SEASONS.—The London Season nominally extends from the beginning of May to about the end of July. At this time Parliament is sitting, the Royal Academy and other picture galleries are open, and nearly all the leaders of society are in town. Later, the great migration commences, and every day the roads and railway stations are thronged by jostling crowds, eager to get to the sea and the moors. At the same time the great invasion of "country cousins" and visitors from America, the Dominions and the Continent sets in. The best time to see London is the spring, when the trees in the Parks are just breaking into leaf, the air is still crisp and cool, and the "show places" are not inconveniently crowded.

SHOPS AND SHOPPING.—A fair lady of the eighteenth century, in a letter to us, aptly described London as "an old lick-pocket." The accusation is certainly no less true to-day than it was then. We can hardly accept the delicate responsibility of advising readers where and how to spend their money, but those who are strange to town may be glad of a few general indications.

The best and most attractive shops are in Regent Street, Oxford Street, Bond Street, Piccadilly and the streets adjacent thereto. Holborn, Cheapside, the Strand, St. Paul's Churchyard, and Tottenham Court Road are also much favoured by shoppers. Outside the central district the chief shopping quarters are the Brompton Road, High Street, Kensington, Sloane Street, and Queensway, Bayswater.

The great **Stores**, where practically everything may be bought, from parasols to pineapples, include the *Army and Navy Stores,* 105, Victoria Street, Westminster, and the *Civil Service Stores*,

425 Strand, and Queen Victoria Street—these were originally co-operative concerns only, but are now open to all; *Selfridge's*, Oxford Street; *Harrod's*, Brompton Road; *Barker's*, High Street, Kensington; *Whiteley's*, Bayswater; *Peter Robinson's*, Oxford Street and Leicester Square; *Waring and Gillows'*, Oxford Street; *Gamage's*, Holborn.

Early Closing.—Shops are compelled by law to allow their assistants a weekly half-holiday. The day of closing varies in different districts, Wednesday and Thursday being the most usual. Nearly all City and West End shops close at 1 p.m. on Saturdays.

STEAMERS.—A number of steam and motor boats make daily passages during the summer from Westminster Bridge to Kew, Richmond, Hampton Court, etc. Luncheon and tea are served on board at moderate prices. See advertisements in the daily newspapers, etc. See also Water-buses, p. 37.

On the higher reaches of the river, the saloon steamers belonging to *Messrs. Salter Bros.* of Oxford make delightful trips in summer through ninety miles of Thames scenery (*see* p. 274.) For full details see the *Guide to the Thames* in this series.

Down the River.—Steamers and motor boats run at intervals during the day from Westminster Bridge to Tower Pier and Greenwich, often doing the trip in less time than would be required by a bus, and providing close-up views of the shipping.

Starting from the Tower Pier steamers make daily trips down river to Southend, Margate, Clacton, Felixstowe, Yarmouth, etc. *See* announcements in daily papers.

SUNDAY IN LONDON.—Continental critics have dealt somewhat harshly with the English Sunday. Take for instance, M. Taine, the French historian: "Sunday in London—the shops are shut, the streets almost deserted; the aspect is that of an immense and well-ordered cemetery. The few passers-by in the desert of squares and streets have the look of uneasy spirits risen from their graves. It is appalling. After an hour's walk in the Strand especially, and in the rest of the City, one has the spleen; one meditates suicide."

Much depends upon one's point of view, but things have changed considerably in recent years, and Sunday need no longer be regarded as a *dies non* even by the sightseer. Information as to **Churches and Chapels** will be found on pp. 20–21. During summer large numbers spend the day, or part of it, on the Thames or other pleasure resorts in the vicinity of London, or even by the sea, the railway and motor-coach companies advertising special excursions. Most of the **Museums and Picture Galleries** are open on Sunday afternoons; both afternoon and evening there are concerts, and many Cinemas are open. In the evening during summer there are band performances in the Parks and in the open spaces controlled by the County Council.

And if on Sunday mornings the deserted City streets still justify M. Taine's description, we may remind the visitor that there is no such time for making leisurely acquaintance with the highways and byways and quaint nooks and corners of this mighty metropolis, while Sunday mornings provides one of the most interesting spectacles in London—the market in Middlesex Street (or Petticoat Lane, *see* p. 240).

VIEW-POINTS, NOTABLE.—All the bridges over the Thames afford fine views. Wordsworth's lines on **Westminster Bridge** at daybreak, commencing "Earth has not anything to show more fair," are well known. An even better view-point is from **Waterloo Bridge**, commanding the fine sweep of the Embankment, with its stately buildings and the majestic dome of St. Paul's. The view eastward from Blackfriars Bridge is marred by a railway bridge, but from a point a short distance along the Embankment the dome is well seen, and one is able to appreciate Wren's masterly grouping of spires in relation to it. The eastern side of **London Bridge** is nearly always lined by spectators, some of whom spend hours in watching the loading and unloading of vessels in the **Pool**.

Of street views, that from **Fleet Street** up Ludgate Hill to St. Paul's would be hard to beat, though the railway bridge is in the way. The view up Fleet Street itself, towards St. Dunstan's Church and the Law Courts, is also worthy of rote, particularly towards sundown. Another entrancing view is that from the end of **Parliament Street,** taking in the Abbey and its "baby," St. Margaret's, Westminster Hall and the Houses of Parliament. The little glimpse down **St. James's Street** from Piccadilly, with St. James's Palace at the foot of the slope, is worth noting. Regent Street—particularly at the Piccadilly Circus end—provides one of the best modern street views in London.

One of the finest Park views is that from a point in **Kensington Gardens** near the refreshment pavilion overlooking the Serpentine. The views from the **Serpentine Bridge** are also very fine. The same may be said of the view from the Buckingham Palace end of **St. James's Park.** The footbridge over the lake also provides a view eastward that of its kind is probably unsurpassed in any city.

Of lofty vantage-points, the most notable are the Monument (p. 242), the Stone Gallery of **St. Paul's Cathedral,** and the tower of the **Roman Catholic Cathedral** at Westminster (p. 115). All (except the last, where a lift is available) involve fatiguing climbs, and should not be attempted unless the day is quite clear. Even then, London's pall of smoke is apt to obscure the outlook. Good all-round views are to be obtained from the roof gardens that are a feature of several of the big stores and hotels and office blocks.

The view in clear weather from the summit of **Primrose Hill** is truly magnificent, especially near sunset. **Parliament Hill,** farther north, also gives a good idea of the "forest of houses"; while from that famous vantage-point, the flagstaff on **Hampstead Heath,** a rural prospect is unfolded that will strike the stranger with amazement. The view from **Richmond Hill** needs no laudation here; but it may be well to beg the visitor to **Windsor** not to skip, as many do, the ascent of the Round Tower, which affords a fine prospect of the winding Thames.

WATER BUSES.—A service of small launches, carrying 150 persons, is, during summer months, operated on the Thames between Tower Pier and Putney, with extensions to Greenwich. Calls are made at Charing Cross, Blackfriars, Lambeth Bridge and Albert Bridge (Battersea). The service is half-hourly, and the fares reasonable.

WATER SUPPLY.—No fewer than 224 million gallons out of the daily total requirement of 320 million gallons are derived from the Thames in the neighbourhood of Laleham, Walton, Hampton, and Staines. The huge reservoirs, of which the largest is the "Queen Mary" at Littleton with an available capacity of 6,679 million gallons, hold 22,329 million gallons (including a new reservoir of 4,450 million gallons capacity, completed 1948).

The daily consumption per head in the area of 540 square miles supplied by the Metropolitan Water Board is about 48 gallons.

SEEING LONDON

Hints for the Hurried Visitor

"fold on fold,
Grey to pearl, and pearl to gold,
Our London, like a land of old,
    The land of Eldorado."

THE metropolis is so vast, its interests are so many and so
intricate and so much of it is ever changing, that it may be
doubted whether any man can truthfully say that he "knows
London." Least of all will the lifelong resident make that
assertion, for if he be of an observant and reflective turn of mind
every journey in an unaccustomed quarter will but add to his
consciousness of abysmal ignorance. In a single suburb—even
the most commonplace to outward seeming—there is matter for
a library; while as to the central portion, with its crowded
interests and constant changes, this closely-packed handbook,
with its rigorous selections and equally rigorous exclusions, is
about as good an illustration as could be offered of the impossi-
bility of emptying the Atlantic with a limpet-shell.

Such being the frame of mind inevitably forced upon those
who spend their working lives in and about London, it may
well be asked despairingly: How can the casual visitor—the
man or woman with one day, two days, three days, a week, or
even a fortnight at disposal—hope in so short a time to gain
an intelligent acquaintance with the sights and features of this
so extensive metropolis, beyond all question the most bewildering
that the world has ever known?

The answer is that the miracle is possible of accomplishment,
is, in fact, accomplished every year by crowds of delighted
strangers, who see more of the "Great Wen" in a few days,
or even hours, than very many Londoners see in a lifetime.
This is due partly to the apathy of Londoners, the majority of
whom, it must be confessed, make but the feeblest response to
the reflection that they are "citizens of no mean city"; partly
to the fact that visitors from a distance have usually studied
such books as this before arrival, and have formed definite

ideas as to the things they wish to see and the things they are content to leave unseen. Of these considerations we should be disposed to attach the greater importance to the second. "System" and "selection"—especially, alas, "selection" with its inevitable corollary, "exclusion"—must be the watchwords of the hurried visitor.

The hustler who has demonstrated to admiring friends that London can be "done" in a day will smile at the leisurely nature of our daily programmes; others will find them far too full. We endeavour to indicate a middle course, allowing time for something more than a mental snapshot of each place, but little for lingering. And an overwhelming consciousness of the "much that lies beyond" prompts us to exhort even the most indefatigable sightseer not for one moment to imagine that "seeing London" and "knowing London" are phrases identical in meaning.

It is premised that the visitor will read these itineraries in conjunction with the notes as to days and hours of admission given in small type under the headings of our descriptions of the various places of interest. Some little care is necessary in this matter, for if economy of time be the governing consideration it is mortifying in the extreme to find on arrival that doors are closed, or will open only on the production of a previously procured order. It is useful to bear in mind also that certain Galleries and Museums *remain open after dark on certain evenings*; but the Houses of Parliament can be seen *only on Saturdays, on Easter and Whitsun Monday and Tuesday, and August Bank Holiday*. It should be said, too, if economy of time be more important than economy of money, that *free days* are best avoided, especially in the height of the season. Apart from fares, sight-seeing in London is cheaper than anywhere, and an occasional sixpence or shilling is generally well spent in avoiding a crowd.

On pp. 45–61 will be found detailed notes on the various transport services. If expense is not so paramount a consideration as time, it is often advantageous to cover intermediate distances by taxi (for fares *see* p. 45), but on congested traffic routes the cab is often little quicker than the bus, and the tube may be quicker than either. In any case in the central parts it is rarely worth while to retain a taxi, as it can be discharged on entering a building, if a lengthy stay is likely, with a reasonable certainty of being able to secure another on leaving. But if a number of places are visited in succession, with only a short stay in each, it will often be found more convenient to direct the driver to wait. For distances of any length the Underground Railways are generally preferable, but given fine weather the buses afford a pleasurable mode of progression and give opportunities for noting objects of interest and the life of the streets that the railway passenger misses.

London at a Glance

It will greatly assist the stranger to keep his bearings in the crowded streets of Central London if he forms at the outset a mental picture of the direction and intersections of the principal thoroughfares. To this end we have prepared a special map (*see* pp. 48–49), showing "London at a Glance," believing that this will be more helpful than pages of elaborate directions. Bear in mind that the river runs from west to east, with a siphon-like northward bend from Vauxhall Bridge to Waterloo; and that the two chief thoroughfares, Oxford Street with its continuations, and the Strand with its continuations, follow approximately the same course from west to east, eventually meeting at the Bank of England. Connection north and south between these two great thoroughfares is provided by Park Lane, Bond Street and Regent Street in the west; by Charing Cross Road and Kingsway and Aldwych, between Holborn and the Strand; and by Chancery Lane at the City boundary. Westminster and Victoria lie to the south of Charing Cross, off these main routes, and connected with the City by the Victoria Embankment and Queen Victoria Street, which converges to meet the two other through routes near the Bank.

In making any necessary modifications or adaptations of the following itineraries one of the principal objects should be to avoid going over the same ground twice.

London in One Day

Assuming that the reader is a "bird of passage," merely breaking his journey, and having a final destination elsewhere, how shall he employ the time at his disposal to the best advantage?

The following are a few alternative modes of spending what must perforce be a very hurried day, the proportion of time given to each place depending, of course, upon whether the pilgrim's "bent" is in the direction of art, architecture, historical association, or "shops" and the life of the streets. The routes start from Charing Cross (Plan II. K. 8), which for sight-seeing purposes may be regarded as the "hub" of London.

Morning	Afternoon
National Gallery.	Regent Street.
National Portrait Gallery.	Oxford Street.
Whitehall (passing Government Offices, Royal United Service Museum and the Cenotaph).	Wallace Collection, Manchester Square.
Houses of Parliament. (*Open on Saturdays and Easter and Whit-sun Mondays and Tuesdays.*)	Drive through Hyde Park and Kensington Gardens.
	Piccadilly.
Westminster Abbey.	Royal Academy.
Westminster (R.C.) Cathedral.	British Museum.
Buckingham Palace (exterior).	Lincoln's Inn (walk through).
St. James's Park.	Law Courts and Temple.
St. James's Palace (exterior).	Fleet Street.
Luncheon in neighbourhood of Piccadilly or Leicester Square.	Ludgate Hill.
	St. Paul's Cathedral.

If it is intended to stay in London overnight, and there are any hours of daylight left, they can be well employed in saunter-ing along the Embankment, with its pleasant riverside gardens, to the starting-point at Charing Cross. Dinner, and perhaps a visit to a theatre, will bring the traveller to the end of the day, and probably of his powers of endurance.

The route outlined has the disadvantage of almost excluding the City. An alternative might be:

Morning	Afternoon
Tower of London.	Law Courts.
Monument.	Temple Gardens.
Bank of England.	Embankment.
Royal Exchange (frescoes).	London County Hall.
Guildhall, Museum & Art Gallery.	Houses of Parliament.
Cheapside.	Westminster Abbey.
St. Paul's Cathedral.	National Gallery.
Luncheon at any of the neighbour-ing restaurants.	

Any remaining hours of daylight could be employed in a stroll in St. James's Park, with a glance at Buckingham Palace and St. James's Palace, and at the many Government Offices.

London in Two Days

The two-day visitor has a bewildering choice of possibilities. He might take the two one-day programmes already sketched, the fact that they overlap to some extent allowing him more ample time for each. Or should he desire to extend the range of sight-seeing, he might proceed somewhat as follows:

First Day	*Second Day*
Charing Cross.	Tower of London.
National Gallery.	Monument.
National Portrait Gallery.	Royal Exchange.
Whitehall.	Bank.
Houses of Parliament.	Guildhall.
London County Hall.	Cheapside.
Westminster Abbey.	St. Paul's Cathedral.
(*Luncheon.*)	(*Luncheon.*)
Imperial War Museum.	Holborn.
Lambeth Palace (exterior).	British Museum.
Tate Gallery.	Oxford Street.
Westminster (R.C.) Cathedral.	Wallace Collection.
St. James's Park.	Regent's Park.
Green Park.	Zoological Gardens.
Hyde Park; Kensington Gardens.	
Victoria and Albert Museum.	
Natural History Museum.	
Science and Geological Museums.	

London in Four Days

All the really "first magnitude" sights in London proper have been included in the foregoing lists. It will depend upon the visitor's taste, and also, perhaps, upon the weather, if sights of second magnitude shall be included, or the time at disposal be devoted to a trip out of London, say to Windsor Castle or Hampton Court.

Of these "second magnitude" sights all the following are in or near the central part of London, and can be easily sandwiched into the programmes already given. The three-day visitor will have to exclude some of them, unless he is content with a very cursory glance:

Chelsea Hospital, Carlyle's House, etc., at Chelsea (can be combined with South Kensington Museums).

Mint (order necessary). Can be combined with Tower.

Oratory, Brompton Road.

St. Bartholomew's Church, Smithfield (oldest in London, except Tower Chapel).

Charterhouse

St. Margaret's, Westminster.

Record Office, Chancery Lane (historical deeds).

Soane Museum and Royal College of Surgeons (order necessary for latter), Lincoln's Inn Fields.

Temple.

Royal United Service Museum, Whitehall.

St. Saviour's Cathedral.

London in from Four to Six Days

The diligent visitor will be able to arrange programmes including all the first-rate and secondary sights already indicated, and to spare a morning or afternoon for a glimpse of South London, including not only Southwark Cathedral, but Dickens's "Borough," the Library of Lambeth Palace, Battersea Park, the Dulwich Picture Gallery, the National Maritime Museum at Greenwich, and the Horniman Museum. For a morning or afternoon trip from Town he will be able to select one or more of the following:

Windsor Castle and Park.
Hampton Court.
Virginia Water.
Kew Gardens.
Richmond.
Burnham Beeches, Stoke Poges, and possibly Penn.
Epping Forest.

Box Hill, Leith Hill, or other beauty spots in Surrey.
A Trip up the Thames, say from Kingston to Windsor, or from Windsor to Maidenhead or Henley.
London Airport (Heathrow).

Most of these trips can be made by public motor as well as by rail. The Tourist Agencies arrange many whole-day coach drives, one of the most popular of which is: Stoke Poges—Burnham Beeches—Maidenhead—Windsor—Hampton Court. Combined motor and launch trips are also arranged, such as car to Stoke Poges—launch Maidenhead to Windsor—car Windsor to Staines—launch Staines to Shepperton—car to Hampton Court and home (*see* also under "Motor Tours," p. 31).

London in a Week

All the foregoing programmes have the advantage of elasticity and the corresponding disadvantage of vagueness. With a whole week at disposal it might be possible to draw up a more rigid programme, including practically everything of general interest. For such a programme the seven West End routes and the City and South London chapters into which this book is divided could be followed fairly closely. Any superfluous shoe-leather might well be devoted, if the weather is fine, to making closer acquaintance with London's parks and open spaces, of which, in our opinion, neither Londoners nor their visitors see half enough. One or two afternoons will probably be devoted to entertainments, but the sightseer will, of course, economize time by reserving these for the evenings or for days when the weather is unfavourable for distant journeys.

In selecting any of the following day tours due regard should be paid to opening and closing of show-places—the Houses of Parliament, for example, can be seen only on Saturdays, Easter and Whitsun Mondays and Tuesdays, and on August Bank Holiday.

First Day. Charing Cross—Northumberland Avenue—Victoria Embankment—Houses of Parliament—Westminster Abbey—St. Margaret's Church—Cenotaph and Government Offices, Whitehall—Royal United Services Museum—Trafalgar Square—National Gallery—National Portrait Gallery.

Second Day. St. James's Park—Marlborough House—St. James's Palace—Buckingham Palace—Green Park—Hyde Park—Kensington Gardens—Kensington Palace—Royal School of Art Needlework—Albert Hall and Memorial—Imperial Institute—Victoria and Albert Museum—Science Museum—Geological Museum—Natural History Museum—Brompton Oratory—Piccadilly—Royal Academy.

Third Day. Regent Street—Oxford Street—Wallace Collection—Regent's Park—Zoological Gardens—Hampstead Heath—Return by Tube to Tottenham Court Road—British Museum—Gray's Inn.

Fourth Day. Strand—Aldwych and Kingsway—Lincoln's Inn Fields (Soane Museum, etc.)—Lincoln's Inn—Law Courts—Chancery Lane—Record Office—Temple—Fleet Street—St. Paul's Cathedral—G.P.O.—St. Bartholomew's Church and the Charterhouse—St. Giles, Cripplegate—London Wall—Guildhall—Cheapside—Bank—Royal Exchange—Monument—Tower of London—Tower Bridge—Mint—Return to Charing Cross by boat or by the Underground or bus.

Fifth Day. Westminster Bridge—London County Hall—St. Thomas's Hospital—Imperial War Museum—Lambeth Palace and Church—Tate Gallery—Chelsea Hospital—Cheyne Walk (Carlyle's House, etc.)—Battersea Park—Victoria—Roman Catholic Cathedral—Westminster School—Church House.

Fifth Day (alternative). Charing Cross to London Bridge by bus or train to Monument station—Southwark Cathedral—The Borough—Tram or taxi to Dulwich Picture Gallery—Boat (from Tower Pier), tram or taxi to Greenwich for Park and National Maritime Museum—London Docks (Conducted tours organised on certain days by the Port of London Authority)—Bethnal Green Museum—Victoria Park—Epping Forest.

Sixth Day. By rail or road to Windsor (state apartments are not always open, but there is plenty otherwise to see). Afternoon steamer down River to Kingston—Hampton Court—Bushy Park.

Sixth Day (alternative). Kew Gardens—Richmond—Kingston—Hampton Court—Windsor Castle and Park—Slough—Burnham Beeches—Stoke Poges.

Seventh Day. Another excursion in the Environs (see "Trips from Town") or see places necessarily omitted in above rounds.

For **Sunday in London** see p. 36.

have to be enforced strictly in the busier quarters of London, and before leaving a car standing it is well to consult a policeman concerning the period during which cars may be so left there, if indeed, they may be left there at all; the police will also direct motorists to the nearest public car park. Particular attention should be paid to the "no-waiting" zones which are indicated by yellow bands painted on lamp-standards, posts, etc. In the central area a number of bombed sites have been cleared and are now in use as car parks. In addition to these and other parking places there are a number of large garages where cars may be left in safety.

LONDON TRANSPORT

In 1933 a comprehensive body, popularly known as "London Transport," was formed with the object of co-ordinating all the various passenger transport services of London and its suburbs as a necessary step towards the solution of London's very serious traffic problem. These services were placed under the control of the London Passenger Transport Board. On 1st January, 1948, under the Transport Act of 1947, the organization passed into the ownership of the British Transport Commission and the management of this huge undertaking placed in the hands of the London Transport Executive. It has, however, continued to be known as London Transport. The area controlled by the Executive is about 2,000 square miles, with a population estimated at 9,800,000 persons.

BUSES

were introduced into London in 1829 by George Shillibeer, from whom they were for some time known as "shillibeers", though they carried on their sides the word "Omnibus", "a carry-all"— usually shortened to "bus." Until 1899 the vehicles were drawn by horses. In that year tentative experiments were made with motor-omnibuses, and from 1905 the use of this class of vehicle became so general that the last horsed bus of the London General Omnibus Company made its final trip on October 25th, 1911. Many of the motor buses now in use are the finest in the world. Smoking is permitted only on upper decks of buses, and at the rear of single-deck buses.

In 1912 the London General Omnibus Company came under the same management as the Underground Railways. In 1933 or later one hundred and seventy undertakings passed to the control of the London Passenger Transport Board. In 1948 ownership passed to the British Transport Commission. A slight idea of the magnitude of the traffic can be gained from the fact that during the year 1950, 7,400 buses and coaches operated a total mileage of $313\frac{1}{2}$ millions, and carried 2,718 million

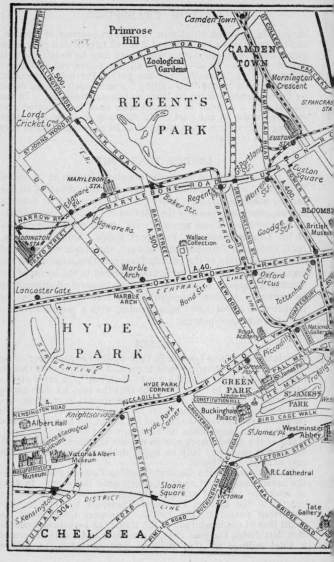

passengers. Put in another way, it may be said that every person in the London Transport area made 277 bus and coach journeys in 1950.

The vehicles bear numbers indicative of the various routes, and blinds display the names of the localities through which they run. The visitor should make himself acquainted with the relative positions of the chief localities by reference to the maps, in order to guard against the possibility of mistaking the direction in which the vehicle is travelling. For the most part vehicles stop only at recognised *Bus Stops*, indicated by plainly marked columns at the kerbside. At *Request Stops* the passenger should indicate his intention of boarding or alighting, as the vehicle will not otherwise stop. Do not attempt either to board or to leave a bus while it is moving.

In entering trams, trolleybuses and buses, especially the latter, hold firmly to the rail till you are either inside or safely on top. This is quite as important if the vehicle is stationary as if moving, for the jerk caused by a sudden start may send you headlong. When desirous of alighting, ring the bell *once* for the driver to stop.

Visitors should endeavour to time their movements so as to avoid using the buses during "rush" hours—say from 7.30 to 9.30 in the morning, and from 4.30 to 7 in the evening (Saturdays 12.30–2.30), according to district—for every vehicle is then loaded to full capacity, and travellers may find it difficult to board the first bus.

Some of the bus journeys are of an astonishing length; for instance, West Croydon Station—Horsham Station (route 414) 32.6 miles: but some Green Line coach routes are considerably longer. There are other such regular daily services to places as far afield as Watford, St. Albans, Epping Town, Brentwood, Windsor, etc., and practically every place of importance within a radius of 30 miles or so is linked by bus or coach routes with the heart of the metropolis, though one or two changes of vehicle may be necessary. On Sundays and Bank Holidays, and on the early closing days in certain districts, extended services are run.

TRAMS AND TROLLEYBUSES

On January 1st, 1948, the entire tramway and trolleybus systems of London and its suburbs operating under the London Passenger Transport Board were, with the buses, passed to the ownership of the British Transport Commission. From 1931, many tramways were converted to trolleybus operation; in October, 1950, substitution of buses for all remaining tramcars began, and before long all of them will have been displaced by oil-engined buses. Meanwhile visitors will probably find interest in using the subway line (*see* p. 189) connecting Southampton Row, Bloomsbury, with the Victoria Embankment and Westminster (journey time 7 minutes), and the very quick and useful services along the Embankment itself, between Blackfriars and Westminster. Trolleybuses are handy for exploring South London—Greenwich, Woolwich, etc.—and such places north of the river as Shoreditch, Islington, etc. Longer runs embrace such resorts as Hampstead Heath, Kew Bridge, and Epping Forest.

THE RAILWAYS OF LONDON

See Railway Map facing p. 45.

There are in the London Transport area some 800 passenger railway stations. The length of passenger lines in the same area is nearly 1,200 miles, or three times the distance from London to Glasgow. Of "tube" and other railway stations served by Underground trains there are 277. It is of interest to note that some 695 million passengers were carried in 1950 in Underground trains, and even these stupendous figures are exclusive of the suburban traffic on main lines. The average number of journeys per head of the population of London by all forms of transport is 501 per annum.

The accompanying map shows all the Underground and other lines, and will repay careful study and constant consultation.

The railways of London are divisible into two groups—those which form the suburban sections of the great trunk lines, and the electrically-driven and purely London railways which are run below street-level and are generally known as—

THE UNDERGROUND

To the sightseer the Underground is chiefly of value for getting quickly to places at a distance; for short point-to-point journeys —unless on a direct line of route—and for seeing the streets themselves, a taxi or a bus is to be preferred. Although the journey times from station to station are short—Euston to Piccadilly Circus, for instance, in 10 minutes—allowance must be made for the time spent in lifts or on escalators and in traversing subways and stairs between them and station platforms, such time on short journeys often equalling or even exceeding that actually spent in the trains. But an Underground journey is often a speedier mode of transit than even a taxi, on account of the congestion of the streets.

From the traveller's point of view the various lines can now be considered a single huge system, though the connections are not so convenient as might have been the case had the principle of co-operation been adopted from the outset. Through bookings are in operation on all the lines, so that from almost any station one may, by changing at the proper point, or points, get to any other station, *whether on the same line or not*. Directions as to stations at which it is necessary to change are given in route outlines displayed on the platforms and in the cars.

This vast network of electric railways comprises two systems —the District Line and the Metropolitan Line—which in places are only a short distance below ground-level, the station platforms being reached from the street by stairways—and four "Tubes" running at considerably greater depths and reached from the street by lifts or escalators. On all lines trains run at intervals of a few minutes, and there is only one class.

To the stranger—and to many Londoners—the Underground Railways form a confusing network, and it will greatly aid the visitor if he can memorize the general directions of the various lines. To this end we have described each route in detail, adding notes on the more important stations.

The simplest route to memorize is that of—

The Central Line

which runs in an almost straight line east and west. Starting from Epping, it proceeds by way of Theydon Bois, Debden, Loughton, Buckhurst Hill, Woodford, S. Woodford and Snaresbrook to Leytonstone, a branch starts at Leytonstone and proceeds via Wanstead, Reabridge, Gant's Hill, Newbury Park, Barkingside and Fairlop to Hainault; a branch starts at Woodford and proceeds *via* Roding Valley, Chigwell, Grange Hill, to Hainault; from the junction the route is to Leytonstone, Leyton, Stratford, Mile End, and Bethnal Green to the Liverpool Street (Eastern Region terminus); it next has a station below the busy roadway at the *Bank*. Thence it passes below Cheapside, Newgate Street (*St. Paul's Station*), Holborn (*Chancery Lane* and *Holborn* (*Kingsway*) stations), and Oxford Street (stations at *Tottenham Court Road, Oxford Circus, Bond Street* and *Marble Arch*). Continuing below the Uxbridge road, on the northern edge of Hyde Park, it has stations at *Lancaster Gate, Queensway, Notting Hill Gate, Holland Park* and *Shepherds Bush*.

At this point the route of the line leaves the Uxbridge road, goes northward past the White City (*White City* station), to *East Acton, North Acton* and *West Acton* and *Ealing Broadway* stations, beside the Western Region main line. After leaving

North Acton a line diverges to *Hanger Lane, Perivale, Greenford, Northolt, South Ruislip, Ruislip Gardens* and *West Ruislip*. Visitors will find the Central Line handy for reaching the neighbourhood of the Royal Exchange, Mansion House, Guildhall, London Bridge, etc. (*Bank* station); St. Paul's Cathedral (*St. Paul's* station), Bloomsbury and the British Museum (*Holborn* (*Kingsway*) station), and the busy shopping district in and around Oxford Street.

At *Bank* station, and again at *Tottenham Court Road*, connection is made with the Northern Line (*see* p. 54). *Oxford Circus* station is shared with the Bakerloo Line (*see* p. 56). At Holborn there is intercommunication with the Piccadilly Line.

The District Line

also runs from east to west, but less directly than the Central London line. The easternmost station likely to interest the visitor is *Tower Hill*, close to the Tower of London. Passing westward below Eastcheap (*Monument* station, for the Monument, London Bridge, etc., and escalator connection with Bank station) and *Cannon Street* (station of same name for Mansion House, Bank of England, etc.; *Mansion House* station for St. Paul's Cathedral, Cheapside, Guildhall, etc.), the line comes close to the river at *Blackfriars* station (for Fleet Street and Ludgate Circus, St. Paul's Cathedral, etc.). Then it runs below the Embankment to Westminster (*Temple* station for the Temple, Kingsway, the Strand; *Charing Cross* station for the Trafalgar Square neighbourhood; *Westminster* station for Houses of Parliament, Westminster Abbey, Whitehall, etc.). The line now turns westward to *St. James Park* station, on the south side of the Park, and *Victoria* (for the Southern Region terminus, Westminster Cathedral, etc.). *Sloane Square* station is handy for Knightsbridge, and *South Kensington* serves "Museum Land."

Stations westward of this point likely to be of service to the visitor are *Gloucester Road* (for the Cromwell Road neighbourhood), and *Earls Court* (for the Exhibitions). Earls Court is an important junction for lines to Putney and Wimbledon, Hammersmith, Richmond, Ealing, Hounslow, Uxbridge, etc.

From *South Kensington* station—

The Metropolitan Line

runs first north and then east, finally rejoining the District Line at *Tower Hill* station to form a loop known as the **Inner Circle.** This half of the circle passes close to the great railway termini on the north side of London and also serves the Kensington and

Bayswater shopping centres, *High Street* (*Kensington*) station being well known to those frequenting Barker's and neighbouring stores. At *Notting Hill Gate* there is a Central Line station just opposite. *Bayswater* is the station for Westbourne Grove and its shops, and *Paddington* that for the Western Region terminus (subway connection). *Edgware Road* station is near the important thoroughfare of that name. The line now runs eastward below the Marylebone and Euston Roads. At *Baker Street* station it links up with the Metropolitan mainline, with trains every few minutes to Wembley, Harrow, Watford, Uxbridge and Rickmansworth, etc. (*see* p. 60). Baker Street station is also handy for Marylebone terminus of the Eastern Region, Madame Tussaud's, Regent's Park, etc. *Great Portland Street* station, at the northern end of that thoroughfare, is close to Regent's Park and the Zoo. *Euston Square* is within a few minutes' walk of the Euston terminus of the London Midland Region, and also serves Tottenham Court Road and Bloomsbury. *Kings Cross* station adjoins the Eastern Region terminus of that name and the St. Pancras terminus of the London Midland Region, and it has interchange with the Piccadilly Line and the Northern Line. *Farringdon* station serves that important market and is handy for the eastern end of Holborn, Ludgate Circus, etc., and *Aldersgate* is within a few minutes' walk of St. Paul's Cathedral. At **Moorgate** station is the terminus of a branch of the **Northern Line,** running northward to Highbury and Finsbury Park. Moorgate station lies close to the junction of Moorgate with London Wall (for the Bank, Royal Exchange, etc.), and *Liverpool Street* station is beneath the Eastern Region terminus of that name. At *Aldgate* Station the line passes beneath that busy highway, and at Tower Hill the District Line is rejoined and the Inner Circle is complete.

These two "east and west lines" are crossed by three deep Tubes running north and south and passing far below the Thames.

The Northern Line

This line, still familiarly **The Hampstead Tube,** serves the residential districts named, bringing them into close touch with the City and the West End. From East Finchley to Morden (*via* the Bank) is a distance of 17¼ miles—the longest tunnel journey it is possible to make on any railway in the world (the Simplon Tunnel is 12¼ miles long). Care should be taken to board the correct train, since the lines diverge at three points.

The southernmost station likely to be used by the casual visitor to London is *Oval*, adjoining the Surrey Cricket Club's headquarters at Kennington. Southward from this point the line runs below the Clapham Road to *Clapham Common*, and following the course of the Balham Road continues through *Balham* to *South Wimbledon* and *Morden*. Going in the other direction from *Oval* (i.e. *towards* London), the line makes for *Kennington* and *Waterloo*, with a station below the great Southern Region terminus at Waterloo, and interchange connections with the Bakerloo Line (*see* p. 56). Leaving Waterloo the Line passes far below the Thames to *Charing Cross* station (handy for the Embankment), with another station (*Strand*) below the main entrance to the Charing Cross Southern Region terminus, and serving Trafalgar Square, the Strand, Whitehall, etc. The course of the line now follows the Charing Cross Road and Tottenham Court Road. *Leicester Square* station is close to the heart of Theatreland, and *Tottenham Court Road* station serves the Oxford Street shopping quarter, Bloomsbury, the British Museum, etc. *Goodge Street* station is about midway along Tottenham Court Road, and *Warren Street* at its northern end, close to Maples' and other large stores. A sharp swing to the right brings the line beneath the *Euston* terminus of the London Midland Region.

Camden Town station (for the Zoo) is an important junction. One line runs northward *via Highgate* and *East Finchley* to *Mill Hill East* and to *High Barnet*; another north-westward *via Chalk Farm* and *Hampstead* (for the Heath) to the garden suburb at *Golders Green*, and thence as a surface railway to *Hendon Central* and *Edgware*. The line from Euston to the Bank first runs eastward to a station serving *Kings Cross* and *St. Pancras* termini of the Eastern and the London Midland Regions respectively (connection also with Piccadilly Tube and the Metropolitan Line); thence continues eastward to the *Angel* at Islington. Then it runs below the City Road and Moorgate, with stations at *Old Street* (for Bunhill Fields, Wesley's House, etc.) and *Moorgate* (for Finsbury Circus, Broad Street and Liverpool Street termini, etc.), to the *Bank*, where there is a very busy station serving also the Central Line and with escalator connection with Monument Station on the District Line. The station, thronged at all hours with City workers, is between the Bank of England, the Mansion House and the Royal Exchange.

From this point the line runs beneath the Thames to *London Bridge* station, below the Southern Region terminus of that name. Beneath Borough High Street (*Borough* station) and

Newington Causeway it passes to the station below the *Elephant and Castle* (interchange with Bakerloo line); and beneath Kennington Park Road (*Kennington* station) it rejoins the branch serving the West End already described.

See reference to a branch of the Northern Line in the Metropolitan Line paragraph.

The Bakerloo Line

derives its name from the fact that in crossing from north-west London to the south-east it serves the termini of the Metropolitan and Southern Region at Baker Street and Waterloo respectively. It extends beyond these stations, however—to *Elephant and Castle* in the south (where it links with the Northern Line, for Clapham and Morden, etc.), and in the north-west to *Queen's Park* station, whence it runs along with the London Midland Region suburban lines to Watford (*see* p. 58). At Baker Street the line diverges also *via St. John's Wood* (for Lord's Cricket Ground) and *Swiss Cottage* to *Finchley Road*, where it joins the Metropolitan Line, and runs *via Wembley Park* to *Stanmore*.

The section between Baker Street and Waterloo is very useful to those exploring the West End. *Baker Street* station (beneath the station of the Inner Circle (*see* p. 54) and the Metropolitan Line) is close to Regent's Park, Madame Tussaud's, etc. Westward are stations below the *Marylebone* terminus of the Eastern Region and the *Paddington* terminus of the Western Region; thence the route closely follows the important highway known as Maida Vale to *Queen's Park* (*see* p. 58).

Cityward from Baker Street, the Marylebone Road is followed to *Regent's Park* station, for the Zoo, Regent's Park, Great Portland Street, etc.; thence the Tube follows Regent Street to Trafalgar Square and passes under the Thames to Waterloo in close proximity to the Charing Cross Railway Bridge.

Oxford Circus station, at the junction of Regent Street and Oxford Street, serves that important shopping quarter, Broadcasting House, Palladium, etc., and is also used by the Central Line. At the southern end of Regent Street is *Piccadilly Circus* station, reconstructed in 1928 with considerable engineering skill. It is in the centre of Theatre-land and is near the Royal Academy, St. James's Park, etc. The *Piccadilly Line* (*see* p. 57) runs north-east and south-west from this point. *Trafalgar Square* station faces the top of Whitehall, at the western end of the Strand, and is within a few yards of the National Gallery, etc. *Charing Cross* station is on the Embankment, and lies below the District Line station. Here, too, the river is crossed by three railways—the Southern Region using the ugly and unwanted bridge, and the Bakerloo and Northern Lines passing far below the Thames by tunnel. *Waterloo* is the busy terminus of the Southern Region (South-Western section, *see* p. 60), and there are stations on the Bakerloo and Northern Lines. For *Elephant and Castle*, the southern-most station on the Bakerloo Line, *see* p. 55.

The Piccadilly Line

One other Tube Railway remains to be described. The Piccadilly Line follows the course of Piccadilly from Piccadilly Circus westward to Hyde Park Corner, but it also extends as far westward as Hounslow West and Uxbridge, running on the surface from Baron's Court, and north-eastward to the populous suburbs of *Holloway* and *Finsbury Park* and on for another 7½ miles to *Cockfosters*. The section best known to visitors begins at *Kings Cross* (below the Eastern Region terminus and close to St. Pancras, London-Midland). The next station is at *Russell Square*, behind the Hotel Russell, in the heart of Bloomsbury, and thence the Tube follows the course of Southampton Row to *Holborn (Kingsway)* station (interchange station with Central Line), at the corner of Kingsway and Holborn, and close to the British Museum, Lincoln's Inn Fields, Holborn Restaurant, etc. A short line extends below Kingsway to *Aldwych* station, in the Strand, and close to Australia House, Somerset House, the Law Courts, etc., but the main route turns south-westward, and with a station at *Covent Garden* (for the Opera House and the Market), crosses the Northern Line at Leicester Square station and the Bakerloo Line at *Piccadilly Circus* station (*see* above). As already stated, the Tube then runs below Piccadilly, with stations at *Green Park* (for Bond Street, Royal Academy, St. James's Palace, etc.), and *Hyde Park Corner*, for the Parks, Buckingham Palace, etc. From *Knightsbridge* station, at the top of Sloane Street, and close to Harrod's Stores, the course is below Brompton Road. At the next station, *South Kensington*, which serves Museum Land, the Piccadilly Line runs close below the District Line and the two run side by side all the way from Barons Court to *Hammersmith*, *Acton Town* and *Northfields*, and thence use the same track to the terminus, *Hounslow West*.

The **Fares** on London Transport rail, bus, and tram services are generally on a scale of 1½d. for the first mile of two stages of approximately half-mile each: 3d. for two miles or four stages: 4d. for three miles or six stages and then increasingly by 1d. or 1½d. for each additional mile. In Central London a passenger may ride about 8 miles for 10d.

On the Green Line Coaches a similar level of fares is in operation. The minimum charge on the coaches from London is 1s. single.

Time-tables, etc.—*Buses, Trams and Trolleybuses.* Times of first and last vehicles are exhibited on the fare-tables within the vehicles. Where bus service interval is 15 minutes or more, time-tables are exhibited on the roadside   In the central area times of last *buses* are exhibited at principal points; *Green Line* on the roadside, and times of first and last trains on the *Underground* within the stations.

Maps of all routes are obtainable on application to London Transport, 55 Broadway, S.W. 1.   **Inquiries** to Public Relations Officer, same address.   **Telephone** inquiries to Abbey 1234.

OTHER ELECTRIC LINES

All the foregoing lines are part of the great Underground system of London Transport.   There are, however, a number of important electric lines serving Greater London and forming the suburban sections of the various Regions of British Railways. (For the Metropolitan Suburban Railway Line, *see* p. 60.)

From **Euston** (I. I. 5) London Midland Region electric trains run north-westward to South Hampstead, Kilburn (High Road), Queen's Park (where the Bakerloo Line joins the L.M.R.), Willesden Junction, Wembley, Harrow and Watford.

From **Broad Street Station** (I.O. 7) (London Midland Region line) trains run to Richmond and to Watford.   The Richmond trains serve Dalston, Highbury, Camden Town, Hampstead Heath, Brondesbury, Willesden Junction, Acton Central, Kew Gardens, Richmond and intermediate stations, whilst the Watford trains serve Dalston, Highbury, Camden Town, Kilburn (High Road), Willesden Junction, Wembley, Harrow and the stations to Watford.

The **Southern Region** suburban system is a network of electrified lines, so ramified as almost to defy description.   Intensive services are run from Waterloo, Charing Cross, Cannon Street, London Bridge, Victoria, Holborn Viaduct, and Blackfriars to all places between these termini and Windsor, Reading, Alton, Guildford, Redhill, Caterham, Sevenoaks and Gravesend.   In addition, several of these very busy main lines have been electrified, comprising those to Portsmouth, Bognor Regis, Littlehampton, Brighton, Eastbourne and Hastings, and to Maidstone and Gillingham.

Electric suburban services in the morning and evening are
thronged by thousands of busy workers getting to and from
the City and West End and should be avoided when possible by
the casual visitor

OTHER LINES NORTH OF RIVER
London Midland Region

EUSTON (Plan I. I. 5) is the terminus of the London Midland Region
Western division. This line—a development of the earliest passenger
railway in the world—provides the route to Ireland *via* Holyhead and
the English portion of the West Coast Route to Edinburgh and Glasgow, serving either by its main line or its branches every place of
importance in the northern and north-western counties, as well as
many in the Midlands.

SUBURBAN TRAINS to Willesden Junction, Wembley, Harrow,
Watford, Richmond, Acton, etc. (see above). The electric line for
local passenger services is linked with the Bakerloo Line at Queen's
Park.

Subway connection at Euston with the *Northern Line* (*see* p. 54). For
Central Line change at *Tottenham Court Road* or *Bank*.

Euston Square (5 minutes' walk) is the nearest station on **Metropolitan Line.**

ST. PANCRAS (Plan I. K. 5) is the terminus of the Midland division,
serving the Midland Counties, and providing the Waverley Route
to Scotland.

SUBURBAN TRAINS to Cricklewood, Hendon, Mill Hill, St. Albans,
Luton, Bedford, etc. Branch line from Kentish Town to East Ham
and Barking, also to Tilbury and Southend.

Subway connection with King's Cross station on **Northern Line, Piccadilly
Line** and **Metropolitan Line. Kentish Town,** on the Highgate branch of the
Northern Line, is also a convenient station for the Midland section, as the two
stations adjoin.

BROAD STREET (Plan I. O. 7), the City terminus of the London
Midland Region, adjoins Liverpool Street (*see* p. 60). For electric
services from Broad Street, *see* p. 58.

Eastern Region

KING'S CROSS (Plan I. K. 5), the terminus of the Great Northern
section. The line runs to Leeds, Bradford and York, affording communication with the north and north-east of England, and forming the
southern portion of the East Coast Route to Scotland.

SUBURBAN TRAINS to Enfield, Cuffley, Hertford; New Barnet,
Potters Bar, Welwyn Garden City and Hitchin.

Subway connection with King's Cross stations (**Metropolitan, Piccadilly** and
Northern Lines). St. Pancras Station (L.M.R.) is adjacent.

LIVERPOOL STREET (Plan I. O. 7) is the terminus of the Great
Eastern section, which serves the Eastern Counties and provides the
routes to the Continent *via* Harwich.

SUBURBAN TRAINS to Tottenham, Edmonton, Enfield; Waltham-
stow, Chingford; Ilford, Romford, Brentwood and Shenfield.

Subway connections with Liverpool Street Stations (Metropolitan and Central
Lines). Broad street Station (L.M.R.) is adjacent.

FENCHURCH STREET (Plan II. O. 8) is the terminus of the London, Tilbury and Southend Section, which serves East London Districts and continues to Tilbury (for ferry to Gravesend), Leigh-on-Sea, Westcliff-on-Sea, Southend-on-Sea and Shoeburyness. There are through electric trains from the District Line to East Ham, Barking, Dagenham and Upminster, and from the Metropolitan Line to East Ham and Barking.

Tower Hill (District Line) is the nearest Underground station and Bank Station (Central and Northern Lines) is a few minutes walk.

Western Region

PADDINGTON (Plan I. F. 7) is the terminus of the **Western Region** main line, which serves the Thames Valley, the West and South-West of England, Birmingham and the Midlands, South and Central Wales. It also provides the routes to Southern Ireland *via* Fishguard, and to the Channel Islands *via* Weymouth.

SUBURBAN TRAINS to Acton, Ealing, Greenford, Southall, Slough, etc., and riverside stations such as Windsor, Maidenhead, and Henley.

Metropolitan and Bakerloo Line stations adjoin the Main Line station, from which connections can be made to all parts of the Metropolis.

MARYLEBONE (Plan I. G. 6) is the terminus of the former **Great Central** section of the Eastern Region. Trains to Rugby, Leicester, Nottingham, Sheffield, Manchester, etc., and to Wembley Hill (also Wembley Stadium), Sudbury, Ruislip, Gerrard's Cross, Beaconsfield, High Wycombe, etc.

Subway connection with Marylebone station on **Bakerloo Line**. Baker Street station on **Metropolitan Line** is a quarter of a mile eastward.

Metropolitan Line

BAKER STREET (Plan I. G. 6) is the terminus of what must perforce be called the "country" lines of the Metropolitan Line (now absorbed in the London Transport organization), familiarly "the Met.," and is also served by "Circle" trains (*see* p. 53). Between Baker Street and Wembley Park, Harrow, Uxbridge and Watford the trains are run by electricity, as also are the trains on the Aylesbury line as far as Rickmansworth, beyond which they are steam-hauled to Chesham and Aylesbury. Many "through" trains are run from these places to and from the City, without change at Baker Street.

Subway connection with **Bakerloo Line**. Change at Oxford Circus for Central Line, at Piccadilly Circus for Piccadilly Line, and at Charing Cross for District Line.

OTHER LINES RUNNING SOUTH OF RIVER

The great trunk lines have upwards of a dozen important termini in London, all linked with each other and with every part of the Metropolis by Underground Railways.

The three railways running southward from London were in 1923 "grouped" under the title of the Southern Railway but are now of course incorporated in the—

Southern Region

WATERLOO (Plan II. L. 9), is one of the largest termini in Europe and serves such points in the South and West as Portsmouth (by electric train) and the Isle of Wight, Winchester, Southampton, Bournemouth, Weymouth, Exeter, Plymouth, Ilfracombe and North

Cornwall. It also links with the steamer services from Southampton to the Channel Islands, Havre (for Normandy, Paris, etc.), and St. Malo (for Brittany). There are also frequent suburban electric services to various parts of south-west and south-east London and the Home Counties. *(See p. 58.)*

The Waterloo and City Railway provides an under-the-Thames link with the Bank Station (page 55); whilst the London Transport Underground system connects Waterloo by "tube" with all parts of the Metropolis including the other main line termini.

LONDON BRIDGE (Plan II. O. 9) besides being a terminus for main line trains to Brighton, Eastbourne, Bognor Regis and other South Coast towns, is also a station at which the trains from Charing Cross and Cannon Street call for Tunbridge Wells, Hastings, Folkestone, Dover, etc. Electric trains are run to the North Kent area, the south-east and south districts serving Greenwich, Woolwich, Dartford, Gravesend, Lewisham, Chislehurst, Orpington, Chatham, and Maidstone, and to such points in Surrey as Croydon, Purley and Caterham, Redhill and beyond. A subway connection links London Bridge with the London Transport Underground services.

VICTORIA (Plan II. H. 10) is a busy terminus with main line services to Brighton, Eastbourne, Hastings, Chatham, Margate, Ramsgate, etc. It is also an important terminal of Continental traffic *via* the Dover–Ostend, Dover–Dunkerque, Dover–Calais, Folkestone–Calais, Folkestone–Boulogne, and Newhaven–Dieppe routes. The London–Paris Sleeping Car Train (the Night Ferry) starts and finishes its journey here: this train allowing passengers to enter their sleeping berths at Victoria and leave them in Paris without change of carriage. There is a subway connection with the London Transport Underground service. For electrically equipped suburban lines see p. 58.

CHARING CROSS (Plan II. K. 8), **CANNON STREET** (Plan II. N. 8), **HOLBORN VIADUCT** (Plan I. M. 7) and **BLACKFRIARS** (Plan II. M. 8) serve the south-eastern suburbs of London and various other parts of Kent including coastal resorts.

Charing Cross is connected by subway with the Strand station of the Northern Line (to Euston, Edgware and High Barnet), and is two minutes' walk from Charing Cross station on the District Line and Bakerloo Line (change at Piccadilly Circus for Piccadilly Tube or at Oxford Circus for Central Tube). Trafalgar Square station on the Bakerloo Line is only two minutes' walk.

The facilities afforded by the main lines from London may be epitomized thus: For excursions to places of interest in Middlesex, Bucks and Herts, the visitor can avail himself of the London and North-Western and Midland sections of the London Midland Region, the Great Northern, Great Eastern and Great Central sections of the Eastern Region and of the Underground lines. For the riverside and western part of the country he will utilize the South-Western section of the Southern Region, the Western Region and the Underground lines. Epping Forest and other parts of Essex are reached by the Great Eastern section of the Eastern Region, the Tilbury section of the London Midland Region, and the Central Line. Surrey, Sussex and Kent are served by the many ramifications of the Southern Region.

AMUSEMENTS

THEATRES, ETC.—CINEMAS—SPORTS AND GAMES.

LONDON is well provided with facilities for indoor entertainment, but, from a summer visitor's point of view, is sadly lacking in outdoor amusements.

THEATRES

Evening performances usually begin at varying times between 6.30 and 7.30 p.m. Matinées, beginning at 2, 2.15 or 2.30, are usual at most houses on two or three days a week. For details see daily newspapers. Seats for most parts of the house should be booked in advance, either direct from the theatre by personal visit, telephone or wire, or at one of the Agents or Libraries. It frequently happens that Agents, owing to their advance bookings, have better seats for disposal than can be secured at the box offices. The price of seats usually includes the entertainments tax. For the cheaper (unreserved) seats it is generally necessary to wait in the *queues*, which, in the cases of popular performances, often begin to form hours before the doors are opened; but at certain theatres even the cheaper seats can be booked. The numbers immediately following the names of theatres in the following list refer to the sketch map on p. 63, showing the situations of most of the West End houses, and the nearest railway stations.

Certain theatres have an established reputation for a particular kind of play, but in others the nature of the performance varies from time to time.

	SITUATION.	TELEPHONE No.
Adelphi (29)	410, Strand, W.C. 2	Tem 7611
Aldwych (23)	Aldwych, W.C. 2	Tem 6404
Ambassadors' (12)..	West St., Cambridge Circus, W.C. 2..	Tem 1171
Apollo (6)	Shaftesbury Avenue, W. 1	Ger 2663
Cambridge (14) .._.	Earlham Street, W.C. 2	Tem 3143
Casino (8)..........	Old Compton Street W. 1...........	Ger 6877
Comedy (38).......	Panton Street, Haymarket, S.W. 1 ...	Whi 2578
Covent Garden (*see*	Royal Opera House (20)	Tem 7961

	SITUATION.	TELEPHONE No.
Criterion (37)	Piccadilly Circus, W. 1	Whi 3216
Drury Lane (22)	Drury Lane, W.C.2	Tem 8108
Duchess (26)	Catherine Street, Aldwych	Tem 8243
Duke of York's (32)	St. Martin's Lane, W.C. 2	Tem 5122
Fortune (21)	Covent Garden, W.C. 2	Tem 2238
Garrick (31)	Charing Cross Road, W.C. 2	Tem 4601
Globe (7)	Shaftesbury Avenue, W. 1	Ger 1592
Haymarket (39)	Haymarket, S.W. 1	Whi 9832
Hippodrome (35)	Cranbourn Street, W.C. 2	Ger 3272
His Majesty's (40)	Haymarket, S.W. 1	Whi 6606
Lyric (5)	29, Shaftesbury Avenue, W. 1	Ger 3686
New (33)	St. Martin's Lane, W.C. 2	Tem 3878

	SITUATION.	TELEPHONE No.
"Old Vic "	Waterloo Road, S.E. 1	Wat 7616
Open-Air Theatre ..	Inner Circle, Regent's Park, N.W. ...	Wel 2060
Palace (9)	Shaftesbury Avenue, W. 1..........	Ger 6834
People's Palace	Mile End Road, E.1.	Adv 4244
Phoenix (10)	Charing Cross Road, W.C. 2	Tem 8611
Piccadilly (3)	Denman Street, W.	Ger 4506
Playhouse (43)	Northumberland Avenue, W.C. 2	Whi 4788
Prince of Wales (36)	Coventry Street, W.1..............	Whi 8681
Princes (15)	Shaftesbury Avenue, W.C. 2	Tem 6596
RoyalOperaHouse(20)	Covent Garden, W.C.2	Tem 7961
St. James's (41) ...	King Street, St. James's, S.W.1......	Whi 3903
St. Martin's (13) ...	West Street, Cambridge Circus	Tem 1443
Sadler's Wells......	Rosebery Avenue, E.C. 1............	Ter 1672
Saville (11)........	Shaftesbury Avenue, W.C. 2	Tem 4011
Savoy (27)	Strand, W.C. 2.	Tem 8888
Scala (1)	Charlotte Street, W.C.	Mus 5731
Stoll (19)..........	Kingsway, W.C.2..................	Hol 3703
Strand (24)	Aldwych, W.C.2	Tem 4143
Vaudeville (28)	404, Strand, W.C. 2	Tem 4871
Westminster	Palace Street, Buckingham Gate, S.W.	Vic 0283
Whitehall (42)	Whitehall, S.W. 1	Whi 6692
Winter Garden (18).	Drury Lane, W.C. 2	Hol 8881
Wyndham's (34) ..	Charing Cross Road, W.C. 2	Tem 3028

Suburban Theatres

We have labelled as "suburban" all theatres not in the proximity of Charing Cross. Nearly every district of importance has one or more houses of entertainment. Some of these equal the West End theatres in comfort and class of performance, while prices of admission are considerably lower.

Bromley, Little, North Street, Bromley.
Century, Archer Street, Notting Hill, W.
Chelsea Palace, Kings Road, S.W. 3.
Embassy, 64, Eaton Avenue, N.W. 3.
Everyman,Holly Bush Vale,Hampstead.
Golders Green, adjoining Tube station.
Grand, Croydon.
King's, Hammersmith, W. 6.

Lewisham, High Road, Lewisham, S.E.
Lyric, Hammersmith, W.
Mercury, Ladbroke Road, W. 11.
Richmond, Richmond Green.
Q Theatre, near Kew Bridge.
Sadler's Wells, Rosebery Avenue, E.C. 1.
Streatham Hill, Streatham, S.W. 2.
Wimbledon, Broadway, S.W.

Variety Theatres, etc.

Matinées generally at 2 or 2.30, evening performance at 6.15, to 6.45. In some houses two performances a night are given, beginning about 6.15 and 8.45 respectively. (One or two houses specialize in "non-stop" performances which usually begin about 1 p.m. and run continuously until about 11 p.m.) Smoking is permitted. Prices are generally lower than in theatres for

Piccadilly Circus and the famous statue *Eros*. A veritable hub of the world, upwards of 50,000 vehicles pass daily.

The Tudor pile of Lambeth Palace has been, for nearly seven centuries, the London residence of the Archbishops of Canterbury.

The Strand, looking eastward. Though with little architectural grace to commend it, the Strand is famous, nevertheless, for its hotels, theatres, cinemas and shops.

Hyde Park Corner, an even busier traffic point than Piccadilly Circus. The reliefs on the triple gateway are copied from the Elgin Marbles in the British Museum.

the corresponding class of seat and are lowest for "non-stop" performances. The numbers immediately following the names in the following list refer to the sketch plan on p. 63.

	SITUATION.	TELEPHONE No.
Coliseum (30)	St. Martin's Lane, near Charing Cross, W.C. 2	Tem 3161
Palladium (2)	Argyll Street, Regent Street, W. 1	Ger 7373
Victoria Palace	Victoria Street, S.W. 1	Vic 1317
Windmill (4)	Gt. Windmill Street, Piccadilly Circus, W.	Ger 7413

Cinemas

In and about the West End are numerous cinemas, large and small. Well-known cinemas are the *Tivoli*, Strand; *Gaumont* and *Carlton*, Haymarket; *Empire, Warner*, and *Odeon*, Leicester Square; *Odeon* and *Marble Arch Cinema*, Marble Arch, W.; *Plaza*, Lower Regent Street; *New Gallery*, Regent Street; *Rialto*; *Astoria*, Charing Cross Road; *New Victoria*, near Victoria Station, etc. Several cinemas specialise in the presentation of News Films.

SPORTS AND GAMES

The Londoner not only works strenuously, but makes the most of his hours of leisure. The weekly half-holiday enacted by a beneficent legislature is generally devoted to games of one kind or another, and during week-ends the river is crowded with pleasure boats, and the roads with motors speeding to the Surrey Hills or the South Coast resorts, or northward to such delectable regions as the Chilterns. We can do no more than mention the headquarters of the various forms of sport, and the leading annual events:—

BADMINTON is played at the Horticultural Hall, S.W.— where the All-England finals are held—at the Alexandra Palace, and elsewhere.

BOATING.—The Serpentine in Hyde Park and the sheets of ornamental water in Regent's Park, Battersea Park, Finsbury Park, Victoria Park and Southwark Park are used for boating, the County Council charge per person being 8*d*. an hour. Parts of the River Lea are also available. But the most popular boating resort among Londoners is the Thames (*see* p. 274) from Hammersmith to Maidenhead and Henley. *See* our *Guide to the Thames*.

The **Oxford and Cambridge Boat Race,** invariably attended by huge crowds, is normally rowed on the Saturday before Holy Week. The course is from Putney to Mortlake, a trifle over 4¼ miles. Oxford, dark blue; Cambridge, light blue. The *Head of the River Race*, in which over 100 boats compete, is rowed at this time of year over the same course and is an excellent sight.

Of the **Regattas,** the most famous is that of Henley, usually held at the beginning of July. Other Regattas are held in July and August at Molesey, Staines, Kingston, Richmond, Marlow, Bourne End, etc.

BOWLS.—Provision is made for this popular game on a number of club grounds. There is a green near Alexandra Gate, in Hyde Park; the L.C.C. maintain public greens, graded "A" and "B", in Battersea Park, Finsbury Park, Ravenscourt Park, and many other open spaces, and provision is also made in most of the suburban parks and recreation grounds.

CRICKET.—Lord's, at St. John's Wood (p. 154), is the property of the Marylebone Cricket Club—the M.C.C. The principal annual fixtures are Eton *v.* Harrow and Oxford *v.* Cambridge, always attracting large crowds. The ground is also the headquarters of the Middlesex C.C. **Kennington Oval** (p. 259), on the south side, is the headquarters of the Surrey C.C. There are many private cricket grounds, and pitches are allotted to regular players in most of the local parks.

DANCING.—It need hardly be mentioned that the metropolis has plentiful provision for dances. From the great costume and other balls at the Royal Albert Hall, Covent Garden Opera House, etc., to the various suburban dance halls there are floors to suit all tastes and all pockets. Many of the larger hotels and restaurants make a feature of dance teas or dance dinners and suppers.

FISHING.—The fresh-water angler can do fairly well in the neighbourhood of London, but a short journey by rail or road is generally necessary. Fishing in the **Thames** is free up to the London Stone at Staines, and beyond that there is also plenty of free fishing, the only places on the main stream where riparian owners have succeeded in maintaining their "rights" being in the Maidenhead district and one or two other small reaches. All tributary streams are strictly preserved. To fish from the weirs it is necessary to obtain a permit from the Thames Conservancy (10s. per annum). For full details see the *Guide to the Thames* in this series. Coarse fish, such as roach, chub, dace, perch, barbel and pike, are fairly abundant. A good deal of re-

stocking is done. The **Lea** is also frequented (especially at
Rye House, Hoddesdon); and the rivers **Colne** and **Chess,** on the
north-western confines of Middlesex, and the Essex **Blackwater**
have many admirers. But enthusiasts will not look for detailed
information in a book of this general character when they are so
admirably served by special publications.

FLYING.—London Airport is at Heathrow, Feltham (*see* p. 17)
but Northolt, Gatwick, Heston, Hatfield, and other aerodromes
are generally busy. "Joy Rides" can be taken on almost any
day when the weather is favourable. For the regular Air
Services *see* p. 17. And *see* p. 263. **Gliding** takes place on
Dunstable Downs, near Whipsnade (*see* p. 275).

FOOTBALL.—The principal London clubs playing the Associa-
tion game are: Arsenal (Gillespie Road, Highbury, N.), Brent-
ford (Griffin Park, Brentford, W.), Charlton Athletic (Greenwich),
Chelsea (Stamford Bridge, Fulham Road, S.W.), Leyton Orient
(Osborne Road, Leyton, E.), Crystal Palace (Selhurst Park,
Croydon), Fulham (Craven Cottage, Fulham, S.W.), Millwall
(The Den, New Cross, S.E.), Queen's Park Rangers (Loftus Road,
Shepherd's Bush, W.), Tottenham Hotspur (Tottenham, N.),
West Ham United (Boleyn Castle, Upton Park, E.). The lead-
ing amateur teams are "Dulwich Hamlet" and "Leytonstone."
Cup Final matches are played in the great Stadium erected at
Wembley Park in connection with the Empire Exhibition. At
Leyton is the Army Sports Ground.
There are several first-class Rugby teams in London. The
Rugby Union International Matches and the Oxford *v.* Cam-
bridge University Match are played at Twickenham. The head-
quarters of the London Rugby Football League are at Mitcham.

GOLF.—There are public 18-hole courses at Hainault Forest,
at Mitcham (Prince's) and in Richmond Park, and practice is
permitted in the early morning on public open spaces like Hampstead Heath and Clapham Common. There are two public
18-hole courses at Hainault Forest and one at Beckenham Place
Park (18-hole). In the various Golf Annuals will be found
a complete list of the golf courses near London. In most cases
visitors introduced by members are allowed to play for a day
or two free, or on payment of a fee of about 2s. 6d. a day (generally more on Saturdays and Sundays). For weekly and monthly
players the charges are reduced.

GREYHOUND RACING.—There are a number of tracks
licensed by the National Greyhound Racing Club. Meetings are
announced in the London papers.

HORSE-RACING.—The race-meeting which most appeals to
the Londoner is undoubtedly the famous **Derby**, normally run
at Epsom on a Wednesday either a fortnight before or a fortnight
after Whitsun, and succeeded two days later by the **Oaks**. On a
Derby Day all the roads and railways leading south from London

are packed with people, and the sight on the course is one never to be forgotten.   **Ascot Week,** a great Society gathering generally attended by the Queen and members of the Royal Family, comes a fortnight after the Derby.   **Goodwood** races begin on the last Tuesday in July.   Other races are held at Alexandra Park, Sandown, Kempton Park, Windsor, Hurst Park, Gatwick, Newbury, etc.   **Pony-racing** at Northolt.

ICE HOCKEY.—Popular matches are played at the Empire Sports Arena at Wembley (and see under Skating), at Earls Court, Streatham, Harringay, etc.

LAWN TENNIS.—Hard and grass courts are provided in many of the public parks and squares, and can be used on payment of a small charge per hour.   The Amateur Championship of the World is generally decided towards the end of June at the All England Lawn Tennis Club at Wimbledon.   The Covered Court Championship and the Amateur Championships in tennis and racquets are usually held at the Queen's Club, West Kensington.

MOTORING.—*See* p. 46.

PUTTING GREENS in many of the parks and squares.

SKATING.—There are rinks at Queensway (Bayswater), Streatham, Earls Court, Richmond, etc., and during the winter the Empire Sports Arena at Wembley becomes a skating rink. Only at rare intervals are the waters around London frozen for a long enough period to give skaters satisfaction.   The chief resorts are the Serpentine in Hyde Park, the lake in Regent's Park, the Hampstead Heath and Highgate ponds, the Welsh Harp water at Hendon, the Long Water at Hampton Court, the Pen Ponds in Richmond Park and Ruislip Reservoir.

SPEEDWAY.—Motor-cycle-racing takes place at Wembley Stadium, Harringay, New Cross, Wimbledon, West Ham.

SWIMMING.—*See* p. 19, under Baths.

HISTORICAL SKETCH

AN exhaustive history of London would be that of the kingdom of which it is the capital; and it is, of course, impossible to find room for anything of the kind here. But there are points in the annals of the city which must be noticed in any Guide to London.

The **name** is probably derived—though there is much dispute on the subject—from the Celtic *Llyn* (pronounced *lun*), a pool or lake (the river at an earlier period expanded into a considerable lake—the part immediately below London Bridge is still "the Pool"), and *din* or *dun*, a hill, fort, or place of strength. The "hill" may have been that on which St. Paul's now stands, or Cornhill, or that crowned by the Tower; but recent research casts doubt on the theory that there was a large settlement here in pre-Roman days, and assigns the origin of London to the Roman Conquest in the first century A.D. Under the Romans *Londinium* arose, a splendid city, one of the nine *coloniæ* of Britain, but inferior in importance at first to Eboracum (York) and Verulamium (St. Albans). Great military roads radiated from the city to various parts of Britain and distances were measured from the *lapis milliaris* in the Forum of Agricola, in the heart of the Roman town (Leadenhall Market covers part of the site of the Forum). The stone, now known as the "London Stone," may still be seen in the wall of St. Swithin's Church, Cannon Street.

The direction taken by the old **London Wall**, dating from the first century A.D., is well known, and can be traced by the modern names of streets. Indeed, considerable sections, composed chiefly of Kentish ragstone and large Roman bricks, may be seen in the thoroughfare still known as London Wall, between Wood Street and Aldermanbury; in the churchyard of St. Giles's, Cripplegate; at the General Post Office, Newgate Street; in the offices of the Oxford University Press, Warwick Square; at the foot of Jewry Street, Aldgate; in America Square, off the Minories; in Trinity Square, and at the Tower itself. That the wall is a reality, and not a figment of the topographer's imagination, may be judged by the fact that contractors for sewers and other underground works find it necessary to stipulate that they shall be allowed to charge extra if they have to cut through or remove any portion of it. Outside the wall, a wide ditch, portions of which can still be traced, provided a further defence.

At the eastern end of the wall, by the river-side, was a strong fort, succeeded later by the White Tower. Thence the wall followed a line slightly westward of the Minories to Aldgate; then it curved to the north-west, between Bevis Marks and Houndsditch ("a ditch beyond the wall") to Bishopsgate, whence it followed the line still known as "London Wall" to Cripplegate. It next took a southern course to Aldersgate, and behind St. Botolph's Church, to Newgate; thence to Ludgate and along Pilgrim Street to the Fleet river (which then flowed in the valley now known as Farringdon Street). It skirted this stream to its junction with the Thames, where another strong fort was erected.* There were three **Gates,** Aldgate, (Ale-gate or All-gate, i.e. open to all), Aldersgate and Ludgate (*Lydgeat,* a postern); and afterwards a postern (Postern Row marks the spot) on Tower Hill. The City Corporation have erected tablets marking the sites of the gates. On the northern side was an outwork or barbican (the modern street, Barbican, preserves its memory). Later, other gates were added, the names of which are still preserved in Billings-gate, Bishops-gate, Moor-gate, Cripple-gate (from the Anglo-Saxon *crepel-gate,* a covered way), New-gate and Dow-gate (Celtic *dwr,* water).

Under the **Saxons** London became the metropolis of the kingdom of Essex. Bede, writing in the early part of the eighth century, refers to London as the "mart of many nations resorting to it by sea and land." The city was constituted the capital of England by Alfred the Great, York and Winchester having previously enjoyed that dignity in succession—the former under the Romans, the latter under the Saxons. In 994, the first bridge across the Thames was built.

The White Tower, in the Tower of London, was erected by William I in 1078, on the site of the Roman fort already noticed. The same king granted a charter to the city (*see* p. 22) confirming the burghers in the rights enjoyed by them under Edward the Confessor. William Rufus in 1097 founded Westminster Hall. King John granted the citizens several charters, and in Magna Carta it was expressly stipulated that London should have all its ancient privileges and customs as well by land as by water.

Wat Tyler's Rebellion took place in 1381, and every schoolboy is familiar with the picturesque part played by the Lord Mayor of that time. Reference must also be made to Jack Cade's Rebellion (1450), immortalized in Shakespeare's *Henry VI*:

* This line corresponds almost exactly with the present boundaries of the City of London, with the exception of the "liberties" or wards still known as "without" added at a later time.

"Now is Mortimer lord of this city!" cried the insurgent leader, when he struck his sword on the London Stone.

In the sixteenth and seventeenth centuries, so rapid had become the increase of London that both Elizabeth and James I issued proclamations against any further extension of the city. In the Strand, between London and Westminster, were many splendid residences of the nobility, with fine gardens reaching to the Thames. The names of most of the streets in the Strand —such as Essex, Norfolk, Burleigh, Buckingham and Northumberland—still preserve these aristocratic associations.

The reign of Mary witnessed the burning of heretics at Smithfield and that of Elizabeth the patriotic rally of the citizens in defence of the country against the Armada. During the Civil War, London sided with the Parliament, and the fateful January 30th, 1649, saw the execution of Charles I at Whitehall. In 1665 London was desolated by the **Great Plague,** which carried off nearly a fifth of the inhabitants; and in the following year the **Great Fire** occurred, destroying more than 13,000 houses, St. Paul's Cathedral, the Royal Exchange, 86 churches and most of the guild halls. The damage was estimated at £10,730,500. Pepys forlornly wrote: "It has been computed that the rents of the houses lost by this Fire in the City comes to £600,000 per annum." According to popular legend the fire began at Pudding Lane and ended at Pye Corner. The lofty Monument near London Bridge marks the spot where the fire broke out. The Tower, Westminster Abbey and Hall, Guildhall, the Temple Church, portions of the Inns of Court, Whitehall, Charterhouse, and about a score of city churches, were almost the only buildings of importance spared by the conflagration. Sir Walter Besant well said:—

"If, as some hold, the cause of the long-continued plague, which lasted, with intervals of rest, from the middle of the sixteenth century to 1665, was nothing but the accumulated filth of London, so that the ground on which it stood was saturated many feet in depth with poisonous filtrations, the fire of 1666 must be regarded in the light of a surgical operation, absolutely essential if life were to be preserved, and as an operation highly successful in its results. For it burned, more or less, every house and every building over an area of 436 acres out of those which made up London within the walls."

But it cannot be denied that the Fire was a great disaster. In rebuilding the city many improvements were effected. Streets were widened and houses of more substantial materials constructed, but London has never ceased to regret that the masterly designs of Sir Christopher Wren and John Evelyn were not carried out in their entirety. St. Paul's Cathedral and fifty-three parish churches were rebuilt by Wren in such a way that, when viewed from such a standpoint as Waterloo Bridge, the lesser fanes, though differing from each other, all harmonize and serve to heighten the general effect of the stately Cathedral dome.

In 1716 it was ordained that every householder should hang a light before his door from six in the evening till eleven. Gas was first used as an illuminant in 1807. In 1767 numbers began to replace the old signs as distinguishing marks for houses.

Most of the City gates and barriers were removed before the end of the eighteenth century, but the most famous of them, Temple Bar, stood in its place until 1878, when, owing to the inconvenience caused to traffic, it was replaced by the present monument. The old "bar" now stands at the entrance to the park at Theobalds, about fourteen miles from London.

To the latter part of the eighteenth century belong some of the finest of the old buildings in London, such as Somerset House, the Mansion House, and the Horse Guards. But the metropolis, as we know it, is very largely a creation of the **Victorian Age,** most of the leading thoroughfares having been widened and improved—many of them actually constructed— and many of the chief public edifices remodelled, if not built, during that period. The formation of wide arteries—such as New Oxford Street and Regent Street, in the early years of the nineteenth century; of Farringdon Street and Queen Victoria Street, later on; of the Shaftesbury and Rosebery Avenues, and of Charing Cross Road; and during the present century the construction of Kingsway—cleared away many notoriously un-savoury localities. Healthful and outlying districts are now made accessible by cheap trains, "tubes," and buses; while in the central areas are many large piles of flats for those who prefer town life to the suburbs.

London in fact is both one of the finest and one of the healthiest cities in the world. In spite of its huge size, the metropolis has almost the lowest death-rate among towns in England with a population of over 200,000, while it is incontestably far healthier than Paris, New York or Rome. In recent years its death-rate has been lower than that of any capital in Europe.

No one needs reminding of the great damage sustained by the Metropolis during the Second World War. Scars are evident, particularly in the St. Paul's Cathedral area, in the many open spaces where once stood many great buildings of commerce. But though the loss in life and material was great, the clearing away of the debris has opened up many a vista of beauty.

The famous old Shot Tower, on the south bank of the Thames by Waterloo Bridge, provides a fine view of London and the river. On the left is the Savoy Hotel to the right of the bridge are Somerset House and King's College.

London (c*).

A view of Trafalgar Square showing Nelson's Column and Landseer's Lions. On the left is the National Gallery, in centre St. Martin's in the Fields and on the right South Africa House.

A quiet corner of Kensington Gardens. The gardens were first laid out in the reign of William III.

THE WEST END

CHARING CROSS AND ITS NEIGHBOURHOOD

HAVING endeavoured to give a general idea of London, and to supply visitors with all information needful to their stay, we will now conduct them through the principal thoroughfares, and do our best to "fairly streets and buildings trace, and all that gives distinction to the place."

There is so much to see in the great "Whirlpool," as George Gissing aptly called London, that the visitor may as well rid his mind at once of any intention of seeing *all*. None the less, by adopting a prearranged and methodical plan, he can greatly lighten his task and ensure that few places of real interest are overlooked. The visitor who has only a limited number of days at his disposal is recommended to refer to the suggested Itineraries on pp. 42-46, with a view to apportioning his time to the best advantage. The series of routes in this and the subsequent section, devoted to the City proper, have been so arranged that every part of Central London is covered, though we do not suppose for a moment that any large number of readers will literally follow in our footsteps. Where no lengthy stay is made in museums or galleries, the journeys can in most cases be accomplished in a morning or an afternoon.

Charing Cross, the centre of the fifteen-mile police radius, and a passing-point of a great number of bus routes, may fairly be considered the "hub" of London, and will make a convenient starting-place for our rambles. Before going farther, let us devote a morning to the neighbourhood.

ROUTE I.—CHARING CROSS—TRAFALGAR SQUARE—NORTHUMBERLAND AVENUE—VICTORIA EMBANKMENT—WHITEHALL—NATIONAL GALLERY

Charing Cross

Plan II. K. 8.
Nearest Stations.—Southern Region terminus of the same name, Strand (Northern Line), Trafalgar Square (Bakerloo Line), Charing Cross (District Line).
Buses connect, either directly or by one or two changes, with all parts of the metropolis.
Note.—West-bound buses stop almost outside the station yard, in the Strand; but *east-bound* buses (for the Bank, London Bridge, etc.) stop in Duncannon Street, in the shadow of St. Martin's-in-the-Fields Church.

"Why, sir," said Dr. Johnson, "Fleet Street has a very animated appearance, but I think the full tide of human existence is at Charing Cross." The remark is hardly less true to-day.

Charing Cross derives its name from the last of the Gothic crosses erected by Edward I to mark the places where the coffin of Queen Eleanor was set down on its way to Westminster. At that time the little village of Charing, or Cheeringe, occupied a half-way position between London and Westminster. The cross was removed in 1647 by order of Parliament. In the forecourt of the railway station is a modern reproduction, but the original stood slightly to the west, on the site now occupied by the statue of Charles I (p. 76).

Trafalgar Square

(Plan II. K. 8)

so named in commemoration of Nelson's great victory, is a large open space, second only to Hyde Park in the estimation of those organising political "demonstrations." It is a pity that a competent landscape gardener is not allowed to transform it by the introduction of a few small lawns and rockeries. The view down Whitehall is fine. The **Nelson Monument** is a granite Corinthian column, surmounted by a statue of Nelson. The statue measures 17 feet 2½ inches; total height of plinth, column and statue is 170 feet 2 inches from the ground.

On the base are bronze bas-reliefs, cast with the metal of captured French cannon, representing scenes from the battles of St. Vincent, the Nile, Copenhagen and Trafalgar. Four colossal lions, modelled by Sir Edwin Landseer, crouch on pedestals at the base. Every year, on the anniversary of Trafalgar (October 21), the monument is decked with wreaths and festoons in commemoration of the victory.

The **Victory's Lamp.**—At the corner of Trafalgar Square nearest the Strand, placed above a curious round stone box which is a miniature police office, is a lamp from Nelson's famous flagship, the *Victory*. The lamp was at the Battle of Trafalgar, but is fitted for a modern light.

A *subway* enables pedestrians to cross the traffic-crowded roadways in safety. Vehicular traffic passes through the Square on the "gyratory" system, a recent census revealed that this is the second busiest spot in London, over 66,000 vehicles passing through in twelve hours.

Below the parapet on the north side of the Square, and quite unknown to the majority of Londoners, are set out the *Standard British Lineal Measures*—inch, foot, yard, chain, etc. Here also are the bronze busts of Admirals of the Fleet Jellicoe and Beatty. Of the statues the best is that of Charles I (*see* p. 76). **Trafalgar Square Station** (Bakerloo) is on south side of Square.

The northern side of the Square is occupied by the **National Gallery** (p. 84), behind which is the **National Portrait Gallery**

(*see* p. 92). To the right is **St. Martin's-in-the-Fields,** sometimes
known as the "Admiralty Church," erected 1721–6 by James
Gibbs on the site of an earlier structure, and well known to
wireless listeners.

The story goes that the parish owes its constitution to Henry
VIII's objection to seeing so many funerals go by his Whitehall
windows, which was the way to the Churchyard of St. Margaret's,
Westminster. This feeling, unreasonable, perhaps, in a widower
of such determination, yet not unnatural, induced him to set
up the parish of St. Martin's-in-the-Fields, with church and
churchyard complete.

One looks in vain now for the "fields." The Grecian portico
is greatly admired, but its effect has been somewhat spoilt by
the curtailment of the steps in front. The greater part of
Buckingham Palace is included in the parish, and overlooking the
sanctuary of the church is a commodious Royal box. The births
of all Royal children born at the Palace are entered in the
register. It will be noted that the vane is surmounted by a
crown. George I was at one time churchwarden of St. Martin's,
the only case of an English monarch who has held such a position.
The register of the old church, still preserved, contains an entry
of the baptism of Francis Bacon (1561). Nell Gwynne was
buried here. So were Robert Boyle, the philosopher; Farquhar,
the comedy writer; Lord Mohun, who was killed in a duel by the
Duke of Hamilton, and who has achieved a dubious immortality
in the pages of Thackeray's *Esmond*; Roubillac, the sculptor;
John Hunter, the surgeon, whose remains were afterwards removed to Westminster Abbey; and many others. The church
is one of the most active in London, and its services are invariably
well attended.

On the eastern side of the Square is **South Africa House,** the
magnificent London headquarters of the Government of South
Africa. The building was opened by King George V in 1933.

On the opposite (western) side of Trafalgar Square is the
Royal College of Physicians (admission by member's order).
The adjoining building was opened by King George V in 1925
as the London headquarters of the **Canadian Government.**
Norway House is the semi-official centre of that country's interests
in London.

From Nelson's Monument there is a fine vista down Whitehall
and Parliament Street towards the Houses of Parliament, and
through the triple **Archway** connected with the New Admiralty
(p. 82) there is a fine view westward along the wide Mall to the
Victoria Memorial and Buckingham Palace. The archway itself,
however, is too hedged with buildings to be seen to advantage
from this side.

The equestrian **Statue of Charles I** in the roadway (where once stood the original Charing Cross, *see* p. 73) is generally regarded as the finest piece of statuary in London. It was cast in 1633, but before it had been erected the Civil War broke out. By the Parliament the objectionable figure was sold as "scrap" to a brazier with the appropriate name of Rivet. An insatiable demand for "relics" of the unfortunate monarch arising, Rivet made a good thing by selling knives and forks with bronze handles, which he pretended were made from the effigy; but with a keen eye to the future he kept the statue intact. At the Restoration it was duly produced from his garden in Holborn, and in 1675 was set up on the site of the old Charing Cross.

The oblique thoroughfare connecting Charing Cross with the Embankment is **Northumberland Avenue,** which by its name commemorates Northumberland House, the town mansion of the Duke of Northumberland, demolished in 1874 to make way for the Avenue. Above the house used to stand the figure of a lion (now at Syon House, Isleworth, *see* p. 272), and it was a favourite joke with the wits of the period to inform credulous strangers that if they watched long enough the animal would be seen to wag its tail.

Also in Northumberland Avenue are the **Constitutional Club** and the **Royal Empire Society** (formerly the Royal Colonial Institute), with a membership of over 16,000, and a library of 250,000 volumes (*see* p. 29), mostly on Empire subjects. Immediately below Charing Cross terminus is the **Playhouse Theatre.** In Craven Street, the thoroughfare between Northumberland Avenue and Charing Cross Station, *Benjamin Franklin*, "printer, philosopher and statesman," resided. At No. 32 *Heine* resided in 1827.

The Victoria Embankment

(See also p. 203)

colloquially "the Embankment," extends from Westminster Bridge to Blackfriars Bridge, a magnificent curve of nearly a mile and a half. It is one of the finest and most air-swept thoroughfares in the metropolis, with attractive gardens, an always interesting outlook on the river, and the not inconsiderable advantage, when sunny days are few, of a south aspect. The broad roadway provides a favourite route for taxis and motors hastening to and from the City, and there is a constant chain of coaches and buses from all parts of London. The neighbourhood of Charing Cross Bridge is a starting-place for many of the motor-coaches to such places as Brighton, Southend, etc. Formerly at high tide the river flowed right up to where the old York Water

Gate (p. 204) still stands, and the area now covered by the Embankment and its gardens was an unsightly expanse of mud. This great improvement, for which Londoners have never been sufficiently grateful to the old Metropolitan Board of Works, was effected in 1864-70, at a cost of a million and a half pounds. Owing to the sloppy nature of the subsoil the cost of maintenance is considerable. The granite protecting wall is 8 feet thick. A mural monument at the foot of Northumberland Avenue worthily commemorates the engineer, *Sir Joseph W. Bazalgette*.

In connection with the Jubilee celebrations of King George V in 1935 the stretch of river between Westminster Bridge and London Bridge was named **The King's Reach**.

Throughout its length the Embankment is planted on both sides with plane trees, and seats face the river. Trams skirt the river-side from Westminster Bridge to Blackfriars Bridge, certain of them turning off at Waterloo Bridge to enter the tunnel beneath Aldwych and Kingsway that connected the southern tramway system with the northern. Beneath the Embankment runs the Underground, with stations at Westminster, Charing Cross, the Temple, and Blackfriars. Close to Charing Cross Railway Bridge the Bakerloo Tube passes beneath the Thames, its Charing Cross Station being below that of the Underground. On the Embankment, facing Charing Cross Station, is a bronze medallion, by Sir G. Frampton, R.A., of *Sir W. S. Gilbert*, the playwright, whose "foe was folly and his weapon wit." His collaborator, *Sir Arthur Sullivan*, is remembered by a monument in the nearby Embankment Gardens.

The Embankment eastward from here is described on pp. 203-4.

Turning in the direction of Westminster Bridge, we pass through pretty gardens with numerous statues, beyond which are new blocks of Government offices (*see* p. 81). Then comes the dignified turreted building, in the Scottish Baronial style, known as **New Scotland Yard,** the headquarters, since 1890, of the Metropolitan Police. It is of Dartmoor granite, hewn by convict labour. The name is popularly derived from the fact that on the site of Old Scotland Yard stood a palace belonging to the Kings of Scotland. In order that northern susceptibilities might not be offended, the spot was actually declared to be a part of Scotland and therefore not a possession of the English monarch—an interesting parallel to the modern holding with regard to foreign embassies, etc.

At one time it was proposed to erect a State opera-house on the site, and remains of foundations are still to be seen in the cellars of Scotland Yard.

On the river-side opposite Scotland Yard is a lofty monument forming the **Royal Air Force War Memorial.**

Continuing to Westminster Bridge, we have the *St. Stephen's Club* (Conservative) at the corner. Flanking the bridge is J. L. Thornycroft's fine group showing *Boadicea* in her chariot: those used to handling horses generally look—in vain—for the charioteer's reins.

Westminster Bridge

(Plan II. K. 9)

one of the widest and most graceful bridges in Europe, consists of seven low segmental iron arches, supported on granite piers. It is 1,160 ft. long and 85 ft. wide, and was opened in 1862. Wordsworth wrote of the view from the bridge of his day (the Charing Cross railway bridge had not then been built): "Earth has not anything to show more fair"; and dull indeed would he be who could fail to admire it now. Looking City-ward we have the noble sweep of the Embankment, lined by green foliage, beyond which rise notable office and other buildings. Looking from the other side of the bridge (up river) we have to the right the Houses of Parliament, with the famous Terrace, overlooking the river. Beyond are several huge blocks of offices, including those of the *Imperial Chemical Industries* and *Thames House.* At the opposite end of the new Lambeth Bridge is Lambeth Palace (pp. 258–9), and closer at hand are the detached buildings of **St. Thomas's Hospital**, which suffered extensive damage during the war. The **Albert Embankment** borders the southern bank of the river from Westminster Bridge to Vauxhall Bridge.

Beside the eastern end of Westminster Bridge is the—

London County Hall

Admission. Parts of the Hall are shown on Saturdays from 10.30 to 12, and 1.30 to 3.30. Also on Bank Holidays until 4.30 (except Boxing Day). The public are admitted to the Council meetings normally on alternate Tuesdays at 2.30 except in recess.

This stately building was opened by King George V in 1922. It is in the English Renaissance style, from designs by *Ralph Knott.* The northern wing was built later and opened in 1933. Increase in the Council's powers and duties have, however, necessitated further accommodation, and the north and south blocks (opened in 1939) were erected in Belvedere Road opposite. The three buildings stand on a ten-acre site and cost five million pounds. Some notes on the London County Council will be found on p. 25.

The principal feature of the interior of the County Hall is the *Council Chamber*, a beautiful hall reached from the main entrance in Belvedere Road by way of a marble ceremonial staircase. Between the Chamber and the river are the Council's Library, Members' Reading Room and other important rooms. Both externally and internally the County Hall is a very fine building, worthy of its site and of its functions. It suffered some war damage. In the northern wing is a Conference Hall and above it the large Education Library for the use of teachers and others connected with the Council's educational service.

During excavations on the site in the summer of 1910 the workmen unearthed a Roman galley, of oak, 50 feet long by 16 feet wide. It is now carefully preserved in the London Museum (*see* p. 123). From the coins found within, the galley is believed to date from about the end of the third century A.D.

Beyond the Hall is the 27-acre site where was held the South Bank Exhibition of the Festival of Britain 1951. Within the site and just beyond the railway bridge is the Royal Festival Hall.

The Royal Festival Hall, built and financed by the London County Council, is constructed of reinforced concrete faced with Portland stone. The large concert hall is equipped with the latest innovations to ensure perfect accoustics and comfort for audience and players, with seats for 3,000. Productions range from symphony concerts to open stage ball t and opera, while a smaller theatre is designed for dramatic productions, concerts and film shows.

From the Hall recross Westminster Bridge. The Houses of Parliament, Westminster Abbey and other buildings hereabouts will require at least a morning to themselves (*see* p. 95), so we will turn along Bridge Street, past **Westminster Station** (Underground Railway) to the corner of **Parliament Street,** the lower continuation of Whitehall. The **Government Offices** at the corner of Parliament Street and Great George Street extend right back to St. James's Park. The blocks fronting Parliament and Great George Streets are occupied by some departments of the **Ministries of Health** and **National Insurance.**

Proceeding up Parliament Street on the west, or left-hand side, we reach a fine quadrangle including the **Home Office,** the **Commonwealth Relations Office,** and the **Foreign Office.** Only persons having business are, as a rule, admitted. Derby Street, on the other side of Whitehall, would take us to **New Scotland Yard,** the river front of which we have already seen

p. 77). In the centre of Whitehall stands that fine symbol of an Empire's sorrow, **The Cenotaph,** inscribed with majestic simplicity, "The Glorious Dead."

The Cenotaph

(Plan II. K. 9.)

This world-famous monument, designed by *Sir Edwin Lutyens, R.A.,* was intended at first merely as a temporary memorial in connection with the Peace Celebrations in July, 1919. Later, in deference to strongly expressed public feeling, it was re-erected in permanent form, "to represent an Imperial Grave of all those citizens of the Empire, of every creed and rank, who gave their lives in the War." As is known it now also commemorates those who lost their lives in the Second World War, the additional inscription "1939–45" having been added in 1946.

At 11 a.m. on Armistice Day (the Sunday immediately prior to November 11th, unless the 11th or 12th of that month is a Sunday) in each year the Cenotaph is the scene of a most impressive ceremony, when the Sovereign, or her representative, and many of the nation's leaders, together with a great concourse of ordinary folk, stand at the shrine for two minutes, while throughout the Kingdom almost perfect silence is maintained, and all traffic is suspended. Large numbers of wreaths are deposited, not only on this occasion, but throughout the year. Every male passer-by will, of course, raise his hat.

We are now opposite historic **Downing Street** (Plan II. K. 9). No. 10, the official residence of the Prime Minister and the usual scene of Cabinet meetings, is a simple mansion of dull brown brick, bearing little outward indication of its importance. Traditionally, the Lord Privy Seal resides in the adjoining house (No. 11), but the rule is not hard and fast, and for some time at least Earl Baldwin, while Prime Minister, lived at No. 11. At the end of the street steps lead down to **St. James's Park** (*see* p. 120). A gateway and subway adjoining No. 10 Downing Street bring one out on the Parade Ground behind the Horse Guards. Across Whitehall from Downing Street, a huge block of Government Offices to house the many Government departments hitherto scattered in various houses in the neighbourhood, occupies the site of **Whitehall Gardens.** Among former residents of Whitehall Gardens was Sir Robert Peel. During his tenure of office he was accustomed to walk across to Downing Street to transact business, and the late Sir Algernon West related:

"It is not so very long ago—indeed, I am told as lately as 1893-4
—that a charge used to appear in the annual estimates presented to
Parliament for a small annuity for the sweeper who kept the crossing
clean, so that the Prime Minister should not dirty his boots on his
passage from Whitehall to the Treasury."

With reference to what has been said as to the former limits
of the river, it is interesting to recall Sir Robert's statement
that his "house was built in 1824, and there were formerly steps
leading to the river. He remembered that on one occasion,
when a boy, preparations were made to remove the family and
valuables by boats on the occasion of a threatened attack by a
mob on his father's house."

Between Downing Street and the Horse Guards is the long
range of buildings housing the **Treasury,** the **Privy Council,** and
other more or less important bodies and functionaries. In the
centre of the road is an equestrian statue of *Earl Haig.* By a
paradox typically British, the buildings from which the affairs
of a mighty Empire are actually administered display none of
the pomp of power, while the **Horse Guards,** now little more than
a guard-house for the Household Cavalry, is always in day-time
sentinelled by imposing Life Guards, whose appearance is calculated to excite awe and admiration in all beholders. The
two mounted sentries at the gate are relieved every hour. The
ceremony is not uninteresting, but a far more imposing spectacle
is provided at a little before 11 every morning (Sundays 10),
when the operation of **Changing the Guard** takes place, and at
4 p.m. when the Guard is inspected. Readers of W. E. Henley
will recall the lines on *The Lifeguardsman;*

> "He wears his inches weightily, as he wears
> His old-world armour; and with his port and pride,
> His sturdy graces and enormous airs,
> He towers, in speech his Colonel countrified,
> A triumph, waxing statelier year by year,
> Of British blood and bone and beef and beer."

The old stone building, dating from 1758, stands on the site
of the tiltyard of Westminster, so renowned in the courtly annals
of Tudor times. A passage under the picturesque clock tower
gives access to **St. James's Park,** and is much frequented by
foot-passengers, but only royalty and a few privileged persons
on the Lord Chamberlain's list are allowed to drive through.

The **Parade Ground** behind, the largest "clear" space in
London (if a space can be described as "clear" which is largely
used for the parking of cars), is the scene of **Trooping the Colour**
on the Sovereign's birthday. Here are *Statues of Field-Marshal*

Earl Kitchener of Khartoum (John Tweed), *Field-Marshal Viscount Wolseley* (Goscombe John, R.A.), and *Field-Marshal Lord Roberts.* On the western side is the **Guards Division Memorial,** unveiled by the Duke of Connaught in memory of the 14,000 Guardsmen who laid down their lives during the Great War. "Never have soldiers more nobly done their duty."

The quadrangular pile, with cupolas, to the north of the Parade Ground, is the **Admiralty.** The wireless aerials above may almost be described as a "nerve centre" of the British Empire, for they provide direct communication with warships in all parts of the globe. Another Admiralty block is at the eastern end of the Mall and forms the fine triple **Archway** (*see* p. 75) through which State processions pass between Buckingham Palace and Westminster. The handsome wrought-iron and bronze gates were designed by Sir Aston Webb, P.R.A. The block is connected with the main building by a bridge, and in addition to the offices in it, the rooms over the Arch house the valuable *Admiralty Library*, containing many rare naval books of all periods and an interesting collection of old signal books.

Facing Whitehall, and separated from the Horse Guards only by the building which serves as the **Paymaster-General's Office,** is the **Old Admiralty,** built by Thomas Ripley, in 1725 to replace the seventeenth-century Admiralty building on the same site. Between this building and the Paymaster-General's Office (1773) is Admiralty House, the official residence of the First Lord of the Admiralty, built in 1786. In the front of the Admiralty courtyard is the screen designed by Robert Adam in 1760, when Whitehall was widened and the old Holbein Gate removed.

Emerging from the Horse Guards we cross Whitehall to the **Royal United Service Institution.** This was founded in 1831 and exists for the promotion and advancement of the science and literature of the three fighting Services. The R.U.S. Museum, which is part of the Institution, is housed in the old **Banqueting House,** the only remaining part of Whitehall Palace.

This beautiful building is an outstanding example of the work of the great architect Inigo Jones. It was built to the order of James I and completed in 1622. Whitehall Palace was originally York House, the residence of Cardinal Wolsey, but on his downfall was sequestrated by King Henry VIII. The Palace was almost entirely destroyed by fire in 1698, but the Banqueting House was saved, although it shows marks of the fire to this day.

Court was held at Whitehall from the reign of Henry VIII, who died there, until the time of William III. Charles I passed through the Hall of the Banqueting House and out of a window, now disappeared, in the extension at the North end, and so on to the scaffold in the

street where he was beheaded on 30th January, 1649. A bust of Charles
I and tablet lately placed over the public entrance mark the approximate site of the window and scaffold. Cromwell held his Parliaments
in the Hall. Charles II was received there at the time of the Restoration, and it was the scene of the St. George's Day banquets of the Order
of the Garter. James II is reputed to have erected the wind-vane
at the North end of the Banqueting House so that he could see "whether
the wind blew Protestant or Papist." Eventually a crisis came and,
seeing there was no chance of getting the support of the French fleet,
for which he had hoped, he fled by night down the river. William and
Mary were received in the Banqueting Hall by "The Grand Convention
of the Lords and Commons of England" on 13th February, 1689, when
they were offered and accepted the Crown. By the time the fire
destroyed the Palace, the Court had already taken up residence at
Kensington Palace. The Banqueting House was subsequently converted into a Chapel and was long known as the Chapel Royal of Whitehall, although it was never consecrated.

In 1893, the use of the Banqueting House was given by Queen
Victoria to the Royal United Service Institution. The new **Wing**
at the South end was built on by Members and their friends, to provide
a lecture theatre, a library and other quarters for the Institution; it
was completed in 1895.

Royal United Service Museum

(Plan II. K. 9)

Admission, 2s., children under 14, 1s. Services in uniform free. Open daily,
    Sundays excepted, from 10 a.m. to 5 p.m.
Nearest Stations.—Trafalgar Square (Bakerloo Line); Strand (Northern Line);
    Westminster (District Line).

The Museum, which is the only one of its kind in the Kingdom,
contains a unique collection of trophies, mementoes and models
covering the history of the three Services from their earliest
days. Note the ceiling of nine massive panels painted by
Rubens.

We pass at once up a short staircase, decorated by paintings
from the Royal Collection, to the **Banqueting Hall,** a superb
specimen of the Later Renaissance, built for James I by the
great architect Inigo Jones, and practically all that remains of
the old Whitehall Palace.

Here are models of the Battle of Waterloo and of the Battle
of Trafalgar, and Chantrey's bust of Nelson on part of the
mainmast of the same famous vessel. Glass cases contain
beautiful models of sailing men-of-war and colourful uniforms
and head-dresses; also relics of such national figures as Drake,
Nelson, Sir John Moore, Wellington, Florence Nightingale,
Wolsey and many others.

In the *Basement*, or Crypt, are the modern exhibits. These
include models of warships from the introduction of steam to
the latest types in the Navy of to-day; of the Mulberry Harbour;
of tanks, armoured vehicles and a Bailey Bridge; and of service
aircraft from early types to the "jet." A magnificent series of

fifteen dioramas depict historic military events from the landing
of Julius Caesar to "D" Day on the Normandy Beach.

The **War Office** occupies the whole of the irregular quadrangle
between Whitehall Place and Horse Guards Avenue, and extends
back to Whitehall Court. It is built of Portland stone, with
groups of Ionic pillars and four circular flanking towers, 156 ft.
high, which mask the architectural difficulty arising from the
fact that not one of the corners is a right angle. The block
contains 1,000 rooms, and there are 2½ miles of corridors. In
the centre of the Whitehall roadway, opposite the War Office,
is appropriately placed a lofty equestrian *Statue of the Duke of
Cambridge*, for nearly fifty years Commander-in-Chief of the
British Army.

Then we pass Great Scotland Yard, the former headquarters
of the Metropolitan Police. Here is the **Central London Re-
cruiting Depot.** Across Whitehall is the **Whitehall Theatre.**

We have now reached again the starting-point of our ramble
at Trafalgar Square, and shall perhaps be disposed to utilise a
spare hour in gaining a superficial acquaintance with the pictures
in our great national collection. A whole morning or afternoon
will hardly suffice to see them properly.

The National Gallery

(Plan II. K. 8)

Admission.—Open free every day—10–6 Mondays to Saturdays, 2–6 Sundays.
  Closed on Christmas Day, Christmas Eve, Christmas Day and Good Friday.

Catalogues, arranged in alphabetical order of painters' names, and with biographical
  notices, 3*s.* 6*d.* Photographs of all pictures are available for purchase at the
  bookstall.

Lectures (free lasting one hour are arranged in consecutive courses. A programme of
  lectures is published monthly giving time-table of lectures and may be obtained
  from the bookstall or by application.

Nearest Stations.—Trafalgar Square (Bakerloo Line), Strand (Northern Line),
  Charing Cross (Southern Region and District Line).

Buses.—With the exception of services using the Holborn and Oxford Street route,
  nearly all the principal bus routes pass through Trafalgar Square.

The National Gallery had its origin in the purchase, in 1824,
by Lord Liverpool's Government, of the Angerstein collection
of thirty-eight pictures. The building, erected 1832–8, has a
length of 460 feet, but is spoilt architecturally by the low elevation and the insignificant dome and "pepper-box" turrets. At
first both the national collection and the pictures of the Royal
Academy were housed here, but the collection had grown so by
1869 that the Academy had to migrate to Burlington House,
and in 1896 the Tate Gallery (p. 117) was built to house the
National Collections of British Art, though there is a representa-

tive display in the building we are about to enter. Various
additions have since been made, including the Duveen Room
and a room to contain the splendid Mond Bequest. Hardly less
important in the public estimation was the introduction, in
1935, of artificial lighting, enabling the gallery to be kept open
during the evening.

Considerable damage was sustained by the building during
the Second World War, by bombing, though happily all of
the pictures were distributed to various places of safety throughout the country or stored below ground. Repair work has pro-
gressed and rooms are re-opened as they are repaired.

The most important presentations, bequests and purchases
have been the Vernon Collection (1847), the Turner Collection
(1856), the Peel Collection (1871), the Wynn Ellis Collection
(1876), the Vaughan Collection (1900), the Cohen Collection
(1906), the Salting Collection (1910), the Carlisle Collection (1913),
the Wertheimer Bequest of nine portraits by J. S. Sargent (1923),
and the Mond and Phillips bequests (1924). Notable acquisitions have been 2057. "Venus and Cupid," better known as the
"Rokeby Venus," presented by the National Arts Collections
Fund; 2285. the large Family Group by Franz Hals, bought for
£25,000; 2457. "The Duchess of Milan," by Holbein, bought by
the National Art-Collections Fund, aided by a grant from the
Treasury, for £72,000; 2790. "The Adoration of the Kings," by
Gossaert of Mabuse, known as "The Castle Howard Mabuse,"
bought for £40,000. In 1918 several fine examples of nineteenth-
century French art were acquired. In 1922 Van Dyck's "George
Villiers, 2nd Duke of Buckingham, and his brother " was acquired.
In 1929 the Titian family group known as the "Cornaro Titian"
was bought for £122,000, and the world-renowned Wilton
Diptych secured for £90,000. With the aid of the National Art-
Collections Fund Rubens's "Watering Place" was acquired in
1936.

The National Collection now includes over 4,000 works, of
which about one-third, being pictures by modern British artists
(from the eighteenth century onwards), must be sought at the
Tate Gallery, at Millbank (see p. 117). At the Tate Gallery also
are displayed nearly all the Turner pictures, except those mentioned on p. 90, and the Wertheimer Sargents. Though still,
as regards the number of its masterpieces, inferior to some of the
great Continental collections, the National Gallery is quite unequalled as a representative collection of the various schools of
painting. It is especially rich in examples of the Italian and

Dutch schools. "The particular and special value of the
National Gallery among European galleries depends largely upon
the unique collection and comprehensive sequence of finished and
unfinished works and studies by Turner, England's greatest
artist, who is also the greatest landscape painter of the world."

Catalogues, with biographical notes, are on sale at the entrance,
but the inscriptions on the pictures themselves, giving name and
school of painter, dates of birth and death, and title, sufficiently
serve the purpose of the general visitor.

In the vestibules are a series of mosaics illustrating various
aspects of modern life and including portraits of film stars,
footballers and other figures; note *Melpohena* (Greta Garbo) in
the central group. On the walls also are hung various representative paintings.

The present disposition of paintings on view and of the arrangement of the various Schools are as follows:—

Rooms I, III, IV, Dome, VIII, IX, X, XI, XVI, II, XXIX,
Italian School.
Rooms V, VI, Duveen, Mond, VII, Dutch and Flemish Schools.
Room XXXII, Spanish School.
Rooms XII, XIV, XV, French School.
Rooms XVII, XVIII, British School.
Duveen Room, German School.

*Space will not permit the enumeration of every picture in this
wonderful collection—the note of which, it should be remembered,
is the consecutive history of painting. We indicate here some of the
more important works but if some are not readily discernible, attendants, on inquiry, will gladly furnish information regarding the
present location.*

Early Italian Schools.—The visitor who has not been initiated
into the history of pictorial art will probably be at first not a
little puzzled to discover what interest attaches to many of the
paintings of the earlier Italian schools. Some of the pictures—
stiff, angular, devoid of proportion and perspective—appear
grotesque and even ludicrous; but they enable the student to
trace the development of medieval art from its crude beginnings
to the wonderful perfection attained in the palmy days of Italian
artistic supremacy, when "the canvas glowed beyond e'en
nature warm," and the works of such painters as Raphael,
Michelangelo, Titian, and their compeers were looked upon as
holding a place among the wonders of the world. After the
fall of Rome, Constantinople became the centre of civilisation
and culture. The Byzantine school of painting was hard and
stiff. There was no attempt at a faithful rendering of nature
in form or colour, of the representation of rounded surfaces nor
of distance by the use of perspective. After the conquest of

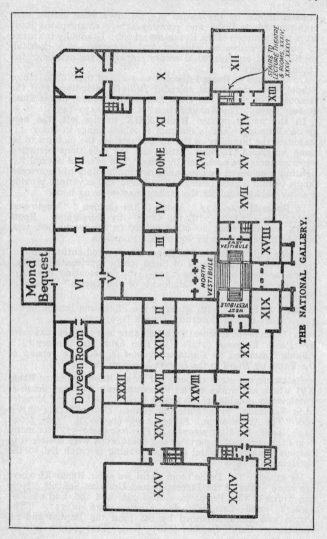

THE NATIONAL GALLERY.

Constantinople by the Latins in 1204, Byzantine artists were transplanted to Italy, and painting slowly emancipated itself from the trammels of the Byzantine school. Gradually the range of subjects embraced widened and increased, and classical, mythological and historical scenes employed the pencils of the Italian painters.

On the walls of **Room I** devoted to works of the North Italian School, note the several splendid *Bellinis*, including (189) the famous "Portrait of the Doge Leonardo Loredan, in his State Robes"; 739. "The Annunciation" *Crivelli* (1430–1493).

In the newly opened **Room XXIX** to the left, the new air-conditioning plant (a diagram of which hangs in Room 11) stabilises the humidity of the air and enables the pictures to be hung un-glazed, thereby cutting out the reflections occurring when pictures are protected by glass. The effect of natural top lighting is achieved by concealing continuous lines of fluorescent lamps behind a glass ceiling. The fabric wall coverings provide a softer background for the Italian masters hung here.

In **Room II** note 1077. "Agony in the Garden," "Virgin and Child," and "Christ with the Cross" by *Borgognone*. **Room XXIX** contains what no other gallery in the world possesses, namely three pictures by Picro della Francisca.

To the right of Room I is **Room III**, devoted entirely to religious works of the School of Siena (early fourteenth century), note altar-piece by *Sassetta* (1392–1450) representing the life of St. Francis, and 1155, "Madonna of the Girdle" *Matteo di Giovanni*.

Room IV is hung with works of the Florentine School, notice 583. "Rout of San Romano" *Uccello* (1397–1475).

In the small room beneath the **Dome** are four gorgeous canvases by *Paolo Veronese* (1528–88). The figure in the centre is "Fame" ascribed to *Guillame Bertelot* (c. 1600), a version of the Fame by *Biard* in the Louvre Museum, Paris.

Retracing our steps through the Dome Room we enter **Room XVI** where are works of the Florentine and Umbrian Schools. Particularly notable are 3918. and 3919. "The Life and Miracles of St. Zenobius," 915. "Mars and Venus," *Botticelli* (1444–1510); 666. "The Auunciation," *Filippo Lippi* (1406–69). 727., 3162., 3230., 4428., the altar-piece by *F. Pesellino* (1422–57)—for many years the component parts of this great work were scattered in various countries; skilful and painstaking research led to the reassembly in 1929.

By crossing the Dome room again we enter **Room XI** where are more works of the Florentine and Umbrian Schools. Note the works of the *Verrocchio* School 781. and 296. and of *Verrochio's* pupil—*Leonardo da Vinci*. Here is 1171. "The Virgin and Child, attended by St. John the Baptist and St. Nicholas of Bari," *Raphael* (1483–1520). This picture is com-

London County Hall, the headquarters of the London County Council. During excavations on the site in 1910 there was unearthed a Roman galley of oak, believed to date from the end of the third century A.D.

Top. The Horse Guards, Whitehall, the picturesque mounted sentries ever an attraction. *Centre.* Admiralty Archway, through which pass State processions to Westminster. *Bottom.* Carlton House Terrace, The Mall.

monly known as the **Ansidei Madonna,** from the Ansidei
family of Perugia, for whom it was painted. It was purchased
from the Duke of Marlborough in 1885 for £70,000, and is one
of the greatest pictures in the world. *Raphael Sanzio,* of Urbina,
was remarkable alike for his prodigious genius and his wonderful
activity. Dying at the early age of thirty-seven, he yet lived
long enough to enrich the world with many masterpieces and to
win for himself the foremost place in Italian art. Here, too, are
Raphael's 744. "Madonna, Child and St. John," and 2919. his
"Procession to Calvary"; note 690. "Portrait of a Sculptor," by
A. del Sarto, perhaps the artist himself.

Room X. Later Venetian School.—The characteristic of the
Venetian painters is their predilection for gorgeous and magnificent scenes; nature adorned with the highest brilliancy of colour,
"They are especially fond of saints who have been cardinals,
because of their red hats, and they sunburn all their hermits into
splendid russet-brown." Then, also, it has been rightly observed
that they had before them the colour of Venice, "that melo-
drama of flame, and gold, and rose, and orange, and azure, which
the skies and lagoons of Venice yield almost daily to the eye."
Among the gems of this school is: 35. "Bacchus and Ariadne,"
Titian (1477–1576). Living to a very great age, Titian is distinguished alike for the greatness of his achievements and the
length of his career. He was one of those fortunate painters
whose merits were fully recognised in their own time. He was
the friend and companion of princes and kings; and it is recorded
that Francis I, visiting his studio, did not disdain to stoop to
pick up the pencil the aged master had let fall. Note 4452.
"The Cornaro Family," acquired in 1929 for the sum of £122,000.
Another of his works, the famous 1944. "Portrait of a Man"
(formerly considered to represent Ariosto), was acquired in 1904
for £30,000. Note 4. "The Holy Family Adoring," and 3948.
"Mother and Child," both by *Titian.* 1313. "The Origin of the
Milky Way," *Il Tintoretto* (1518–94). 1041. "The Vision of St.
Helena," 268. "Adoration of the Magi," 294. "The Family of
Darius," all by *Paolo Veronese* (1528–88). 1450. "The Holy
Family," *Sebastiano del Piombo* (1485–1547). Here also are
697. *Moroni's* famous "Portrait of a Tailor," and other portraits
from the same brush.

Turning to the right we find—

Rooms XII, XIV, and **XV,** which are devoted to works of the
French School. In Room XII are canvases by *Claude (Gelée,*
1600–82), and the *Poussins (Nicholas,* 1594–1665, and *Gaspard
(Dughet),* 1613–75). 30. "Seaport: the Embarkation of St.
Ursula," and other pictures by *Claude.* 1449. "Cardinal
Richelieu," *Philippe de Champaigne* (1602–74), of which there
is a replica in the Louvre.

Note the *Lancrets* in Room XIV and 1090. "Pan and Syrinx,"

F. Boucher (*Boucher* is well represented in the Wallace collection, *see* p. 147).

In recent years a number of valuable pictures by modern French artists have been added to the national collection. The greater number are shown at the Tate Gallery (p. 117), but here in Room XV, *Manet* (1832–83) is represented by the two soldier pictures 3294 A. and B.   Note 3286. "Baron Schwiter," by *Delacroix*.

Rooms XVII and **XVIII** contain representative examples of the **British School,** but the greater number of British works in the national collection are at the Tate Gallery (*see* p. 117).

Room XVII is principally devoted to portraits. *Gainsborough*: 3812. and 1811. "The Painter's Daughters," The Misses Mary and Margaret Gainsborough; 683. the famous portrait of Mrs. Siddons; Note also *Reynolds'* 111. "Lord Heathfield," 79. " The Three Graces decorating Hymen," 5750. "Sir Watkin Williams-Wynn with his mother." See also 1162. " Shrimp Girl," the " Marriage à la Mode," series and "Calais Gate," by *Hogarth* (1697–1764).

Room XVIII is notable for its landscapes, including several fine Turners. At his death *J. M. W. Turner* (1775–1851) left all his pictures to the National Gallery, "provided that a room or rooms be added to the present National Gallery, to be, when erected, called Turner's Gallery." By far the greater number of the master's works, numbering in all over five hundred, will be found at the Tate Gallery (*see* p. 117), but here he is worthily represented by some of his most gorgeous and characteristic canvases. 538. "Rain, Steam and Speed," 534. "San Benedetto: looking towards Fusino," 497. "Crossing the brook." The many *Constables* speak for themselves—130. "The Cornfield," 1207. "The Hay Wain," 2651. "Salisbury Cathedral." Note also 2674. "The Poringland Oak" by *John Crome*.

Passing through the Vestibules we pause in an endeavour to identify the various well-known sportsmen, artists, film-stars, etc. who figure in the mosaics. Here are such well-known works as 4257. "Queen Charlotte" *Sir T. Lawrence*, and 1315. "Admiral Pulido Pareja," attributed to *Velasquez*.

Retracing our steps through Room I we come to—

Rooms V, VI, Mond, Duveen, VII. Dutch and Flemish.— The distinguishing features of this school are the strict fidelity to nature, wonderfully accurate delineations of real life, and marvellous preservation and freshness of the works after centuries. Notice especially the works of Rembrandt, Rubens, Ruisdael, Jan Vermeer, Peter de Hooch, Cuyp, P. Potter, and Van Dyck.

Room V is devoted to works of the seventeenth century. Note *P. Potter's* "Landscape" 8490, and 1390. "The Shore at Scheveningen," 2561. "View near Haarlem" by *Jacob van Ruisdael*. The world-famous "Avenue," *Hobbema* (1638–1700) will be found in Room VI. Here also are 835. 834. "Courtyard and Interior of a Dutch House" *P. de Hooch*; 1251. "Portrait of a Woman" and 2529. "Lady with a Fan" both by *Franz Hals*.

Among the many famous *Rembrandt* pictures with which the Mond Room abounds will be found 775. "Portrait of an Old Lady"—Francoise van Wasserhoven (?); 45. "Woman taken in Adultery," 54. "A Woman Bathing," 1674., 1675. "Portraits of Jacob Jacobsz. and Margaretha Trip," and 672. and 221. two self-portraits. Note also 4042. "Man in Fur Cap" *Carel Fabritius.*

In the **Duveen Room** now repaired after the war damage, some interesting examples of the **German School** will be found at the far end of the gallery. The principal are: *Holbein's* "Duchess of Milan" and "Ambassadors" 1314. Representing the Netherlands School is *Jan van Eyck* (1390–1441) see 186. "Portrait of John Arnolfini and his Wife," 2790. "The Adoration of the Kings," *Mabuse* (1470–1541), known as "The Castle Howard Mabuse."

Room VII contains many wonderful works by *Rubens*—"Rape of the Sabines," "Judgement of Paris," "Brazen Serpent," etc., and his one-time assistant *Van Dyck*. Note 1172. *Van Dyck's* great (144 in. x 114 in.) portrait of Charles I, painted for Charles at his Court. "One remembers only, in looking upon this picture of him, Charles's graces, not his faults." Also by *Van Dyck* is 49. "Portrait of an Artist (?)". Note also "Triumph of Silenus," a joint work. In this room too, are some pictures which have overflowed from the Italian rooms—note particularly 2923. *Caracci's* "The Three Maries" and 172. *Caravaggio's* "Christ at Emmaus."

Straight ahead in **Room IX** we see a representative collection of the **Spanish School**. The National Gallery possesses many of the greatest works of Velasquez and Murillo, and has also acquired some characteristic examples of El Greco. 1129. "Philip IV of Spain," 1148. "Christ at the Column," and 2057. "Venus and Cupid" (The Rokeby Venus), all by *Velasquez* (1599–1660). "The Immaculate Conception" by *Velasquez* lent by the Misses Frere. 1457. "Christ driving the Traders from the Temple"; 3476. "The Agony in the Garden." *El Greco,* 1473. "Donna Isabel Cobos,' by *Goya.*

It is now necessary to retrace our steps passing through the vestibule where photographs of the pictures may be bought.

Leaving the National Gallery (note the fig-trees flourishing in the gardens), we turn to the left, passing the copy of Houdon's statue of *Washington,* presented by the State of Virginia. It is dwarfed by its surroundings, and a more suitable site should be found. We turn to the left at the corner opposite the Church of **St. Martin's-in-the-Fields** (*see* p. 75), and make our way to the National Portrait Gallery. Facing the entrance to the Gallery is a much-discussed statue to Nurse Cavell (*see* p. 129).

The National Portrait Gallery

Plan II. K. 8.
Access.—Trafalgar Square (Bakerloo), Charing Cross (Southern Region and District Line), Strand (Northern), Leicester Square (Piccadilly).
Admission.— Open all year, except Good Friday, Christmas Eve and Christmas Day. Mondays to Fridays, 10–5; Saturdays till 6 p.m.; Sundays, 2–6 p.m., Free.
Lectures.—*See* Announcements in building.
Lift to all floors.
Catalogues.—5/–, and short guides available.

The National Portrait Gallery was founded in 1856, but the first permanent building was the gift of Mr. W. H. Alexander in 1896; an extension was given in 1933 by the late Lord Duveen. The collection contains nearly 4,000 portraits of eminent men and women of all ranks and ages. Royal personages, statesmen, poets, judges, writers, scientists, warriors, actors, all who have played a part in national history are represented. The word "portrait" is read in its widest sense, for not only does the collection include paintings, drawings and photographs, but numerous presentments in bronze and marble as well. There are also cases containing medals. The Gallery comprises three floors and a basement.

The works are arranged viz:

Top Floor   Henry VII to George V.
             Sixteenth century–Twentieth century.

First Floor Arts and Sciences.
             Eighteenth century–Twentieth century.
             Recent acquisitions.

East Wing   Kit-Kat Club Portraits.

On entering take the lift to the—

Top Floor

Entering **Room 7** we see portraits of the Tudor Monarchs including Henry VII, Henry VIII, Edward VI, Mary I and Elizabeth. The first two Queens of Henry VIII are also here, together with Cardinal Wolsey and Thomas Cromwell, Cranmer, Latimer and Ridley, and Cardinal Pole, and also Mary Queen of Scots. At the end of the room is a family group of Sir Thomas More with his descendants. Around the full-length portrait of Elizabeth are gathered her favourites and secretaries of state, including Leicester and Essex and Walsingham, Burghley and Salisbury. **Room 8** covers the reigns of James and Charles I, the civil war and the Commonwealth and includes Inigo Jones, Ben Jonson, John Donne, Buckingham with his family, and on the end walls Charles I and Henrietta Maria. In this room also are portraits of the great Lord Bacon and Shakespeare with other men of art and learning. **Room 9** contains a company the like of which is seldom seen for it includes Thomas Hobbes and Isaak Walton, Isaac Newton and William Dampier, Christopher Wren, Dryden, Locke, Bunyan, Pepys and Purcell. The seventeenth century ends in **Rooms 10 and 11** with the period of the Restoration, the Revolution of '88 and the reign of William and Mary, and Queen Anne. Judge Jeffreys, of "Bloody Assizes" fame is in **Room 11.** Also here is the Duke of Marlborough.

Returning now to **Room 6** we see the portraits of the first three Georges with notabilities of the middle of the eighteenth century.

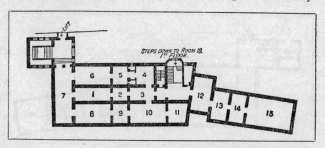

PLAN OF TOP FLOOR

Room 5 contains statesmen of the latter part of the eighteenth century and includes the younger Pitt, Charles James Fox, Burke, Wilkes, George Washington, Benjamin Franklin and Lord North. In **Room 4** are the Admirals Lord Nelson, Rodney, Duncan, Hood and Howe; Clive and Warren Hastings, and founders of the Commonwealth overseas. In these rooms (4 and 6) can be seen works by the great masters of portraiture, Gainsborough and Reynolds and their contemporaries. In **Room 3** and on the staircase landing are a number of busts and statues.

Proceeding to the West Wing we find in **Room 12** three large groups, Pitt addressing the House in 1793, The first House of Commons after the Reform Bill of 1832, and the Lords in 1820.

In **Room 13** is a portrait of the Duke of Wellington and nearby are other generals distinguished in the Peninsula and at Waterloo. Here also are statesmen of the early nineteenth century. **Room 14** shows the growth of the Commonwealth with the explorers, churchmen and reformers of the middle of the century, and **Room 15** contains leading statesmen of the last century, Lord Durham, Lord Melbourne, Palmerston, Gladstone, Disraeli,

Cobden and Bright, Lord Salisbury, Joseph Chamberlain and John Burns. In company are Cecil Rhodes, General Booth, the seventh Earl of Shaftesbury. Queen Victoria and Edward VII are in this room.

Adjacent to Room 12 is a staircase which descends to the

First Floor

which illustrates the arts and sciences from the beginning of the eighteenth century. We turn left for **Room 24** which contains some notable busts including a terra-cotta of William Hogarth. In **Room 25** we see Dean Swift, Hogarth again, Alexander Pope, Samuel Richardson, Sterne, Handel, the

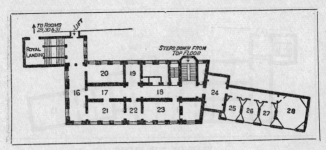

PLAN OF FIRST FLOOR

preachers Isaac Watts, Wesley and Whitefield, Cowper and Arkwright, the inventor. In **Room 26** are Dr. Johnson and several of his contemporaries, and famous men of the theatre. **Room 27** contains a galaxy of literary genius and writers of the late eighteenth–early nineteenth century period.

Room 28 concludes with Faraday and Darwin, Kipling and Thomas Hardy. Gilbert and Sullivan, Ellen Terry and Henry Irving. Returning past the staircase there is a long corridor hung with drawings; in the first half actors, artists, writers and musicians of the eighteenth century and in the second a fine series of modern drawings of artists, writers and scholars.

Beyond is **Room 16** where recent acquisitions are shown.

A short flight of stairs gives access to the **Royal Landing,** where is a picture of the late King George VI and his Family. In the **East Wing** in **Room 19** we find the series of portraits of the members of the Kit-Kat Club, painted 1700–20. On the **Ground Floor** are the naval and military commanders of the twentieth century.

WESTMINSTER

ROUTE II.—WESTMINSTER—THE HOUSES OF PARLIAMENT—ST. MAR-
GARET'S CHURCH—WESTMINSTER ABBEY—THE ROMAN CATHOLIC
CATHEDRAL—THE TATE GALLERY.

THE present **City of Westminster**—constituted a municipality in 1900, though it has been a city by royal charter for centuries—extends from the river to Oxford Street, and from Temple Bar to Kensington. In this excursion we shall only traverse a small part of it. Westminster, the reader should remember, was a busy spot long before London had being. Hemmed in to the east and west, the river here spread in a wide and shallow stream, near the north brink of which was a small eyot, overgrown with briars and brushwood, known as Thorney Island, or the Isle of Brambles. As it was impossible to cross the river with safety for miles on either side, the Britons established a ford at this point, and built houses for the accommodation of travellers, and marts at which they might obtain necessaries. The Romans, following their example, brought the main roads, Watling and Dover Streets, into connection with the ford, a reminder of which we still have in the adjacent Horseferry Road.

We will assume that the round, which will occupy a full day, is begun at **Westminster Bridge** (p 78), in the shadow of "Big Ben." Across the river is the long façade of the **London County Hall** (p. 78). Walking a few yards westward, to the corner of Parliament Street, we have on our left one of the most striking and picturesque scenes in the Metropolis, or, indeed, in any capital. On the left are Westminster Hall and the stately Houses of Parliament, with their fretted pinnacles; to the south is the venerable Abbey, partly hidden by St. Margaret's Church, the greyness of the stone set off by the smooth green lawns of **Parliament Square.** Beyond the trees on the far side of the Square is the Middlesex Guildhall.

The congestion of traffic in the square had long been a problem, but now considerable alterations have been made. The portion previously known as the Canning enclosure has been reduced and here now stand the statues of *President Lincoln*, by Gaudens, and *George Canning* (1827); and the road moved further west to make a larger central lawn. The old trees on the west side of the Square form an avenue along the raised terrace where, facing the Houses of Parliament, are the statues of *Sir Robert Peel* (1850), *Lord Beaconsfield* (1881) always fondly decked with flowers and wreaths on Primrose Day (19th April) and the *Earl of Derby* (1869). From the paved walk, on which stands the statue of *Lord Palmerston* (1865), a fine vista of the north front of the Abbey is obtained. Against Westminster Hall is a fine statue of *Oliver Cromwell* (1658) by Thornycroft.

In the shadow of the tall Clock Tower is **New Palace Yard,** the quadrangle from which Members enter the Houses of Parliament. It was one of the two courtyards of the old Palace of Westminster built by Edward the Confessor and occupied by the sovereign of England until Henry VIII took possession of Whitehall. **Old Palace Yard,** between the Abbey and the Houses of Parliament, to which we must make our way to secure admission to the present legislative chambers, was another courtyard of the Palace, though its identity has almost been lost in the roadway.

The Houses of Parliament

Plan II. K. 9 and 10.
Admission.—The Palace of Westminster is open to the general public on Saturdays, Easter Monday and Tuesday, Whit Monday and Tuesday and August Bank Holiday, providing the Houses of Parliament are not sitting on these days. Entrance by the Norman Porch adjoining Victoria Tower from 10 a.m. to 3.30 p.m.
Strangers' Galleries.—When Parliament is sitting, persons of either sex desirous of listening to the debates in the House of Commons can gain admission to the Strangers' Gallery (should there be any vacant seats) after 4.15 p.m. (11.30 a.m. on Fridays), by applying at the Admission Order Office in the Central Lobby. To ensure admission on any important occasion, it is advisable to apply to a Member for an *Order in Advance.* These are issued six days beforehand to forty Members alphabetically for each sitting day. Members, therefore, receive two Orders approximately every sixteen sitting days. Orders must be signed by a Member and bear the name and address of the holder.
   Admission to the *Special Gallery* and *Under the Gallery* is only granted on the personal application of a Member to the Serjeant at Arms.
   Commonwealth visitors desirous of listening to debates should apply to their High Commissioners, likewise foreigners to their Embassy or Legation.
   The House usually meets at 2.30 p.m. and rises at 10 p.m. (Friday 11 a.m. to 4 p.m.).
   For debates in the *House of Lords* there is limited accommodation at 2.40 p.m on Tuesdays and Wednesdays, and at 4.10 p.m. on Thursdays.
Nearest Station.—Westminster (District Line).
Buses on Victoria–Trafalgar Square routes, or running over Westminste Bridge, pass through Parliament Square.

St. Stephen's Chapel, built by Edward III, was for centuries the meeting-place of the House of Commons—a fact which explains the still frequent allusions to "St. Stephen's." The old building having been destroyed by fire in 1834, designs were invited for a new structure, and of the ninety-seven sent in that of *Barry* was selected, the first stone being laid in 1840, and the building completed in 1857. The House of Lords was used for the first time on the 15th April, 1847, the House of Commons at the commencement of the 1852 Session. The building is in the richest Gothic style (Tudor or Perpendicular), and occupies an area of 8 acres. It contains 11 courts or quadrangles, and cost £3,000,000. The principal façade, overlooking the river, is 940 feet in length. Unfortunately, the external stone (magnesian limestone) is too soft for the climate, and extensive repairs have become necessary.
   The **Clock Tower,** overlooking Westminster Bridge, is 316 ft.

The Houses of Parliament, from the river. Barry's magnificent building was completed in 1857. The clock tower on the right contains Big Ben whose resonant note is familiar to millions of radio listeners throughout the world.

London (*d*).

The Houses of Parliament and Westminster Hall. Westminster Hall was the scene of the trial of Charles I. Some of the original oak roof remains, wood for which was obtained from British trees planted in the sixth century.

high and 40 ft. square. When the House is sitting a light is shown from the Clock Tower by night, and a Union Jack flies from the Victoria Tower by day.

The **Clock,** which has four dials, each 22½ ft. in diameter, was constructed by Dents, under the direction of the late Lord Grimthorpe. It is one of the finest timekeepers in the world. During a recent year on 118 days the error of the clock was not greater than two-tenths of a second, on 105 days it was between two-tenths and a half a second, and on 49 days it was from a half to one second wrong. The minute hands are 14 ft. long, the hour hands 9 ft.; the figures are 2 ft. long, and the minute spaces 1 ft. square. The hours are struck on the famous **Big Ben,** so named in compliment to Sir Benjamin Hall, First Commissioner of Works at the time the bell was cast. It weighs 13½ tons, and in calm weather its resonant note may be heard over the greater part of London. Wireless broadcast has made its notes familiar throughout the world. The quarters are struck upon four smaller bells.

The **Central Tower,** 300 ft. high, is used as a ventilating shaft. The great **Victoria Tower,** at the south-west angle of this great block, is 336 ft. high and 75 ft. square. The archway beneath, 50 ft. high, forms the **Royal Entrance,** and is used by the Sovereign when opening Parliament. Note in old Palace Yard, Marochetti's fine *Statue of Richard Cœur de Lion.*

Beyond, the **Victoria Tower Gardens** extend to Lambeth Bridge. A notable feature is *Rodin's* fine sculpture, *The Burghers of Calais.* It is unfortunate that the pedestal is 17 ft. high. Here, too, is a statue of *Mrs. Pankhurst,* one of the pioneers of the "Votes for Women" movement.

The **Public Entrance** is by the door adjoining the Victoria Tower, whence we ascend the Royal Staircase to the **Norman Porch,** a small square room with groined roof supported by a beautiful central pillar. A door on the right leads to the **Queen's Robing Room,** decorated with frescoes and panels representing the Legend of King Arthur. Her Majesty and her attendants, on the occasion of opening Parliament, proceed in procession to the House of Lords by way of the **Royal Gallery,** a handsome hall, 110 ft. long, paved with beautiful mosaics, and having a richly-gilded panelled roof. On the walls are two large frescoes by Maclise—"The Death of Nelson" and "The Meeting of Wellington and Blücher after Waterloo." Two bronze figures on the right by John Tweed, form the Peers' War Memorial. The title of J. S. Copley's "Death of the Earl of Chatham" is a misnomer, for Pitt did not die until some time after the seizure depicted.

We next enter the **Prince's Chamber,** panelled with dark wood. The **House of Lords** is sumptuously decorated; and a "gilded chamber" indeed. It is 90 ft. long, 45 ft. broad, and 45 ft. high, and is lighted by twelve stained-glass windows containing portraits of the kings and queens of England. In the niches between the windows are statues of the barons who compelled

King John to sign Magna Carta. The frescoes represent "Edward III conferring the Order of the Garter on the Black Prince," "The Baptism of Ethelbert," and "Judge Gascoigne committing Prince Henry to the Tower." The red morocco benches of the 550 noble lords entitled to sit in the House are ranged right and left of the **Throne,** the cross-benches being reserved for princes of the blood. Seats on either side of the Throne, at the south end, are for Ambassadors and distinguished visitors. The cushioned ottoman immediately in front is the famous **Woolsack,** on which the Lord Chancellor sits. At the other end of the house is the **Bar,** at which the faithful Commons attend to hear the speech from the Throne, and to hear the Royal Assent to the Bills they have passed. Above are galleries for strangers and the Press.

Beyond the **Peers' Lobby** is the **Peers' Corridor,** leading to the Central Lobby and containing frescoes relating to the Stuart period by *C. W. Cope*—

Funeral of Charles I. (*first on left*).
Parting of Lady Russell from her husband, Lord William Russell, before his execution (*first on right*).
Expulsion of Fellows of a College at Oxford for refusing to sign the Covenant (*on left*).
Departure of the *Mayflower* for New England (*on right*).
Defence of Basing House by Cavaliers (*on left*).
Departure of London Trained Bands to relieve the garrison of Gloucester (*on right*).
Charles I raising his Standard at Nottingham (*last on left*).
Speaker Lenthall defending the Rights of the House of Commons against Charles I, when he attempted to arrest the five members (*last on right*).

The octagonal **Central Lobby,** 60 ft. in diameter and 75 ft. high has a vaulted stone roof, inlaid with Venetian mosaics. Above the doors leading to the Lords and the Commons respectively are mosaics by Sir E. Poynter representing St. George and St. David. Other mosaics represent St. Andrew of Scotland and St. Patrick of Ireland. The niches contain statues of English sovereigns, while ranged around are statues of statesmen.

Immediately opposite the door by which we entered the Central Lobby is the **Churchill Arch,** made of stonework from the former war-damaged Commons Chamber, and leading to the **Commons' Corridor,** lined like the Peer's Corridor, with eight large frescoes by E. N. Ward, R.A.:—

Alice Lisle concealing fugitives after the Battle of Sedgmoor (*first on left*).
Jane Lane assisting the flight of Charles II (*first on right*).
The Last Sleep of Argyll (*on left*).
The Execution of Montrose (*on right*).
The Lords and Commons presenting the Crown to William and Mary (*on left*).

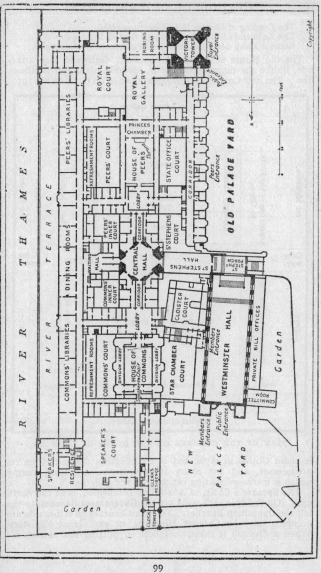

THE HOUSES OF PARLIAMENT

The Landing of Charles II at Dover (*on right*).
The Acquittal of the Seven Bishops (*last on left*).
General Monk declaring for a free Parliament (*last on right*).

The old **House of Commons** chamber, destroyed May 1941, was, unlike the magnificent Lords, severely plain and business-like.   The new Commons' Chamber, opened on October 26, 1950,

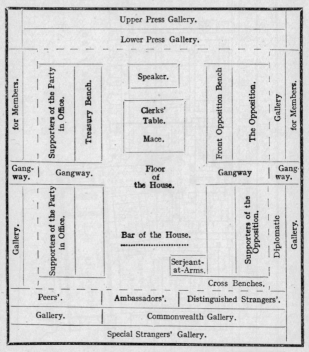

PLAN OF THE CHAMBER OF THE HOUSE OF COMMONS.

is again Gothic in style, but is considerably different from its predecessor, and has many improvements, not least among which is increased seating capacity in the galleries.

The **Speaker's Chair,** of Australian blackwood, is at the north end.   On the Speaker's right are the **Government Benches,** to the left the **Opposition Benches.**   The front benches on either side are occupied only by Cabinet Ministers, or ex-Cabinet Ministers. When a division is taken members supporting the motion file

into the "Aye" lobby, to the right of the Speaker, the "Noes" to
the other side. A bell rings beforehand to warn members who
may be in other parts of the House, the doors are then locked,
and the voters are counted by "tellers" as they return to their
seats. Below the Speaker sits the Clerk of the House, and at the
other end of the table reposes the **Mace,** the symbol of the House's
dignity and privileges. Over the Speaker's Chair is the **Reporters'
Gallery.** The **Peers'** and **Distinguished Strangers' Galleries** are
at the other end, while the **Members' Galleries** are on either
side (for admission *see* p. 96).

Return to the Central Lobby, where a door on the right side
leads to **St. Stephen's Hall,** occupying the site of the old St.
Stephen's Chapel (p. 96), where the Commons met for centuries.
Brass studs in the floor mark the position of the Speaker's chair
and table; and in appropriate reference to the great struggles
in our Parliamentary history which were here fought, the walls
of the hall have been decorated with a series of paintings relating
to "the Building of Britain," while at the ends are mosaics by
R. Anning Bell, R.A., representing "St. Stephen, King Stephen
and Edward the Confessor" (a group having reference to the
founding of St. Stephen's Chapel), and "Edward III giving
instructions for the rebuilding of St. Stephen's Chapel."

In order that the mural paintings may be viewed in historical
sequence, it is best to proceed at once to the far end of the Hall
and to begin with the fourth picture on the right:

King Alfred's Ships attack Danish invaders, 877 (*Colin Gill*).
Richard I leaves England to join the Crusade (*Glyn Philpot, R.A.*).
King John gives consent to Magna Carta, 1215 (*Charles Sims, R.A.*).
The English people gather secretly to read aloud Wycliffe's English
Bible (*George Clausen, R.A.*).

Now crossing to the north side of the Hall we have—

Sir Thomas More refuses to grant Henry VIII a subsidy, 1523
(*Vivian Forbes*).
Queen Elizabeth commissions Sir Walter Raleigh to sail for America
and discover new countries, 1584 (*A. K. Lawrence*).
Sir Thomas Roe, envoy to the Moghul Emperor, lays the foundation
of British influence in India, 1614 (*W. Rothenstein*).
The English and Scottish Commissioners present to Queen Anne the
Articles of Union, 1707 (*W. T. Monnington*).

Steps at the east end of the hall lead to **St. Stephen's Porch.**
On the right is—

Westminster Hall

Admission.—Westminster Hall is open to the Public on Saturdays from 10 a.m. till
one hour before the House meets on days when the House is sitting. On all
other weekdays it is open from 10 a.m. to 4 p.m. (Christmas Day and Good
Friday excepted).

Westminster Hall, next to the Tower and Westminster Abbey,
is the most historic building in London. It was begun by William
Rufus in 1097 and enlarged by his successors. Richard II, in

1397, caused it to be rebuilt, and added the grand **Oak Roof,** rightly described as "one of the finest feats of carpentry extant." Only British oak grown in the Sussex Weald was used, and the trees must have been planted not later than the sixth century. The wood, having in the course of centuries become seriously decayed, has been judiciously patched and reinforced with steel. Much of the Norman masonry was cut away to provide for the fourteenth-century windows still visible, and in 1644 the Norman walls were still further mutilated and relined with stone. Small doors have been cut in the newer stone lining, so that antiquaries may examine the older work at will. Westminster Hall is probably the largest hall in the world with a roof unsupported by pillars, excepting, of course, modern steel structures. Its length is 238 ft.; breadth, 67½ ft.; height, 90 ft. A considerable part of the roof was damaged by fire during air raids.

The historical associations of the Hall are full of interest. From 1224 until 1882 the Law Courts were held within and around. The hall was the scene of the trial and condemnation of Charles I and of the proclamation of Cromwell as Lord Protector. Here, a few years later, Cromwell's head was brought from Westminster Abbey, with those of Bradshaw and Ireton, and impaled on an iron-tipped pike on the southern gable for something like a quarter of a century. The Protector's head was blown down during a heavy storm in 1686 and secreted, it is said, by a sentry. It is still preserved in this country and was exhibited to one of the learned societies in 1911. In Westminster Hall were tried and condemned William Wallace, Lord Cobham, Sir Thomas More, the Protector Somerset, the Earl of Essex, Sir Thomas Wyatt, Guy Fawkes, and the Earl of Strafford. It was the scene, too, of the acquittal of the Seven Bishops (1688), and of the long trial of Warren Hastings. King George VI lay in state here in February, 1952.

Tablets on the stairs and in the middle of the Hall mark the posts where Wallace, Charles I and Strafford stood during their trials, and record the lying-in-state of King Edward VII and King George V.

From the east side of the staircase landing a flight of steps leads down to **St. Stephen's Crypt** (or the **Chapel of St. Mary),** a remnant of old St. Stephen's which escaped the fire of 1834 and after a long period of neglect has in recent years been restored and is again used for services and marriages. It is a richly decorated, vaulted apartment, 90 ft. in length, 28 ft. wide, and 20 ft. high.

Emerging in Old Palace Yard, we cross the road to—

St. Margaret's Church

Plan II. K. 9.
Access.—See Houses of Parliament, p. 96.
Admission daily between 11 a.m. and 4 p.m., but not during weddings or other special services. Entrance by west and east doors. Visitors are expected to contribute to the maintenance and restoration of the church. (For services *see* p. 20.)

St. Margaret's is the Parish Church of the House of Commons. Members, headed by the Speaker (whose pew is immediately in front of the lectern), attend service here on special occasions. The window over the east door, which replaces the Caxton Window (destroyed by blast during an air raid) commemorates *Captain the Hon. E. A. Fitzroy*, Speaker of the House of Commons from 1928 to 1943, who is buried in the chancel.

The church is well known as the scene of many society weddings, and its famous bells are also rung whenever the Sovereign drives past in state. This custom goes back at least as far as the reign of King Edward VI.

St. Margaret's is of special interest to Americans—more so, perhaps, than any other London church. It contains a memorial tablet to *Sir Walter Raleigh*, the founder of Virginia, who was beheaded in Old Palace Yard in 1618, and whose body was interred in the chancel: he is also commemorated by the *West Window*, presented by American citizens in 1882. A mosaic commemorates Bishop Phillips Brooks of Massachusetts, who often preached here. Of unique interest is the sculptured monument near the west door to *Sir Peter Parker*, Baronet. Captain of H.M. Frigate *Menelaus*: it depicts his death in action against the Americans on August 3, 1814. The American Ambassador reads the Lessons at the annual service here on Memorial Day.

Tradition relates that the church was founded in 1064 by King Edward the Confessor for the use of the laity, the Abbey Church being intended for the monks. It was served by clergy from the Abbey, and was not constituted an independent parish until 1840. The church was rebuilt in the reign of Edward I, and again rebuilt on the eve of the Reformation (c. 1490–1523), the architect being Robert Stowell. In the eighteenth century the exterior was cased in Portland stone, and the tower reconstructed. But the restoration effected by Archdeacon Farrar, under the guidance of Sir Gilbert Scott, repaired much of the damage done by previous restorers, and the interior, with its graceful Perpendicular arches, gives a very fair impression of Stowell's original design.

The glory of the church is the *East Window*, representing the Crucifixion. It is generally considered one of the most beautiful examples of stained glass in England, and has a curious history.

It was part of the dowry of Catharine of Aragon, and was made in the Low Countries at the orders of her father, King Ferdinand of Spain, who intended it for the chapel which Henry VII was building in the Abbey: but by the time of its delivery Catharine was married to Henry VIII, who bestowed the window upon Waltham Abbey. At the Dissolution of the Monasteries, it was removed to the private chapel of New Hall in Essex, which passed through a succession of owners: during the Civil War General Monk had the window taken down and buried in chests. Later it was sold for 50 guineas to Mr. John Conyers of Copt Hall, Essex, from whose son it was bought in 1758 for 400 guineas by the Churchwardens of St. Margaret's out of a Parliamentary grant of £4,000 for the repair and decoration of the church. But relations between the Abbey authorities and St. Margaret's had long been strained, and the Dean of Westminster seized the opportunity to institute legal proceedings against the Churchwardens, on the grounds that the window was a "superstitious picture," and that he had not been applied to for a faculty for its erection. The lawsuit dragged on, judgment being finally given for the Churchwardens.

The central panel of the Reredos is a copy, carved in lime-wood (1753), of Titian's picture, "The Supper at Emmaus," at Penshurst. The Font (1641) is by Nicholas Stone. A tablet near the east door given by the Roxburgh Club in 1820, commemorates *William Caxton*, who was buried here in 1491. The church contains a number of very fine monuments and memorials of great historic interest.

The Registers (not shown) contain entries relating to the marriages of John Milton and Samuel Pepys. John Wilkes, M.P., became a Churchwarden in 1759. The north aisle was severely damaged by an oil-bomb in September, 1940, and much of the modern glass has been destroyed by blast.

Also on the west side of Old Palace Yard and close by King Henry VII's Chapel of the Abbey is the magnificent new **National Memorial to King George V,** unveiled by King George VI on October 22, 1947. It is a full-length figure of the King standing on a large plinth. It was sculptured in Portland stone by Sir William Reid Dick, K.C.V.O., R.A., with Sir Giles Gilbert Scott, O.M., R.A., acting as architect. King George V is portrayed in the uniform of a Field-Marshal, wearing the Garter Robes and holding the Sword of State. In connection with the memorial is a philanthropic scheme for the provision of playing fields throughout the country.

WESTMINSTER ABBEY

Plan II. K. 9 and 10.
Access.—All buses on routes serving both Victoria and Charing Cross pass the Abbey. Trams to Westminster Bridge.
  Nearest "Underground" Station—*Westminster* (District Line).
Admission.—The Abbey is opened daily throughout the year at 8 a.m., and closes in the Winter months (1st October to 31st March) at 6 p.m.; in the Summer months (1st April to 30th September) at 7 p.m.
  The Royal Chapels are open to visitors on week-days from 10.30 a.m. to 2.30 p.m. and also during the Summer months from 3.45 p.m. to 5.30 p.m. (During Winter 3.45 p.m. to 4.30 p.m.)
  On Sundays visitors are admitted to the Nave and Transepts between the hours of Divine Service.
  Organized and conducted parties are not permitted on Sundays.
  The nave and transepts are open to the public free. The charge for admission to the Ambulatory and Chapels is 1s., children, 6d., except on Mondays, when they are open free. *They are not open to the public on Sundays.* On paying days parties are conducted by the vergers round the Royal Chapels at intervals of 15 minutes, starting from the south gate of the Ambulatory. Tickets must first be obtained at the little table close by. The Cloisters can be seen at any time. The public are not admitted to view the monuments on Sundays, Good Friday, Christmas Day, or during the hours of divine service.
Services.—*Week-days:* Holy Communion (generally in the Chapel of St. Faith) at 8. Matins, 10; Evensong, 3 p.m. The boys attending Westminster School have a service daily at 9 a.m.
  Sundays: Holy Communion at 8; Matins, 10.30; Holy Communion, 11.30; Evensong, 3; Special Service with Sermon, at 6.30.

Westminster Abbey, last resting place of kings, queens, famous men and women. Entering the great door in the magnificent West Front a view of great beauty is beheld.

London (d*).

Westminster Cathedral (Roman Catholic) . . . "beyond all doubt the finest church that has been built for centuries." The great Campanile (St. Edward's Tower) is **273** feet high.

WESTMINSTER ABBEY 105

Dimensions—Total length, including Henry VII's Chapel, 513 ft.; breadth across transepts, 200 ft.; internal height of nave, 102 ft.; height of western towers, 225 ft.

According to tradition, the first church on the site was built between the years 605 and 610 by Sebert, King of the East Saxons, and was consecrated by St. Peter himself, who suddenly appeared for the purpose, rewarding the ferryman who carried him across the river with a miraculous draught of salmon. Being built on the west side of the City of London, it was called the "West Minster." In the time of St. Dunstan (960) we find a Benedictine Monastery established. Edward the Confessor is, however, usually regarded as the founder of the church. He was crowned in the Abbey, as has been every monarch since, with the exception of Edward V., and Edward VIII. Here, too, a few days after the consecration of the building he had done so much to rear, the Confessor was buried, and henceforth, for hundreds of years, until the time of George III, the Abbey was the last resting-place of kings and queens. In later generations it has become much more than that, for room has been found for England's leading statesmen and warriors, poets, artists and men of letters—all, in fact, whom the nation delights to honour. In addition are numerous monuments, but it by no means follows from the existence of a monument that the person commemorated was actually interred in the Abbey.

Like all our great churches, the Abbey has been the growth of centuries. In the main, the present building is the work of Henry III, who pulled down all the eastern part of the Confessor's church in order more worthily to enshrine the body of the saint. The western portions were added at various periods between 1340 and 1483. The north and west cloisters, and the Jerusalem Chamber, near the south-west tower, were built by Abbot Litlington in the reign of Edward III. The magnificent chapel at the eastern end was added by Henry VII, between 1502 and 1512. The towers at the western end were added in 1738-9, it is believed from designs by Hawksmoor, one of Wren's pupils. The central tower designed by Wren is still wanting. Since the seventeenth century masons have been at work replacing, stone by stone, the decayed exterior, with the result that externally, in the words of Mr. L. E. Tanner, "the church is a copy, not by any means faithful, of the original." In recent years the exterior has been cleaned and treated for preservation against the smoke-laden atmosphere.

The form of the Abbey is that of a Latin cross, but the choir extends beyond the transepts almost to the middle of the nave. Behind the high altar is the Chapel of the Confessor, the "burial-place of kings," and beyond that again the noble Henry VII's Chapel. Round the Confessor's Chapel runs a spacious Ambulatory, from which open numerous other chapels.

Entering the church by the great West Door the visitor has a view of the interior of great beauty. It is from here, the west end of the nave, that one obtains the most characteristic views of the Abbey.

Here too, immediately in the foreground, is that touching symbol of a nation's grief and remembrance:

The Grave of the Unknown Warrior

All that is necessary is said by the inscription:

BENEATH THIS STONE RESTS THE BODY
OF A BRITISH WARRIOR
UNKNOWN BY NAME OR RANK
BROUGHT FROM FRANCE TO LIE AMONG
THE MOST ILLUSTRIOUS OF THE LAND
AND BURIED HERE ON ARMISTICE DAY
11 NOV: 1920, IN THE PRESENCE OF
HIS MAJESTY KING GEORGE V
HIS MINISTERS OF STATE
THE CHIEFS OF HIS FORCES
AND A VAST CONCOURSE OF THE NATION

THUS ARE COMMEMORATED THE MANY
MULTITUDES WHO DURING THE GREAT
WAR OF 1914–1918 GAVE THE MOST THAT
MAN CAN GIVE LIFE ITSELF
FOR GOD
FOR KING AND COUNTRY
FOR LOVED ONES HOME AND EMPIRE
FOR THE SACRED CAUSE OF JUSTICE AND
THE FREEDOM OF THE WORLD

THEY BURIED HIM AMONG THE KINGS BECAUSE HE
HAD DONE GOOD TOWARD GOD AND TOWARD
HIS HOUSE

The slab is of black marble, quarried from one of the Belgian battlefields. On a pillar close by is suspended the *Ypres Flag*, which was carried in France during the War and for the first twelve months rested on the grave. Below is the *Congressional Medal*, bestowed on the Unknown Warrior by the United States Government in 1921.

Commencing our tour of the church we turn to the right and see, in the south-west corner of the nave, the **Warriors' Chapel** (St. George's Chapel) which has been set apart in memory of those who fell in the 1914–18 War. Here is the memorial erected by the Imperial War Graves Commission to the One Million Dead of the British Empire. Here, too, lie the ashes of Field-Marshal Viscount Plumer and Lord Allenby. At the entrance are the memorial books containing the names of civilians who lost their lives in the 1939–45 War. Above is the memorial to President Roosevelt, unveiled 1948. On the pillar east of the chapel hangs the contemporary portrait of King Richard II— *the earliest known portrait of an English sovereign.*

Above the neighbouring door in the **South Aisle of Nave** is the

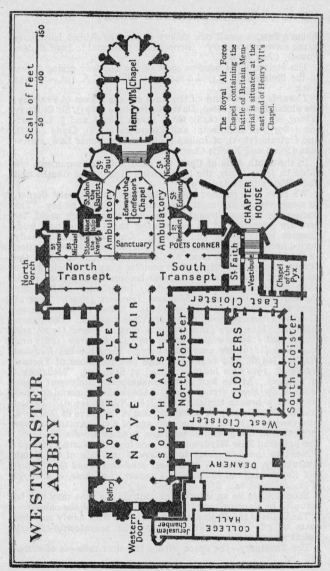

WESTMINSTER ABBEY

Scale of Feet
0 50 100 150

Henry VII's Chapel

The Royal Air Force Chapel containing the Battle of Britain Memorial is situated at the east end of Henry VII's Chapel.

St. Paul
St. Nicholas
St. John the Baptist
Edward the Confessor's Chapel
St. Edmund
Abbot Islip
St. John the Evang.
Ambulatory
St. Benedict
Ambulatory
St. Andrew
St. Michael
Sanctuary
POETS CORNER

CHAPTER HOUSE

North Porch
North Transept
South Transept
St. Faith
Vestibule
Chapel of the Pyx

CHOIR
North Aisle
South Aisle
North Cloister
East Cloister

NAVE
North Aisle
South Aisle

CLOISTERS
North Cloister
South Cloister
West Cloister

Belfry
DEANERY

Western Door
Jerusalem Chamber
COLLEGE HALL

Abbot's Pew, a small oak gallery erected by Abbot Islip early in the sixteenth century.   Beneath is a memorial to Lord Baden-Powell, *Chief Scout.*

The stained-glass window west of the doorway giving access to the **Cloisters** (p. 113) is a memorial of Y.M.C.A. 1914-18 War work.

Towards the east end of the nave are the graves of Peabody, the philanthropist (1869), David Livingstone (1873), Sir C. Barry (1860), Sir G. Scott (1878), G. E. Street (1881), and J. L. Pearson (1897), all architects; and Lawrence (1879), Clyde (1863), and Outram (1863), of Indian Mutiny fame; Bonar Law, statesman (1923) and Neville Chamberlain.

In the **South Aisle of Choir** the most notable monuments are those to *Isaac Watts,* the hymn-writer (1748), and *Charles* and *John Wesley* (1788 and 1791).

We have now reached the **South Transept, or Poets' Corner,** to many visitors the most interesting part of the Abbey.   The transept is famous throughout the English-speaking world, for here are memorials of all our greatest bards and writers, from Chaucer to Tennyson and Kipling.   Only a few are actually buried here, but this is the spot chosen for such commemoration as art can give.   The tomb of *Chaucer* (1400), from which the Corner "derives the origin of its peculiar glory."   Ironically, he was buried here not as a poet, but because he happened to be Clerk of the Works at Westminster.   Immediately in front are the graves of *Browning* (1889) and *Tennyson* (1892).   Near at hand is a bust of *Longfellow* (1882).   *Milton* (1674), *Edmund Spenser* (1599) and *Gray* (1771) are close together.   The monument of *Shakespeare* (1616) adjoins that of *Burns* (1796) and *Wordsworth* (1850), while *Dickens* (1870), *Thackeray* (1863) and *Macaulay* (1859) are near each other.   Here too lies *Rudyard Kipling* (1936), and below the aisle rest the ashes of *Thomas Hardy* (d. 1928; his heart is buried at Stinsford, "Mellstock" in Wessex).   At the foot of the Shakespeare monument is the tomb of *Sir Henry Irving* (1905).   Above the memorial to *Scott* (1832) is a bronze medallion of *John Ruskin* (1900).   In the middle of the transept a white slab marks the grave of *Old Parr,* who died in 1635, at the reputed age of 152.   Australians are interested in the memorial to *Adam Lindsay Gordon* (d. 1870). The beautiful **Rose Window** is best seen from the North Transept.

Next to the monument to *Dryden* is the gate of the **South Ambulatory,** *from which parties are conducted round the Chapels and Royal Tombs at intervals of a quarter of an hour, at a charge of* 1s., *children,* 6d.   *Mondays, free, no guides.*

Should there be an interval of waiting, the time may well be occupied in glancing round the central portion of the church.

The **Stalls of the Choir** are noteworthy, in their newly acquired coats of gilt and colour.   In 1935 the seventeenth-century Pulpit was restored to use.

The **Sanctuary**—the space within the altar rails—is of extraordinary interest, for here all the sovereigns of England since the Conquest have been crowned. The Altar and Reredos were designed by Sir G. Scott, the sculptured figures being by Armstead, the mosaics by Salviati. The seats for the officiating clergy rest on a part of the tomb of *King Sebert*, the Saxon founder of the church. On the same side (south) is the tomb of *Anne of Cleves* (1557), the fourth wife of Henry VIII. On the north side are the three fine tombs, similar in design, of *Aveline, Countess of Lancaster* (1273), *Aymer de Valence, Earl of Pembroke* (1324), and *Edmund Crouchback, Earl of Lancaster* (1296).

Returning to the South Ambulatory, we begin the round of—

The Royal Tombs

A glance at the plan will show that the central portion of the, eastern end of the church is occupied by Edward the Confessor's Chapel, round which run the South and North Ambulatories, or walking-places, and from these open out a number of minor Chapels, three on the south and three on the north. King Henry VII's Chapel is at the extreme eastern end. Many of these tombs were long thought to be covered merely with the grime of centuries, but recent investigations have proved the "grime" to be a heavy varnish intended to protect the colouring of the tomb and canopy, now again revealed.

Entering the South Ambulatory, then, we see first on the left the traditional tomb of *King Sebert* (p. 105). Note above it the old paintings—fine examples of the brilliant restoration work carried out here recently.

Passing a small altar-tomb over the graves of four children of Henry III and four of Edward I, we reach the **Chapel of St. Edmund,** King of the East Anglians, which has been principally used as a burial-place for relatives of sovereigns. The tomb of *William de Valence, Earl of Pembroke,* half-brother of Henry III (1296), still retains portions of the beautiful Limoges enamel with which it was originally decorated. In the Chapter House can be seen a representation of the figure when the decorations were complete.

The **Chapel of St. Nicholas** is dedicated to the young Bishop of Myra, the patron saint of children. It contains the private vault of the Percy family of Northumberland, members of which still have a right (not always claimed) to be interred in the Abbey —the only persons in England possessing such a privilege. Note the tombs of the *Widow of the Protector Somerset* (1587) and of *Sir George Villiers and his Wife* (1605 and 1632). Across the aisle is a thirteenth-century painted altarpiece—"the most remarkable example of medieval painting known."

We now ascend a flight of twelve stone steps, at the foot of which is the vault of the *Earls of Clarendon,* to—

The Chapel of King Henry VII

the most magnificent portion of the Abbey and doubly magnificent since its restoration. The first stone was laid on the
24th January, 1502-3, but the chapel was not completed until
ten years after the king's death. The entrance gates are of
bronze, mounted on oak and embellished with the "roses" united
by the marriage of Henry with the Princess Elizabeth of York,
the portcullis, fleur-de-lis and other Tudor badges. The vaulted
roof, with its airy network and luxuriant ornamentation, fantas-
tic and fairy-like, is almost unrivalled for beauty. Washington
Irving has well said: "On entering, the eye is astonished by the
pomp of architecture, and the elaborate beauty of sculptured
detail. Stone seems, by the cunning labour of the chisel, to
have been robbed of its weight and density, suspended aloft, as
if by magic, and the fretted roof achieved with the wonderful
minuteness and airy security of a cobweb." The beautiful stalls
appertain to the *Knights of the Bath*; the lower seats are for
their esquires (three to each knight). No installation had been
held from 1812 until the ceremony was revived by King George
V on July 22, 1913. Above the stalls are suspended the gorgeous
banners, swords, helmets, and scarves of the Knights, all newly
made for the ceremony. Some of the carvings on the stalls are
very grotesque. Nearly a hundred richly-carved niches, each
containing a small statue, run round the Chapel below the
clerestory windows. At the eastern end is the beautiful **Tomb
of Henry VII** (1509) and his wife, Elizabeth of York. The tomb
was the work of a Florentine sculptor, Pietro Torrigiano, but
the screen is of English workmanship. *James I* (1625) also lies
in the vault below, and a little in front, beneath the altar, is
the grave of the founder's grandson, the youthful *Edward VI*.
The graves of George II (1760) and Caroline of Anspach (1737),
are in the western part of the Nave, but without monuments.

The magnificent High Altar—a reproduction of Torrigiano's
original—was the Jubilee Gift (1935) of the Order of the Bath.

The Apse consists of five small Chapels, in which are several
monuments. In the middle chapel were buried in 1658 *Oliver
Cromwell*, his mother and sister, and other Puritan leaders; but
their bodies were exhumed and dishonoured after the Restoration.
This chapel, now the Royal Air Force Chapel, contains the
Battle of Britain Memorial, dedicated to those gallant few who
died in the Battle of Britain of the Second World War. The
armorial badges of the Squadrons concerned are shown and in
the adjoining chapel is the Roll of Honour containing the names
of 1,497 airmen of Britain and her allies who fell in the battle.

The South Aisle contains, amongst others, a monument to
Mary Queen of Scots (beheaded 1587, and first buried in Peter-
borough Cathedral; reinterred here in 1612). In the vaults of
this aisle lie Charles II, William III, Mary II, Queen Anne,

and various other royal personages. Wall tablets near the door commemorate Lord Cromer (1841–1916), the "Regenerator of Egypt," Lord Milner (1854–1925), "Servant of the State," and Lord Curzon.

In the North Aisle are buried in the same tomb *Queen Mary* (1558) and *Queen Elizabeth* (1603). Let into a glass-covered recess in Elizabeth's tomb is the Essex Ring, given by the Queen to the favourite as a pledge of clemency should he at any time need it. It was his endeavour to return the ring which led to his execution. Near-by rest the Princes murdered in the Tower; *Addison* (1719), and others.

In Henry VII's Chapel and protected by an iron grille is the **Coronation Chair**, one of the most famous pieces of furniture in the world. It was made for Edward I, and had beneath it, until it was stolen on Christmas Day 1950, the **Stone of Scone**, which was brought from Scotland in 1296, and led later, on the accession of James I, to the fulfilment of the ancient prophecy:

"If Fates go right, where'er this stone is found,
The Scots shall monarchs of that realm be crowned."

Tradition declares it to be the identical stone upon which Jacob pillowed his head at Bethel. Upon it the kings of Scotland were crowned for many centuries, and it has served the same purpose for every English monarch from the time of Edward I to the present day. The stone is 26 ins. long, 16 ins. wide, and 11 ins. thick, and was attached to the chair by clamps of iron. Discovered again in 1951 it is stored elsewhere in the Abbey. At the Coronation the chair, then covered with cloth of gold, is moved to the other side of the screen, before the high altar. Near the chair are the sword (7 ft. long) and wooden shield of Edward III.

From Henry VII's Chapel we pass into the **North Ambulatory.** A short flight of steps leads up to the **Chapel of Edward the Confessor**, where lie the bodies of no fewer than six kings and six queens. In the middle is the large *Shrine of the Confessor* (1066), erected by command of Henry III in 1269, and for centuries an object of veneration to the devout. Few traces are left of its former magnificence. On the north side lies his Queen, *Editha* (1075). Observe that all the kings here are placed not below, but *above* the ground. The other monarchs, starting from the north side, are *Edward I* (1307), inscribed *Malleus Scotorum*, "hammer of the Scots" (when the tomb was opened in 1774 the body was found to be 6 ft. 2 in. in length); *Henry III* (1272); *Queen Eleanor*, first wife of Edward I (1290); *Henry V* (1422), the hero of Agincourt, "too famous to live long"; *Queen Philippa*, wife of Edward III (1369); *Edward III* (1377); and *Richard II* (1399), and his Queen, *Anne of Bohemia*. The **Chantry of Henry V** demands special notice. By a curious coincidence, apparently undesigned, it is in the shape of the modern letter H. The tomb, surmounted by a headless wooden effigy, is beneath the arch and close to the top of the stairs by which we enter the Chapel. Overhead hang the king's shield, saddle and helmet.

Passing again to the North Ambulatory, we cross to the small **Chapel** or **Shrine of St. Erasmus,** with its beautiful fifteenth-century clustered columns. This forms the entry to the **Chapel of St. John the Baptist,** where the most interesting tomb is that of *Thomas Cecil, Earl of Exeter* (1622), and his first wife. Space was reserved on the left for his second wife, but with proper spirit she declined to be buried here, as the place of honour was already occupied.

Abbot Islip's Chapel is distinguished by the frequent repetition of his name and rebus, "I slip"—an eye with a bough clasped by a hand and a man slipping from a tree.

Passing the huge cenotaph of *General Wolfe* (1759), the hero of Quebec, we enter—

The **Chapels of St. John the Evangelist, St. Michael** and **St. Andrew,** on the east side of the North Transept. Here are many interesting monuments and tablets, that to *Lady E. Nightingale,* by *Roubillac,* attracting most attention. Note also the fine monument to *Sir Francis Vere* (1608), with its kneeling knights, and the tablet to *Lord Rayleigh* (1842–1919), the eminent scientist. Near the exit is the memorial to *Sir John Franklin* (1847), with Tennyson's fine epitaph.

Close by is another doorway to the church, from which a path passes close to St. Margaret's Church. The entrance bears the name of **Solomon's Porch,** though the original porch, erected in the reign of Richard II, was entirely transformed by Wren, and Sir G. Scott was responsible for the present triple portico.

The **North Transept** is generally known as the **Statesmen's Aisle.** Sadly obscured by monuments is the *Bunyan Memorial Window,* representing scenes from the *Pilgrim's Progress.* Note the beautiful window in the South Transept.

We now turn into the **North Aisle of the Choir,** frequently called the **Musicians' Aisle,** on account of the number of organists and composers buried or commemorated in it. Hereabout also are graves of eminent scientists, *Sir J. F. Herschel* (1871), *Charles Darwin* (1882) and *Lord Kelvin* (1907). In 1936–7 a new **Organ**—one of the finest in the world—was installed. This, like its predecessor, stands on each side of the choir.

We now enter the **North Aisle of Nave** containing windows commemorating famous engineers. About half-way down the aisle a small stone in the centre of the walk marks the grave of "*Rare Ben Jonson*" (it is thought by some that the inscription was intended to be *ORARE Ben Jonson*) (1637), and near-by are the *R.A.M.C.* War Memorial and window. Another window, the gift of the Hon. J. W. Gerard, is "In memory of British prisoners who died in Germany, 1914–18, a tribute from the American Ambassador in Berlin, 1909–17."

At the west end of the North Aisle is the N.W. or Belfry

Tower, which contains a very fine peal of bells. They are the heaviest in London. At the end of the aisle near the Belfry, is the grave of Ernest Bevin.

We have now accomplished the round of the Church, but several features of the great Abbey of which it merely formed a part remain to be seen.

The **Cloisters,** consisting of four "walks," and dating from the thirteenth to the fifteenth century, though portions are even older. Here are tombs of many abbots, with nearly obliterated inscriptions, and about a hundred other tablets and memorials.

From the east walk a pointed archway, with mutilated figures (note on left the Roman sarcophagus), admits to—

The **Chapter House,** an octagonal chamber, 58 ft. in diameter, with stone seats all round and a single central pillar. In order to protect the fine floor, visitors don overshoes before entering the Chapter House. The Chapter House was begun in 1250, and from 1377 to 1547 was the meeting-place of the House of Commons. The glass cases contain ancient documents, royal and ecclesiastical seals, etc. J. Russell Lowell (1819–1891) is commemorated by a window and tablet above the entrance stairway, and another tablet commemorates the noble-minded Walter Hines Page (d. 1918), United States Ambassador to Great Britain during the 1914–18 War.

In the **Crypt** (the Ancient Treasury) below the Chapter House are the Coronation Copes, altar fronts and other beautiful "ornaments" of the Abbey. (*Not at present open to the public.*)

Adjoining is the **Chapel of the Pyx,** so named because here was kept the pyx, or box, containing the standard gold and silver coins. Access is gained from the East Cloister by a door secured by six locks. The Chapel was part of the original building of Edward the Confessor.

Beyond is the **Museum** in the Norman Undercroft *open daily* (*except Sundays*) *from* 10.30 *a.m.—6d., children, 3d.*), a range of five vaulted bays also containing much of the original stonework of Edward the Confessor's building. Here is placed a remarkable collection of **Wax Figures** of eminent persons interred in the Abbey.

It was a medieval custom to carry wax effigies of the deceased in funeral processions. Among them are William and Mary in their coronation robes (the king standing on a cushion, as was his wont, to increase his height); Queen Anne; Queen Elizabeth; Charles II; Lord Nelson (the effigy was made *after* his burial in St. Paul's, to lure sightseers back to the Abbey); Pitt, Earl of Chatham (also made after the funeral); Frances Theresa, Duchess of Richmond, "La Belle Stuart," in the robes worn by her at Queen Anne's coronation (she it was who sat for the figure of Britannia on our coins); the Duchess of Buckingham, in robes worn by her at the coronation of George II, with her infant son, and also her third son, the last Duke of Buckingham.

Other cases contain a quaint and interesting similar assortment of royal effigies, but earlier in date and all of wood. There are also various relics of earlier buildings, coins, etc.

A passage on the left, just beyond the Undercroft entrance, leads to the **Little Cloisters,** surrounded by residences of the clergy.

At the south-west end of the Abbey, and forming part of the Deanery, is the **Jerusalem Chamber.** Here Henry IV died in 1413, on the eve of starting for the Holy Land, thus fulfilling the prophecy that he would die in Jerusalem (*vide* Shakespeare's *King Henry IV, Part II*). The Chamber can only be viewed by order from the Dean.

Turning to the left on leaving the Abbey by the door in the North Transept, we pass along the Green to the western end. The open space here is the **Broad Sanctuary,** a great resort in former days of people who sought the protection of the Church against the civil power. Edward V was born in the Sanctuary in 1470. An archway on the south leads to **Dean's Yard,** where is **Westminster School,** refounded by Queen Elizabeth in 1560.

The large College Hall is the dining-room (the tables are said to be made from timber of the Spanish Armada). There are 40 foundationers or king's scholars and about 200 Oppidans or Town Boys. The *Westminster Play*, given annually just before Christmas, has usually a witty epilogue alluding to current events. The time-honoured custom of *Tossing the Pancake* ("Pancake Greaze") takes place annually on Shrove Tuesday, the boy who succeeds in getting the largest piece being rewarded with a guinea by the Dean.

On the south side of Dean's Yard is the **Church House,** "the central business house of the Church of England."

On the north side of the Broad Sanctuary long stood Westminster Hospital, founded in 1720, the first of the voluntary hospitals, now replaced by a fine new building in quieter surroundings close to the Embankment at Lambeth Bridge (*see* p. 259). The site is to be used for a new Colonial Office building. The beautiful Renaissance edifice adjoining the old site is the **Middlesex Guildhall,** rebuilt in 1913. Note the friezes representing Magna Carta, Henry III granting a charter to Westminster, and Lady Jane Grey accepting the Crown from the Duke of Northumberland. The **Methodist Central Hall,** an imposing square block in the Renaissance style, is frequently used for concerts, exhibitions, etc. The dome is the third largest in London, being exceeded only by those of St. Paul's Cathedral and the British Museum Reading Room. It has a diameter of 90 ft., and the height to the lantern is 220 ft.

Tothill Street leads to **St. James Park Station** and the huge block housing the offices of **London Transport**. The sculptures by *Jacob Epstein* have provoked more than a little comment.

In **Victoria Street** are the offices of many famous engineering firms. In the building at the corner (since reconstructed) was framed the Act of Union by which the Dominion of Canada was constituted in 1866-7. This building occupies the site of Caxton's house in the Almonry, where he showed the first printing press to Edward IV in 1477. On the left of Victoria Street, farther down, are the *Army and Navy Stores*.

Towards the western end of Victoria Street, Ashley Gardens (left) bring one in a few yards to—

Westminster Cathedral

Plan II. I. 10.

Admission.—The Nave and Chapels may be inspected freely, but visitors will, of course, refrain from walking about during services. Organised parties of visitors may only be conducted by a member of the Cathedral staff.

Tickets of admission to the tower (*Lift*, 1s.) may be obtained from the Cathedral Porter.

Services.—Low Masses: 6.30, 7, 7.30, 8, 8.30, 9; Prime and Terce, 10.10 a.m.; 10.30, Capitular High Mass, followed by Sext and None; 3.15, Sung Vespers, Compline and Benediction; 6, Matins and Lauds (of following day); 8, Sermon and Benediction.

Sundays: Masses at 6. 6.30, 7, 7.30, 8, 8.30, 9; Prime and Terce, 10.10; 10.30 (High Mass at High Altar, followed by Sext and None); 12 (Low Mass with Sermon), 3.15 (Vespers and Solemn Benediction), and 7 (Compline, Sermon, Benediction, at High Altar), 8.30 p.m. (Matins and Lauds).

Dimensions.—Exterior: Length, 360 ft.; width, 156 ft.; height of nave, 117 ft.; height of campanile, 284 ft. Interior: Length, 342 ft.; width across nave, aisles, and side chapels, 149 ft. (nave only, 60 ft.); height of domes, 112 ft.; diameter of domes, 60 ft. The building covers an area of 54,000 sq. ft.

This vast and imposing, yet simple, structure of brick and stone, in the Early Byzantine style, was designed by J. F. Bentley, whose early death in 1902 robbed him of the satisfaction of seeing his work complete. The foundation stone was laid by Cardinal Vaughan on the 29th June, 1895. The structure was opened for use in 1903, but as under the laws of the Roman Catholic Church no place of worship may be consecrated unless completed as to fabric and free from all debt, the actual consecration ceremony did not take place until June 28, 1910. Much remains to be done to the interior, and many years will elapse before the decorations are complete. In the opinion of Norman Shaw, the Cathedral is "beyond all doubt the finest church that has been built for centuries. Superb in its scale and character and full of the most devouring interest, it is impossible to overrate the magnificence of the design."

The dominating external features are the great **Campanile** (or St. Edward's Tower), 273 ft. high (top of cross, 284 ft.), and the dignified **West Front**, with its finely balanced pillars and arches.

The mosaic Tympanum over the main doors was designed by *R. Anning Bell, R.A.* At present the interior, though awe-inspiring in its vastness and in the majestic simplicity of its design, strikes one as bare and sombre; but when the work of incrustation is complete, and the lower surfaces are covered with coloured marbles and the vast domes and vaulting with mosaics, the effect will be indescribably rich and grand. The **Nave** is the widest of any church in England, and owing to the fact that the sanctuary is 4½ ft. above the level of the nave, every part commands an uninterrupted view of the High Altar, with its imposing marble and mosaic baldachino, on which the light is cleverly concentrated. In 1937 the great Crucifix, weighing 2 tons, was restored to its original position at the entrance to the Sanctuary. If the Cathedral had no other feature of interest, the beautiful marble pillars (nearly all the gifts of various benefactors) would well repay a visit. All the pillars have elaborately carved caps of white Carrara marble, no two alike. The side-chapels are elaborately decorated. Adjoining the *Chapel of the Blessed Sacrament* (to the left of the High Altar) is a white marble monument to Cardinal Vaughan (d. June, 19, 1903). The screen and gates in this chapel, surmounted by a gold pelican, are very beautiful. In a corresponding position on the other side of the Sanctuary is the *Lady Chapel.* On the right as one enters the nave are the *Chapel of St. Gregory and Augustine,* the *Chapels of St. Patrick and the Irish Saints* and of *St. Andrew and the Saints of Scotland,* and the *Chapel of St. Paul;* on the left are the *Chapel of the Holy Souls* and the *Chapel of St. George and the English Martyrs* containing memorial panels to the fallen of both world wars, and the *Chapel of St. Joseph* where Cardinal Hinsley lies buried. The finely sculptured *Stations of the Cross* are by *Eric Gill.* The *Great Organ,* with beautiful marble screen is in the West Gallery.

Below the choir is the Crypt, or St. Peter's Chapel, also with fine columns. Here are monuments covering the remains of *Cardinals Wiseman* and *Manning,* transferred from their original place of interment at Kensal Green. Those who make the ascent of the Tower (*lift*) will be rewarded with a magnificent view over London. The tower is about 60 ft. higher than the western towers of Westminster Abbey, but is 30 ft. lower than the Clock Tower of the Houses of Parliament. *Archbishop's House* adjoins the Cathedral, in Ambrosden Avenue.

In Francis Street are the London headquarters of **Toc H.**
Slightly to the east, at the top of Rochester Row, is the **Greycoat School,** founded 1698. The neighbouring **Burdett-Coutts and Townshend School** is of interest, especially to Australian visitors, as the *Alma Mater* of Mr. W. M. Hughes, the distinguished Commonwealth statesman. He also acted as a pupil teacher here before emigrating to Australia. **Vincent Square** forms a playground for the boys of Westminster School. On the west side is the **Horticultural Hall,** used for exhibitions, Badminton, etc. The Horticultural Society's new hall

is in Greycoat Place. In Horseferry Road is the Home Office **Industrial Museum** of safety appliances, etc. (*week-days*, 10-4 *free*).

For the **Victoria Station** of the Southern Region, *see* p. 61.

In Grosvenor Gardens is an excellent statue of **Marshal Foch,** by *Georges Malissard.*

Here also are the headquarters of the *Royal National Life-boat Institution.*

Prominent in Buckingham Palace Road is Airways House of the **British Overseas Airways Corporation;** here too are the *National Training College of Domestic Subjects*; the **Public Baths** and **St. George's Library**; one of London's largest **Motor Coach Stations,** and the **Royal Sanitary Institute.** The Institute is specially concerned with questions of public health. The **Parkes Museum of Hygiene** is *open free daily,* 10-5; *Saturdays,* 10-1.

Vauxhall Bridge Road, to the east of Victoria Station, leads to **Vauxhall Bridge.** Turning to the left from Vauxhall Bridge along Millbank, we reach—

The Tate Gallery

Plan II. K. 11.
Access.—By 88 bus from Oxford Circus, Piccadilly, Trafalgar Square or White-hall to the side of the Gallery. From Victoria Station, by bus or tram down Vauxhall Bridge Road (alighting at the Bridge and turning left along Millbank). From Westminster Station, approximately ten minutes' walk past the Houses of Parliament and along the Embankment.
Admission.—Open free week-days from 10-6, Sundays, 2-6.
Lectures.—Tuesdays and Thursdays at 3.
Refreshments.—Luncheons, teas, etc., in the Rex Whistler restaurant in the basement.

This famous gallery contains in addition to the National Collection of British Painting, for which it was built, the National Collection of Modern Foreign Painting and the National Collection of Modern Sculpture. The original building, designed by Sidney R. J. Smith, was presented to the nation, together with 65 pictures, by Sir Henry Tate (d. 1900) and opened by King Edward VII, then Prince of Wales, on July 21, 1897. It was enlarged, also at Sir Henry Tate's expense, in 1899. Additional galleries, to house the Turner Bequest, were provided in 1910 by Sir Joseph Duveen, the elder, and his son, Lord Duveen of Millbank. The latter also defrayed the cost of an extension, completed in 1926, to contain the Modern Foreign paintings, and the new Sculpture Hall, completed in 1937.

The collection of British paintings, numbering over 3,000 works, is representative of artists from the seventeenth century to the present day, and is especially notable for its unrivalled examples of Blake, Turner, Alfred Stevens, J. S. Sargent, the Pre-Raphaelites, and leading contemporary painters. Its development owes much to the gifts of private individuals and of the Contemporary Art Society and National Art-Collections Fund. It also includes a number of pictures transferred from the National Gallery, Trafalgar Square, and the purchases made annually

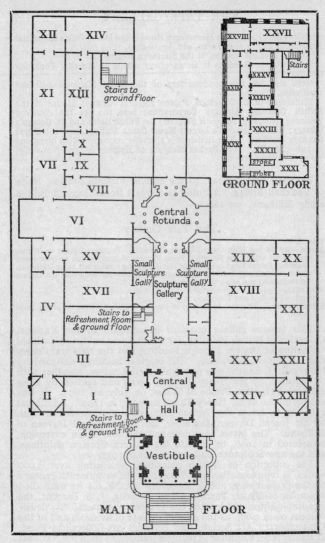

GROUND FLOOR

XXVIII · XXVII
Stairs
XXIX · XXXV · XXXIV
XXX · XXXIII
XXXII
STORE · XXXI
STORE

XII · XIV
Stairs to
ground floor
XI · XIII
X
VII · IX
VIII
VI
Central
Rotunda
V · XV
Small
Sculpture
Gally.
Small
Sculpture
Gally.
Sculpture
Gallery
XIX · XX
XVII
XVIII
IV
Stairs to
Refreshment Room
& ground floor
XXI
III
XXV · XXII
II · I
Central
Hall
XXIV · XXIII
Stairs to
Refreshment Room
& ground floor
Vestibule

MAIN   FLOOR

THE TATE GALLERY

118

under the terms of the Chantrey Bequest. Among the best-known works are *Hogarth's* "Calais Gate," *Reynolds'* "Lord Ligonier," *Gainsborough's* "Watering Place," *Stubbs'* "Gentleman Holding a Horse," *Crome's* "Slate Quarries," *Turner's* "Petworth Park," *Constable's* "Marine Parade, Brighton," *Millais'* "Christ in the House of His Parents," *Watts'* "Hope," *John's* "Smiling Woman" and *Spencer's* "Resurrection."

The collection of Modern Foreign Painting was founded on the bequest of 39 pictures by Sir Hugh Lane in 1915, and the endowment of £50,000 provided by Samuel Courtauld in 1923 for the acquisition of late nineteenth-century and early twentieth-century French paintings. Its representation of the Impressionist and Post-Impressionist Schools is one of the most celebrated in Europe, and includes *Manet's* "Serveuse de Bocks," *Renoir's* "La Première Sortie," *Seurat's* "Une Baignade," *Van Gogh's* "Sunflowers," *Cézanne's* "Cézanne Chauve," *Picasso's* "Jeune Fille en Chemise" and *Matisse's* "The Forest."

The collection of Modern Sculpture contains the gift by Rodin to the British nation in 1914, and among other well-known works includes *Maillol's* "The Three Nymphs," *Despiau's* "Mademoiselle Schulte," *Gill's* "Prospero and Ariel," *Epstein's* "Visitation," *Moore's* "Reclining Woman," *Renoir's* "Venus Victrix" and several works by *Degas*.

In April, 1951, the Lower Galleries (approached through the Sargent Gallery) were rehung with water-colours and drawings by English artists from the eighteenth century to the present day, and one room with examples by foreign artists from Ingres to Klee.

In 1941 the Tate Gallery was severely damaged in successive air-raids but all the galleries were re-opened by 1948. The organisation of special exhibitions has become a feature of the Tate's policy.

Reproductions, Post-Cards, Catalogues and other publications are obtainable at a stall near the entrance to the Gallery.

Eastward from the Tate Gallery the Victoria Embankment extends to Westminster Abbey and the Houses of Parliament, passing **Lambeth Bridge,** and I.C.I. House, the fine headquarters of the *Imperial Chemical Industries* (note the fine nickel doorways and the busts of Alfred and Ludwig Mond, and others). The Board of Trade have offices in the same building.

THE PALACES AND CLUBLAND

ROUTE III.—ST. JAMES'S PARK—BUCKINGHAM PALACE—THE LONDON MUSEUM—ST. JAMES'S PALACE—MARLBOROUGH HOUSE—PALL MALL —THE HAYMARKET—LEICESTER SQUARE—SHAFTESBURY AVENUE.

STARTING again from Charing Cross, let us cross the top of Whitehall and pass through the handsome **Admiralty Arch,** with its triple gateway (*see* p. 75), to—

St. James's Park

Plan II. I. & K. 9.
Nearest Stations.—Trafalgar Square (Bakerloo Line), Strand (Northern Line
St. James's Park (District Line).   Green Park (Piccadilly Line).
Buses connect Trafalgar Square and Charing Cross with all parts of London.

The **Mall,** leading from the Admiralty Arch to Buckingham Palace, flanked on either side by an alley, with double rows of plane trees, forms a splendid processional road on occasions of State pageantry.

St. James's Park (93 acres) is one of the oldest and in the opinion of many the most beautiful of London's pleasure grounds. Up to the reign of Henry VIII it was a marshy expanse, with a hospital for lepers, dedicated to St. James the Less, on its northern boundary. That sagacious monarch built a palace for himself (St. James's) on the site of the hospital, and converted the marsh into a deer-park. Charles II played *paille-maille* on the broad roadway known as the Mall, and employed the French landscape gardener, Le Notre, to convert the deer-park into a garden. It was still, however, far from being a pleasant place until George IV commissioned Nash, the architect, to improve it. A lake extends nearly the entire length, and is the haunt of many varieties of wild-fowl. The bridge commands one of the most exquisite views in London.

On the eastern side of the Park are the **Foreign Office** and other Government buildings, the **Horse Guards Parade** and the **New Admiralty** (*see* p. 82). On the south the Park is bordered by **Birdcage Walk,** probably deriving its name from an aviary maintained by Charles II. The flower beds on this side of the Park are among the best in London.

The **Bird Life** of London is remarkably varied—thanks in great degree to the sanctuary provided by the many Parks. Willow warblers, whitethroats, spotted flycatchers, kingfishers, chaffinches, sandpipers,

[Herbert Felton.

One of the most beautiful of London's pleasure grounds is St. James's Park.
This view across the lake, the haunt of many varieties of wildfowl, shows in the
background a glimpse of (left) the War Office and the Foreign Office.

The Gatehouse, St. James's Palace—"Our Court of St. James's" to which foreign ambassadors are still accredited—together with the Presence Chamber and Chapel Royal are all that now remain of Henry VIII's original edifice.

wrynecks, and other more or less uncommon birds—uncommon certainly in cities—have all made their homes or been seen within half a mile of Hyde Park Corner during recent years. Not many years ago a pair of kestrels built a nest in the tower of St. Michael's, Cornhill, in the heart of the City, while another pair made their home in the western towers of Westminster Abbey.

At Storey's Gate is the **Institution of Mechanical Engineers,** while close at hand, in **Great George Street,** is the **Institute of Civil Engineers.**

Outside No. 13, **Queen Anne's Gate,** is a quaint little *Statue of Queen Anne,* and in many ways this thoroughfare wears an air that is in marked contrast to the great modern buildings on every hand. At Nos. 40/42 are the headquarters of the **National Trust for Places of Historic Interest or Natural Beauty.** Towering high above the Park is the huge block of residential chambers known as *Queen Anne's Mansions,* among the loftiest in London. Students of architecture are more interested in the neighbouring pile (*see* p. 114) built for the "Underground" but now the headquarters of London Transport.

To the west are the **Wellington Barracks,** the headquarters of the Brigade of Guards, comprising the Grenadier and Coldstream Guards and the Scots, Irish, and Welsh Guards.

When not in khaki, all the Guards regiments wear scarlet uniforms with blue facings, but the various units may be distinguished by their cap-bands, or when guard-mounting, by the plumes in their bearskins, that of the Grenadiers being white, that of the Coldstreamers red, the Irish blue, while the Scots have none. The Welsh Guards wear a white plume with a horizontal strip of green. The Brigade of Guards furnishes the Queen's Guard, i.e., the Palace sentries. The protection of the person of the Sovereign is the function of the Household Cavalry, who (stationed at Knightsbridge Barracks) may be distinguished by their blue tunics and red helmet plumes.

Prior to 1944 the **Royal Military Chapel,** commonly called the Guards' Chapel, was regarded as the most beautiful military chapel in the world. During the time of Divine Service on the morning of Sunday, June 18, 1944, the chapel was hit by a flying-bomb, and of its former magnificence only the east end remains. To this a temporary nave has now been added and the whole structure gives an impression of amazing dignity. Happily the memorial altar to King George V, the altar silver, gift of King George VI, and all the priceless gold plate belonging to the church and the magnificent mosaics behind the altar have all been preserved.

The main service of the day on Sundays is at 11 a.m. and to this the public are admitted without ticket, and at it one of the

Guards' bands always provides the music. The other services are led by organ and choir. The chapel is open on week-days from 9.30–12.30 and 2–4.30, Saturdays, 12 noon.

At its western end St. James's Park is overlooked by—

Buckingham Palace

(Plan II. I. 9)

the front of which was in 1913 reconstructed in Portland stone from designs by *Sir Aston Webb, P.R.A.* The Palace derives its name from a mansion erected by John Sheffield, Duke of Buckingham, in 1703, when keeper of the Mulberry Garden planted in connection with James I's scheme for founding a British silk industry. The house was purchased by George III some sixty years afterwards, when his family had outgrown St. James's. His son and successor, George IV, commissioned his favourite architect, Nash, to remodel it, but the Palace was little used until 1837, when Queen Victoria chose it as her town residence. King Edward VII made constant use of it, an example which was followed by King George V and Queen Mary, and later, in 1937, by King George VI and Queen Elizabeth. King Edward VII was born in the Palace, on the 9th November, 1841, and died here on the 6th May, 1910. With the wing added in 1847, the Palace forms an extensive quadrangle, the east front, facing the Park, being 360 ft. long. The ceremony of Changing the Guard (alternate days at 10 o'clock) invariably attracts here a crowd of interested spectators.

The gardens and lake at the back of the Palace occupy the whole of the triangle, about 40 acres, between Constitution Hill and Grosvenor Place. The *Royal Mews* may be seen on Wednesday (2–4 p.m.) by those who have written, beforehand, to the Superintendent, enclosing an addressed envelope for the reply. Two weeks' notice should be given.

In front of the Palace stands the **Queen Victoria Memorial,** designed by the late *Sir Thomas Brock, R.A.* The central figure of the Queen (13 ft. high) is carved from one solid block of marble, and has to the left and right groups representing *Justice* and *Truth,* while facing the Palace is a group symbolic of *Motherhood.* The whole is surmounted by a winged figure of *Victory,* poised on a sphere supported by the figures of *Courage* and *Constancy.*

A semicircular colonnaded screen, having a radius of about 100 ft., encloses the **Queen's Garden,** in which the statue stands, and around which traffic circulates on the gyratory system. The wrought-iron gateways bear the names and heraldic emblems of the principal countries of the Empire, by whom they were given.

From Buckingham Palace the tree-bordered **Constitution Hill,** 95 ft. wide, runs obliquely to Hyde Park Corner (p. 136), where is the **Wellington Arch** crowned by a large bronze quadriga, representing Peace, by *Adrian Jones, M.V.O* This group is unique among the London statues because the silhouette is practically the same from both sides of the arch, a *tour de force* which is seldom accomplished in monumental sculpture.

The **Green Park** (Plan II. H. and I. 9) is a triangular space of 53 acres, between Constitution Hill and Piccadilly. Its eastern side is formed by the Queen's Walk, overlooked by the massive Devonshire House and *Ritz Hotel*, and, to the south, by—

Lancaster House

(Plan II. I. 9)

Formerly Stafford House, Lancaster House was presented to the nation by the late Lord Leverhulme for the purpose of housing the **London Museum.** Now, however, the main collections are exhibited at Kensington Palace (*see* p. 138), but it is hoped to re-open the basement of Lancaster House as a branch museum for the display of the Roman boat, the transport and architectural exhibits and other specimens which are too big or unsuitable for Kensington Palace. Illustrated catalogues (which for the periods for which they have been prepared provide a general picture of past London life and history) as well as postcards may be obtained on application to the Director at Kensington Palace.

Of Lancaster House itself it may be said that it was long regarded as the finest private residence in London (though the top storey (a later addition) is hardly worthy of the lower portion); and its interest has been enhanced as the result of the damage and destruction of recent years. The house was originally built for that Duke of York whose column looks down on St. James's Park from Waterloo Place (p. 125). He did not live to see its completion and the property passed in 1841 to the Duke of Sutherland.

The building was requisitioned by the Foreign Office in 1941 and is used for International Conferences.

Adjoining Lancaster House on the east is—

St. James's Palace

(Plan II. I. 9)

"Our Court of St. James's," to which foreign ambassadors and ministers are still accredited, stands on the site of the leper hospital referred to on p. 120. It has long ceased to be the sovereign's official residence, but the western portion, known as **York House,** has been so used by members of the Royal Family, including the Duke of Windsor (when Prince of Wales) and the Duke of Gloucester. Henry VIII's palace, begun in 1532, is said to have been designed by Holbein, but was forsaken for **Whitehall** on the downfall of Wolsey, and did not become the official residence of the sovereigns of England until the reign of William III. Little of the old palace now remains. In 1809 a fire destroyed the eastern wing; and all that is now left of Henry VIII's edifice are the picturesque Gateway facing St. James's Street, the Presence Chamber and the Chapel Royal.

Here lived not only Henry VIII, but Edward VI, Elizabeth and Mary. On the morning of his execution Charles I attended divine service in its Chapel, walking thence through the Park, guarded by a regiment of foot, to the scaffold at Whitehall. George III was married and George IV born here; William IV and Queen Adelaide made it their principal residence. The building was less distinguished during the reign of Queen Victoria, being used only for courts, levees, and other ceremonies. Here the oath was administered to King Edward VII on his accession, to King George V in 1910, to King Edward VIII in January, 1936, to King George VI in December of the same year, and to Queen Elizabeth II in February, 1952.

Overlooking Friary Court is the balcony from which, on the death of a sovereign, the proclamation is made. "The King is dead! Long live the King!"

The **Chapel Royal** is entered from the Colour Court. The services on Sunday mornings (see p. 20) are open to the public.

Adjoining the palace is—

Clarence House

the official London residence of Queen Elizabeth II, at the time of her accession.

The house was built in 1825 for King William IV, then Duke of Clarence. Since then it has been the London residence of the Duchess of Kent, mother of Queen Victoria, the Duke of Edinburgh her second son, and his brother the Duke of Connaught.

Marlborough House

is on the other side, separated from St. James's Palace only by the roadway. It was the London home of King Edward VII from his marriage in 1863 to 1902; from that date until 1910 was the residence of King George V, then Prince of Wales; from 1911 until her death the London residence of Queen Alexandra. It is now the home of Queen Mary. It was built by Wren in 1709 for the great Duke of Marlborough and "Sarah," but alterations have deprived it of its original character.

Marlborough House Chapel is known as **The Queen's Chapel** from the fact that about 1623 Inigo Jones was ordered to "prepare with great costliness" a chapel for the services of the Infanta of Spain, the intended bride of Charles I, so that she, as a Roman Catholic, could hear Mass. This marriage did not take place, but later the chapel was opened with great ceremony for Charles's queen, Henrietta Maria.

Under William and Mary permission was given by the Bishop of London for German Lutheran services to be held.

The Chapel is often alluded to as the Danish Chapel. In 1880 it was placed at the disposal of the Danish colony in London by Queen Alexandra.

The memorial of Queen Alexandra facing St. James's Palace was the work of the late *Sir Alfred Gilbert*.

By the roadway between Marlborough House and St. James's Palace we return to the Mall, where we turn to the left and along the Mall we pass below **Carlton House Terrace:** at No. 13 and subsequently at No. 11 Mr. W. E. Gladstone resided for many years; at No. 10 is the **Union Club** (social and non-political), founded in 1822, and here also is the home of the **Savage Club. Waterloo Place** occupies the site of Carlton House, so famous in Regency annals and scandals. The **Duke of York Column,** a granite pillar, 112 ft. high, commemorates the second son of George III, he of the "marching" proclivities.

It is a curious fact that the monument bears no inscription. Although a "national" memorial, the greater part of the bill was paid by the simple expedient of stopping one day's pay from every officer and man in the British Army. Unkind comment of the time explained the height of the monument by the Duke's habit of keeping away from his creditors! Among other monuments in and around the square note that of *Captain Scott* (1912), the Antarctic explorer; it was the work of Lady Scott, and was erected by officers of the Fleet. The equestrian bronze figure of *King Edward VII* was sculptured by *Sir Bertram Mackennal*, with *Sir Edwin Lutyens* as architect.

Waterloo Place being close to the headquarters of London's motoring world, a curious interest attaches to the stones erected there by desire of the Iron Duke to assist clubmen of his day to mount their horses.

The corner on the right is occupied by the **United Service Club** ("The Senior"). On the other side of Pall Mall, at the foot of Regent Street, are the **Crimean Monument** and *Statues of Florence Nightingale,* the "Lady of the Lamp" (d. 1910), and of *Sidney Herbert,* who was Secretary for War at the time of her devoted labours. On the corner to the north side of Pall Mall are the headquarters of Cox's, the Army bankers, now amalgamated with Lloyds Bank. Hereabouts are the large offices of numerous banks and insurance companies.

Pall Mall

(Plan II. I. and K. 8 and 9)

the heart of Clubland, is generally believed to derive its name from the ball game of *paille-maille,* played by Charles II and his merry associates in St. James's Park. Strangers may care to be informed that the pronunciation should be *pell mell,* not *pawl mawl.* We can do little more than enumerate the great clubs which are its distinguishing feature (*see* also pp. 23–4). The **Athenaeum** celebrated its centenary in 1924. The frieze adorning the building is a replica of that of the Parthenon. The wits of the day hailed with delight Decimus Burton's refusal to carry out the wishes of members: "Instead of an ice-house he gave them a frieze." At No. 106 is the **Travellers' Club,** and at No. 104 the **Reform Club,** the premier club of Liberalism. At No. 89 are the luxurious premises of the **Royal Automobile Club.** Then we have the **Oxford and Cambridge Club** (No. 71). **Marlborough House,** already mentioned has an entrance in Pall Mall.

On the other (north) side we have at Orleans House (No. 52) the **Marlborough-Windham Club,** being a post-war amalgamation of the former Marlborough, Windham and Orleans Clubs; at No. 36 the **Army and Navy,** familiarly known as the "Rag," and at the opposite corner (No. 30) the **Junior Carlton,** occupying the greater part of the south side of—

St. James's Square (Plan II. I. 8). This fine square, to the north of Pall Mall, was laid out early in the eighteenth century, and retained the favour of the aristocracy until a quite recent period. Now, however, many of the fine Georgian houses are tenanted by business firms.

In an old building, just behind No. 31, at the south-east corner, George III was born in 1738. Near-by is the new **Norfolk House** at present occupied by a section of the Ministry of Labour. On the wall will be seen the plaque commemorating the use of Norfolk House as General Eisenhower's headquarters during the planning of the invasion operations of World War II. On the north side of the square No. 10 (Chatham House) is noteworthy as having been the residence of three Prime Ministers, namely, William Pitt, Lord Derby and W. E. Gladstone. In 1923 the house was anonymously presented by two Canadians as headquarters of the **Royal Institute of International Affairs,** formed to encourage and facilitate the study of foreign affairs. Outside are link extinguishers, reminders of the London that existed before lamp-posts and electric light standards. In the Square, too, are the **East India and Sports Club** (No. 16), numerous other clubs, and a number of Government and Royal Commission offices. It was from the balcony of No. 16 that the news of the victory at Waterloo was announced. At No. 14 is that invaluable institution to literary workers and lovers of books, the **London Library,** founded in 1841. There are at present about 475,000 volumes on the shelves. Town members are entitled to take ten volumes at a time: country members fifteen volumes. Entrance fee, £3 3s.; annual subscription, £4 4s.

In **King Street**, west of the Square, is the **St. James's Theatre,** where the late Sir George Alexander achieved so many triumphs. The street is the headquarters of some of the most famous dealers in works of art and antique furniture.

St. James's Street leads upwards from the fine gateway of St. James's Palace to Piccadilly. Here are some of the oldest clubs, though in most cases their quarters have been rebuilt. On the left, ascending, we have, at the corner of Cleveland Row, the **Thatched House Club,** and at the next corner (No. 74) the **Conservative Club.** Also on the left are the **Carlton Club,** headquarters of the Tory party, in their new quarters, **Brooks's,** and the **Devonshire.** On the right are **Boodles'** and **White's.**

No. 22 St. James's Place (tablet), a *cul-de-sac* on the east, was the residence of Samuel Rogers, the banker-poet. At Spencer House are the temporary quarters of the well-known auctioneers *Christie, Manson and Woods*.

In Park Place is the headquarters of the **Overseas League.**

Jermyn Street runs parallel to Piccadilly on the south. It is a busy little thoroughfare and affords an interesting route to Lower Regent Street, where we turn down to the right at the *Plaza Cinema* and so regain Waterloo Place.

As we descend the hill, there is a nice view of the Duke of York's Column, pleasantly backed by the greenery of St. James's Park and the venerable towers and spires of Westminster. Beyond the Crimean Monument (*see* p. 125) we turn (left) into **Pall Mall East,** and follow it past the foot of Haymarket. On the north side, in Suffolk Street, is the gallery of the **Royal Society of British Artists,** where spring and autumn exhibitions are held. In the open space formed by the junction of Pall Mall East and Cockspur Street is an equestrian *Statue of George III.* The artist has perpetrated the costume of the period (the uniform of an officer of the Royal Horse Guards, Blue), and while the likeness of the king is excellently preserved, equal justice is done to the wig and pig-tail. It is strangely ironical that the chief American shipping offices should have grown up around this memorial of the obstinate monarch who was so largely responsible for the severance of the United States from England.

The **Haymarket** (Plan II. K. 8) (available only for vehicles proceeding *southward*), hardly so rural in aspect as its name would imply, has at its lower corner the *Carlton Hotel*, one of the most sumptuous establishments in London. It stands on the site of the old Her Majesty's Theatre, demolished in 1893, and replaced by the adjoining **His Majesty's Theatre,** with which the late Sir Herbert Tree was so long associated.   On the eastern side is the **Haymarket Theatre**; on the left are the *Carlton* and *Gaumont Cinemas*.   In Panton Street is the **Comedy Theatre**.

On the corner of Whitcomb Street and New Coventry Street is *Fanum House*, the headquarters of the **Automobile Association**.

New Coventry Street leads to the north side of **Leicester Square** (Plan II. K. 8), long famous as a theatrical centre but now known for its cinemas.   The Square derives its name from Leicester House, "the pouting-place of princes," where George II, when Prince of Wales, having quarrelled with his father, set up an opposition Court, an example dutifully followed by his son Frederick, father of George III.   The open space, then known as Leicester Fields, was long a favourite resort of duellists. The Square is now laid out as an ornamental garden, with a statue of Shakespeare in the centre, and busts of Reynolds, Hunter, Hogarth and Newton, all of whom lived hereabouts, at the corners.   The former *Empire*, on the north side of the Square, has been rebuilt as a cinema, and a similar fate has overtaken the old Alhambra, whose site is occupied by the *Odeon Cinema*.   *Daly's Theatre*, too, has been replaced by the *Warner Cinema*.   On the south of the Square are the **Royal Dental Hospital** and the *Leicester Square Theatre (cinema)*.

In the south-east corner of the Square Hogarth had his studio. At No. 47 (west side: house demolished 1937), Sir Joshua Reynolds lived from 1761 until his death.   So numerous were his callers and sitters that, as Cunningham records, "Sir Joshua gave his servant six pounds annually of wages, and offered him a hundred pounds for the door"—i.e. the gratuities.   At No. 28 lived John Hunter, the famous surgeon, whose anatomical collection, bought by the Government for £12,000, is now at the Royal College of Surgeons (p. 193).   In St. Martin's Street, south of the Square, Sir Isaac Newton lived from 1710 to 1727.

An unauthenticated anecdote records that a hungry friend, being shown into the dining-room, where Sir Isaac's dinner was laid, grew tired of waiting, and consumed the chicken, leaving the bones under the cover.   When at last the great man entered, he removed the cover, and, seeing the bones, exclaimed: "How absent we philosophers are!   I really forgot that I had dined." The house was afterwards occupied by Dr. Burney, father of the lively Fanny, subsequently Madame D'Arblay.   It was demolished in 1913.   On the site is now the **Westminster Public Library.**

Leaving the Square at its north-east corner by way of Cranbourne Street, we reach the **Hippodrome**, a popular house of entertainment, at the corner of Charing Cross Road.

Marble Arch, with a glimpse of Hyde Park. Originally intended as the portal for Buckingham Palace, the gateway was made too narrow to admit the State coach. It was placed here in 1851.

[*Dixon Scott*

Pride and joy of London's children, Sir George Frampton's
statue of Peter Pan in Kensington Gardens is eagerly sought
out by youthful visitors.

Charing Cross Road (Plans I. K. 7 and II. K. 8) runs between Charing Cross and Tottenham Court Road. It is intersected about a quarter of a mile from Oxford Street by **Shaftesbury Avenue,** leading from Piccadilly Circus to Broad Street and High Street, and so into New Oxford Street and Holborn. At the point of intersection, *Cambridge Circus*, is the **Palace Theatre:** close at hand the **Cambridge Theatre** and the **Phoenix.**

In High Street, near the northern end of Shaftesbury Avenue, is the Church of **St. Giles-in-the-Fields,** originally built as the chapel of a leper hospital by Matilda, Queen of Henry I, and reconstructed for the third time in 1734. As in the case of St. Martin's (p. 75), the "fields" are now far to seek. Here are the tombs of Andrew Marvell, Shirley the dramatist, and George Chapman, **the** first translator of Homer; also of "Unparalleled Pendrell," **who** helped Charles II to escape after Worcester. Hogarth's "Idle Apprentice" recalls the old churchyard. Until the construction of New Oxford Street, the main highway to the West went round by the present Broad Street and High Street, and malefactors on their way to Tyburn were given their last cup of ale from the steps of St. Giles's Church. It was in St. Giles's parish that the Great Plague originated in 1665.

Both Shaftesbury Avenue and Charing Cross Road contain a number of modern playhouses. Near the southern end of the latter is **Wyndham's Theatre,** and, nearer to Trafalgar Square, the **Garrick.** Adjoining is the **Westminster City Hall,** the municipal headquarters of the City of Westminster. Opposite is the angle formed by the Portrait Gallery and Orange Street is a memorial garden to Henry Irving, opened by Sir Laurence Olivier in 1951.

In the centre of the roadway, at the foot of St. Martin's Lane, is the **Nurse Cavell Memorial,** the work of the late *Sir George Frampton, R.A.* It bears Nurse Cavell's memorable words shortly before her execution: "Patriotism is not enough; I must have no hatred or bitterness for anyone." In **St. Martin's Lane** is the **Coliseum,** a huge house of entertainment. On the west side, the **New Theatre** and the **Duke of York's Theatre.**

PICCADILLY TO KENSINGTON

ROUTE IV.—PICCADILLY—THE ROYAL ACADEMY—PARK LANE—HYDE
PARK—KENSINGTON GARDENS—KENSINGTON PALACE

WE will assume this time that the start is made from **Picca-dilly Circus** (Plan II. I. 8). This famous spot has been to a great extent transformed during recent years, very striking modern buildings having replaced the more humble shop premises dating from Nash's time (*see* also p. 142). Change of another kind has overtaken the famous old *London Pavilion*—now a cinema. Great as the alteration is above ground, the circular **Subway** below the Circus is even more remarkable with its attractive shop windows and its unending swirl of pedestrians. Its construction was a miracle of engineering ingenuity. Picca-dilly Circus is a very important traffic "hub," both above and below ground, main thoroughfares and "tube" railways radiating hence to north, south, east and west. *Piccadilly Circus Station* is used by more than 25,000,000 passengers yearly. Upwards of 48,000 road vehicles alone pass through the Circus in the course of a day; the "roundabout" system is in use here, the central point being occupied by the late Sir Alfred Gilbert's graceful statue of *Eros* to the memory of Lord Shaftesbury.

On the south side of the Circus is the **Criterion Theatre**; a few yards eastward of the Circus is the enormous *Corner House Restaurant*. To the north-west, with entrance in Glasshouse Street, is the *Regent Palace Hotel*.

Resisting for a while the blandishments of rebuilt Regent Street, (*see* p. 142), we turn along—

Piccadilly
(Plan II. H. 9 and I. 8)

one of London's most attractive thoroughfares, though it, too, has to a great extent been rebuilt. It is said to derive its name from the pickadils, or ruffs, worn in the early Stuart period. Commencing at Piccadilly Circus, it extends westward for nearly a mile to Hyde Park Corner, and is continued as Knightsbridge, Kensington High Street and Kensington Road to Hammersmith, after which it forms the great Bath Road to the West of England. It is thronged at nearly all hours of the day. The eastern portion is occupied by shops, but the western portion, skirting the Green

Park, is overlooked by fine mansions and clubs. At the junction of Piccadilly with Piccadilly Circus we have the striking modern building of *Messrs. Swan & Edgar.* On the north side is the imposing *Piccadilly Hotel.* A few yards westward on the opposite side and lying a little back from the road is the bomb-damaged fane of **St. James's Church.** It was built by Wren in 1684, and had a very fine interior, with font and altar carvings by Grinling Gibbons. The church was badly, though not irreparably, damaged in October 1940, and services (8.15, 11 and 6) are now held in the South Aisle. The carvings and organ case happily escaped damage. The *Garden of Remembrance,* given by the late Viscount Southwood, in commemoration of the courage and fortitude of the people of London during the Second World War, and opened by Her Majesty Queen Mary in May 1946, has seats whereon it is pleasant to rest awhile and reflect in peace. The charming little bank building beside the church was the work of Sir Edwin Lutyens. At No. 195 are the galleries in which are held the exhibitions of the **Royal Institute of Painters in Water Colours** and the **Royal Institute of Oil Painters.** Occupying the ground floor of the same block is *Prince's Restaurant.* Another restaurant farther west and on the opposite side of Piccadilly, is *Hatchett's.* Here used to stand the old "White Horse Cellars," the starting-place of West of England coaches.

On the north side of Piccadilly, between Sackville Street and Burlington House, is the quaint, old-fashioned **Albany,** so frequently figuring in novels of the last century. These bachelor chambers have had many distinguished tenants, including Byron, George Canning, Bulwer Lytton and Lord Macaulay (the famous *History* was written here).

At No. 20, **Savile Row,** to the north, Sidney Smith resided from 1827 to 1832; No. 14 was the last home of Sheridan; and at No. 12 Grote lived and wrote his *History.* The Row is famous for its tailoring establishments.

The Royal Academy of Arts

Plan II. I. 8.

Admission.—The Summer Exhibition of contemporary art (1s. 6d.) is held from the first week in May to the middle of August (9 a.m. to 7 p.m.). Loan exhibitions are held in the autumn and winter (usually 10–6). The Gibson and Diploma Galleries are reached by a staircase to right of main entrance (free daily from 11 to 4).

Catalogues.—Official Catalogue, 1s.

Nearest Stations.—Green Park (Piccadilly Line), Piccadilly Circus (Piccadilly and Bakerloo Lines).

Buses —A large proportion of the bus services pass through Piccadilly Circus, a few minutes distant, and many run along Piccadilly, past the doors of Burlington House.

Burlington House was rebuilt early in the eighteenth century by Richard Boyle, Earl of Burlington, and purchased by the Government in 1854 at a cost of £140,000. A number of extensions have since been made, and a storey added. The Royal Academy occupies the inner or northern portion, while various learned societies are accommodated in the blocks on either side. The best known of these societies is the **Royal Society**, incorporated by Royal Charter in 1662. Its roll of Fellows and Presidents includes such illustrious names as those of Newton, Halley, Davy, Darwin, Kelvin, and many others. Members append the letters F.R.S. to their names. The Society's Library contains about 50,000 volumes, some fine portraits and busts, Newton's telescope, the original model of Davy's safety lamp, and other objects of interest. Admission by order of a Fellow. Other bodies include the **Geological, Chemical, Royal Astronomical and Linnean Societies, the Society of Antiquaries of London, and the British Association for the Advancement of Science.** The libraries and museums of these Societies can generally be seen on application.

Crossing the inner court, we reach the part best known to the public. The **Royal Academy of Arts** was founded by George III in 1768, its first President being Sir Joshua Reynolds, and was first established in Somerset House. From 1838 to 1869 the annual exhibitions and schools were held in the National Gallery. There are forty Royal Academicians (who add R.A. to their names) and about thirty associates (A.R.A.), as well as a number of retired and foreign Academicians and Associates. The **Annual Exhibition** (familiarly "The Academy") usually opens on the first Monday in May, and is preceded by the "Private View" —a Society function in which dress plays at least as important a part as Art—and the "Academy Dinner," generally attended by royalty, and by leading politicians of all parties. The pictures to be shown are chosen by a "Selection Committee," whose judgments of course do not always commend themselves to the general body of artists. The works must have been finished in the last few years and not exhibited elsewhere in London. In the upper part of the building occupied by the Academy and open (free) throughout the year, are the **Gibson and Diploma Galleries,** with a very interesting collection of pictures presented by Academicians on their election, the Gibson Collection of Sculptures, and some valuable old masters. A study by *Leonardo da Vinci* is a special attraction and there are palettes and other mementoes of many famous artists.

On the west side of Burlington House is the **Burlington Arcade,** for the most part sacred to hosiers, bootmakers and jewellers. The **Royal Arcade** is a similar structure connecting Old Bond Street and Albemarle Street. The **Piccadilly Arcade,** on the south side of Piccadilly, provides a shop-lined covered way between that thoroughfare and Jermyn Street.

Continuing westward, we pass the foot of **Old Bond Street**, where are many famous shops—notably jewellers—and the galleries of a number of well-known art dealers. In recent years Bond Street has been invaded by motor-car dealers. It runs northward to Oxford Street, the upper and wider portion being known as **New Bond Street**. On No. 147, New Bond Street is a tablet recording that Nelson lived there, but the house has been entirely rebuilt. The famous thoroughfare—

"Where each who wills may suit his wish,
Here choose a Guido—there his fish."

takes its name from Sir Thomas Bond, its builder in 1686.

In Conduit Street, connecting Bond Street and Regent Street, are the headquarters of the **Royal Society of Painters in Water Colours**, whose exhibitions are always largely attended.

Albemarle Street is so named from the second Duke of Albemarle, son of General Monk. Near the top is the **Royal Institution**, founded in 1799 for the promotion and teaching of science. The lectures given to juvenile audiences in the weeks succeeding Christmas always attract wide attention. Next door, at No. 20, is the **Davy-Faraday Laboratory**, presented by the late Dr. Ludwig Mond. At No. 23 is the **Royal Society of Portrait Painters**. At No. 7 are the headquarters and exhibition rooms of the **National Book League**. Nearby in Grafton Street at No. 15A, lived Sir Henry Irving (*plaque*).

St. James's Street, running south from Piccadilly to Holbein's fine gateway at St. James's Palace, we have described on p. 127. Wimborne House, No. 22, **Arlington Street** was long the town mansion of the Marquess of Salisbury. No. 5, now an annexe of the Devonshire Club, was for years the residence of Sir Robert Walpole, and later of his son, Horace Walpole. The *Ritz* is one of the most sumptuous of London's hotels. The restaurant overlooks the **Green Park** (p. 123), which borders the south side of Piccadilly all the rest of the way to Hyde Park Corner, affording the favoured occupants of houses on the other side a magnificent view across to Westminster. *Green Park Station*, on the Piccadilly Line, has replaced Dover Street Station. Across the way is the enormous block of *Devonshire House*, perpetuating the name of the town residence of the Duke of Devonshire, which long occupied the site. A beautiful memento of the old Devonshire House is the fine iron gateway on the other side of the road, in the railings of Green Park.

Berkeley Street (Pope lived for a time at No. 9) leads to **Berkeley Square** (Plan II. H. 8), noted for its plane trees, and

reminding one of Thackeray's "Jeames of Barkley Square."
Although the character of the Square has changed, some of the
houses on the west side still have associations of interest, the past
being especially recalled by the quaint ironwork and the torch
extinguishers in front of the doors. The southern side of the
Square is filled by *Lansdowne House*, the huge block which
houses a department of the War Office. On the east side the still
larger *Berkeley Square House* houses the **Ministry of Transport.**

West of Berkeley Square, in Farm Street, is the **Church of
the Jesuit Fathers,** where Cardinal Manning was received into
the Church of Rome. In Charles Street, Berkeley Square, is
Dartmouth House (35), the home of the **English-Speaking Union.**

Continuing along the north side of Piccadilly, we pass the
foot of **Clarges Street,** taking its name from Nan Clarges, the
needle-woman, whose father was a blacksmith, and who married
General Monk and became Duchess of Albemarle. No. 85
Piccadilly, on the corner, is the **Turf Club.**

Beyond **Half Moon Street,** deriving its peculiar name from a
long lost tavern, at one time of considerable repute, are the
Naval and Military Club (No. 94, formerly occupied by Lord
Palmerston) and the **American Club** (No. 95).

White Horse Street leads to **Shepherd Market,** which has been
described as "a modest little country town . . . small but busy . . . a
strange survival set in this most aristocratic quarter." Though in
great part rebuilt it still retains a pleasantly rural flavour, and is
characteristic of many oases in London which unexpectedly greet the
explorer who forsakes the main thoroughfares.

Continuing along Piccadilly, we pass the **Public Schools Club**
(100), **St. James's** and **Bachelors** (106), **Royal Aero** (119),
Cavalry (127) and other clubs. At No. 128 is the **Royal Air
Force Club.** In the stately mansions between Hamilton Place
and Apsley House several members of the Rothschild family
reside. No. 145 was the residence of King George VI at the
time of his accession, and where Queen Elizabeth II was born.

Apsley House (Plan II. H. 9), the residence of the Duke of
Wellington, was presented to the Great Duke by the nation in
1820, **as part of** his reward. It is now to be presented back to
the nation and part used as a Wellington Museum.

It was originally built in 1785 as a red-brick mansion for Lord
Chancellor Bathurst, who, it is said, in order to secure the land,
had to buy out the proprietor of an apple-stall, an old soldier
to whom George II, in an excess of generosity, had given the
site as a reward for bravery at the battle of Dettingen. During
the Reform Bill agitation the mob smashed the windows, so
the Duke had them encased in iron shutters. Later, when the

changeable crowd followed him with cheers from Constitution Hill, he took no notice until the shutters were in sight, when he bowed sarcastically and passed into the court without a word.

In the roadway island opposite is a fine equestrian **Statue of the Duke of Wellington,** by Boehm.

Park Lane (Plan II. G. and H. 8 and 9), overlooking the eastern side of Hyde Park, was long famous for its splendid mansions, many of them filled with some of the world's most celebrated pictures and statuary, but its character has changed in recent years and it is now notable on account of the huge buildings in modern style which have replaced such famous residences as Grosvenor House (long the London home of the Dukes of Westminster), and Dorchester House, wherein Mr. Whitelaw Reid resided when American Ambassador. Although these huge piles, such as *Grosvenor House* and the *Dorchester Hotel*, have been much criticized, they have architectural distinction, a fact which is forcibly brought home to those who trouble to compare them with other large buildings in the vicinity.

Just within the Stanhope Gate of Hyde Park is the **Cavalry War Memorial,** with a striking sculpture of St. George and the Dragon, by *Adrian Jones, M.V.O.*

Between Park Lane and Bond Street lies the "blue-blooded" and reverently regarded district of **Mayfair,** for which the visitor may look in vain in the Directory, for it has no parochial or other official recognition. The name is the only survival of the old May Fair, an annual scene of debauchery suppressed at the end of the eighteenth century.

In **Curzon Street** (Plan II. H. 8), on the site of Sunderland House, stood a Chapel long famous for marriages at a minute's notice. Hasty beauties and eager swains were here tied together with the utmost celerity; and it is said that no fewer than 6,000 pairs were thus united in one year. The beautiful Miss Chudleigh was wedded in this fashion to the Duke of Kingston; and the still more beautiful Miss Gunning, the youngest of the lovely sisterhood who turned the heads of young Englishmen at that period, came hither with the Duke of Hamilton, half an hour after midnight, and was married with a bed-curtain ring.

At the corner of this street and South Audley Street Leconfield House occupies the site of Chesterfield House, where the famous letters were penned, and in a room of which E. M. Ward's well-known picture represents Dr. Johnson impatiently awaiting an audience. At 25 **Brook Street,** Handel lived for nearly forty years. Nearly all his works were composed within its walls, including the *Messiah* (1741). A movement is on foot to secure

and nationalise the house. In this street is *Claridge's Hotel*.
Grosvenor Square (Plan II. H. 8) is one of the finest in London.
No. 1 is the huge **United States Embassy.** Lord Lytton, the
novelist, lived at No. 12; *Rienzi* and *The Last Days of Pompeii*
were written at 36, Hertford Street.   Here also is the **Roosevelt
Memorial,** unveiled by Mrs. Roosevelt, 12th April, 1948.

We now return to **Hyde Park Corner** (Plan II. H. 9—station
on Piccadilly Tube), another of London's landmarks, and one
of the world's busiest traffic centres.   Vehicular traffic passes
the "Corner" on the gyratory system.   A recent census showed
that some 83,000 vehicles pass this point between 8 a.m. and
8 p.m.—or nearly 100 a minute.   The large building at the
corner of Grosvenor Place is **St. George's Hospital.**   At the
entrance to the Green Park (p. 123) is the **Wellington Arch,** surmounted by Adrian Jones's imposing quadriga.   The arch is
matched in grace by the screen entrance to Hyde Park, a triple
gateway erected in 1826 from the designs of Decimus Burton.
The reliefs are copied from the Elgin Marbles.   On the road
"islands" are memorials to fallen members of the **Machine Gun
Corps** and of the **Royal Regiment of Artillery.**

Hyde Park
(Plan II. F., G. and H. 8 and 9)

has an area of 361 acres, and is joined on the west by **Kensington
Gardens** (Plan II. E. and F. 8 and 9), with 275 acres, the two
together forming London's finest lung.   From Park Lane to
Kensington Palace is about a mile and a half, while from Marble
Arch to Hyde Park Corner is the best part of a mile.   What
London owes to this delightful stretch of greenery can never be
told.   Prior to the Dissolution the park formed part of the
Manor of Hyde, and was the property of the Abbey of Westminster.   By Henry VIII it was converted into a deer-park and
under the Stuarts it was used for horse-racing.   King William
and Queen Anne caused a number of improvements to be made;
but it is to Queen Caroline, the consort of George II, that we
owe its most attractive feature, the **Serpentine,** an artificial
sheet of water, stretching from Lancaster Gate in a south-
easterly direction to the **Dell,** opposite Albert Gate, and having
with the Long Water an area of 41 acres.   Notice boards point
the way to the various gates (*see* plan, pp. 144–5).

Cars may use the avenues through the Park, but carts and lorries
are not permitted to enter.   Cyclists may use all roads open to wheeled
traffic.   The speed of motor vehicles is limited to *twenty miles an hour*,
and they are not allowed to use the road between the Achilles statue
and the Powder Magazine.

Chairs.—A 3*d.* ticket entitles one to the use from 9–2, or 12–5, or 4 to close, of a chair in Hyde Park, Kensington Gardens, St. James's, or the Green Park. Season tickets—15s. all Royal Parks, 10s. one park only.

Bathing (Mixed) is allowed in the Serpentine *Lido* free, from 6 a.m. to 10 a.m. daily (including Sundays). A charge of 6*d.* (children free) is made between 10 a.m. and 8.30 p.m. daily (including Sundays)—closing time varies with advancement of season.

Boating can be enjoyed for 1s. 6*d.* to 4s. per hour (boathouse on north side, close to the Humane Society's Receiving House).

Bowling.—1s. per hour per person.

Putting.—Tickets obtainable at 2*d.* per round.

Teas, light luncheons, etc., can be obtained at the Ring Tea House, between the Marble Arch and the Serpentine, and also at the Tea House in Kensington Gardens, near the Serpentine Bridge.

Entering from Hyde Park Corner, we have on the left the well-known **Rotten Row,** a corruption of *route du roi,* a course of a mile and a half reserved for riders. The drive adjoining is thronged on fine afternoons in the season with cars of many types. On the north side of the Serpentine is the **Ladies' Mile.** The **Bandstand** is occupied on summer evenings by a first-class band. The **Ring Tea House,** a little north of the Serpentine, is popular in summer. The "Ring" was a great resort of rank and fashion in Stuart and Commonwealth times.

As already mentioned (p. 120) the bird-life of London is remarkably rich, and in 1925 an "official" Bird Sanctuary was opened a few hundred yards west of the Superintendent's House in Hyde Park. The Sanctuary forms a **Memorial of W. H. Hudson,** "writer and field naturalist"; but the pretty bird bath is, in the opinion of many, marred by *Epstein's* panel of Rima (*see* Hudson's *Green Mansions*).

The **Flower Beds** are in spring and summer a blaze of colour, the displays of flowers attracting thousands of admirers.

Their leafy glades and vistas give to Kensington Gardens a charm denied to Hyde Park, the northern part of which is for the most part bare and flat. Advantage is taken of this fact by the promoters of political meetings and demonstrations, which often attain to huge proportions. At week-ends and on summer evenings the corner nearest the Marble Arch is generally the venue of a number of earnest orators, each with his knot of more or less appreciative listeners. It is a side of London life of which little is seen at other times, and the visitor in search of mild amusement may be recommended to take a stroll in this direction.

The Marble Arch
(Plan II. G. 8)

at the north-east corner of the Park, was intended by George IV to form the portal of Buckingham Palace, but by a miscalculation it was made too narrow to admit the State coach. It cost

£80,000, and the gates another £3,000. The arch was placed in its present position in 1851. This is another of the busy corners of London, a recent census showing that between 8 a.m. and 8 p.m. no fewer than 60,000 vehicles passed. With a view to relieving this congestion, the park boundary was some years ago set back, leaving the Marble Arch in the centre of a spacious "circulating area."

To the west of Hyde Park are—

Kensington Gardens

which with their broad avenues and charming water scenery give sudden surprises of landscape scarcely surpassed for beauty in any part of England. The gardens, first laid out in the reign of William III, were considerably enlarged in that of George II. At this period Queen Caroline appropriated about 300 acres of the old Hyde Park and separated them from the park by a fosse and sunken wall.

The Serpentine is crossed at the entrance to Kensington Gardens by a five-arched stone **Bridge,** the view from which on either side, with its combination of water and woodland, is exquisite. On the Kensington Gardens side of the bridge is a popular *Refreshment Pavilion*; and on the other side is the **Powder Magazine.** The **Round Pond,** with an area of 7 acres, is beloved by juvenile yachtsmen. At the end of the **Broad Walk,** 50 ft. wide, between the Round Pond and Kensington Palace, is a white marble *Statue of Queen Victoria* by Princess Louise. The huge equestrian statue by G. F. Watts, 12 ft. high, representing *Physical Energy*, is a replica of the central portion of the Rhodes Memorial on the slope of Table Mountain, Cape Town. Youthful visitors especially will seek out with eagerness the *Statue of Peter Pan, by Sir George Frampton, R.A.* In the Children's Playground is an "Elfin Tree," with gnomes, fairies, etc.

Kensington Palace

Plan II. E. 9.
Nearest Stations.—High Street, Kensington (Underground); Queensway (Central Line).
Buses serving Kensington High Street or Notting Hill Gate pass the ends of the Broad Walk.
Admission.—The State Apartments are open to the public March-September on Saturday and Sunday afternoons from 2 p.m. to 6 p.m., Charge, 1s. Sunken gardens free.

Here Queen Victoria was born (May 24, 1819) and spent her childhood: and here on the morning of June 21, 1837, she received the news of her accession to the throne. Here, too, was born on the 26th May, 1867, the Princess May, now Queen Mary. William III purchased the mansion, then known as Nottingham House, from Lord Chancellor Finch; and Sir Christopher Wren was employed to extend and adapt it as a royal residence. King William, Queen Mary, Queen Anne, her husband (Prince George of Denmark), and George II all died here. Under George I an additional suite of state rooms was constructed by Wm. Kent. Several suites of rooms in the Palace are still occupied by relatives of the Royal Family.

The two floors beneath the State Apartments in the southern and eastern wings of the Palace form the new home of—

The London Museum

The main collections of the Museum were moved in 1950 to the Palace, where they are now open to the public. Certain exhibits remain at Lancaster House (*see* p. 123).

The following is a summary account of the Collections, which are designed especially to illustrate the history and the social and domestic life of London in all periods, the exhibits ranging from unpolished flint weapons of the Stone Age to modern dolls and toys.

Stone, Bronze and Iron Ages. A wide range of early flint and metal tools and weapons discovered in the London district and including particularly a fine series from the River Thames.

Roman Period (A.D. 43 to about A.D. 400). The collection illustrates the history of the Roman city whose name, Londinium, may be seen in contemporary script on a late first-century jug in the Museum. The city destroyed by Boudicea (Boadicea) in A.D. 61 was an undefended commercial town of small extent, though, late in the first century an independent fort had been built in the Cripplegate area. The walls were not added until after A.D. 140 (when the city was increased in size) and were strengthened by the addition of bastions in the fourth century. Lamps, writing materials, brooches, articles of toilet, domestic utensils, grave furniture, etc., illustrate the life of Roman London, and are complementary with the large Guildhall Museum collection.

Dark Ages (Saxon to early Norman). Little is known of buildings or other structures belonging to this pnase of London's history, but the collection includes pottery, implements and weapons from various parts of the City and beyond, as well as objects from pagan Saxon cemeteries at Mitcham, Ewell and elsewhere.

Medieval Period (Twelfth to fifteenth centuries). A wide range of specimens illustrating the varied life of the time in which London became of increasing importance as a port and commercial centre. The collection provides in effect a picture of the medieval life of England as a whole.

Tudor and Stuart. Objects of outstanding interest at this time are the Gresham steelyard (1572), the Cheapside Hoard of Elizabethan jewellery (which is described in a separate published catalogue), the Tangye collection of Cromwellian relics and documents, the "London" Cup (1670) and the Pepys chessboard.

Eighteenth and Nineteenth Centuries. Apart from the general collections illustrating the later history of London the artistic products of these periods, the Bow and Chelsea porcelains, Battersea enamels and glass are of particular interest. The Museum's costume collection is of very great importance and includes coronation robes and other clothes belonging to Queen Victoria and other members of the Royal Family. There is a collection of toys extending backwards to the sixteenth century, as well as collections illustrating Parliament and the London Stage. London topography and architecture are illustrated by a large collection of prints and drawings.

In that mellow part of Kensington which lies between the Gardens and Holland Park are many delightful residences favoured by successful lawyers, literary men and artists. At No. 2, Palace Gardens (Plan II. D. 9), close to the west boundary of the gardens, Thackeray died in 1863. At No. 16 (formerly 13), Young Street, on the other side of High Street, *Vanity Fair*, *Pendennis*, and other works were written. Lord Macaulay died at Holly Lodge, Campden Hill, in 1859.

Slightly farther west, in extensive grounds bordering the Kensington Road, is **Holland House,** built in 1607.

At the Commonwealth it passed to General Fairfax, and Cromwell and Ireton were often here. Addison and his wife, the Countess of Warwick, came here in 1716, and it was in 1719, that he died, and the house passed from the Warwick family to Henry Fox, the father of the famous statesman, Charles James Fox. For a long period it was the recognised rallying-place of the Whigs, and the most brilliant social and literary centre in London. The house sustained considerable damage in 1940–41 and is unoccupied. In 1951 the house and part of the estate were bought by the London County Council for use as a public park.

A turning just beyond the grounds of Holland House leads to Holland Park Road, where at No. 12 (north side) is **Leighton House** (Plan II. C. 10), designed and used as a residence by Lord Leighton, P.R.A. (d. 1896). In 1925 the house and its contents were generously presented by Mrs. Russell Barrington to the Kensington Borough Council, who have also acquired the freehold of the property. The house, damaged during the war, was re-opened in 1951 for use as a museum for concerts and exhibitions.

The house contains several oil paintings by Lord Leighton, a large collection of his original drawings and sketches, and proof engravings and photographic reproductions of his principal pictures. The chief feature is the beautiful Arab Hall, with playing fountain. The tiles were collected by Lord Leighton and his friends during visits to the East, and most of them are three hundred years old, while two are of the fourteenth century. The Damascene windows, with their gorgeous colouring, are very fine.

We can make our way back to Charing Cross either by train from Kensington High Street, or by bus along Kensington Gore and Knightsbridge. The latter route affords an opportunity for noting a few features of interest omitted on our outward ramble through the parks. **Kensington High Street** is a favourite shopping quarter, with many large stores, including *Barker's*.

Kensington Gore takes its name from *Gore House*, almost as famous as Holland House in the early part of the last century as a literary and political centre. The word Gore, has no sanguinary significance. It is used in the sense, known to dressmakers, of "a wedge-shaped piece"—in this case a plot of ground.

The **Royal Albert Hall** (Plan II. F. 9) was built 1867–71 as a memorial of the Prince Consort, at a cost of £200,000.

It is one of the largest halls in the world, and will comfortably seat 8,000 people, with another 1,100 in the orchestra. Though frequently used for political demonstrations, boxing contests, and other great gatherings, it is principally famous for musical performances on a large scale. Not every singer or speaker emerges successfully from the ordeal of facing that vast audience. In the arena alone there is space for 1,000 persons, while the amphitheatre holds nearly 1,400. Above are three rows of boxes, many of them private property, and still higher are the balcony and a picture gallery and promenade. The magnificent **Organ**, built by Willis and recently enlarged, has over 10,000 pipes and is probably the largest organ in the world.

On the west side of the Hall is the **Royal College of Organists,** to the right of which is **Queen Alexandra's House,** and opposite, the Imperial College Union. In the district immediately south of the Albert Hall are several important colleges, as well as the South Kensington Museums (see pp. 170–81).

Opposite the Albert Hall, just within Kensington Gardens, is the **Albert Memorial** (Plan II. F. 9), erected to the memory of the Prince Consort.

The memorial cost £120,000, and was designed by Sir Gilbert Scott, on the model of an Eleanor cross. The pedestal is adorned with 178 marble relievos of musicians, poets, painters, architects and sculptors of all times. Among the public undertakings with which the Prince identified himself was the Great Exhibition of 1851, held in Hyde Park. Hence the statue holds a copy of the exhibition catalogue.

Lowther Lodge is the home of the **Royal Geographical Society.** The Museum contains mementoes of Captain Scott's Antarctic expedition and many other objects of geographical interest. There is an excellent reference library. Note the statue of Sir Ernest Shackleton, facing Exhibition Road.

At No. 25, Princes Gate is the **Royal School of Art Needlework,** *open free daily,* 10–5.30 *except Saturdays.* No. 14 is the residence of the United States Ambassador to the Court of St. James. At No. 16 are the headquarters of the **Royal Photographic Society.**

Passing **Knightsbridge Barracks,** we reach the *Hyde Park Hotel,* opposite which the **Brompton Road** runs off in a south-westerly direction to Cromwell Road and the South Kensington Museums (p. 170); while **Sloane Street** leads due south to Chelsea. No. 60, Knightsbridge (with pillared portico) is the home of the **Royal Thames Yacht Club.** The fine mansion on the eastern side of Albert Gate (58), is the **French Embassy,** built originally for George Hudson, the "railway king."

REGENT STREET AND REGENT'S PARK

ROUTE V.—REGENT STREET—OXFORD CIRCUS—THE WALLACE COL-
LECTION—MARYLEBONE ROAD—REGENT'S PARK—THE ZOOLOGICAL
GARDENS—EDGWARE ROAD—BAYSWATER ROAD.

AGAIN starting from Piccadilly Circus, let us turn up Regent
Street and further explore "Shopland."

Regent Street

Plans I and III. 7 and 8.
Nearest Stations.—North end: Oxford Circus (Central and Bakerloo Tubes). South
    end: Piccadilly Circus (Bakerloo and Piccadilly Tubes).
Buses from all quarters pass through the street or touch Piccadilly Circus (at the
    southern end) or Oxford Circus (to the north).

Both Regent Street and Regent's Park owe their existence
to a magnificent whim of George IV, who, as Prince Regent,
lived in Carlton House, which stood on the spot now occupied
by the southern half of Waterloo Place. He conceived the idea
of building a villa on or near Primrose Hill (then a rural spot),
and projected a fine new road, three miles long, to connect it
with Carlton House. The villa never became a reality; but
Regent Street did, and the New or Regent's Park followed.
The street was laid out in 1813–20 by the architect Nash, of
whom it was said:

> "Augustus at Rome was for building renown'd,
>   For of marble he left what of brick he had found;
>   But is not our Nash, too, a very great master,
>   He finds us all brick and he leaves us all plaster?"

After a century of service, Nash's buildings have in recent
times been razed, their place being taken by marble and ferro-
concrete "palaces" that make Regent Street without question
the finest shopping thoroughfare in the world. The architect
mainly responsible was Sir Reginald Blomfield. It would be
difficult to beat the fine view from Piccadilly Circus into Regent
Street, with the splendid sweep of the Quadrant and the fine
building of the County Fire Office, and the observant loiterer
will find many interesting details in doorways, balconies, etc.

Overlooking Piccadilly Circus are the blocks housing Swan &
Edgar's. Next comes the *Piccadilly Hotel*, with frontages both
to Regent Street and Piccadilly. Glasshouse Street on the right
leads to the *Regent Palace Hotel* (Messrs J. Lyons & Co.), and

to **Golden Square,** familiar, in name at least, to readers of
Nicholas Nickleby. Farther north is **Great Marlborough Street,**
with a noted police court where the seamy side of West End
life is focused. A notably beautiful Tudor building in Great
Marlborough Street forms part of *Liberty's* premises. Children
love to watch the clock, St. George engaging the Dragon at each
quarter hour and slaying him at the hour. Note the fine frieze
on the Regent Street front of Liberty's premises. Near at hand,
in Argyll Street, is the **Palladium.**

Hanover Street, on the west side of Regent Street, brings one
to **Hanover Square,** where are the headquarters of several learned
societies, and a striking modern building forming the headquarters of the Celanese Corporation. In George Street, south
of the Square, is the church of **St. George's, Hanover Square,** the
scene of so many fashionable marriages. It dates from 1725,
and contains several stained-glass windows made in Mechlin at
least two centuries earlier.

Among the marriages recorded in the registers are those of Sir
William Hamilton to Nelson's "Emma" in 1791; Benjamin Disraeli
to Mary Ann Lewis in 1839; George Eliot in 1880; "Theodore Roosevelt, twenty-eight, widower, ranchman," and "Edith Kermit Carow"
Dec. 2, 1886); and Lord Oxford and Asquith (1894).

Oxford Circus

(Plan I. I. 7)

one of the busiest bus and tube centres, has, like Regent Street
itself, been transformed by the rebuilding of business premises.
Above and below ground, it is a busy spot: 36 million passengers
used the Tube station during a recent year; important improvements have made it capable of handling 50 million passengers
per annum. Here Regent Street crosses **Oxford Street** (p. 157),
and then continues northward, as Langham Place and Portland
Place, to the Marylebone Road. On the western side is the
Polytechnic, founded by Quintin Hogg in 1882 and rebuilt at a
cost of £90,000 in 1911 as a memorial of King Edward VII.
This institution has something like 11,000 students attending
its many classes. The Cameo-Polytechnic Cinema is situated in
the building. At the head of Regent Street is **All Souls' Church,**
with its peculiar "extinguisher" spire, designed by Nash. Damaged during the war it was re-dedicated and re-opened after
restoration in April 1951. On the eastern side of Regent Street
is **Queen's Hall,** gutted during the war. With seating accommodation for 3,000 it was here that many of the principal London

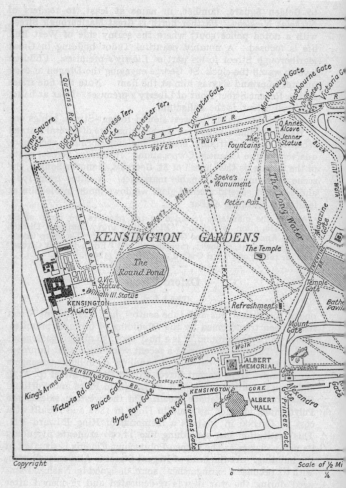

KENSINGTON GARDENS

The Round Pond

The Temple

The Long Water

Speke's Monument

Peter Pan

The Fountains

Anne's Alcove

Jenner Statue

North Walk

BAYS WATER

Queens Rd.

Black Lion Gate

Inverness Ter.

Porchester Ter.

Lancaster Gate

Marlborough Gate

Westbourne Gate

Victoria Gate

Orme Square Gate

THE BROAD WALK

Budge's Walk

Q. Vic. Statue

William III. Statue

KENSINGTON PALACE

Refreshments

Temple Gate

Mount Gate

Bowling Grn.

Colbrookdale

ALBERT MEMORIAL

Flower Walk

Fort Gate

Gore

ALBERT HALL

Alexandra Gate

Prince's Gate

King's Arms Gate

Victoria Rd. Gate

Palace Gate

Hyde Park Gate

KENSINGTON RD.

Queen's Gate

KENSINGTON

Queen's Gate

Magazine Gate

Scale of ½ Mi

0   ¼

HYDE PARK AND F

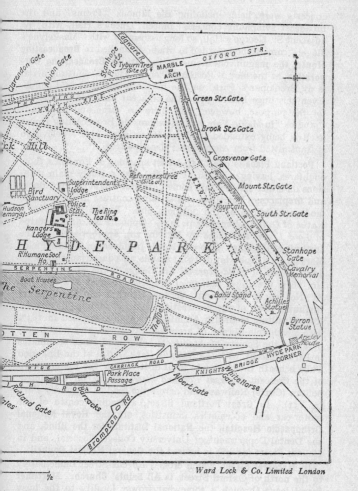

Ward Lock & Co. Limited London

½

concerts were held, including the famous "Proms" and the broadcast symphony concerts: indeed, Queen's Hall, with the adjacent St. George's Hall, so long associated with "Maskelyne's Magic" came to be regarded as studios attached to **Broadcasting House,** the magnificent home of the **British Broadcasting Corporation,** at the foot of Portland Place. The transmitting aerial is at Brookman's Park, on the northern outskirts of London. Even this huge building and the adjacent halls are insufficient for the purpose, however, and there are large and important "studios" in Maida Vale and elsewhere and Broadcasting House itself is being extended to twice its original size. Television is transmitted from Alexandra Palace (p. 228).

Portland Place is one of the most spacious of London's thoroughfares, having a width of 120 ft. The severely plain mansions on either side contain some beautiful Adam ceilings, doors and fireplaces. But there is a striking contrast in some of the modern buildings at the northern end. In the roadway is a statue of *Quintin Hogg* (*see* p. 143). Opposite No. 92 is a statue of *Lord Lister,* and close by (at No. 28), appropriately, is the **Institute of Hygiene.** Opposite No. 47 (residence of the late Field-Marshal Earl Roberts: d. 1914) stands an equestrian statue by John Tweed of *Field-Marshal Sir George White* (d. 1912). At No. 26 is the *Royal Society of Tropical Medicine and Hygiene.* At No. 59 is the **Mount Vernon Hospital** and the **Radium Institute.** One of the contrasting modern buildings houses the **Royal Institute of British Architects** (No. 66), founded in 1837, with a valuable library of architectural works, and now incorporating the Society of Architects. Portland Place terminates in **Park Crescent,** with the *Regent's Park Station* of the Bakerloo Tube beneath the garden in front of it. Near the eastern horn of the Crescent is *Great Portland Street Station,* on the Metropolitan (Circle) Railway, and across the road is Regent's Park (p. 151). In **Great Portland Street,** a leading centre of the motor-car and accessories industries, are the **Royal National Orthopaedic Hospital,** the **National Institute for the Blind,** and the Dental Department of University College Hospital, and in Hallam Street (44–46) is housed the **General Medical Council.**

In **Margaret Street,** which crosses Regent Street immediately to the north of Oxford Street, is **All Saints' Church.** Mortimer Street leads through a somewhat frowsy locality to the busy **Middlesex Hospital,** recently rebuilt. At No. 76, Charlotte Street (tablet), Constable, the great landscape painter, lived from 1822 until his death in 1837. Here, too, is the **Scala**

Theatre. In **Fitzroy Square** are the headquarters of the **British Drama League,** with a valuable library, and **St. Luke's Hostel,** a nursing home for the clergy and their families.

On the other (western) side of the upper part of Regent Street we have **Cavendish Square,** an important feature of which is the **Cowdray Club,** for nurses and professional women. **Harley Street, Wimpole Street,** and other thoroughfares in the neighbourhood are noted for the large number of consulting physicians and specialists residing in them. The imposing Grecian building at the corner of Wimpole Street and Henrietta Place is the headquarters of the **Royal Society of Medicine.** The parent Society was founded in 1805; the present organisation is a fusion of fifteen former societies. The library contains over 100,000 volumes. In nearby Stratford Place is the **National Gallery of British Sports and Pastimes** founded by the late Walter Hutchinson in 1949.

The streets hereabouts have interesting associations:

Holles Street, connecting Cavendish Square with Oxford Street, was the birthplace of Lord Byron in 1788. The site of the house (formerly No. 24) forms part of the premises of Messrs. John Lewis and Co.

No. 50 Wimpole Street (tablet) was the home, before her marriage, of Elizabeth Barrett Browning and has been immortalised in that famous play *The Barretts of Wimpole Street*; Henry Hallam's *Constitutional History of England* and *The Literature of Europe in the 15th, 16th and 17th Centuries* were written at No. 67 (tablet), where he resided from 1819 to 1840; and at No. 82 Wilkie Collins died in 1889. At No. 73, Harley Street, lived Sir Charles Lyell, the great geologist, and later, W. E. Gladstone; No. 38 (formerly 13) was the home of Barry Cornwall and Adelaide Anne Proctor; William Beckford, the eccentric author of *Vathek*, lived at No. 100. Anthony Trollope died at 34, Welbeck Street; No. 48 (tablet) was the residence of Dr. Thomas Young, the Egyptologist. No. 23, Queen Anne Street (tablet) was the home of J. M. W. Turner. In Devonshire Street, farther north, lived Sir John Herschel, the great astronomer (No. 56—tablet); while No. 1, Devonshire Terrace, at the corner of High Street and Marylebone Road (tablet), was the home from 1839 to 1851 of Charles Dickens. Here he wrote, among other works, *The Old Curiosity Shop*, *Martin Chuzzlewit* and portions of *Dombey and Son* and *David Copperfield*.

In Wigmore Street is **Wigmore Hall,** well-known to music-lovers, and in Mandeville Street the **Trinity College of Music.**

Bentinck Street leads into **Manchester Square,** on the north side of which is **Hertford House,** the stately mansion containing—

The Wallace Collection

Plan I. H. 7.

Nearest Stations.—Bond Street (Central Line), Baker Street (Metropolitan Railway and Bakerloo Line).

Buses passing along Oxford Street or Baker Street bring one within a minute's walk of the Collection. Alight at Selfridge's or at George Street.

Admission.—Free. Open daily from 10 a.m. to 5 p.m.; Sundays, 2 to 5. Closed on Good Friday, Christmas Eve and Christmas Day.
Catalogues of Paintings, Miniatures, Sculpture, European Arms and Armour, can be obtained at entrance.

The Wallace Collection, perhaps the largest and finest Collection of works of art ever presented to any country by a private individual, was bequeathed to the nation by Lady Wallace, on condition that the Government provided a building for it in central London, and made the necessary arrangements for its upkeep. It was eventually decided to purchase the freehold of Hertford House where the collection had been installed during Sir Richard Wallace's lifetime, and adapt it for the purpose of a public gallery. It was opened by the Prince of Wales (afterwards Edward VII) in June 1900. The Collection was formed mainly by Richard, fourth Marques of Hertford, and supplemented by Sir Richard Wallace, to whom it had passed by bequest. Lord Hertford resided chiefly in Paris where he assembled most of the French works of art of the seventeenth and eighteenth centuries which give the Collection its particular character. The paintings of this period include important works by Watteau, Boucher and Fragonard, whilst the collection of French furniture is unique outside France and the Sèvres porcelain is only rivalled by the Royal collection at Windsor Castle and Buckingham Palace. In addition there is a remarkably representative collection of paintings of all European schools, the Dutch school being particularly well represented. Sir Richard Wallace enriched his inheritance chiefly by the addition of a fine collection of Renaissance sculpture and works of art, majolica, Limoges enamel, bronzes and ivories. In addition he acquired the collection of continental arms and armour, which is unequalled outside the Royal and Imperial Collections of Europe and is an important supplement to the national collections of arms and armour housed in the Tower of London.

Passing the turnstile, we go through the door at the right to—

Room I–II.—English portraits and French furniture, pictures and Sèvres porcelain of the eighteenth century, notably two great chandeliers signed by J. Caffieri.

Room III.—Italian sculpture, bronzes and majolica, French Renaissance furniture, illuminations, and miscellaneous goldsmith's work.

Room IV.—French paintings and sculpture of the seventeenth century. In the centre are ivories, medals, goldsmiths' work and wax miniatures, mostly of sixteenth and seventeenth centuries.

Room V.—European Arms and Armour. In the centre, the equestrian suit made at Nuremberg for Otto Heinrich, Count Palatine of the Rhine in 1532–6. An outstanding collection of firearms, cross-bows and swords mainly of seventeenth and eighteenth centuries is exhibited in the wall cases.

Room VI.—In the centre the complete war harness for horse and man made about 1475–85 for the von Freyberg family,

Schloss Hohenaschau (Upper Bavaria). In the wall cases are important pieces mainly of the eighteenth century.

Room VII is also devoted to European armour, fifteenth and sixteenth centuries.

Room VIII.—Oriental arms and armour.

Founders' Room.—Portraits and other works of art connected with the founders of the Collection and its benefactors.

Room IX.—French furniture of the eighteenth century and paintings by *Canaletto* and his followers. In the centre, a case of porcelain and rock crystal.

Room X.—French furniture; Italian paintings and sculpture of the Renaissance period. In the corridor water colours by *Bonington.*

Room XI.—The collection of miniatures is displayed in cases in the centre of the room which is hung with French nineteenth century pictures relating to the Napoleonic regime.

We now return to the Entrance Hall and ascend to the first floor by the Grand Staircase. This is of marble and decorated with a balustrade of wrought iron and gilt bronze made for Louis XV's *Cabinet des Medailles* (now part of the Bibliothèque Nationale) in Paris. The walls, landing and conservatory above are decorated with Boulle furniture, French bronzes and outstanding paintings by *François Boucher.*

At the top of the staircase, to the left, is the entrance to—

Room XII, hung with works by *Guardi* and *Canaletto.* In the centre are outstanding pieces of Sèvres porcelain. Against the wall to the left is a large Boulle cabinet of the Louis XVI period.

Room XIII.—Dutch portraits and landscapes.

Room XIV.—Dutch genre subjects.

Room XV is completely hung with pictures by Dutch seventeenth-century landscape painters including *Hobbema, Cuyp* and *Willem van der Velde.*

Room XVI is hung with many of the most celebrated pictures.

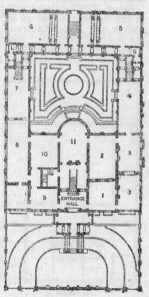

WALLACE COLLECTION: THE
GROUND FLOOR.

The portraits are particularly worthy of note and include.

"Mrs. Robinson" (Perdita) by *Gainsborough* and *Romney*; "Nelly O'Brien" and "Mrs. Carnac," by *Reynolds*; "Philippe le Roy rnd his Wife," by *Van Dyck*; "The Laughing Cavalier," by *Franz Hals*; *Rembrandt's* portrait of his son, "Titus" and his two portraits of "Jean Pellicorne" and his wife and children; "The Lady with a Fan" and "Don Balthasar Carlos on Horseback," by *Velazquez* and "Isabella Brandt," by *Rubens*. Other pictures include "Perseus and Andromeda," by *Titian*, the most important Italian picture in the collection painted in 1554 for Philip II of Spain; "The Annunciation," by *Philippe de Champagne*; "The Rainbow Landscape," by *Rubens*; "The Halt During the Chase" and "A Fête in a Park," by *Watteau*; "A Dance to the Music of Time," by *Poussin* and other outstanding works by *Rubens, Van Dyck, Claude, Jan Steen, Pieter de Hooch, Hobbema, Reynolds* and *Gainsborough*.

Room XVII.—French paintings of the nineteenth century, including works by *Prudhon, Delacroix, Gericault* and others.

Room XVIII.—Outstanding French paintings and furniture of the eighteenth century by *Watteau, Lancret, Pater, Boucher, Nattier* and *Vigée Le Brun*. Paintings by *Fragonard* include the famous "Swing," "The Souvenir" and "The Fountain of Love." In the centre of the room are two cases containing the collection of snuff boxes. Notable amongst the furniture is Marie Antoinette's *sécrétaire* from the Petit Trianon by *Riesener*.

Room XIX.—French furniture and paintings of the eighteenth century including portrait of "Madame de Pompadour," by *Boucher*, and a series of panels painted for her Paris *hôtel* by the same artist.

Room XX.—Contains more French furniture and an important collection of oil paintings by *Bonington*. Over the chimney-piece is "Portrait of Mrs. Robinson" (*Perdita*) by *Reynolds*.

In the corridor between Rooms XX and XXI are more water colours by *Bonington*, and a case containing Sèvres porcelain from the service made for the Empress Catherine II of Russia.

Room XXI.—French furniture with Boule marquetry, notable clocks, paintings and porcelain.

Room XXII.—French furniture and paintings by *Pater Greuze* and *de Troy*.

WALLACE COLLECTION: THE
FIRST FLOOR

Facing Spanish Place, a few yards north of the Wallace Collection, is **St. James's Roman Catholic Church,** built in 1890 to replace the old Spanish Embassy Chapel.

In Portman Square is Home House, generously presented by Mr. Samuel Courtauld to the trustees of the **Courtauld Institute of Art,** to serve as a temporary headquarters pending the construction of the Institute which is to form part of the new London University Building (*see* p. 159).

West of Hertford House is **Baker Street,** a busy thoroughfare connecting Oxford Street with the Marylebone Road and Regent's Park, and containing the studios of some of the leading photographers. On the west side is a car park. The site was formerly occupied by the **Portman Rooms,** a resort of Beau Brummell and other famous men of his period, and much used for dances, etc.

No. 31, Baker Street (tablet) was the birthplace of Lord Lytton, the novelist. No. 12, Seymour Street (tablet) was the residence (1861-4) of M. W. Balfe, the composer. No. 14, York Place (tablet) was the residence of William Pitt and Lady Hester Stanhope, 1803 and 1804.

Baker Street Station (Plan I. G. 6), as well as being an important station on the Underground Railway, is the starting-point of the Metropolitan Railway line to Wembley Park, Harrow, etc. (*see* p. 60). Note the fine premises and tower of the *Abbey National Building Society.*

The **Marylebone Road** (Plan I. G. and H. 6), with its continuation **Euston Road** (Plan I. I. and K. 5 and 6), runs from Edgware Road to King's Cross. Formerly a thoroughfare of little attractiveness, it has been widened and now contains some fine buildings. It is important, too, because here are no fewer than four of the principal railway termini. A quarter of a mile to the west of Baker Street is **Marylebone Station,** the terminus of the Great Central Section of the Eastern Region of British Railways. Almost facing the station entry is the **Marylebone Town Hall,** a classical building, of Portland stone. Marylebone (Maryle-bourne) derives its name from the old Tyburn stream, which flowed from Kilburn to the Thames. A small obelisk in the churchyard of **Marylebone Parish Church,** a short distance east of Baker Street, marks the grave of *Charles Wesley* (1788). Almost opposite is **Madame Tussaud's,** the famous waxwork exhibition. At York Gate is the **Royal Academy of Music,** granting the coveted degrees of A.R.A.M. and L.R.A.M. The Academy was founded in 1822 and incorporated by Royal Charter in 1830.

Upper Baker Street leads directly to the Clarence Gate of—

Regent's Park

Plan I. G. and H. 4, 5, and 6.
Nearest Stations.—Baker Street and Great Portland Street (Metropolitan); Baker Street, Regent's Park and St. John's Wood (Bakerloo Line); Chalk Farm or Camden Town on the Northern Line.

This is one of the largest of the London parks, having, with Primrose Hill to the north, an area of 473 acres. It was laid out by Nash for the Prince Regent, after whom it is named, in accordance with the same royal plan which led to the construction of Regent Street (*see* p. 142). Around the Park runs a pretty road, two miles in circuit, known as the **Outer Circle**. The much smaller **Inner Circle** encloses the gardens formerly maintained by the Royal Botanic Society, but now open to the public and known as **Queen Mary's Gardens**. A very successful modern innovation is the **Open-Air Theatre**. On the western side of the Park is a large, many-armed **Lake**, with islands and bridges. Between this and Queen Mary's Gardens is **Bedford College**, affiliated to London University, the most important college for women in London. *St. John's Lodge* is now occupied by the *Institute of Archæology*. An attractive feature of the Park is the **Broad Walk**, from near the Marylebone Road entrance to the Zoological Gardens. Its flower-beds present at nearly all seasons a display of great beauty, and the chestnut avenue in spring rivals the more famous avenue in Bushy Park.

Winfield, the modern house on the western side of the Park, has replaced St. Dunstan's Lodge, which gave its name to the famous **St. Dunstan's** institution for men blinded in the Great War and which is in part carried on in buildings near the Inner Circle.

The Zoological Gardens

Admission.—The Gardens are open daily from 9 a.m. until sunset or 7 p.m. when sunset is later. From November 1st to February 28th the opening time is 10 a.m. Admission, 2s. 6d. except on Mondays (other than Bank Holidays), when only 1s. 6d. is charged. Children, 1s. and 6d. Admission to Aquarium, 1s. Adults, 6d. Children: Mondays 6d. (adults and children), except Bank Holidays, Admission on Sundays: all day by ticket or by payment from 2.30 p.m.
Bath Chairs and Push Chairs can be obtained at the Kiosk near the Zoo Shop.
Entrances.—The *Main Entrance* is in the Outer Circle of Regent's Park. The *North Entrance* is in Albert Road, on the northern side of the Regent's Canal. The *South Entrance* is near the head of the Broad Walk.
Car Park opposite main entrance (Plan I. H. 5).
Nearest Stations.—Camden Town (Northern Line) is the nearest station, thence 74 bus to the North Gate Entrance. Great Portland Street (Metropolitan Line) and Regent's Park (Bakerloo Line) stations are about a mile from the South Gate Entrance, buses 3 and 53 running from these stations to Gloucester Gate, which is within 5 minutes' walk of the Zoo. Bus service No. 74 connects Baker Street Station with the North Gate Entrance.

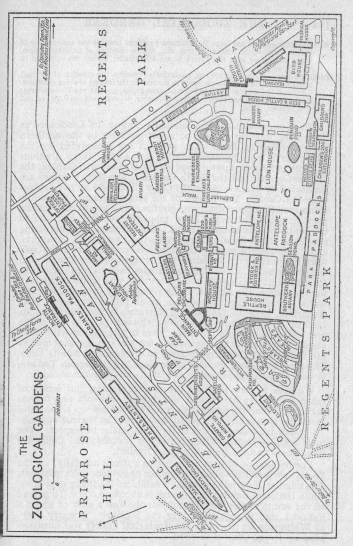

THE
ZOOLOGICAL GARDENS

PRIMROSE HILL

REGENTS PARK

REGENTS PARK

Refreshments.—There are large Refreshment Pavilions towards the eastern side of the Gardens, where luncheons, teas, etc., can be obtained at moderate prices. There is another near the Parrot House and smaller buffets are scattered in various parts.

Feeding Times.—With many visitors, particularly juveniles, the question of personal refreshment is here for once eclipsed in interest by the feeding of other creatures. The usual times are as follows: Pelicans, 2.30; eagles, 3.30 (except Wednesdays); lions, tigers and other beasts of prey, 3 (winter, 2); seals and sea-lions, 12 and 3.30 (winter, 2.30).

The Zoological Gardens, familiarly known to Londoners as "the Zoo," occupy an area of about 34 acres in the northern part of Regent's Park. The grounds are intersected by the Outer Circle and by the Grand Union Canal, three divisions being thus formed, known respectively as the North Garden, the Middle Garden, and the South Garden. The three portions are connected by tunnels under the Outer Circle and by two bridges over the Canal. The houses of the larger animals: elephants, rhinoceroses, hippopotamuses, giraffes, etc., are in the middle portion; while the bears, lions, monkeys, reptiles, etc., are in the southern part of the Gardens. The northern strip bordering the Grand Union Canal accommodates the cranes, owls, pheasants, etc. The western part of this section is connected by a footway (forming part of the Primrose Hill bridge over the Canal) with the giraffe house. The **Mappin Terraces** have tiers of enclosures for the animals, rising one above the other, with walks in between for the public, the animals being retained by deep ditches and walls, without the aid of the usual prison-like bars. The **Aquarium**, beneath the Mappin Terraces, is the largest of its kind in the world, and its 3,000 inhabitants provide one of the greatest attractions of the Zoo. Here in large tanks with thick glass inspection fronts, may be seen fish and specimens of marine life that are of absorbing interest to children and adults alike. The Reptile House, situated quite close to the Mappin Terrace, is very well-equipped, and is one of the finest in the world.

We give a plan showing the various houses, but limits of space forbid any attempt at description. Parents and friends taking children are advised to coach themselves up beforehand as to the habits and degrees of ferocity of the various animals. To betray ignorance here is to forfeit all claim to respect. The most popular section with juveniles is probably the **Children's Zoo**, where various animals may be fondled.

The number of visitors exceeds two millions annually, for the Zoo is now London's almost sole place of outdoor entertainment. The number of vertebrate animals exhibited is usually over 3,000 while the total number of inmates is about 10,000. To attend to the wants of the varied family at the Zoo a staff of about a hundred men is required. (For the Society's "country Zoo" at **Whipsnade** see p. 275.) The **Zoological Society** was incorporated by Royal Charter in 1829.

Close to the South Entrance to the Zoo is the interesting

Royal Chapel of St. Katherine (rebuilt), containing some splendid wood-work. From Stephen's reign the Queens of England have been patrons of St. Katherine's, which forms part of the dowry of a Queen Consort.

To the north of Regent's Park rises the grassy slope of **Primrose Hill** (*see* p. 37). Close to the north-west confines of the Park, and reached by the St. John's Wood Road, is **Lord's Cricket Ground** (Plan I. F. 5), the headquarters of English cricket. The ground took its name from an early owner; it is now the property of the Marylebone Cricket Club—the M.C.C. The gateway forms a memorial of *W. G. Grace*. Here are played in June and July the Eton and Harrow, Oxford and Cambridge, and other great matches.

St. John's Wood Road slopes down to the **Edgware Road,** a great trunk road—part of the old Watling Street—running in a north-westerly direction from the Marble Arch to Kilburn and Cricklewood, thence on to Hendon and St. Albans, and eventually through the Midlands to Holyhead. **Edgware Road Station** (Metropolitan and District Lines; Plan I. F. 7) may be entered either from Chapel Street or the Marylebone Road (p. 151). A few yards to the north is the Bakerloo Tube station.

Another important thoroughfare in this direction is the **Harrow Road,** which branches off from the Edgware Road beyond Chapel Street, and leads north-westward through Paddington to Willesden, and thence on to Harrow, passing **Wembley Stadium,** erected in connection with the British Empire Exhibition and now used for Greyhound and Speedway racing, Football matches and similar important sporting events. The Stadium is most directly reached by rail from Baker Street or Marylebone stations. Adjoining it is the **Empire Swimming Pool** (skating and ice hockey in winter) and Sports Centre. **Kensal Green Cemetery** (Plan I. A. and B. 5), about 2 miles from Edgware Road, covers about 70 acres, and contains over 40,000 graves. Among the host of notabilities here interred may be mentioned Leigh Hunt, Thackeray, Tom Hood, Anthony Trollope, John Leech, and the Duke of Cambridge.

Turning southward along the Edgware Road, in the direction of the Marble Arch, we have on the right **Praed Street,** leading to **Paddington Station** (Plan I. F. 7), terminus of the Western Region line, connected with the Bakerloo Tube and with the Paddington (Praed Street) and Paddington stations of the Metropolitan Line. Close at hand is the large **St. Mary's Hospital.** Set into the wall of *Lloyds Bank*, 195, Edgware Road, at the corner of Star Street, is an old stone marking "half a mile from Tyburn Gate" (see over).

At the **Marble Arch** (p. 137), the Edgware Road joins Oxford Street, which here changes its name to the **Bayswater Road,** forming the northern boundary of Hyde Park and Kensington Gardens. At the intersection of the roadways stood the famous, or infamous, **Tyburn** gallows, the scene of countless executions.

The exact site is indicated by a tablet on Hyde Park railings. The first recorded execution was that of William FitzOsbert, or "longbeard" (1196). Here also, to name only a few, William Wallace, the Scottish patriot (1305); Perkin Warbeck, the pretender (1499); Elizabeth Barton, the "Holy Maid of Kent" (1534); the notorious highwayman, Jack Sheppard (1724), were done to death. Two notable Roman Catholic martyrs were Dr. John Story (1571) and Oliver Plunket, Archbishop of Armagh (1681). A movable gallows was about 1760 substituted for the old fixed structure. After 1783 all executions took place at Newgate.

Near Marble Arch are the *Odeon* and *Marble Arch Pavilion Cinemas, Maison Lyons Restaurant* and the *Cumberland Hotel.*

Westward the busy roadway is overlooked by the stuccoed frontages of Hyde Park Gardens and Lancaster Gate. At No. 10 Hyde Park Place is the **Smallest House in London.** A short distance from the Marble Arch is the secluded old *St. John's Burial Ground.* The tombstones and monuments have been removed and ranged round the walls, which latter, by the way, were long patrolled at night by "Charlies" (watchmen) on account of the depredations of "body snatchers." At the entrance to the burial-ground is the *Chapel of the Ascension,* founded by the late Mrs. Russell Gurney, not for services, but expressly for "rest, meditation and prayer." The building, considerably damaged by bombs, and not at the moment in use, was elaborately decorated with Scriptural paintings by Frederic Shields (d. 1911).

The cathedral-like fane of **Christ Church, Lancaster Gate,** is opposite the gate of the same name. A notable feature of **Queensway** (more familiar under its former name—Queen's Road) is *Whiteley's* great store (now owned by Selfridge's).

By continuing westward along the Bayswater Road, or taking Central Line from Lancaster Gate or Queensway stations, we reach **Shepherd's Bush** (Plan II. A. 8), by no means so rural as its name suggests. It is the site of the "White City," erected for the Franco-British Exhibition of 1908. The Stadium, in Wood Lane, is used for athletic meetings, greyhound racing, etc.

From the **Marble Arch** buses go along the western part of **Oxford Street** to Regent Street, passing *Selfridge's* (on the left) and several other well-known establishments of the kind (*see* p. 157).

In Duke Street is the **King's Weigh House Chapel,** built to replace the famous chapel of that name in the City.

OXFORD STREET AND HOLBORN

ROUTE VI.—OXFORD STREET—SOHO—TOTTENHAM COURT ROAD—UNIVERSITY OF LONDON—BLOOMSBURY—THE BRITISH MUSEUM—HOLBORN.

WE will assume this time that the start is made from **Oxford Circus** (*see* p. 143), at the junction of Oxford Street with Regent Street.

Oxford Street

Plan I. H. and I. 7.

Stations, commencing at west end, Marble Arch, Bond Street, Oxford Circus, Tottenham Court Road and Holborn (Kingsway). All these are on the Central Line which runs below Oxford Street throughout its length. At Oxford Circus connection is made with the Bakerloo Line, at Tottenham Court Road with the Northern Line, and at Holborn with the Piccadilly Line.

Buses.—A constant stream of buses from all parts of London passes through Oxford Street.

This has always been the principal traffic artery between the west and north-west of London and the City. Beneath it runs the Central Line Railway. Although Oxford Street proper, from the Marble Arch to Tottenham Court Road, is only a mile long, it forms part of a great highway extending from the Bank to Shepherd's Bush, and thence *via* Acton and Ealing to Uxbridge and so to Oxford. In Oxford Street are some of the best-known shops in London, including *Peter Robinson's*, *John Lewis's*, *Marshall and Snelgrove's*, *Bourne and Hollingsworth's*, *D. H. Evans's*, *Waring and Gillow's*, *Selfridge's*, and many others. Some idea of the value of sites here may be gathered from the statement that £40 a square foot is a not unusual price. Considerable war damage and the setting up of numerous small businesses has transformed the appearance of Oxford Street, but it is nevertheless a favourite shopping quarter.

Eastward from Oxford Circus is **Wardour Street,** once noted for its old furniture and curiosity shops, but now the headquarters of the cinema trade. It lies near the heart of the **Soho** quarter, almost entirely occupied by foreigners of various nationalities, and famous for its restaurants. It is also becoming noted for the number of its motor garages. In recent years the foreign quarter seems to have overflowed to the other side of Oxford Street, about Charlotte Street. At the north-west angle of **Soho Square** is the **French Protestant Church ;** on the east side is the Roman Catholic **Church of St. Patrick.** The Duke of

Monmouth's house—it will be recalled that "Soho" was his battle-cry at Sedgemoor—stood on the site of the present Hospital for Women.

At No. 51, **Frith Street,** south of the Square, Mozart lived as a boy. Hazlitt died at No. 6 in 1830. In **Dean Street,** to the west, are the ruins of **St. Anne's Church,** notable as the burial-place of William Hazlitt (d. 1830), and of the unfortunate Theodore, King of Corsica, who died at Soho in 1756, as tablets on the west wall of the tower record.

Close to the junction of Oxford Street with Tottenham Court Road are the *Frascati Restaurant* and the *Oxford Corner House,* one of Lyons's great restaurants. At the opposite corner is the **Dominion Theatre,** used principally as a cinema.

Tottenham Court Road (Plan I. I. and K. 6 and 7), with a number of important furnishing establishments—such as *Maple's* and *Heal's*—runs northward for rather more than half a mile to the Euston Road, and is thence continued as the Hampstead Road, leading, *via* Camden Town, to Hampstead Heath. At the corner of Great Russell Street is the **Central Young Men's Christian Association,** with halls for meetings, restaurants, a splendidly equipped gymnasium, swimming baths, social rooms, a boys' department, and bedrooms with 240 beds for young men. Many classes are held for business training, and in various ways the Association renders excellent service to the young men of London. In 1929 Queen Mary laid the foundation stone of the neighbouring **Y.W.C.A. Central Club** for London's business girls. The building was designed by Sir Edwin Lutyens. About half-way down Tottenham Court Road is the **Whitefield Tabernacle,** an important "institutional" church of the Congregational body.

Any street to the right will lead into **Gower Street,** where are many hostels and boarding-houses for the students and business people of the district. A memorial on the wall of University College reminds us that near the spot Richard Trevithick ran in 1808 the first steam locomotive to draw passengers. (The actual spot was in Euston Grove.) At the far end is the fine building which houses the **School of Hygiene and Tropical Medicines,** and a few paces further up on the right is the **Royal Academy of Dramatic Art.** The theatre attached to the academy was badly damaged by bombs, but repairs are in hand. It faces on to Malet Street.

University College, near the north end of Gower Street, is incorporated in the University of London and has accommodation for upwards of three thousand students. Attached to it are important scientific laboratories. The cost of the **Institute of Anatomy** was defrayed out of a munificent gift from the Rockefeller Foundation.

The University of London

Founded in 1836 as an examining and degree-conferring body, it became a teaching University in 1900, and consists of 10 specialised institutes and 35 "schools." Students attending the Institutions can obtain internal degrees, and provision is made at Birkbeck and one or two other Colleges for students only able to attend evening classes. In addition, certain institutions, not controlled by the University, may accept internal students for courses under Recognised Teachers. In the 1949–50 session there were more than 22,000 internal students; and over 28,000 students studying for external degrees, which may be taken without attendance at a University Institution. The Extra-Mural Department of the University organises extension lectures and tutorial classes. The University is mainly non-residential, but it is planned to extend residential accommodation as soon as possible; some of the Colleges have hostels and the University itself has three hostels, *Nutford House, Canterbury Hall,* and *Connaught Hall,* the last two being in the Bloomsbury area.

In 1927, with the assistance of a magnificent gift from the Rockefeller Foundation, a site of about eleven and a half acres was acquired, stretching from the north front of the British Museum to Gordon Square and from Malet Street on the west to Russell and Woburn Squares on the east, for the erection of a home worthy of the University. On June 26, 1933, the foundation stone was laid by King George V. The buildings now complete and in occupation, include the **Senate House,** which houses the Administrative Staff of the University and serves as the ceremonial headquarters; the **Tower,** 210 feet high, which houses the bookstack of the **University Library,** containing over 500,000 volumes; and the **Institute of Education, Institute of Historical Research** and **School of Slavonic and East European Studies** to the north of the Tower. Beyond this main block, are the **School of Oriental and African Studies** and **Birkbeck College.** Other buildings to be included on the site are the **University Hall,** which will be used for the principal academic functions; the **Students' Union** (at present temporarily housed in Woburn Square); and other specialised institutes. Torrington Square itself will be retained as a University garden, round which these buildings will be erected. When finished, the scheme will represent one of the finest examples of planned development that any city can show. Other buildings in the neighbourhood house a number of University institutions, including the **Institute of Advanced Legal Studies,** the **Institute of Commonwealth Studies,** and the **Institute of Germanic Languages and Literatures,** all in Russell Square.

Adjoining Chaucer House (the headquarters of the Library Association) in Malet Place, is the **National Central Library.**

Facing University College in Gower Street is **University College Hospital,** rebuilt in the form of a diagonal cross, at the cost of the late Sir J. Blundell Maple. At the junction of Gower Street with the Euston Road is **Euston Square Station** (Plan I. I. 6), on the Underground. **Euston Station** (Plan I. I. 5; *see* p. 58), a terminus of the London Midland Region of British Railways, is a short distance eastward. Across the road are the **Friends' House** and the **Wellcome Research Institute.** Close at hand, in **Gordon Square** (Plan I. K. 6), is **Dr. Williams's Library,** containing about 40,000 volumes, chiefly theological and historical, which may be borrowed freely by ticket-holders. Adjoining is the **Catholic Apostolic Church,** of cathedral-like proportions. On the east side of Woburn Square is **Christ Church,** with a reredos in memory of Christina Rossetti, the poetess (d. 1894).

We are now in the well-known quarter of—

Bloomsbury

more favoured by visitors than any other part of London. Many houses provide "apartments," and there are a large number of hotels and boarding houses, though many of these are giving place to huge blocks of residential flats. The popularity of the district is accounted for partly by the fact that it is within easy reach of the City and West End and of the great railway termini; and partly by the attractiveness of the numerous **Squares,** each with its lovely lawns, flower-beds and luxuriant trees.

The largest, **Russell Square,** has figured in several well-known novels, notably *Vanity Fair.* The east side of the Square is occupied by the *Russell* and *Imperial Hotels*; elsewhere are the headquarters of a number of well-known societies. In Queen Square, with entrance from Guilford Street, is the **Royal Institute of Public Health**; farther down Guilford Street are the new buildings of the **Royal Children's Hospital.** London House, Guilford Street, is a hall of residence for British men students from all over the Empire.

In Tavistock Square, north of Russell Square, are the headquarters of the **British Medical Association.** Note the beautiful memorial gates in the courtyard. Across the road, at Woburn House, is the **Jews' College**; the *Library and Museum* on the first floor are open Mondays to Thursdays, 2–5; Fridays and Sundays 10–2; closed Saturdays and Jewish holidays. Also in Tavistock Square is the Ministry of Labour's **Appointment Bureau.** Close at hand are the headquarters of the **National Free Church Council.**

[Central Press

The mecca of all Londoners and visitors alike, Regent Street is the finest shopping thoroughfare in the world.

[Central Press

Oxford Street is another famous shopping street and is lined with many of the best-known emporiums in London.

London (f).

The British Museum contains priceless treasures and antiquities from all parts of the world. Here, are the Elgin Marbles from the Parthenon at Athens. The famous Reading Room can accommodate some 500 readers.

Southampton Row (Plan I. K. 7), leading from Russell Square to Kingsway, is one of the most important arteries between North and South London. Here are the *Bedford*, the *Imperial* (with Turkish Baths), and a number of other hotels, much resorted to by provincial visitors. At the junction of Southampton Row with Theobald's Road the tramway emerges from below Kingsway (*see* p. 189). Here are the imposing offices of the *Liverpool Victoria Friendly Society*. The **Central School of Arts and Crafts** is under the London County Council. Nearby is the **Baptist Church House**, with a statue of John Bunyan at the corner. Between Southampton Row and Bedford Row is **Red Lion Square**, the east end of which received heavy damage during the war. Its pleasant open garden is a popular meeting place for office workers in the lunch-hour.

On the other side of Southampton Row **Great Russell Street** leads past **Bloomsbury Square**, in which is the **College of Preceptors**. No. 6, Bloomsbury Square (tablet), was the residence of Isaac D'Israeli; and No. 31 that of Sir Anthony Panizzi, the famous chief librarian of the British Museum.

The British Museum

Plan I. K. 7.

Admission.—The Museum is open free on week-days from 10 a.m. to 5 p.m. and on Sundays from 2.30 to 6 p.m.
It is closed on Christmas Day and Good Friday.

The Reading-Room (*see* p. 162) is only available to ticket-holders, but visitors may obtain permission to go as far as the doorway and see the room, on application to the officials at the Entrance Hall. It is open daily from 9 a.m. to 5 p.m. except during the week beginning with the first Monday of May.

Catalogues, Handbooks, Pictorial Postcards, other Reproductions and Photographs are on sale at the Entrances. The general Guide, with plans, is quite sufficient for the ordinary visitor. Handbooks to Sculptures, Coins, Antiquities and other departments, can be bought. Some of these are excellent and double the interest of a visit. Casts of sculptures, etc., can be obtained.

Guide-Lectures.—These are not at present available.

Nearest Stations.—Holborn (Central and Piccadilly Lines), Tottenham Court Road (Central and Northern Lines), Euston Square (Metropolitan), Euston (London Midland Region), Russell Square (Piccadilly Line), Goodge Street (Northern Line).

Buses.—All buses running along New Oxford Street, Tottenham Court Road or Southampton Row pass within a few yards of the Museum. Alight at Museum Street or Great Russell Street.

Trams.—From North and South London to Southampton Row.

The Museum originated in 1753 with the purchase of the library and collection of Sir Hans Sloane and of the Harleian manuscripts, a public lottery having been set on foot for the purpose of raising the necessary funds. Added to by the Cottonian collection of manuscripts, which had long been public property, the Museum, the Harleian MSS. and the Royal Library, arranged in Montague House, was opened to the public in 1759. Many libraries and collections of natural objects, coins and antiquities were added—especially the magnificent library collected by George III (1823), and the renowned Elgin Marbles (1816)—and the Museum became one of the most extensive and valuable in Europe.   A new building being imperatively required, the erection was entrusted to the brothers Smirke, with the result that, between the years 1823 and 1847, Montague House disappeared, and the present structure took its place.   The great Reading Room was built in 1857; the White Wing, on the east, in 1884.   A further extension, the King Edward the Seventh Galleries, on the north, was opened in 1914; and Lord Duveen presented a new gallery to house the marbles from the Parthenon.

Some considerable damage was suffered by the Museum during the war, though, fortunately, such damage was confined to the actual buildings.   Many of the priceless treasures and antiquities were evacuated to various parts of the country or, where possible, stored in the basements of the Museum.   As and when repairs are executed rooms and galleries are being re-opened.

One enters the Museum from Great Russell Street and crosses the courtyard to the Ionic portico.   The figures on the pediment are by *Westmacott*, and represent the progress of the human race and the development of Art, Science, etc.   The entire front is 370 ft. in length, and has an Ionic colonnade of 44 columns.

In the Main Entrance Hall alert officials guard a doorway inscribed "Ticket-Holders only."   This leads to the famous **Reading Room,** a huge circular hall, accommodating between 450 and 500 readers, who sit at desks radiating like the spokes of a wheel from two concentric circles, in the inner of which sit the officials, while the printed *Catalogue,* mounted in about 1,400 sheaf-volumes, is ranged round the outer circle and overflows into the inner.   The dome is 106 ft. high, and has a diameter of 140 ft., only 2 ft. less than the dome of the Pantheon, Rome. About 25,000 of the volumes most in request, such as dictionaries, encyclopædias, bibliographies, etc., are ranged round the Room itself and may be consulted without filling up a form.   For other works it is necessary to look under the names of authors in the Catalogue.   When the name of an author is not known, the excellent *Subject Index* will frequently give the needful clues for books acquired subsequently to 1880.   A copy of every book published in the United Kingdom has to be sent here.   There is a Newspaper Repository at Colindale, near Hendon, to which are sent all newspapers and periodicals published.   Thackeray's opinion has probably been echoed by many a literary worker :

"It seems to me one cannot sit down in that place without a heart full of grateful reverence.   I own to have said my grace at the table, and to have thanked Heaven for this my English birthright, freely to partake of these bountiful books, and to speak the truth I find there."

Persons desirous of becoming "Readers" must apply to the Director,
specifying the purpose for which they wish to use the Room, which is
confined to research not possible elsewhere, and enclosing a recommenda-
tion from a person of recognised position. Tickets are renewable every
twelve months, and are not granted to persons reading for examinations
or competitions, or under 21 years of age.

Also to be noted in the Entrance Hall are the colossal Buddha,
Chinese of the fifth century, and the famous Amaravati Sculpture
from S. India.

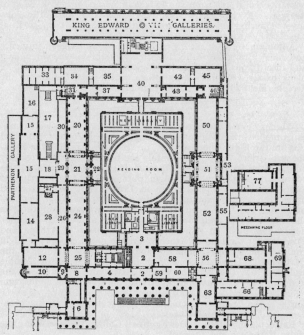

BRITISH MUSEUM: GROUND FLOOR

It would require months to become acquainted with this vast national
storehouse, and we can do little more than give clues of the best
to be seen in a brief visit. Various publications are sold in the entrance
in Montague Place, each being a veritable mine of information.

From the main doorway of the Museum we turn left into—
The Sculpture Galleries. The first is (4) the **Roman Gallery,**

with a number of inscribed stones found in England, and portrait busts of Augustus, Nero, and other worthies and unworthies familiar to us by name from childhood. In (8), the **Græco-Roman Room** beyond, are Roman copies and imitations of Greek sculpture. In the small ante-room (9) may be seen the famous *Demeter of Cnidus* and in the room beyond (10) sculptures from the *Mausoleum,* one of the Seven Wonders of the Ancient World. The **Assyrian Saloon** (28), contains slabs and figures discovered by Sir A. Layard, and the **Nimrud Gallery** contains sculptures from the Palace of Assur-Nasir-Pal, King of Assyria. In the centre is a case containing antiquities discovered during an expedition to Nimrud (Kalhu) 1949–50 from the British Archæological School in Iraq.

Adjoining these is the Egyptian Gallery housing an immense and most interesting collection of Egyptian statues, sarcophagi and inscriptions, including the famous Rosetta Stone, a slab of black basalt with three inscriptions, which gave the key to the decipherment of the Egyptian hieroglyphics.

The Elgin Marbles

We next enter the ante-room of the **Elgin Rooms,** which contains models, diagrams and drawings of the Acropolis. Beyond this are the Elgin Rooms proper, in which are arranged the Panathenaic frieze and pedimental sculptures which originally adorned the Parthenon at Athens. These were brought to this country in 1801–3 by Lord Elgin, purchased by the Government and deposited in the Museum in 1816. They were executed under the supervision of Pheidias, the controller of Pericles' buildings, and have been regarded as the greatest sculptures in the world. The sculptures, from the east and west pediments, depict the Birth of Athena and The Contest of Athena and Poseidon for the land of Athens. At the north end of the Elgin Room is the **Metopes Room** housing 15 of the 92 metopes of the Parthenon. These all come from the south side of the Temple and illustrate the fight between Lapiths and Centaurs at the wedding feast of Peirithous, typifying the triumph of civilisation over barbarism, a popular subject with the Greeks. To the south, is the Ephesus Room containing sculpture from the great Temple of *Diana of the Ephesians.*

Retracing our steps to the Egyptian Gallery and ascending the stairs at the far end to the—

Upper Floor

We find on the left the apartments known as the **First to Fifth Egyptian Rooms.** Interest is chiefly excited here by the mummies, both of men and animals, of which there is a very large collection, dating from about 3600 B.C. to A.D. 500, inscriptions and paintings from ancient tombs and objects of daily life and art.

From the Egyptian Rooms we continue through to the **Babylonian Room,** containing the Museum's share of the discoveries at Ur and other Sumerian and Babylonian antiquities.

From the middle Egyptian room a bridge and short staircase

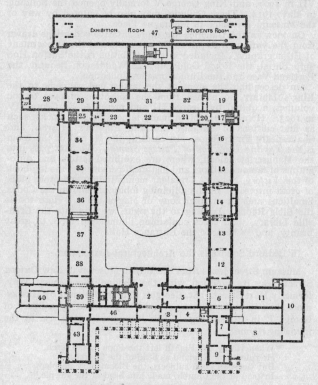

BRITISH MUSEUM: FIRST FLOOR

give access to the Exhibition Galleries of the **Department of Prints and Drawings and Oriental Antiquities.** The Students Room of the Department of Prints and Drawings is open to ticket holders only, Monday–Friday, 10–4; Saturday, 10–1. Note the busts of Sir Hans Sloane and Charles I at the entrance.

A staircase leads down to

The King Edward VII Galleries

The memorial stone of this extension was laid by King Edward VII in 1907, and King George V formally opened the building in May, 1914. These Galleries may also be entered by way of the Museum Entrance in Montague Place.

On view in the Galleries are representative collections drawn from the various Antiquities Departments and the Department of Ethnography. Included in the exhibition is the Sutton Hoo Ship Burial, the Royal Gold Cup, the Waddesdon Bequest, the Portland Vase and the Eumorfopoulos Collection.

On descending the steps at the farther end we come to the **King's Library,** so named from the collection of over 60,000 volumes, acquired by George III and presented by George IV in 1823. Here are exhibited many famous English books, such as first editions of *Paradise Lost* and *Pilgrim's Progress*, and Shakespeare First Folios. In cases at the N. end of the room is the *Tapling Collection of Postage Stamps*. We next pass into the **Manuscript Saloon,** where are exhibited letters and autographs of famous authors and historical personages, the log-book of the *Victory*, Nelson's Trafalgar memorandum and other MSS. of great interest. In the adjoining lobby are shown the Codex Sinaiticus and an original copy of Magna Carta. Here too is the **Bible Room.** Turning to the right, we pass into the **Grenville Library,** with cases containing illuminated MSS. of great beauty, and so back to the Entrance Hall.

In Bedford Square is the **Architectural Association.**

Museum Street leads from the British Museum to New Oxford Street near its junction with the oblique Bloomsbury Way, formerly Hart Street. **St. George's Church,** designed by Hawksmoor, has an extraordinary steeple, surmounted by a figure of George I, in Roman toga. This incongruity gave rise to the following rhyme:

> "When Harry the Eighth left the Pope in the lurch,
> He ruled over England as head of the Church;
> But George's good subjects, the Bloomsbury people,
> Instead of the Church, made him head of the steeple."

Further eastward, at the corner of High Holborn and New Oxford Street, is the **Holborn Town Hall,** with a public library adjoining. Eastward, beyond the *Holborn Restaurant* and Kingsway, are the **Holborn Empire** and the Holborn Stadium; neither at present in use.

Bloomsbury Way would bring us back to the southern end of **Southampton Row** (p. 161), from which electric trams, on emerging from the subway, run along an important line of thoroughfare which starts with the **Theobald's Road,** the north side of which was flattened by bombs early in the war (leaving a great open space leading up to Guilford Street), and is continued as Clerkenwell Road and Old Street to Shoreditch. Lord Beaconsfield was born at No. 22, Theobald's Road (tablet), in 1804.

Rosebery Avenue runs thence in a north-easterly direction to the *Angel* at Islington. At the top of **Guilford Street** long stood the **Foundling Hospital,** founded in 1739 by Thomas Coram, a retired sea captain, for "exposed and deserted children." The Hospital is now established at Berkhamsted, Hertfordshire. Appropriately, the Bloomsbury site is now a children's playground.

In Great Ormond Street are the **Royal Children's Hospital** and the **Homœopathic Hospital.**

The streets hereabouts have many interesting literary and artistic associations. At No. 32, Brunswick Square, lived John Leech, the caricaturist. Ruskin lived at 54, Hunter Street. At 13, Great Coram Street, Thackeray lived before going to Kensington. In 1925 the Dickens Fellowship acquired No. 48, Doughty Street (Plan I. L. 6) as the **Dickens House and Library** (*open week-days* [*Bank Holidays excepted*] 10–12.30, 2–5 p.m. *Admission*, 1s.). Here Dickens lived from 1837–9, writing the final portions of the *Pickwick Papers,* the whole of *Nicholas Nickleby* and *Oliver Twist,* and the commencement of *Barnaby Rudge.* The Museum contains a most interesting and valuable collection of Dickens relics and a very complete Dickens library. *Bleak House* and *Little Dorrit* were written while Dickens was living in Tavistock Square. The British Medical Association headquarters mark the site.

From Doughty Street, John Street leads us back to Theobald's Road, which we cross to **Bedford Row,** a short but wide road, tenanted almost entirely by solicitors. At the top turn left into—

Gray's Inn (Plan I. L. 7), one of the four great Inns of Court originally founded for the education and lodging of law students, to one or other of which all barristers are "admitted." Gray's Inn occupies an extensive area, from Holborn to Theobald's Road. Most of the offices line the western side of Gray's Inn Road and overlook the pleasant gardens, with their fine plane trees and well-kept lawns, laid out by Francis Bacon, who was admitted a member of the Inn in 1576, at the age of fifteen, and held the high office of Treasurer for nine years. The contorted catalpa trees near the centre are said to have been planted by him. In the Elizabethan **Hall,** destroyed during the war, but now rebuilt, Shakespeare's *Comedy of Errors* is believed to have been acted in 1594. The adjoining Chapel was destroyed with the Hall and **at** the same time the Library was badly gutted with the loss of many thousands of books. Against the South wall of the hall is a statue of Francis Bacon, by *F. W. Pomeroy, A.R.A.* It was originally erected to mark the tercentenary of his election as Treasurer (1608).

Gray's Inn Road is a dingy and unattractive thoroughfare running northward to King's Cross, passing the **Royal Free Hospital** and the **Eastman Dental Clinic**, a valuable institution due to the generosity of Mr. George Eastman of Rochester, New York, U.S.A.

Turning to the right on emerging from the Inn into the Gray's Inn Road we come, in a few yards, to where stone pillars—**Holborn Bars**—mark the City Boundary. A striking bronze statue, executed by *Albert Toft*, forms the **War Memorial of the London Fusiliers.**

Holborn

(Plan I. L. and M. 7)

the eastward continuation of New Oxford Street, takes its name from the *Old Bourne*, or burn, a tributary of the Fleet River, which formerly flowed through the hollow now spanned by the Viaduct. Here are some good shops, including *Gamage's*. The large red-brick block occupied by the *Prudential Assurance Company* marks the site of Furnival's Inn, where Dickens was living when he began the *Pickwick Papers*.

Chatterton, the boy poet, committed suicide in a garret in **Brooke Street,** immediately west of the Prudential offices. At the north end of this street is **St. Alban's Church**, formerly noted for its ritualistic services. It suffered considerable damage during the war and the services are now held in a chapel at the side of the church.

Opposite Gray's Inn Road are some of the **Oldest Houses in London,** dating from the Elizabethan period, though they have recently undergone a complete renovation. Their projecting timbered fronts form the street side of **Staple Inn.** An archway beneath gives access to the quaint little Inn. Though long an inn connected with the law, it owes its name to an earlier use, when it served as a kind of custom house, where wool was

[Will F. Taylor

Staple Inn, Holborn, where are some of the oldest houses in London. It owes its name to the time when as a kind of custom house, wool was weighed and dues collected here.

London (ʃ*).

The Brompton Oratory of St. Philip Neri is largely attended, even by non-catholics, on account of its musical services.

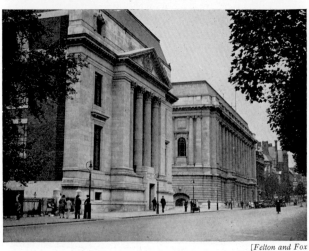

The Geological and Science Museums in Exhibition Road with exhibits of absorbing interest to young and old alike.

weighed and the dues upon it collected. No. 10 is of special interest, for it was here that "Mr. Grewgious" of *Edwin Drood* lived.

"Staple Inn," wrote Dickens, "is one of those nooks the turning into which from the dashing street imparts to the relieved pedestrian the sensation of having put cotton wool in his ears, and velvet soles on his boots." The old Hall, formerly occupied by the *Institute of Actuaries*, was destroyed by a flying bomb in 1944.

Farther east, close to Fetter Lane, stood Barnard's Inn. The site is occupied by the **Mercers' School,** the fourteenth-century hall of the inn being utilised as a dining-room. The school has a history extending over four centuries and a half. Dean Colet of St. Paul's, and Sir Thomas Gresham, founder of the Royal Exchange, were scholars.

Either of several bus routes or the tube, Central Line (from Chancery Lane Station, a short distance westward), will enable us to return, in a few minutes, to our starting-point at Oxford Circus.

THE SOUTH KENSINGTON MUSEUMS AND CHELSEA

ROUTE VII.—BROMPTON ROAD—THE ORATORY—VICTORIA AND ALBERT MUSEUM—SCIENCE MUSEUM—NATURAL HISTORY MUSEUM—IMPERIAL INSTITUTE AND LONDON UNIVERSITY—CHELSEA.

ONE more excursion will complete our sight-seeing in the West of London, and leave us free to devote some attention to the City and South London. This trip to South Kensington, or "Museum Land," must perforce be omitted by the hurried visitor, but no one with time to spare should fail to make himself acquainted with our great national collections.

From Charing Cross we may go by Underground to South Kensington Station, or from Piccadilly Circus by the Piccadilly Line to the same destination. The bus ride *via* Piccadilly, Knightsbridge and the Brompton Road is one of the most interesting and enjoyable in the Metropolis. **Piccadilly** has already been described (p. 130). At **Albert Gate** (p. 141) we turn in a south-westerly direction along the **Brompton Road,** passing on the left *Harrod's Stores*. In about half a mile from Albert Gate we reach—

The Church of the Oratory

Plan II. F. 10.
Admission free at all times when the Church is open, and to all the services. Open daily from 6 a.m. to 9.30 p.m. Sundays, 8.30 p.m. During the services, visitors are not allowed to walk about the Church for the purpose of seeing it.
Services.—Sundays: Masses at 6.30, 7, 7.30, 8, 8.30, 9 and 10 a.m.; High Mass 10.45; Low Mass and Sermon, 12; Vespers and Benediction, 3.30; Sermon and Benediction, 7 p.m.
Week-days; Mass, 6.30, 7, 7.30, 8, 8.30 and 10 a.m.; Benediction, Saturdays, 4.30 p.m.; Evening Service and Sermon, 8 p.m. (except Saturdays).
Nearest Station.—South Kensington (District and Piccadilly Lines).

Dedicated under the title of the Immaculate Heart of Mary, this church is commonly called the Oratory because it is served by the Fathers of the Oratory of St. Philip Neri. Built from the designs of H. Gribble in the style of the Italian Renaissance, it was opened by Cardinal Manning in 1884. The exceptionally wide nave has twelve statues of the Apostles which came from the cathedral at Siena. The Lady Altar, in the north transept, merits a detailed examination. Erected in Brescia in 1693, it was brought to this country in 1886. Over the altar of St.

Philip Neri, founder of the Oratory, is a copy of the picture of the Saint by Guido Reni. The high altar is well proportioned and liturgically correct. The fine organ was destroyed by fire in 1950, but its reconstruction was begun immediately. On the West side of the Oratory grounds, overlooking the Brompton Road, is the *Statue of Cardinal Newman* (1801–90), who, after his conversion to Catholicism (1845) introduced the Institute of the Oratory into England.

Beyond is the long façade of—

The Victoria and Albert Museum

Plan II. F. 10.

Admission.—Open free on week-days, except Good Friday and Christmas Day from 10 a.m. to 6 p.m. On Sundays from 2.30 to 6 p.m. The Library and Print Room are closed on Sundays.

Catalogues, etc.—Guides to collections at various prices. These, as well as photographs and pictorial postcards, are on sale at the bookstalls adjoining the Entrances. Plaster casts of various works of art, including objects in the Museum, can be obtained to order.

Frequent guide lectures are given.

Nearest Station.—South Kensington (District and Piccadilly Lines).

Buses.—Any bus passing along Brompton Road or Knightsbridge (by the latter alight at Brompton Oratory) will serve. Also Route 49.

The Victoria and Albert Museum is a Museum of Fine and Applied Art of all countries, styles and periods; it includes Architectural Details, Arms and Armour, the Art of the Book, Carpets, Costumes, Drawings, Embroideries, Engravings, Furniture, Glass, Gold and Silversmiths' Work, Ironwork, Ivories, Jewellery, Lace, Lithographs, Miniatures, Musical Instruments, Oil Paintings, Pottery and Porcelain, Tapestries and Woodwork. It is organised in eleven departments:—architecture and sculpture; ceramics; engraving, illustration and design; library; metalwork; paintings; textiles; woodwork; Indian section; circulation and museum extension services; and has a number of outstations.

The National Collection of Post-Classical Sculpture, of Watercolours and of Miniatures, the National Art Library and the National Lantern Slide Loan Collection are included in the Museum. The entire Museum covers an area of 12 acres, so that even the sightseer who devotes a whole day to the purpose can hardly hope to take more than a superficial glance at these vast collections. For parallel reasons we cannot possibly describe the contents of this treasure house in detail. The most we can do is to guide the visitor through the maze of courts and galleries, noting briefly the contents of each, so that he may at least form an idea of the collections and may also know where to find those sections in which he is particularly interested.

Before entering by the main portal in Cromwell Road, it is well to take a glance at the exterior of the fine building designed by *Sir Aston Webb*, *P.R.A.* It is in the Renaissance style, with domes and towers. The lofty central lantern has the outline of an Imperial Crown and is surmounted by a figure of Fame. The niches between the first-floor windows are occupied by figures of thirty-two famous British painters, craftsmen, sculptors and architects. Over the great archway are also various emblematic and royal statues.

The Museum is slowly recovering from the complete dislocation of the war years, and the galleries are steadily being re-arranged and opened to the public. They are being re-arranged into two distinct groups: **The Primary Collections,** exhibiting masterpieces of all the arts brought together by style, period or nationality, so arranged as to show the development of the arts through the ages; and **The Study Collections** arranged on the basis of the departments mentioned on page 171, but the objects are grouped together within the various classes of sculpture, ceramics, metalwork, paintings, textiles, woodwork, etc.

When all the galleries have been re-opened it will be possible to trace the development of the arts in Europe, from the late Classical and Early Christian periods, through early Medieval art, Italian and Northern Gothic and the Renaissance. European art will be divided into (*a*) English objects from about 1520 to mid-nineteenth century, and (*b*) Continental material from 1570 to early-nineteenth century. Far Eastern and Islamic Art will have special galleries.

For convenience it is best to look on the collections as divided into three main blocks—those in the South portion (nearest entrance in Cromwell Road), those in the West (Exhibition Road entrance) and the Central Galleries.

We outline below the routes to the principal galleries—

In the **South Portion** the visitor turns to the right from the main entrance, and descends the stairs to the Lower Ground Floor. In **Rooms 8–10** is the Museum's collection of oil paintings.

Ascending to the Upper Ground Floor we find English sculpture **(Room 64)**, European small sculpture **(63)** and a miscellaneous collection of Continental sculpture in **Rooms 50 and 64**, and the cast courts **(Room 46)**.

Rooms 121–126 illustrate the history of the decorative arts, particularly furniture, in England from 1750–1820. Art in the eighteenth century was marked by a love of lavish ornament; Chippendale was the most famous interpreter of this style and several pieces of furniture based on his designs will be found in these rooms.

The chimney piece, the pair of pedestals (W. 24 and A–1934) and the cabinet (W. 43–1949) from Robert Adam's designs illustrate the classical revival which began early in George III's reign.

Rooms 137-142 display the collections of the Department of Ceramics, covering all the " arts of fire," including pottery and porcelain, glass vessels, stained glass and enamel-painting.

It is now necessary to return, via the Main Staircase, to the Main Entrance Hall.

In the Central portion, the room immediately ahead of the Main Entrance is reserved for Recent Acquisitions.

Beyond this in Room 43 are exhibited examples of Early Medieval Art divided into three sections: Late Antique and Early Christian Art, Byzantine and Sassarian Art, and Western Early Medieval Art. Outstanding objects in each section are an ivory Diptych, "The Miracles of Christ," Early Christian; Byzantine bronze gilt triptych, "The Virgin and Child enthroned": and an Anglo-Saxon Reliquary Cross in walrus ivory on gold. Rooms 22-24 are devoted to Italian and Northern Gothic Art, note the early fourteenth-century English silk embroidery hanging between the pillars before entering Room 23. Note also the Pisano marbles in Room 22, the ivories in Room 23 and the silver-gilt Studley Bowl on the window side of Room 24. Examples of Spanish Gothic Art and Carpets are found in Room 25: the stairway from this room is lined with fifteenth, sixteenth and seventeenth century Spanish Carpets and leads to the Library. It is the National Art Library and is the largest of its kind in the world, containing 250,000 works on art and its allied subjects, and a large collection of photographs. The Library houses the Dyce and Forster Libraries; *students are admitted free to the library but regular readers must obtain a ticket.*

Room 38 is the Goth c Tapestry Court, the collection is particularly rich in Flemish weaving from the first years of the sixteenth century. The earliest tapestry on show, the "Story of Troy" is on the West Wall. Note the three splendid "Triumphs," displayed behind glass to give the effect of hanging naturally on a wall, yet protected from the atmosphere. The triumphs of Chastity over Love, Death over Chastity, Fame over Death, and Time over Fame was a popular subject for representation in the fifteenth and sixteenth centuries. An earlier style of tapestry than the "Triumphs" was the pictorial representation of the Miracle and Morality plays. The "Pity restraining justice from striking sinful man," comes from the second tapestry of the set depicting the "Deadly Sins." Four more pieces of this set are to be seen at Hampton Court.

The large tapestries are housed here whilst the several smaller ones will be found in the Gothic and Northern Gothic Rooms, including two early fifteenth-century Arras pieces and the famous gold and silver tapestry "Adoration of the Infant Saviour."

On the north and west sides of the quadrangle are Rooms 11-20 devoted to Italian Renaissance Art.

To left in Room 42 and adjoining corridor are examples of Islamic Art. Islam, religion founded by Muhammad after his flight from Mecca to Medina in A.D. 622 formed basis for civilisations in Asia, N. Africa and Spain, and samples of work done are shown here.

In Room 41 are some of the finest water-colours by British artists in the Museum, so arranged as to show a picture of the development of this art through two centuries. Among some of the finest are: *Paul Sandby's* "Windsor Castle," P. 7-1945: "The End of the Mall-Spring Gardens," by *Thomas Rowlandson*, P. 110-1931: all drawings by *John Robert Cosens*, including "View in the Island of Elba," 3042-1874: *Thomas Girtin's* "Kirkstall Abbey" 405-1885, and "Durham

Castle and Cathedral," P. 33–1928: *Turner's* "Hornby Castle, Lanca-shire," FA. 88, and later Turners, including "Lake of Brienz," 980–1900: "Chirk Aqueduct," by *John Sell Cotman* 115–1892, also his "Landscape with river and cattle," 93–1894.   In the adjoining **Room 47** is displayed the fine collection of John Constable's works.   This collection chiefly originated from the gifts made by Constable's children and other benefactors.

Turning right into the large **Octagon Court, Room 40,** we have a temporarily arranged selection of the Museum's large number of historic costumes, dating from early seventeenth century to the 1920's. There are also cases of costume dolls, a pinewood panelled room from Hayne's Grange, Bedfordshire (*c.* 1620), and part of a dining-room painted by *Paul Sandby* in 1793.

Retracing our steps past the wonderful Constable landscapes we gain **Room 48a** where are displayed the Raphael cartoons lent by the late King.   These seven cartoons by Raphael (1483–1520) are amongst the most important surviving examples of High Renaissance art.   Ten such cartoons were commissioned by Pope Leo X, as the designs for tapestries, mainly illustrating episodes in the lives of St. Peter and St. Paul, which were to be hung in the Sistine Chapel of the Vatican on ceremonial occasions.   Upon completion the designs were sent to Brussels, where Pieter van Aelst wove from them the original set of tapestries, rich with gold and silver thread, which, after many vicissi-tudes, are now on exhibition in the Vatican Picture Gallery.   During the Second World War specially built shelters in the Museum building were made to house these cartoons which were too large and fragile to be transported out of London.

Also in this court hangs a Mortlake tapestry of the Miraculous Draught of Fishes, lent by the Duke of Buccleuch.

Descending the stairs at the end of the corridor, Room 47, we find examples of Continental Art between late sixteenth and eighteenth centuries, in **Rooms 1–4.**   Note the Nevers and Delft ware and the Venetian glass in Room 1; the tapestries in Rooms 2 and 4: and the French panelling in Room 3.

The West portion.   For ease of reference the visitor is now presumed to be inside the Exhibition Road Entrance which gives direct access to the galleries open in this portion of the Museum.   Ascending the first flight of stairs we have straight ahead the newly arranged Tudor galleries, where examples of the various arts have been brought together to show the general character of the period.

The exhibits in **Rooms 52–54** illustrate the love of colour, richness and ornate design which characterised Tudor and Early Stuart Art after the full flood of the Renaissance had swept over England.   Note the Bradford Table Cover (T. 134–1928), the Woollen pile carpet, with arms of Queen Elizabeth (243–1908), Queen Elizabeth's Virginals (19–1887), the silver-gilt Mostyn Salt (146–1886), and Vyvyan Salt (M.273–1925), the oak Machell Bedstead from Westmorland (W.12–1943), and the rich book-bindings in Room 52; the lavishly embroidered gauntlets of the Woman's Leather Gloves (907–1904) Room 53; and in Room 54 The Great Bed of Ware (W.47–1931) and the State Room of Old Palace, Bromley, completed in 1606 for James I (248–1894).

Rooms 55 and **57a** are devoted to Portrait Miniatures.   The Museum houses the National collection and all the great British miniaturists

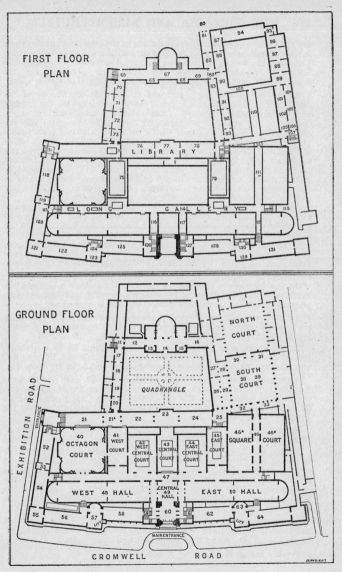

FIRST FLOOR PLAN

80
81
82
83
65
66 67 68 69
70
71
72
73
L I B R A R Y
76 77 78
75
79
L O N G   G A L L E R Y
51
118
119
113
120
116 117
121
122 124 125 126 127 128 130 131
123 129

87 88 94 95 96 97 98 99
89 90 100 104
91 110 101 105
92 102 106
93 103 107
111

GROUND FLOOR PLAN

NORTH COURT
11 12
13 14 15 16
17
18 QUADRANGLE
19
20
21 21ᴬ 22 23 24 25
40 OCTAGON COURT
41 WEST COURT
42 WEST CENTRAL COURT
43 CENTRAL COURT
44 EAST CENTRAL COURT
45 EAST COURT
46ᴬ SQUARE 46 46ᴮ COURT
27 28
26 29
30 31
38 39 SOUTH COURT
32
33
52
53
54
55
WEST 48 HALL
56 57 58 59 60 61
CENTRAL 49 HALL
EAST 50 HALL
62 63 63ᴬ 64
LIFT
LIFT
MAIN ENTRANCE

EXHIBITION ROAD
ENTRANCE

CROMWELL   ROAD

COPYRIGHT

THE VICTORIA AND ALBERT MUSEUM

are shown here: and almost every decade in the long range of 300 years is represented by a portrait of some person, characteristic of his time. These include two by **Holbein,** the Younger, the founder of the National School of Anne of Cleves and Mrs. Pemberton. There is also the famous unfinished portrait of Queen Elizabeth I by *Isaac Oliver*.

Rooms 56–58 are newly arranged to illustrate the history of the decorative arts in England from the Restoration to the middle of the eighteenth century. Particularly notable are the elaborately carved stand of the japanned cabinet (W. 29–1912) and the mirror above (W. 37–1949), and the Calverley toilet service (240. 240m–1879), being typical of the revolt against puritanical austerity which marked this period. Other interesting objects include a carved oak cupboard with the Prince of Wales feathers and the letter A, reputed to stand for Prince Arthur, eldest son of Henry VII; candlestands by Robert Adam; and table attributed to James Moore, cabinet-maker to the Crown. Many foreign craftsmen and designers, e.g. Grinling Gibbons, Daniel Marot, etc., were also working in England and the Continental influence of these immigrants asserts itself in the design of much of the furniture, silver and pottery exhibited here. In **Room 58** are three panelled rooms from No. 3 Clifford's Inn (c. 1686), No. 26 Hatton Garden (c 1730) and No. 5 George Street (1750–60), furnished in a style characteristic of their period; the splendid gilt Music Room was removed from Norfolk House just before the war, the interior decoration of which, by Matthew Brettingham, illustrates the rococo phrase prevalent in the eighteenth century.

On the floor above in **Room 74** the Art of the Book is represented, exhibits include examples of manuscripts, writing and illumination; printing; book-illustration and decoration; and bookbinding.

Turning to the left out of Room 74 there are four (**Rooms 70–73**) which are used for special exhibitions arranged by the Department of Engraving, Illustration and Design.

To the right, after leaving Room 70, are **Rooms 68–69** containing the collections of Continental Domestic Silver arranged by country, note the late sixteenth century Venetian ewer and basin in Room 69.

Arranged chronologically round **Rooms 65–67** are examples of English Silversmiths' work of which the following are of especial importance; the Pusey horn and the Howard Grace Cup, English 1525–6 (**M.** 2680–1931), though the more important pieces are exhibited in the Primary Collections.

Room 89 displays English Church Plate, and illustrates the work of English silversmiths in the service of religion.

Rooms 81–93, to the left, house the remainder of the metalwork exhibited and form part of the Study Collections. Here are displayed pewter, Sheffield plate, brass and bronze work, Russian and Ethiopian metalwork, Continental ecclesiastical silversmiths' work, Far Eastern and Near Eastern metalwork (including arms and armour) and European arms and armour, and other metalwork. In Room 93 are clocks, barometers and watches (Study Collection).

Rooms 91–92 contain jewellery, rings and snuff boxes of which the Armada Jewel, made in 1588 (M. 81–1935) is of particular interest **Room 132** on the second floor is devoted to Theatre Arts.

For the **Indian Museum,** *see* p. 178.

Outstations of the Victoria and Albert Museum include Bethnal Green Museum, *see* p. 235, the Wellington Museum, Apsley House, *see* p. 134, Ham House, Richmond (open 1st April to 31st October: Weekdays 10–6, Sundays 2.30–4, admission 1 *s.*, children who must be accompanied by an adult, 6*d.*, admission to grounds free); and Osterley Park—the house originally built in 1577 by Sir Thomas Gresham, remodelled by Robert Adam in 1761 is now open as a museum.

Leaving by the Exhibition Road doorway we see across the road the—

Geological Museum

Open free, daily, 10–6; Sundays 2.30–6 p.m. Closed Christmas Day and Good Friday.

The building, which forms the headquarters of the Geological Survey, is light and airy and the contents of the Museum are admirably displayed. The centre of the ground floor is occupied by a great rotating geological globe and cases of gemstones and ornamental stones. Round these are some excellent models and dioramas of British scenery, and beyond these and on the first floor are maps, photographs and specimens illustrating the geology of various parts of Britain, the collections being arranged territorially. The exhibits in the upper galleries are designed to illustrate Economic Geology and Mineralogy.

Behind the exhibition galleries are the offices of the Geological Survey and a large Reference Library (open to the public, free, Monday to Friday, 10–5, Saturday, 10–1).

A few yards northward, and almost opposite the **Royal School of Art** is the entrance to—

The Science Museum

Open free, daily, 10–6; Sundays, 2.30–6 p.m. (Closed Christmas Day and Good Friday.)
Lectures free daily (except Sundays) at 11.15 a.m. and 3.15 p.m.

Owing to deterioration of the older sections of the premises the Museum exhibits are now housed in the Eastern Block and in the Western Galleries. A new Centre Block is under construction, but in the meantime the loss of exhibition space formerly available in the old building has prevented many of the pre-war exhibits from being put on view.

To the right on entering is **Gallery I**, reserved for special exhibitions, usually of topical interest. On the left beyond the Foucault Pendulum, stairs lead down to the **Children's Gallery**, with fascinating dioramas and working models. Here also are the Illumination and the Bryant & May fire-making collections and also the mining exhibits in a realistic setting.

The bulk of the other main collections are on the floors indicated below but are subject to change of location as a result of redecoration and rebuilding.

Ground Floor.—Stationary Engines, including beam engines by James Watt and the original Parsons' steam turbine, Mechanical Road Vehicles, Railway Transport with Stephenson's "Rocket" and working models, Electrical Engineering.

1st Floor.—Textile Machinery, Hand Implements and Machine Tools, Electrical Communication, Metallurgy, Agricultural Machinery, Gas Industry, Writing, Typewriting, Printing and Paper-making.

2nd Floor.—Sailing Ships, Merchant Steamers, Steam Ships of War, Small Craft, Marine Engines, Time Measurement and Weights and Measures, Industrial Chemistry.

3rd Floor.—Meteorology, Photography and Kinematography, Chemistry, Mathematics, Astronomy, Geodesy and Surveying, Optics, Heat, Acoustics, Electricity and Magnetism, Electron Physics, Atomic Physics.

Science Library.—Open free Monday to Saturday, 10 a.m. to 5.50 p.m. (Closed Sundays and Bank Holidays, Christmas Day and Good Friday.) Contains about 360,000 volumes, and 17,000 journals and publications of learned societies, about half of them current.

Western Galleries.—These Galleries, which adjoin the Imperial Institute at the western end of Imperial Institute Road, on the north side, contain the Aeronautical Collections. These Collections include a replica of the original aeroplane in which the Wright brothers, in 1903, made their historic "first flight." Other notable machines of later date are here: the British aeroplane which was the first to make a transatlantic flight, that with which the Schneider Trophy was won in 1931, and the first successful jet-propelled aeroplane.

The collection of historical aircraft is exhibited in two hangars acquired by the Science Museum at West Byfleet, Surrey.

North of the Science Museum is—

The Indian Museum

a branch of the Victoria and Albert Museum, and with the same hours of opening. There are important exhibits of Indian sculpture, painting and textiles, and special rooms devoted to the music, theatre and dance, and religions of India.

Adjoining the building is—

The Imperial Institute

Plan II. F. 10.

Admission.—The Exhibition Galleries (stories and scenes of the people and the countries of the British Commonwealth) are open free week-days 10-4.30, Empire Films may be seen in the *Cinema*, free, from 12.45 p.m. to 1.30 p.m.; 3-3.45 (Saturdays, 2.30 and 3.30 and Sundays, 2.30 p.m.-6 p.m.). Guide Lecturers, free, are available for schools and parties on application to the General Secretary. Canteen.

Nearest Station.—South Kensington (District and Piccadilly Tube). (*See* footnote, p. 180).

The Imperial Institute was founded in 1887 as a memorial of Queen Victoria's golden jubilee. Its primary purposes were two-fold, firstly to give scientific and technical advice in the interests of the economic development of the natural resources of the Empire, and secondly educational, to provide visual aids to a knowledge of the life, scenery and industries of the Empire.

Since 1st April, 1949, as a direct result of recommendations adopted by the Commonwealth Scientific Conference of 1946, the scientific and technical activities of the Institute have been transferred to the control of the Secretary of State for the Colonies; the Institute retaining its educational functions centred in its Exhibition Galleries and other visual aids to a knowledge of the Commonwealth. From the same date the Minister responsible for the administration and finance of the Institute is the Minister of Education, who includes in the Estimate for his Department an annual grant-in-aid from Parliament to supplement the annual grants to the Institute from Overseas Empire Governments and the annual income from its invested endowment funds.

The scientific and technical activities are now undertaken by the following bodies: Colonial Products Advisory Bureau (Plant and Animal), and the Mineral Resources Division, Colonial Geological Surveys, and continue to be accommodated in the Imperial Institute building.

The **Library and Reading Rooms** are open to inquirers from 10 a.m. to 5 p.m. week-days, 10-1 Saturdays. The Library contains a large collection of works of reference relating to raw materials and their uses, and is regularly supplied with the more important official publications of all countries of the Empire and of many foreign countries, and with over 800 technical and scientific periodicals.

Each of these two scientific departments issues a quarterly journal. They are entitled respectively *Colonial Plant and Animal Products* and *Colonial Geology and Mineral Resources,* and together take the place of the *Bulletin of the Imperial Institute.*

In the Imperial Institute Buildings is the home of the **Warburg Library** and **Institute,** appealing especially to art lovers and students of European civilisation. The Library and the collection of photographs are open to students on week-days, 10–6, Saturdays, 10–1.

On the other (south) side of the road is the main block of the **Imperial College of Science and Technology,** founded under Royal Charter in 1907 and incorporating several older institutions. The courses of instruction are intended to prepare students for industrial careers in which scientific knowledge is essential. The College is affiliated to the University of London.

To the north, in Exhibition Road, is the **City and Guilds of London Central Technical College,** now incorporated with the Imperial College. In Prince Consort Road, immediately south of the Albert Hall, is another imposing block occupied by the **Imperial College of Science and Technology.** Here, too, is the **Royal College of Music,** opened in 1894, providing a musical training to some 500 pupils and awarding the diploma of L.R.C.M. On the ground floor is shown the Donaldson Collection of Musical Instruments (*open free daily in term-time, except Saturday,* 11–2 *and* 3–5). The **Albert Hall** has already been described (p. 141).

The most inveterate sightseer will probably be by this time in a state of collapse, but there still remains to be seen what many people regard as the most fascinating of the treasures of South Kensington.

We turn south down **Exhibition Road,*** a broad, straight thoroughfare leading from Kensington Gardens and deriving its name from the Great Exhibitions for which the site was long used. Beyond the home of the Geological Survey and Museum we have on our right the sunken garden surrounding—

The Natural History Museum

Plan II. F. 10. Suffered considerable damage during the war, but most of the Exhibition Galleries have now been re-opened.

Admission.—The Museum is open free daily from 10 to 6 throughout the year. Sundays from 2.30 to 6 p.m. Closed Christmas Day and Good Friday.
  Students' Tickets, giving special facilities, are issued on application to the Director, subject to certain conditions.

Library.—The Museum Library is available only to accredited students on application to the Director.

Publications.—Complete lists of all Museum publications will be forwarded on application to the Director. These include scientific catalogues and monographs, as well as Guide Books, Economic Pamphlets, Instructions for Collectors, and Picture Postcards.

Lecture Tours.—Tours covering one or more of the Galleries take place daily at 3 p.m., except Sundays.

Refreshment Room on first floor at head of staircase.

Nearest Station.—South Kensington (Underground and Piccadilly Line). (*See* footnote.) Buses, Nos. 14, 30, 45, 49, 74, 96.

  * A subway runs from South Kensington station, passing below Exhibition Road and serving most of the Museums, etc.

The great terra-cotta building was designed by Alfred Water-house and completed in 1880.

The Natural History Museum, or British Museum (Natural History), to give it its official title, is the principal centre in the British Empire for the general study of natural history. It comprises the five Natural History Departments of the British Museum: Zoology, Entomology, Geology (Palaeontology), Mineralogy, and Botany; it also includes the finest existing collection of natural history books and periodicals. The public galleries contain selections of specimens from the collections of the five departments of the Museum, dealing, respectively, with existing forms of animal life (Zoology and Entomology), existing forms of plant life (Botany), the crust of the earth on which plants and animals subsist (Mineralogy) and with extinct and fossil plants and animals (Geology).

The Central and North Halls contain exhibits of general interest (displays frequently changed), including British Mammals, Viruses, Insect Pests and exhibits dealing with Early Man.

The Zoological Galleries include the Mammal Gallery and Balcony on the first floor, the new Bird Gallery and British Bird Pavilion: sections illustrating the variety of insects, starfishes, molluscs and other invertebrates; Reptile and Fish Galleries, and the Whale Hall where a 91-foot model Blue Whale is displayed.

The Mineral Gallery, although not yet open in its entirety, shows a systematic collection of minerals as well as special exhibits of precious metals, gem stones, meteorites large and small, and models showing atomic structure, etc.

In the Geological Department a small gallery near the entrance, illustrating the Succession of Life from its origin to the emergence of man, leads into the Fossil Plant and Fossil Reptile Galleries. The great Dinosaurs are shown in a separate gallery, a series of dioramas adds interest to the fine specimens in the Fossil Fish Gallery. Among the fossil mammals and birds, the remains of archaeopteryx are of outstanding interest, and there are fine skeletons of moas, extinct elephants and the sabre-tooth tiger.

The Museum is not only a place of absorbing interest to the general visitor, but is also a great index to natural objects, and as such a world centre of scientific and economic research.

Having thus dutifully "done" the Museums, we could make our way past South Kensington station to Chelsea (see p. 182). Or from the Albert Hall we may take bus westward through Kensington High Street—a popular shopping quarter. Slightly farther west (see p. 140) are Holland House and Leighton House. Still farther west is Olympia, the scene of the Royal Tournament and of other important shows and exhibitions. Nearer to Museum-land is Earls Court, another great show-place, wherein large exhibitions, rallies and displays are held.

By reason of its size, construction and up-to-date methods of lighting and heating it is possible to produce gigantic spectacles.

Some displays take advantage of the effects to be obtained by the great *Swimming Pool*, which measures approximately 200 ft. by 100 ft. The building can also be used to house boxing contests, for which there is a seating capacity of approximately 20,000, thus providing the largest indoor arena in Europe. The *Empress Hall* is used for ice skating, ice hockey and the presentation of spectacles on ice; also for pageants and dancing, for which purpose it can accommodate about 7,000 people.

By continuing westward along the Hammersmith Road we should pass, opposite Brook Green, **St. Paul's School,** an important public school for boys, founded by Dean Colet in 1509, and removed from behind St. Paul's Cathedral to this site in 1884. **Nazareth House,** adjoining, is the headquarters of a Catholic community known as the Sisters of Nazareth, devoting themselves to the care of the poor.

Hammersmith, chiefly known to-day as a busy railway, trolleybus and bus centre, has many interesting associations. The **Lyric Theatre** is associated with many successful revivals of old plays such as *The Beggar's Opera*. Near at hand is the **King's Theatre.** At Hammersmith the Thames is spanned by a fine Suspension Bridge, and on the Middlesex bank are the boathouses of several well-known rowing clubs. Moored off the Middlesex bank is the training ship *Stork* (450 tons), under the auspices of the Navy League. Beyond the boat-houses is the Upper Mall, with many delightful riverside residences of an earlier period. No. 26 bears a tablet recording that it was the residence of William Morris, "poet, craftsman and socialist" (1878–1896). Another house records that "the first electric telegraph, 8 miles long, was constructed here in 1816 by Sir Francis Ronald, F.R.S."

To the south of Kensington lies old-world—

CHELSEA

with its many literary and artistic associations. It is best reached by way of Sloane Square station. Whole volumes have been written about this fascinating quarter, and we can do no more than indicate a few of its leading features. At Chelsea, then a country village, lived Sir Thomas More, among his frequent visitors being Henry VIII, Holbein and Erasmus. Beaufort Street, to the north of the present Battersea Bridge, occupies part of the site of his house. Other distinguished residents at various periods were Dean Swift, Sir Richard Steele, Addison, John Locke, Sir Robert Walpole, Gay, Newton, Smollett, Sir Hans Sloane, whose collection originated the British Museum, J. M. W. Turner, Leigh Hunt, Thomas Carlyle, D. G.

Rossetti, George Eliot, General Gordon, J. McNeil Whistler, and scores of others.

From Sloane Square station turn to the left along **King's Road**, named after King Charles II. In a few yards will be seen the former Duke of York's School (now the headquarters of several Territorial regiments), founded in 1801 for the support and education of the sons of soldiers, and removed in 1909 to Dover.

Taking the next left-hand turning we reach the Royal Hospital Road, in which is the principal entrance to the world-famous—

Royal Hospital, Chelsea

Admission free on week-days from 10 to 12, and from 2 to 4 or later if the public gate is open. Visitors are admitted, so far as room permits, to the Sunday service in the Chapel at 10.50 a.m.
Nearest Station.—Sloane Square (Underground).

In 1682 Charles II, at the instigation of Sir Stephen Fox, used the site of a theological college for an asylum for old and invalid soldiers, employing Sir Christopher Wren as architect. The buildings form three spacious quadrangles, facing the river. In the central quadrangle is a statue of Charles II in Roman toga by Grinling Gibbons. Accommodation is normally provided for about 550 inmates, and there are a great number of "out-pensioners." In winter the aged warriors are clothed in dark blue coats: in summer the colour is scarlet.

The show parts are the large Hall and the Chapel, though the courtyards where the picturesque old warriors sun themselves, and fight their battles o'er again, should also be seen. The **Hall** contains a collection of tattered flags, captured in battle, portraits of Royalty, cases of unclaimed medals, and some old leather "black Jacks." The **Chapel,** the scene of Herkomer's picture, "The Last Muster," contains a fine altar-piece, carvings by Emmett and Morgan, an altar-cloth presented by William IV, and a further collection of flags, among which are several British Regimental colours, and Eagles captured from the French during the Napoleonic Wars. The Communion service was bought in James II's reign. The **Council Chamber** (*open on Saturday afternoons and after Sunday morning service*) has a fine collection of Stuart portraits by Van Dyck, Lely and Kneller.

During World War II, twenty-six bombs fell within the Hospital precincts, causing extensive damage to the buildings; luckily the Hall and Chapel escaped almost intact. At present, pending reconstruction, nearly 200 pensioners are accommodated in premises temporarily leased at Leatherhead.

Between the Hospital and the river are some attractive **Gardens** with shady avenues, admission to which is free. They occupy part of the site of the old Ranelagh Gardens, the scene of so many merry junketings in the eighteenth century. The **Chelsea Flower Show** is held here in May. To the east is the **Chelsea Suspension Bridge,** rebuilt in 1935–7. In Chelsea Bridge Road are the **Chelsea Barracks,** occupied by the Guards, and the **Lister Institute of Preventive Medicine.**

Turning westward along the pleasant **Chelsea Embankment,** with **Battersea Park** (p. 259) on the opposite bank, we shortly reach the **Chelsea Physic Garden,** given by Sir Hans Sloane in 1722 to the Apothecaries' Company as "a physic garden, so that apprentices and others may better distinguish good and useful plants from those that bear resemblance to them and yet are hurtful."

Since 1899 the Garden has been maintained by the Trustees of the London Parochial Charities for the study of botany and for providing material and opportunity for botanical investigation. Specimen plants of great botanical value are grown here for distribution to various colleges and institutes. The Garden is accessible to teachers and students on week-days from 9.30 to 5 or sunset. Orders for a single visit can generally be obtained on application to the Clerk to the Committee of Management, 3, Temple Gardens.

Cheyne Walk (pronounced "Chainey"), a terrace of red-brick Queen Anne mansions overlooking the river, has many interesting associations. At No. 4 lived and died Maclise the painter; here, too, George Eliot died in 1880, after a residence of three weeks only. In the Embankment Gardens a fountain, surmounted by a bust by Ford Madox Brown, recalls the fact that Dante Gabriel Rossetti (1828–1882), lived at No. 16, known as the "Queen's House," from an erroneous tradition that it was the residence of Catherine of Braganza, Charles II's neglected wife. A *Statue of Thomas Carlyle* by Boehm marks the foot of **Cheyne Row,** a spot which no literary pilgrim omits to visit. **Carlyle's House** (No. 24—formerly 5—Cheyne Row) was purchased by public subscription in 1895. *Open daily,* 10–6, *or dusk if earlier, at a charge of* 1s. (*Saturdays,* 6d.), *or* 6d. *each for parties of ten or more.* The house contains a number of interesting personal relics, furniture, etc. It is held by the National Trust.

In Danvers Street, near the foot of Beaufort Street, linking **Battersea Bridge** and the King's Road, has been re-erected **Crosby Hall,** an interesting relic of medieval London removed from Bishopsgate Street in 1908. The hall was built in 1466 by Alderman Sir John Crosby, and occupied by Richard of Gloucester when he plotted the murder of the two princes and his own accession. Later it was bought (but not occupied) by Sir Thomas More, and it is on the site of his last home that

[*Herbert Felton*

The fine Renaissance style building of the Victoria and Albert Museum in Cromwell Road. It covers an area of 12 acres and is a treasure house of exhibits of Fine and Applied Art of all countries of the world, styles and periods.

Carlyle's House in Cheyne Row, Chelsea, which no literary pilgrim omits to visit.

the Hall now stands. It forms part of an international hall of residence and clubhouse for women graduates studying in London under the British Federation of University Women.

West of Cheyne Row is Lawrence Street, where the manufacture of the famous old *Chelsea China*, which fetches almost fabulous prices, was carried on. Monmouth House, Lawrence Street, was the residence of Fielding and of Smollett, and here Gay wrote *The Beggar's Opera*. At the corner of Church Street is **Chelsea Old Church,** built early in the fourteenth century. During the war it was almost completely destroyed, though most of the contents of value were salvaged, among which are many ancient monuments, which have suffered varying degrees of damage, and some chained books, including a "Vinegar Bible." However, the Thomas More Chapel remains and will be restored. The headless remains of Sir Thomas More may possibly be in the tomb he himself erected here, in blissful ignorance of the impending tragedy, but it is very doubtful. His head, we know, was interred at St. Dunstan's, Canterbury, after being exposed for fourteen days on London Bridge. In Church Street is the *Rectory*, where the brothers Charles, George and Henry Kingsley passed their boyhood.

Cheyne Walk extends beyond Battersea Bridge, and here, at the extreme western end (No. 118—tablet by Walter Crane), Turner, the great landscape painter, spent his last years and died. Up to his last illness, it is said, he would always endeavour to get on to the balustraded roof to see the sun rise over London and at the close of the day to watch it set in splendour beyond Putney. J. M. Whistler lived at No. 96.

In the shadow of the Imperial Gas Works, farther west, is the picturesque **Sandford Manor House,** a residence of Nell Gwynne and, later, of Addison. Recently it has been admirably restored. It is not, however, to be regarded as a show place, being in use as a residence.

By following any northward turning from the river we should strike King's Road again. In Manresa Road is the **Chelsea Public Library,** containing interesting prints of bygone Chelsea.

South-westward, King's Road leads through **Parsons Green** to **Putney Bridge,** the starting-point of the Oxford and Cambridge Boat-races. Lining the Surrey bank are the London quarters of a number of famous rowing clubs. On the Middlesex bank, close to the bridge, is **Fulham Palace,** the official residence of the Bishops of London. Nearly opposite, on the Surrey side, are the beautiful grounds of the **Ranelagh Club.**

CHARING CROSS TO THE CITY

ROUTE VIII.—THE STRAND—COVENT GARDEN—ALDWYCH AND KINGSWAY —TEMPLE BAR—LINCOLN'S INN FIELDS—THE TEMPLE—FLEET STREET —LUDGATE CIRCUS—THE VICTORIA EMBANKMENT.

TURNING this time City-wards, let us follow the Strand and Fleet Street, a line of thoroughfare surpassing even Oxford Street in the volume of traffic constantly passing between west and east. The latter part of the route, after passing Temple Bar, is within the City of London, and therefore outside the strict limits of this section of the Guide, but it will be better for purposes of continuity to regard Ludgate Circus as marking the boundary.

The Strand

Plan II. K. and L. 8.

Nearest Stations.—Western end, Trafalgar Square (Bakerloo Line); Strand (Northern Line); Charing Cross (Southern Region—terminus); Charing Cross (District). Eastern end, Aldwych (Piccadilly Line); Temple (Underground).

With its medley of hotels, theatres and shops, the Strand is one of the most famous thoroughfares in Europe, but sadly lacking in architectural dignity. With the falling-in of leases, a certain amount of rebuilding has taken place, and the opportunity used, where possible, to widen so important an artery. There is still, however, great congestion, notwithstanding the fact that east-bound traffic is "by-passed" through Aldwych. The intelligent visitor has only to pause in any doorway and watch the crowds of all ranks, ages, conditions and nationalities that surge by, to have an epitome not merely of metropolitan but of national and world life.

In Elizabethan times, and long afterwards, the Strand was bordered by aristocratic mansions, with gardens extending down to the river-side. The names still survive in such streets as Burleigh Street, Villiers Street, Bedford Street, Southampton Street, etc. Indeed, there is hardly a street in the neighbourhood of the Strand the name of which would be sought unsuccessfully in the British peerage. From Charing Cross to Temple Bar, where the famous griffin in the middle of the roadway marks at once the commencement of the City and of Fleet Street, the Strand is almost exactly seven-eighths of a mile long.

Northumberland Avenue we have already dealt with (p. 76). **Charing Cross Station** (Southern Region) has in its courtyard a copy of the old Charing Cross (p. 73). Though still a busy terminus, the station is no longer the starting-point of the Continental boat trains with their far-reaching connections—traffic which made the name Charing Cross almost a synonym for important railway junctions. In the forecourt is an entrance to the Strand station of the Northern (Underground) Line.

In William IV Street is the **Charing Cross Hospital.** Rhodesia House, at the corner of Agar Street, is the London headquarters of the **Government of Southern Rhodesia.** The building was erected as the home of the British Medical Association (*see* p. 160), for whom Epstein sculptured the statues which still remain. A little farther along the Strand are the headquarters of the High Commissioner for **New Zealand** (on the left). On the right is the **Tivoli Cinema,** among the most important in London.

To the south, between the Strand and the river, lies the quarter known as **The Adelphi,** built by the brothers Adam in 1768-70, and long one of the architectural glories of London. Unfortunately the hand of Progress has been laid on the Adelphi and the Terrace and other pleasant thoroughfares have been replaced by modern blocks. In John Adam Street is the **Royal Society of Arts,** established in 1754 for the encouragement of arts, manufactures and commerce.

On the north side of the Strand, opposite Adam Street, is the **Adelphi Theatre,** and just beyond the **Vaudeville.** On the opposite side of the Strand is the huge block of offices for *Shell-Mex and B.P. Ltd.*—best seen from the Embankment, however. The site was previously occupied by the Hotel Cecil. Next door is the **Savoy Hotel,** extending from the Strand to the Embankment. In the east block is *Simpson's Restaurant,* making a speciality of English food cooked in the English style. The **Savoy Theatre** was long identified with the burlesque operas of Sir W. S. Gilbert and Sir Arthur Sullivan. Reconstruction has made this one of the most charming of London's theatres. The huge *Strand Palace Hotel* (Messrs. Lyons & Co., Ltd.) occupies the site of the old Exeter Hall, famed for its religious meetings. The **Chapel of the Savoy,** reached by Savoy Hill, on the right, now the Chapel of the Royal Victorian Order, stands on part of the site of the ancient Palace of the Savoy, given by Henry III to his uncle Peter, Earl of Savoy. It afterwards passed to John of Gaunt. King John of France, the captive of Poitiers, died here in 1364, and the Palace is believed to have been the scene of Chaucer's marriage. The palace was burnt down in the reign of Richard II by Wat Tyler. Henry VII in the year 1505 built a hospital on the site, and the church we see to-day was the chapel. It is the private Chapel of the Sovereign by right of the Duchy of Lancaster. Savoy Hill became well-known as the home of the British Broadcasting Corporation, with the famous "studios" of the London Station (2LO); but in 1933 the Corporation moved to its magnificent premises in Portland Place (*see* p. 146). Next to Savoy Hill and facing the Embankment is the **Institute of Electrical Engineers.**

Either of the thoroughfares running northward from the Strand would bring us in a few minutes to **Covent Garden Market** (Plan II. K. 8), the chief market in London for fruit, vegetables and flowers. It takes its name from the fact that it was of old the Convent Garden of St. Peter's, Westminster (the Abbey). After that Convent was, with so many others, disestablished and disendowed, the site remained vacant, and in course of time stalls were erected for the sale of vegetables against the wall of the garden of Bedford House, in the Strand. In 1631 the Earl of Bedford built around it the quadrangle (about three acres in extent); and the Piazza, designed by Inigo Jones, was long the favourite lounging place of fashionable men about town. The market buildings were erected in 1831, but have been extended and improved in recent years. The central avenue is lined with shops, in a few of which fruits and flowers are displayed for retail sale. Early each morning, when the wholesale market is in full swing, a very animated scene may be witnessed. The Piazza and the taverns connected with it were conspicuous in the social, literary and dramatic history of the eighteenth century. On the western side of the market is **St. Paul's Church,** built by Inigo Jones in 1633. In the churchyard were buried Samuel Butler, the author of *Hudibras*; Sir Peter Lely, who painted the portraits of so many frail beauties of the Stuart Court; Wycherley, the dramatist; Dr. Arne, the composer of "Rule, Britannia"; Grinling Gibbons, the woodcarver; Charles Macklin, the actor; and John Wolcot ("Peter Pindar"). Here, too, are the ashes of Dame Ellen Terry (d. July, 1928).

Running parallel with the Strand, between Bedford Street and Southampton Street is **Maiden Lane,** a narrow street in which Voltaire lodged, and where Andrew Marvell was living when he refused Charles II's bribe of £1,000 to support the then Government. J. M. W. Turner, the great landscape painter, was born at No. 20, his father being a hairdresser. *Rule's Oyster House*, on the north side, is a favourite haunt of theatrical and literary people, and has many interesting old play-bills, portraits, caricatures, etc. At 27, Southampton Street (tablet),

David Garrick lived from 1750 to 1772, prior to his removal to Adelphi Terrace. In Garrick Street, on the north-west side of the market, is the **Garrick Club**, possessing a valuable collection of portraits of famous actors. This street leads into **Long Acre,** long a centre of horse and harness dealers and coach-builders, but now a haunt of car dealers. The labyrinth of streets hereabouts is rather confusing to strangers; we are in the neighbourhood of the notorious **Seven Dials,** at one time the haunt of the most disreputable of London's residuum, and even now none too savoury. Long Acre runs in a north-easterly direction, and after crossing Drury Lane is continued as **Great Queen Street** to **Kingsway.** In Great Queen Street is the magnificent **Freemasons' Hall,** erected at a cost of about a million pounds as a Peace Memorial and dedicated by H.R.H. the Duke of Connaught in July, 1933. In Drury Lane we have the famous and historic **Drury Lane Theatre** (Plan II. L. 8—main entrance in Catherine Street), the painted pillars of its colonnade well calculated to put waiting "pittites" in a mood to appreciate the spectacular glories within. This, the fourth theatre on the site, can seat 2,500 persons. Across the road is the **Fortune Theatre.** One of the doorways in its frontage leads to the adjoining **Church of Scotland,** and it has been remarked that so well has the architect done his work that only notice boards distinguish the entrance to the church from the way into the pit. Towards the northern end of Drury Lane is the **Winter Garden Theatre.** In Bow Street is the **Royal Opera House,** used also for ballet, dances, etc. **Bow Street** will always be associated with the famous "Bow Street runners"; and with Fielding, the novelist, and his brother, Sir John Fielding, the blind magistrate. In **Wellington Street,** by which we can return to the Strand, is the site of the Lyceum Theatre, so long associated with Sir Henry Irving and Dame Ellen Terry. The building is now used as a popular dance salon.

Kingsway and Aldwych

Plan I. L. 7 and II. L. 8.
Stations.—North end, *Holborn* (*Kingsway*) (Piccadilly and Central Lines); south end, *Aldwych* (Piccadilly Line), Temple (District Line).
Tramway.—Beneath the whole length of Kingsway runs the Tramway Subway, a link between the trolley buses and trams of North and South London (*see* p. 50). The northern end of the subway emerges at Southampton Row; the southern on the Embankment below Waterloo Bridge. There are intermediate stations opposite Bush House and near Holborn Station (Central Line).

These thoroughfares were constructed by the London County Council in 1905 to provide direct communication between North and South London. **Kingsway,** lined almost throughout with tall and stately blocks of offices, starts from the junction of High Holborn with Southampton Row. It extends southward in a straight line for a third of a mile and then forms a crescent, known as **Aldwych,** the western horn of which debouches into the Strand almost opposite Waterloo Bridge, while the eastern horn enters the Strand at St. Clement Danes Church.

In a large block at the south end of Kingsway are the headquarters of the **Royal Air Force.** Across the road is the huge portal of **Bush House.** The **Stoll Theatre** was erected by Oscar Hammerstein of New York at a cost of £200,000, and opened in 1911 as the London Opera House. An ice rink has since been constructed on the stage, and the theatre is the scene of numerous ice-ballets and similar performances. At the opposite corner of Sardinia Street is a huge ten-storied block serving as the **Offices of the Public Trustee.** For **Lincoln's Inn Fields,** see p. 193. **Kingsway Hall,** on the opposite side of Kingsway, is used by the Methodist body (see p. 20) and also for concerts and lectures. For **Great Queen Street,** see p. 189. **Holy Trinity Church** is the successor of a building dating from 1831, which was undermined by the Tube railways and had to be condemned as unsafe. The **Church of St. Anselm and St. Cecilia,** a Roman Catholic fane at the northern end of Kingsway, was opened in 1909 to replace the historic Sardinian Chapel, which stood near-by.

At the western end of Aldwych is the disused Gaiety Theatre, once famed for its musical plays. **India House,** a fine building forming the London headquarters of the Indian Government, was designed by Sir Herbert Baker, A.R.A., and the manner in which it conforms to the adjoining Bush House and yet includes much distinctive detail is admirable. In Aldwych are the *Waldorf Hotel* and two playhouses, the **Aldwych Theatre** (noted for farce), and the **Strand Theatre,** and in Catherine Street is the charming **Duchess Theatre.** Aldwych owes its name to the fact that the district was in Saxon times the site of a Danish settlement. The lofty and massive **Bush House** is among the largest single buildings in London. It is mainly occupied as offices. The principal portico faces up Kingsway and is undeniably impressive. It bears the inscription, "To the friendship of English-speaking people," and is surmounted by symbolic figures by *Malvina Hoffman.* The roof of Bush House commands magnificent all-round views of London. In Houghton Street on the left is the **London School of Economics,** a branch of London University. On taking a right turn either through the courtway of Bush House or through Melbourne Place we come to the prominent island site of **St. Mary-le-Strand Church.** Built by Gibbs in 1717 it is an edifice worthy of such a site, though it is now somewhat overshadowed by the great bulk of Bush House. Thomas à Becket was for a time rector here.

At the junction of Aldwych and Wellington Street with the Strand, westward from the church, Lancaster Place leads south

to the fine new **Waterloo Bridge** (Plan II. L. 8). Designed by
Sir Giles Gilbert Scott, building was commenced in 1938 after
many years of controversy over the safety of the previous bridge.

Retracing our steps eastward along the Strand there is, on the
right, the dignified façade of **Somerset House,** occupying the site
of the palace begun in 1547 by the Protector Somerset, who,
however, did not live to see its completion, the headsman of
Tower Hill abruptly closing his career.

The proud and unscrupulous Duke provided some of the
materials by pulling down the cloisters of St. Paul's, with the
charnel-house and chapel, flinging the bones to rot in what is
now the Bunhill (Bonehill) Fields Cemetery (p. 225). After
Somerset's death the palace became royal property. Inigo
Jones, the great architect, died here in 1652. In 1775 it was
rebuilt at a cost of £360,000 as a home for the Royal Academy,
the Royal Society, and other learned bodies, and into the interior
decorations of this fine example of English classical architecture
such men as Reynolds, Gainsborough, and Cipriani put some of
their finest work. The south and principal front, 780 ft. long,
presents a noble façade in the Palladian style, with a terrace
which, before the construction of the Embankment, was lapped
by the waters of the Thames. The eastern wing was added in
1828 and the western wing, with frontage to Wellington Street,
in 1854–6. The building houses the Head Office of the *Inland
Revenue,* the *Probate Registry* where Wills are kept and may be
inspected for a small fee, and the *Office of the Registrar General of
Births, Deaths and Marriages.*

The eastern portion with a separate entrance is occupied by
King's College, founded in 1828, and now affiliated to London
University (*see* p. 159). There are several large halls and a
number of laboratories and class-rooms.

At No. 5, Strand Lane, a narrow passage at 163, Strand, is
what has for long been thought to be a **Roman Bath,** one of the
few relics of the Roman period in London. Recently, however,
some doubt has been thrown on its origin. It has a continual
flow of spring water and is about 15½ ft. long, 6½ ft. wide, and
5 ft. deep. Key from Room 393c, County Hall.

Close at hand is the *Aldwych Station* of the Piccadilly Tube
Railway. This line, merely a link between Aldwych and
Holborn stations, is a spur from the main line, it being always
necessary to change at Holborn for onward routeing.

On the opposite side of the Strand and at the eastern end of
Aldwych is **Australia House,** an imposing building in Doric
classical style erected by the Commonwealth to serve as offices
for the various States. The foundation-stone was laid in 1913,
and the formal opening took place in 1918, both ceremonies

being performed by King George V. The colonnaded building is so well proportioned that at a first glance its hugeness is scarcely apparent. There are ten floors. Much of the stone and wood-work is Australian, as are also the beautiful marble pillars. The site cost nearly £400,000 and the total cost amounted to nearly £1,000,000.

Across the wide road facing the entrance to Australia House is the **Gladstone Memorial,** of bronze, designed by the late *Sir Hamo Thornycroft, R.A.* Surrounding the figure of Gladstone are four seated figures representing Education, Brotherhood, Aspiration and Courage.

In a prominent island site is the shell of **St. Clement Danes Church.** The church was erected in 1681, from the designs of Wren, on the site of a much earlier building, traditionally said to have been the burial-place of Harold Harefoot and other members of the Danish colony settled here in Saxon times. It suffered terrible damage during the war. Services are now held in the Church Hall, Portugal Street, Kingsway. Alongside the entrance pathway to the church are some old tombstones set into the pavement. The tower contained the famous old peal mentioned in the nursery rhyme: "Oranges and Lemons, said the bells of St. Clement's," but these fell from their place during the bombing and were cracked. The pulpit, carved by Grinling Gibbons, is now in St. Paul's Cathedral. Amidst the ruins there is a brass tablet to the memory of William Pennington Bickford, who was rector for over thirty years and who instituted an annual Oranges and Lemons Service for children.

Outside the east end of the church is a bronze **Statue of Dr. Johnson,** who regularly attended service at St. Clement Danes.

Between Aldwych and the Law Courts stands what is left of **Clement's Inn,** an ancient Inn of Chancery in the garden of which Falstaff and Shallow "heard the chimes at midnight."

The Royal Courts of Justice

Plan I. L. 7.
Nearest Stations.— Aldwych (Piccadilly Line) and Temple (District Line).

The Royal Courts of Justice, generally called the "Law Courts," extend back to Carey Street. The style is what is known as Monastic Gothic, and the building, exclusive of site, cost little short of a million pounds, most of which was provided out of unclaimed funds in Chancery. The principal entrance, facing the Strand, has a fine recessed archway, flanked by towers in which are the entrances to the public galleries of the various Courts. There are twenty-three of these, serving the Queen's

St. Clement Danes is now but a shell, though the tower remains more or less intact. In it was the famous old peal mentioned in the nursery rhyme " Oranges and Lemons."

The Royal Courts of Justice at the eastern end of the Strand. Anyone may ascend the steps in the towers on either side of the entrance and take a seat in the public galleries.

Kingsway, lined with stately blocks of offices, was constructed by the L.C.C. in 1905 to provide direct communication, via the Aldwych, between North and South London.

Bench, the Chancery, and the Probate, Divorce and Admiralty
Divisions and the Court of Appeal. These, however, proved
insufficient, and five new Courts are being erected.

The Courts are entered by way of the mosaic-paved *Central
Hall,* which is 238 ft. long and 80 ft. high, and has a fine rose
window in the gable. Here is the marble statue of *Sir William
Blackstone* presented to the Bar of England by the American
Bar Association in 1924. Only barristers and solicitors and
persons connected with the cases are allowed in the body of the
Courts and in the Central Hall, but anyone may ascend the steps
in the towers and take a seat in the public galleries. The
Central Hall is shown to the public during vacations. The
Judges' entrance is at the back, in Carey Street.

On the west side is a pleasant stretch of greensward, thrown
open in the daytime, alongside which we may pass to the steps
leading up to **Carey Street,** where is the **Bankruptcy Court,** with
which no reader will desire to be too closely acquainted. Serle
Street leads onward to **Lincoln's Inn Fields** (Plan I. L. 7), almost
the largest of London's "Squares," the magnificent plane trees
of which afford grateful shade on a summer day. (Tennis courts,
grass, 1s. 6d.; hard, 2s. Fee, 2s. 6d. per year; 6d. per day, book-
able in advance. Miniature golf and basket-ball are also played.)
The gardens were laid out early in the seventeenth century, and
were long a noted resort of duellists. Lord William Russell was
executed here in 1683. A tablet under the summerhouse in the
centre marks the spot, but according to the late Sir G. L. Gomme
it is inaccurately placed. Most of the houses are now occupied
by solicitors, but at one time this was the most fashionable place
of residence in London, and several of the existing mansions
were built for members of the nobility. Tablets commemorate
several notable residents. No. 58 was for some years occupied
by Dickens's biographer, Forster, and in *Bleak House* is introduced as the office of the ill-fated Tulkinghorn.

On the south side are the **Land Registry,** and the **Royal College
of Surgeons** erected in 1835 from the designs of Barry. It contains the museum of anatomy founded by John Hunter, the
famous surgeon, who died in 1793. The collection, which has
been greatly augmented since Hunter's death, is one of the most
remarkable in the world. It is for the purpose of medical education and is divided into two main categories, Anatomy and
Pathology. While open to medical practitioners and students,
others can obtain tickets of admission for educational purposes
from the Secretary or Conservator. Some of the exhibits are
decidedly gruesome. In the Anatomy room are contrasted the
skeleton of Bryne, the Irish giant, 7 ft. 7 in. high, and that of

Caroline Crachami, who died when ten years of age, having attained the height of only 20 in. The library contains over 110,000 volumes.

In the north-east corner of Lincoln's Inn Fields is the **Institute of Auctioneers and Estate Agents,** a very attractive modern building. At No. 13 is **Sir John Soane's Museum** (Plan I. L. 7), *open free from 10 to 5 on Tuesdays to Saturdays inclusive. Closed August. Other times apply personally or by letter to the Curator.*

The Museum is in the private house of the famous architect, built by him in 1812 and left with all its contents under a private Act of Parliament which became effective on his death in 1837. Soane, the architect of the old Bank of England, is usually considered the most original architect of the late Georgian period. The collections are mainly of architectural significance and comprise some 20,000 drawings from the sixteenth to nineteenth centuries and a library of 8,000 volumes. The Egyptian and Roman antiquites, curiously arranged, include the great Sarcophagus of Seti I (1370 B.C.). Among the paintings the most important are Hogarth's *Rakes Progress* and *Election* series, a notable Canaletto and works by Watteau, Reynolds, Turner and Lawrence. The Unique Picture Room, designed with folding walls, the Crypt and Monk's Parlour, remain unchanged since Soane's time.

This side of Lincoln's Inn Fields is known as *Canada Walk*, commemorating the near-by establishment, during World War II, of the **Royal Canadian Air Force.**

Opposite, and within the gardens, is a memorial seat to *Margaret MacDonald* (d. 1911), wife of the late Ramsay MacDonald, the first Labour Premier in this country—one of the few London memorials to women other than queens.

To the east of the square is **Lincoln's Inn** (Plan I. L. 7), another of the four great Inns of Court. The others are Gray's Inn, Holborn (p. 168), and the Inner and the Middle Temple (p. 197). These four "societies," governed by Benchers, alone have the power of "calling to the bar." Prior to the erection of the present Law Courts, the Court of Chancery held its sittings here. Entering by the picturesque gateway from Lincoln's Inn Fields, we have on the left the **New Hall** and **Library** of red brick, built in 1845. In the Hall is a large fresco entitled "Justice, The Hemicycle of Law Givers," executed gratuitously by G. F. Watts. It was restored in 1927. The collection, founded in 1497, is the largest and finest law library in London, containing over 70,000 volumes and a number of valuable MSS, bequeathed by Sir Matthew Hale and others. Passing the pleasant gardens (note the fine wrought-iron gates), we come to the **Chapel,** erected from the designs of Inigo Jones in 1623, and containing some good stained-glass windows and wood carvings. The **Old Hall** dates from 1506, and recent very thorough restoration—amount-

ing almost to rebuilding—has revealed the original work, long
covered with plaster and stucco. Readers of Dickens will like
to recall that here was heard the case of Jarndyce *v.* Jarndyce.

The Gatehouse opening on to Chancery Lane was built in 1518
by Sir Thomas Lovell, whose arms appear above, together with
those of Henry VIII and Henry de Lacy, Earl of Lincoln. The
gateway was restored in 1899. Close to the gateway, a tablet
on the wall of No. 24, Old Square, recalls the residence of John
Thurloe, Cromwell's Secretary of State.

Chancery Lane (Plan I. L. 7) connects Fleet Street with
Holborn. The upper part of the western side is overlooked by
the somewhat dingy offices of Lincoln's Inn (and *see* p. 194).
Near the Fleet Street end is the **Law Society's Institution.** The
fine Tudor building on the opposite side of the Lane is the **Public
Record Office.** (*The public are freely admitted to the Museum
containing the more famous treasures, between 1 and 4 p.m. daily,
except Saturdays and Sundays. Organised parties at other times
by arrangement. Search rooms open 10 to 5.30; Saturdays 10
to 2: except for searches subject to payment of Fees when the hours
are 10 to 4.30 and 10 to 1*). Here are stored the state papers and
records formerly kept in the Chapter House of Westminster
Abbey, the Rolls Chapel, and other places. Records of a later
date than 1842 may be seen on payment of fees. Other Records,
and Records of Government Departments down to years specified
by the Departments themselves, may (with a few exceptions) be
inspected free of charge by holders of Students' tickets. The
collection includes among other interesting MSS. the original
volumes and ancient covers of *Domesday Book*, most of the documents connected with the "Gunpowder Plot," including the
warning sent to Lord Monteagle, and Wellington's report from
the battle of Waterloo. The Museum occupies the site of the
old Rolls Chapel.

At No. 6 Chancery Lane, we may without modesty remind
the reader, are the Headquarters of the Publishers of this guide,
and of over one hundred similar volumes dealing with various
parts of this country and abroad, of Mrs. Beeton's cookery
books and numerous children's books and other works.

Near-by is **Clifford's Inn,** one of the most peaceful corners of
London until in 1935 the greater part of the site was covered
by a modern block of offices.

Near the Holborn end of Chancery Lane, Southampton Buildings provide another entrance to **Staple Inn** (p. 169). This

street leads also to the **Patent Office,** where inventions, designs and trade marks are registered. The excellent library (over 340,000 vols.), rich in scientific works, journals, transactions, etc., both British and foreign, may be used by anyone on signing the visitors' book (*open daily, except Sunday*). **Fetter Lane** (Plan I. M. 7), to the east, running approximately parallel with Chancery Lane, though hardly an inviting thoroughfare, has some interesting associations. It is variously said to derive its name from the *faitours*, or beggars, once infesting it, and a colony of *feutriers* (felt-makers or saddlers). Dryden and Otway, the poets, at one time lived here, and here John Gerard (1545–1612) had his herbal garden. He was a surgeon as well as superintendent of the gardens of William Cecil, Lord Burghley. He was one of the first (according to his *Herball* of 1597) to experiment with "Turkey wheat" (American maize), sweet potatoes, Jerusalem artichokes, not to mention his interest in tulips, which were also natives of "Turkey" in his day. The *Royal Scottish Corporation* building in Fleur-de-Lis Court boasts an unusual luxury among city offices. —a front garden.

We regain our main line of route in Fleet Street, but it will be advisable to retrace our steps for a few yards westward to the spot opposite the Law Courts where a monument in the roadway marks the site of the old **Temple Bar** (Plan II. L. 8). This famous portal to the City, which callous Londoners allowed to be carted away to private grounds at Theobald's Park, Cheshunt, was built by Wren in 1670, and was long used for the exhibition of conspirators' and criminals' heads, notably those who were "out" in 1745. It had, however, more pleasing associations. As one writer well says:

"The shadow of every monarch and popular hero since Charles II's time rested for at least a passing moment at the old gateway. Queen Anne passed here to return thanks at St. Paul's for the victory of Blenheim. Here Marlborough's coach ominously broke down in 1714, when he returned from his voluntary exile. George III passed through Temple Bar, young and happy, the year after his coronation; and again, when old and almost broken-hearted, he returned thanks for his partial recovery from insanity; and that graceless son of his, the Prince Regent, came through the Bar in 1814, to thank God at St. Paul's for the downfall of Bonaparte. Queen Victoria sued for admission to the City at Temple Bar on November 9th, 1837, when she attended the Lord Mayor's banquet after her accession."

It is strange that a king should have to ask for admission to his own capital, yet such is the real significance of Temple Bar and other points on the city boundary. In accordance with

ancient custom, it is still the practice whenever the Sovereign
visits the City in state for the Lord Mayor to receive her here,
at Holborn Bars, or at the boundary on the Embankment (p.
20), and to tender the sword of state, which Her Majesty is
expected to return immediately. A small reproduction of the
old gateway hangs before a neighbouring restaurant. The
present ugly monument is usually known as the "Griffin,"
though, as a matter of heraldic fact, the supporters of the City
arms are dragons—held by some calumnious individuals to
typify the rapacity of the citizens.

Adjoining the Law Courts we have the *Branch Bank of
England*, while on the south side is *Child's Bank*, the successor
of the building where the fair but frail Nell Gwynne kept her
account, and which figured as "Tellson's" in Dickens's *Tale of
Two Cities*. At the entrance to the Inner Temple, facing the
foot of Chancery Lane, is No. 17, Fleet Street, with a projecting
upper storey. The house was built in 1610. On the first floor
is a chamber known as **Prince Henry's Room,** which may be
visited, free, on weekdays from 10 to 5. It is believed to have
been used as the Council Chamber of the Duchy of Cornwall.
In view of the interest attached to the house, the London
County Council, with the assistance of the Corporation, purchased
the building in 1900, when it was on the point of demolition, and
restored the premises at a cost of £30,000.

The Temple

(Plan II. L. and M. 8)

is one of the most interesting places in London. Between busy
Fleet Street and the broad Embankment are a venerable church,
Gothic halls, piles of stately buildings, quadrangles, spacious
lawns, trees and flower gardens, and a shady nook where plays
a little fountain close to rockeries and flowers. The Temple has
the flavour of a university town, mingled with associations of
the old Crusading times and the literary history of the eighteenth
century. "It is the most elegant spot in the metropolis,"
wrote Charles Lamb, who was born in Crown Office Row. "What
a cheerful, liberal look hath that portion of it which, from three
sides, overlooks the greater garden—that goodly pile 'of building strong, albeit of Paper hight,' confronting, with massy
contrast, the lighter, older, more fantastically shrouded one,
named of Harcourt, with the cheerful Crown Office Row (place
of my kindly engendure) right opposite the stately stream which

washes the garden-foot with her yet scarcely trade-polluted
waters . . . a man would give something to have been born in
such places."

In 1185 the Knights Templars, that remarkable Order which
so successfully combined the priestly and the military characters,
removed from Holborn to the banks of the Thames, and built
the famous Church. After the abolition of the Order, in 1312,
Edward II gave the property to Aymer de Valence, Earl of
Pembroke, whose tomb may be seen in Westminster Abbey.
On his death the knights of the rival Order of St. John of Jerusalem—the Hospitallers—became possessed of the property, and
in 1346 leased it to the doctors and students of the law, who
have ever since, with characteristic tenacity, retained it. In
1609 James I abandoned his rights in favour of the corporations
of the Inner and Middle Temple. The Inner Temple was so
called to distinguish it from the Outer Temple, beyond the
City boundary, the Middle Temple being between the two. The
Outer Temple has long ceased to have any official recognition,
though the name is still applied to a block of offices adjoining
Temple Bar. The heraldic device of the Inner Temple is a
winged horse (*Pegasus*), that of the Middle Temple the holy lamb
(*Agnus Dei*). Wags have it that "the lamb sets forth the
innocence; the horse the expedition of the lawyers."

The Temple Church

Note.—Pending war damage repairs, in progress, the church is not open to visitors.

There are two parts, the characteristic "Round Church" of
the Templars, of which there are only four examples in this
country (Church of the Holy Sepulchre, Cambridge; St. Sepulchre's, Northampton; Little Maplestead, Essex; and this); and
the Early English Choir. The former, 58 ft. in diameter, was
built by the Templars and consecrated by Heraclius, Patriarch
of Jerusalem, in 1185. It is in the Transition-Norman style.
The choir dates from 1240. The Norman porch, at the Western
end, is much admired. The tiled pavement, with the oft-repeated
emblems of the Temple, the painted ceiling and the nine tombs
of Crusaders, with recumbent figures in full armour, were the
chief features of the interior. Most of the stained-glass windows
were modern but only a few remain. In the stair leading up
to the circular triforium is a small penitential cell with slits
through which the choir is seen. In this narrow prison dis-
obedient Templars were confined; and there is a grim tradition
that those who had broken their vows were here starved to
death, while day by day the services of the church were chanted
in their ears. The standing of the church is peculiar. It is
private—the joint property of the Inner and Middle Temple
Societies (whose emblems, the winged horse and the lamb,

decorate the ceiling of the choir)—and exempted from episcopal jurisdiction by a Papal Bull. The rector, known as "the Master," holds office not by reason of induction or institution, but by virtue of Letters Patent issued by the Sovereign. Within the church were memorials of John Selden (1654) and Richard Hooker (1600), and outside, to the north of the choir a stone marks the position of the **Grave of Oliver Goldsmith** (1774). Poor Noll wrote many of his best works and died at No. 2 Brick Court near-by (house destroyed). His neighbour was Sir Wm. Blackstone, of the *Commentaries*. Thackeray rented chambers for a time in the same block. The **Master's House,** the site was at the north-east corner of the church, was completely destroyed during the war, but it is to be rebuilt. It was first built in 1667 and was one of the most beautiful houses in London.

Near-by are the ruins of **Inner Temple Hall** (1870), designed by Smirke, and the adjoining **Inner Temple Library,** a Gothic building (1862) which contained about 70,000 volumes, including the Petyt collection, bequeathed in 1707 by a former keeper of the Tower records. Damage was suffered during the war and most of the Library was lost but re-building is now in progress.

Middle Temple Hall, restored after war damage, was built in 1572, and has a magnificent oak roof, richly carved. It contains a fine oak screen. On a dais at the end of the Hall, Shakespeare is believed to have acted in *Twelfth Night* early in 1602. The long table that stands here, made from an oak in Windsor Park, was the gift of Queen Elizabeth I to the Benchers. Upon it she is said to have signed the death-warrant of Mary, Queen of Scots. The smaller table was constructed from the timbers of Drake's ship, *The Golden Hind.* A temporary building in Brick Court now houses what is left of the **Middle Temple Library.** (Some 60,000 or more volumes were lost when the building was heavily damaged.)

Apart from feeling distress at having seen so much wanton destruction, it is nevertheless restful to stroll for a while through the various courts and quadrangles, with their interesting associations. It was in **Fountain Court** that Ruth Pinch, of *Martin Chuzzlewit* was accustomed to meet her brother Tom, "with the best little laugh upon her face that ever played in opposition to the fountain and beat it all to nothing." The old fountain familiar to Dickens was removed many years ago. Of the host of eminent names, legal and otherwise, associated with the Temple, we need only mention Raleigh, Pym, Ireton, Beaumont, Wycherley, Burke, Sheridan, Moore and Cowper. Dr. Johnson had rooms in Inner Temple Lane, the modern Johnson's Buildings marking the site; and Charles Lamb was born in Crown Office Row. A fountain and statue on the lawns overlooking the Embankment commemorate his connection with the Temple.

The pleasant **Temple Gardens,** formerly reaching right down to the river, but now separated from it by the Embankment, have been rendered immortal by Shakespeare in *Henry VI,*

Part I, as the scene of the quarrel between Plantagenet and Somerset, when the white and red roses—those fatal emblems of civil war—were plucked and adopted as badges. Appropriately, a *Temple Rose Show* was long held each summer in the gardens.

From the quiet of the Temple with its stately buildings and green lawns it is but a step to the bustle of—

Fleet Street
(Plan I. L. and M. 7)

famous the world over as the journalistic centre of London. In or near it are the offices of nearly all the great newspapers and periodicals, where hosts of busy toilers are at work both day and night. The name is, of course, derived from the old *Fleet River* (now debased to the rank of a common sewer, of which the last portion flows below Farringdon and New Bridge Streets) which flowed from Hampstead to Holborn and entered the Thames at Blackfriars. Readers of Pope's *Dunciad* will recall the not very pleasant references:

"To where Fleet Ditch, with disemboguing streams
Rolls the large tribute of dead dogs to Thames."

and again:

"Sons of a day! just buoyant on the flood,
Then numbered with the puppies in the mud."

Fleet Street itself, owing to successive widenings, is almost entirely modern, but the explorer has only to turn into any of the quaintly-named courts and byways on either side to find an abundance of Queen Anne and Georgian houses.

On the north side is **St. Dunstan's Church**, rebuilt 1831–3. Some monuments from the church which formerly occupied the site are preserved within, including a brass of 1530. Note the beautiful lantern tower, very similar to the famous Boston "Stump." The projecting clock was returned to the church in 1935 after having for some years adorned St. Dunstan's Lodge, Regent's Park—that same house which during the Great War became famous as headquarters of work among blinded men (*see* p. 152). A little knot of sightseers generally waits to see the clubbed giants strike the quarter-hours. The clock was the first ever to have minute divisions. The figure of Queen Elizabeth I over the school door on the east side of the church formerly adorned the old Lud Gate on Ludgate Hill. The church was immortalised by Dickens in *The Chimes*, and has associations with Izaak Walton, of *Compleat Angler* fame, who "resided for some years in Fleet Street, at the corner of Chancery Lane (west side), and, between 1652 and 1664, was overseer of the poor and

Fleet Street, " the Street of Ink," and a well-known view of St. Paul's. Centre of the journalistic world, there are grouped hereabouts offices of all the great newspapers.

[*G. Wilson and W. Scott*

From the bustle of Fleet Street, Middle Temple Lane leads to the old-world quietude of the Temple quadrangles.

London (g*).

[Gerald Wilson

The Bank of England and the Royal Exchange, another of London's busy traffic points.

[J. Allan Cash

The Victoria Embankment and the vast Shell-Mex building. Cleopatra's Needle rises prominently from the river-front.

a sidesman and vestryman of this parish." The memorial window was erected by the principal angling associations. A monument close to the railings commemorates *Lord Northcliffe*.

On the opposite side is *Gosling's Bank* (Barclays), the windows bearing the sign of the old "Three Squirrels," where Warren Hastings, Clive, Pope, Samuel Richardson, Camden, Ellenborough, Sir Philip Francis, and many other famous men kept their accounts. The *Cock Tavern* displays as sign a gilded chanticleer, the original of which, carved by no less a hand than that of Grinling Gibbons, is preserved inside.

Fetter Lane has already been noticed (p. 196).

Crane Court, on the north side of Fleet Street, witnessed the first meeting of the Royal Society. In **Wine Office Court** is the celebrated *Old Cheshire Cheese*, always associated with Johnson and Goldsmith. American and Continental visitors like to find their way to this quaint old hostelry—still with the pristine simplicity of wooden benches and sanded floor. No. 7, Wine Office Court is **Dean Wace House,** the headquarters of the National Church League. A tablet on No. 17, **Gough Square,** beyond the head of the Court, marks the house where Dr. Johnson lived from 1748 to 1758, and where he toiled over his great Dictionary. The house has been carefully restored to its eighteenth-century condition, and may usually be inspected, together with a number of MSS., autographs, first editions, etc., of great interest to Johnsonians. The Great Cham died in Bolt Court, hard by. Within the doorway of No. 71, Fleet Street (south side), is inscribed on marble tablets, for some reason unknown to us, a complete copy of Thomas Hood's famous poem, *The Song of the Shirt*.

Whitefriars Street and **Bouverie Street,** now given over to printers and their myrmidons, lead down to the former Alsatia, so vividly described by Scott in *The Fortunes of Nigel*. On the left of Fleet Street are the magnificent building of the *Daily Telegraph and Morning Post* and the modern offices of the *Daily Express*. T. P. O'Connor (1848–1929) is fittingly commemorated by a bronze bust on the wall of *Chronicle House*.

With a frontage to Fleet Street and a longer one to Salisbury Court is a huge new block of offices used by the *Associated Press and Reuters*, completely dwarfing **St. Bride's Church** to the east, though the beautiful spire of this famous church rises to a height of 223 ft. The church, badly damaged during the war, but due to be restored, was rebuilt by Wren in 1680 and was one of the finest specimens of the Italian style in England. In the central aisle is the flat tombstone of Samuel Richardson. Lovelace, the author of "Stone walls do not a prison make," and "I could not love thee, dear, so much, Loved I not honour more," was buried in the old church, destroyed during the Great Fire. By reason of its memorials to literary men the church has been called "the Cathedral of Fleet Street." Among the entries in the register of christenings was one recording the baptism of Samuel "the son of John Peapis and his wife Margaret," on March 3, 1632–3. It is now generally accepted that the infant was no other than Samuel Pepys of the immortal *Diary*, and that he first saw the light in a house in Salisbury Court. In a house, now demolished, overlooking the churchyard, John Milton lived. In **Salisbury Square,** Richardson, the father of the English novel, carried on his printing business; and here is the site of **Warwick House,** almost completely gutted by fire during the war, the former headquarters of the publishers of this Guide. In this Square, too, are the offices of the **Church Missionary Society.**

The eastern termination of Fleet Street is **Ludgate Circus** (Plan I. M. 7) at the foot of Ludgate Hill. Many will look with interest at the *Edgar Wallace Memorial* tablet, at the corner of Fleet Street and St. Bride Street. **Farringdon Street,** leading northward to King's Cross, covers the old Fleet River (p. 200). On the east side, on a site partly occupied now by the Memorial Hall, stood the infamous Fleet Prison for debtors, rendered immortal by Dickens as the scene of the incarceration of Mr. Pickwick. The **Memorial Hall,** long the headquarters of the Congregational body, was built in 1874 in memory of the "fidelity to conscience" of the 2,000 ministers ejected from the Church in 1662 by the Act of Uniformity.

Southward from Ludgate Circus is **New Bridge Street** leading to Blackfriars Bridge. A few yards on the right in Bride **Lane** is the **St. Bride Foundation Institute,** containing a general lending and reference library, recreation-rooms, swimming-bath, etc. To the south Bridewell Lane recalls the old **Bridewell,** a palace (*vide* Shakespeare's *Henry VIII*) presented by Edward VI to the City Authorities and afterwards used as a house of correction. In Tudor Street are the headquarters of the **Institute of Journalists.**

Blackfriars Bridge

is one of the widest and busiest road bridges in London. More than 41,000 vehicles and over 60,000 pedestrians pass this busy corner every day. There are subways for pedestrians.

The bridge takes its name from the thirteenth-century monas-

tery of the Black Friars. In 1450 Henry VI's Parliament
assembled here and three-quarters of a century later it was the
scene of the court held by Wolsey and the Papal Legate to try
the divorce case of Henry VIII and Katherine of Aragon, a
scene that lives for ever in the pages of Shakespeare's *Henry
VIII*. At the northern end of the Bridge is the *Blackfriars
Station* of the District Line, with the *St. Paul's–Blackfriars*
station of the Southern Region adjoining.

At this point the Fleet River flowed into the Thames, and
interesting relics of old quays, etc., were excavated during the
erection of the huge building on the opposite corner—the headquarters of Messrs. Lever Bros., Ltd.

The Victoria Embankment

is a wide thoroughfare running beside the river from Blackfriars
Bridge to Westminster.   On the right, overlooking the Embankment, is **Sion College** founded in 1630 and containing a library
of over 300,000 volumes, especially rich in theological works.
The **City of London School**, for boys, faces the river; the girls'
school is in Carmelite Street.   In this locality are a number of
imposing buildings and blocks of offices; it is almost another
Fleet Street, so numerous are the newspaper and publishing
premises.   In John Carpenter Street is the **Guildhall School of
Music and Drama**, maintained by the Corporation of London.

Returning to the Embankment and continuing westward we
obtain on the right pleasant glimpses of **Temple Gardens** (p. 199).

Nearly opposite the western boundary of the City (marked by
a tablet) is moored **H.M.S. President,** the headquarters of the
London Division of the Royal Naval Volunteer Reserve.   It
has the longest pay list in the Navy, as the names of officers
serving at the Admiralty or engaged on special service at home
or abroad are borne on its books.   At Temple Stairs is moored
the *Wellington*, formerly an Admiralty sloop, now the Livery
Hall of the Honourable Company of Master Mariners.   Behind
the *Temple Station* of the District Railway is the tasteful little
building originally designed by the late J. L. Pearson for use as
the Astor Estate Office, and now the **Incorporated Accountants'
Hall.**   It is surmounted by a gilded caravel.

Nearly opposite the station is moored the famous *Discovery*,
the ship in which Captain Scott voyaged to and from the Antarctic.   She now serves as a hostel and training ship for Sea
Scouts.   The small museum contains photographs, charts and
relics of the *Discovery* in her Polar days, and of Captain Scott

and those who sailed in her. A gangway connects the ship with the Embankment. (*Admission [daily] Mondays to Fridays, inclusive, 2–4 p.m.; Saturdays, 10 a.m.–2 p.m.; 1s.; children, 6d. Closed occasionally for periods of one week for training courses.*)

Again on the north side we reach another of the series of Embankment Gardens and note the fine river front of Somerset House (p. 191). Passing under Waterloo Bridge, which we have seen from the Strand at the beginning of our tour, we note the Belgian Monument, which commemorates the hospitality shown by this country to Belgians during the 1914–18 War.

Continuing on the left is that famous Egyptian obelisk known as **Cleopatra's Needle,** brought to this country in 1878.

This and the companion monolith now in New York originally stood before the great temple of Heliopolis many centuries before the time of Cleopatra. The "Needle," of red granite, is 68½ ft. high, and weighs 180 tons. The inscriptions relate its history. While the obelisk was being towed to England the steamer had to abandon it on account of bad weather, but it was subsequently recovered. At the foot are two large bronze sphinxes (perforated during the 1914–18 War by fragments from an aerial bomb).

On the other side of the road are the **Embankment Gardens,** one of the sunniest and most delightful spots in London, much frequented during the luncheon hour by workers from the many neighbouring offices. In summer refreshments can be obtained and there are evening band performances.

Beyond the Gardens are seen in their fine situation the Savoy Hotel and the neighbouring *Shell-Mex* building with its huge clock. They are better appreciated from this side.

Indisputable evidence of the fact that all this "good dry land" has been filched from the river is afforded by the presence at the far end of the Gardens of the beautiful **York Water Gate,** designed by Inigo Jones for York House, the seat of the first Duke of Buckingham and the birthplace of Bacon (1561).

The river is here spanned by the unsightly **Charing Cross Railway Bridge,** and an adjoining footway for pedestrians. Near here stood the blacking factory at which Dickens worked in boyhood. The bridge superseded the Hungerford Suspension Bridge, the ironwork of which was utilised for the lofty Suspension Bridge now spanning the Avon at Clifton. Compared with Paris, London is poorly provided with bridges, and for many years "the question of the bridges" is likely to form an integral part of the London Traffic Problem.

Any of the streets on the right lead up to the Strand from whence it is but a short walk to Charing Cross, the starting-point of our tour.

THE CITY

"I pray you, let us satisfy our eyes with the memorials and the things of fame that do renown this City."—Twelfth Night.

FOR the exploration of the City proper (for boundaries, see plan on pp. 48–49) we can hardly choose a better starting-point than the triangular spot in the very heart of London commonly spoken of as—

The Bank
(Plan II. N. 8)

The significance of the name should not go unnoticed, for although "the Bank" originally implied solely the Bank of England, the neighbourhood is now so closely packed with British and foreign banks and financial organisations as to merit the designation "The Bank of the World." That this is no empty phrase will be appreciated by all who have followed the powerful influence of "The Old Lady of Threadneedle Street" (i.e. the Bank of England) in the solution of the many tangled financial problems which have troubled the world in recent years.

Both above and below ground this is a busy spot—although a recent census showed eleven places in London that were even busier. Here converge no fewer than seven of the most important thoroughfares, each filled from morn till night with an unending stream of buses, cars, lorries, cyclists and pedestrians. A recent official count gave an average at the Bank of over 3,000 vehicles an hour; while underground over 600 trains a day bring people to or from this busy centre. It was not until late 1947 that a system of traffic light control was introduced, but even so those representatives of law and order in the form of the City police force are still on hand in case of need.

Dexterity of no common order is required to get across the roadways in safety, and pedestrians, especially strangers, are strongly advised to make use of the circular Subway from which short stairways give access to all the diverging thoroughfares.

The Subway also gives access to the Bank Stations of the Central and Northern Lines.

The Bank of England
(Plan II. N. 8)

occupies the whole of the site of just over three acres between Threadneedle Street, Princes Street, Lothbury and Bartholomew Lane. The accommodation of the original one-storey building having become inadequate, a new and lofty structure was erected between the wars within the fortress-like walls with which Sir John Soane surrounded the site, and which have a solidity calculated to inspire confidence in the breast of the most timid investor. It will be observed that, for purposes of security, they are entirely windowless, all the rooms immediately behind them being lighted by skylights; but even a Raffles who succeeded in passing this barrier would be baffled at the extraordinary series of defences surrounding the vaults, which include concentric walls of steel and concrete, enormously strong. To make assurance doubly sure the Bank is guarded at night by a picquet mounted by the Brigade of Guards.

The Bank was founded in 1694 as a private corporation doing the ordinary business of a bank, to which were subsequently added exclusive right of note issue in England and Wales and the duties of Registrar for Government Stocks. On March 1st, 1946, the Bank passed to public ownership. Now it does practically no private commercial business, but is mainly concerned as Banker to the Government and to other banks.

Opposite the Bank, in the angle formed by Threadneedle Street and Cornhill is—

The Royal Exchange

Plan II. N. 8.
Admission.—The interior court is open(free) daily to all, except on certain afternoons.

This is the third building of the kind which has occupied the site. The first Exchange, founded by Sir Thomas Gresham, and opened by Queen Elizabeth in 1571, fell a victim to the Great Fire of 1666; and a similar fate overtook its successor in 1838. The present building, designed by Tite, was opened by Queen Victoria in 1844. The steps of the Royal Exchange are one of the places from which a new sovereign is always proclaimed on his accession. In front stands a memorial, designed by Sir Aston Webb, P.R.A., to London troops who fell in the 1914–18 War. Close by is an equestrian *Statue of the Duke of Wellington* (riding without stirrups) by Chantrey. The interior of the Exchange is a large quadrangular court, with a tessellated pavement which formed part of Gresham's building and, like the pavements of several City churches, was spared by the Fire. The Court was originally planned into "walks" patrolled by the various merchants. But the "Silkman's" walk has vanished as completely as those of the Salters and the Barbadoes, and except for some tallow and grease business about 4 p.m. on Wednesdays, but little Exchange business is done here. The ambulatory is decorated with a famous set of 32 spirit-varnish Frescoes by distinguished artists. The visitor is strongly advised not to miss seeing these pictures—anyone may go in. The pictures are plainly labelled, the subjects relating to the history and development of London.

The hall also contains statues of Queen Victoria, Elizabeth I, Charles II, and Connor's bust of Abraham Lincoln. As already remarked, the exchange business of London has long outgrown this hall and the brokers have migrated to the Baltic and other Exchanges.

The Royal Exchange has a famous peal of Bells, recast in 1921. After silence since 1939, a new chime was inaugurated by the Lord Mayor in 1950.

Some damage was done to the roof during the war, and it was here, in the roadway, that London witnessed its largest crater.

Rebuilding has transformed the appearance of this once familiar corner of London. The Royal Exchange and the Mansion House remain as relics of an age which loved Classic porticoes; all around are soaring examples of the new architectural spirit, and the conjunction of styles raises some interesting points for architectural students.

The Mansion House

Plan II. N. 8.
Admission.—The Egyptian Hall, etc., are shown (circumstances permitting to visitors, *on Saturday afternoons only*, making previous application by letter addressed to the Lord Mayor's Secretary.

The Mansion House, the official residence of the Lord Mayor, was first occupied in 1753. The architect was George Dance, the "Clerk to the City's Works." The foundation stone was laid in October 1739. It has a fine Corinthian portico, from the platform of which official announcements are often made. The principal room is the *Egyptian Hall*, which is used for public meetings connected with charities of a National character, and also it is in this room that London's Chief Citizen stands hospitality.

In the north-east corner of the building is situated the Mansion House *Justice Room*, where the Lord Mayor presides daily.

On the corner formed by King William Street and Lombard Street stands the Church of St. Mary Woolnoth, rebuilt in 1716 by Hawksmoor, a pupil of Wren. It is of special interest to Canadians as the church of British Columbia in London. John Newton, joint author with Cowper of the *Olney Hymns*, was once rector, and was buried here with his wife, but their remains were removed in 1893 to Olney. Beneath the church run the Northern and Central Tubes, the exterior of the station harmonising with the church.

Indecision is fatal at this busy spot, for the loiterer is likely to be swept off his feet. Let us therefore turn westward along the Poultry and Cheapside to St. Paul's Cathedral and Ludgate Hill, and so join the last route of our West End section.

ROUTE IX.—CHEAPSIDE— GUILDHALL — GENERAL POST OFFICE — ST. PAUL'S CATHEDRAL—LUDGATE HILL—OLD BAILEY—QUEEN VICTORIA STREET—CANNON STREET.

On the right of the **Poultry** (Plan II. N. 8) is the magnificent headquarters building of the *Midland Bank*, designed by *Sir Edwin Lutyens* and rightly described as a masterpiece. The street in its modern aspect gives little indication of its former character, when the old Chepe was from end to end an open market. This and neighbouring thoroughfares still bear the names of the commodities once displayed for sale in them. On the north side are Milk Street, Wood Street, Ironmonger Lane and Honey Lane, and to the south is Bread Street. The name of **Cheapside** (Plan I. N. 7) is an obvious derivation from the Anglo-Saxon *ceapian*, to sell or bargain. Though less than a quarter of a mile in length, Cheapside is one of the most important city thoroughfares, and is lined with shops. Jewellers, tailors and hosiers especially favour it. A tablet on Nos. 40–41 marks the side of the old *Cheapside Cross*. In **Old Jewry,** on the right, are the headquarters of the **City Police** (*see* p. 33). The name recalls a synagogue built by Jews who were subsequently driven farther east. During the 1939–45 war, when the building next to the police headquarters was destroyed, an ancient "wailing wall" was discovered. It had been in use as one of the main walls of the building. Close at hand, with main entrance in Prince's Street, is **Grocers' Hall,** the headquarters of the old and wealthy Grocers' Company, or "Pepperers," and at the corner of Ironmonger Lane is the site of the **Mercers' Hall.** Although the offices of this company still stand, the Hall itself, rebuilt in 1884, was burnt out early in the war. Fortunately most of the Grinling Gibbons carvings were saved. The Mercers are considered the senior of the City Livery Companies.

At **King Street** we turn rightward for—

The Guildhall

Plan I. N. 7.
Admission.—The Great Hall is open all day and may be freely seen. The Art Gallery is open Mondays to Saturdays, 10–5; the Library and Commercial Reference Room, 9.30–5; and the Temporary Museum, 10–5.
Nearest Stations.—Bank (Central and Northern Lines), Moorgate (Metropolitan, etc.), Mansion House (District).

This famous civic palace is chiefly associated in the popular mind with the great banquet on Lord Mayor's Day (November 9), when important political pronouncements are frequently made by members of the Government. It has been the scene of some of the most stirring episodes in our history. Nearly every crowned head in Europe—when crowned heads were more common—was fêted within these walls; and many of our leading statesmen, soldiers and sailors have here been honoured with the freedom of the City—an honour esteemed second only to honours received from the hands of the Sovereign. The Guildhall, begun about 1411, was partly destroyed by the Great Fire in 1666, and was again very badly damaged on the night of December 29, 1940, when among other losses the roof of the Great Hall was destroyed. This has now been replaced by a temporary roofing. As we cross the Yard a good view is obtained of the fine fifteenth-century porch. Until 1910 the east wing bore no sort of resemblance to the west wing, but this was remedied, and with the exception of the roof the entire south front appears according to the eighteenth-century design of George Dance, R.A.

The **Great Hall** is used for the election of the Lord Mayor and Sheriffs, and for many civic and political gatherings. Since the destruction of the Council Chamber it has also been used as a Chamber for the Common Council. The famous wooden figures known as *Gog and Magog* which formerly stood in the gallery were lost when the roof was burned. Damage and loss was also sustained by the many windows depicting scenes from the history of the City and there are now only two intact. Ranged round the hall are monuments (damaged) to Wellington, Nelson (inscription by Sheridan), Chatham (inscription by Burke), Wm. Pitt, and Lord Mayor Beckford. In the north-west corner are standard measurements of a foot and a yard, and let into the floor of the hall are plates marking a chain (66 ft.) and 100 ft.

The old **Council Chamber** and the **Aldermen's Court Room,** were destroyed.

The **Guildhall Library,** founded in 1425, is maintained as a public reference library. The principal library is a magnificent hall in Victorian Gothic style, 100 ft. long and 50 ft. high, with book-lined bays on either side. The roof, with arched ribs, the stained-glass windows, and the fine chimney-pieces merit special attention. On state occasions the Lord Mayor receives distinguished guests in this room. The Library has an estimated total of 130,000 volumes and, as one would expect, is especially rich in works on London and Middlesex. A well-furnished **Commercial Reference Room** adjoins.

At the head of the stairs leading down to the Basinghall Street entrance is a collection of clocks, watches, etc., belonging to the Clockmakers' Company.

The **Temporary Museum,** in a room adjoining the Library, contains selections from an extensive collection including articles of archæological and civic interest bearing on the history of the City.

The **Art Gallery** (temporary building) is entered from Guildhall

Yard, of which it forms the eastern side. The collection here includes works of the nineteenth-century British School and works illustrating the civic history, social life and topography of the City. Plaques erected by the City Corporation remind us that the Guildhall Chapel stood here from 1299–1822, and Blackwell Hall from 1356–1820.

On the opposite side of the Yard is the *Guildhall Police Court.* in Guildhall Buildings is the *City of London Court.*

The **Irish Chamber** is the headquarters of the Irish Society, actually a highly important committee of the City Corporation. It is entirely independent in its jurisdiction. The Corporation appoints it, but has no further control over it, as its powers are defined by statute. Its function is to administer the City's Irish estates—a relic of the part taken by London in the "plantation of Ulster" 300 years ago. These are mainly in Coleraine and, as the name itself suggests, Londonderry. Under the society's charter the whole of its revenue, which is large, must be spent in those districts.

At the corner of Guildhall Yard stands the Church of **St. Lawrence Jewry,** built by Wren in place of one destroyed by the Great Fire. It suffered considerable damage in December 1940. For more than two centuries the Lord Mayor and Corporation have attended service here on Michaelmas Day, prior to the election of a new Lord Mayor. The weather vane in the form of a gridiron, in allusion to the legendary history of St. Lawrence, was retrieved from the churchyard where it had fallen, and is now in the temporary Chapel that has been built beneath the tower. St. Lawrence Jewry is the official Church of Canada (the Daughters of the Empire), New Zealand and South Africa, and contained the official flags and pews of the Dominions.

Gresham Street (Plan I. N. 7) runs from the north-west corner of the Bank of England to St. Martin's-le-Grand along a course roughly parallel to Cheapside. The first turning on the right is Aldermanbury. The Church of **St. Mary, Aldermanbury,** now but a shell, contained the tomb of the infamous Judge Jeffreys. Milton was married here in 1656 to his second wife, though his spell of happiness was of short duration. In the churchyard is a memorial to Herminge and Condell, who acted with Shakespeare and edited the First Folio edition of the plays. Nearly all the offices and warehouses hereabouts are tenanted by firms connected with the wholesale drapery trade; a notable exception being the *Chartered Insurance Institute.*

Eastward along Gresham Street, at the corner of Basinghall Street, is **Gresham College,** founded under the will of Sir Thomas Gresham, and rebuilt in 1913.

Near the Post Office end of Gresham Street is the **Goldsmiths' Hall,** rebuilt from Hardwick's designs in 1835. The hall contains notable pictures of sovereigns, and a goblet out of which Queen Elizabeth I is said to have drunk at her coronation. The "hall-mark" of the Company, a leopard's head, is familiar to all fortunate enough to possess gold plate or ornaments. At the corner of Gresham Street and Wood Street is the site of the former **Haberdashers' Hall.** This Company has done much for education in the past.

Returning now to Cheapside, we note on the south side the ruins of the famous **Bow Church,** or, to give its full name, the Church of St. Mary-le-Bow.

A person born within the sound of Bow Bells is a "Cockney," or Londoner pure and simple. It was the sound of Bow Bells, if we are to believe tradition, that lured the runaway apprentice, Dick Whittington, back from Highgate, to be Lord Mayor of London. In 1905, after a long interval of disuse, the *Whittington Chimes* were restored, from a setting provided by Sir Charles V. Stanford. The church was rebuilt by Wren after the Great Fire, the steeple, being 235 ft. high, generally considered his masterpiece. Many authorities, indeed, regarded it as the finest Renaissance campanile in the world. Below the church is a *crypt* showing Roman, Saxon and Norman work. It forms a series of "bows," or arches, and the ecclesiastical court which formerly met here became in consequence known as the Court of Arches (now removed to the Sanctuary, Westminster). The tablet on the west wall relating to John Milton was removed from the Church of All Hallows, Bread Street, on its demolition.

In **Milk Street,** north of Cheapside, Sir Thomas More was born in 1480. At the corner of Wood Street and Cheapside still flourishes the famous **Plane Tree** referred to by Wordsworth in "Poor Susan." The western end of Cheapside suffered considerable damage during the war, many offices hereabouts being destroyed at the same time as the **Saddlers' Hall,** which stood on the corner of Foster Lane; **St. Vedast's Church** (Wren), a few paces up Foster Lane, suffering a like fate. The church, however, is not entirely without hope of restoration. In **Old Change,** to the south is **St. Augustine's Church,** still another of the Wren churches to suffer damage or destruction. The Rev. R. H. Barham, author of the facetious *Ingoldsby Legends*, was rector here at the time of his death.

Several important thoroughfares converge at the west end of Cheapside. **Aldersgate Street** (Plan I. N. 7), with its memories of Milton and John Wesley, runs northward to the Metropolitan station of the same name, and is thence continued as the **Goswell Road,** of Pickwickian associations, to the *Angel* (now a Lyons

restaurant) at Islington (*see* p. 228).   The southern part of
Aldersgate Street is known as **St. Martin's-le-Grand,** a name
familiar in all quarters of the globe as the headquarters of our
great postal system.   The name is a relic of a wooden church
dedicated here in 1050.

The General Post Office

Plan I. M. and N. 7.
Nearest Stations.—St. Paul's (Central Line), Aldersgate Street and Barbican
(Metropolitan), Mansion House (District Line).

The enormous postal business of London is carried on in no
fewer than nine extensive blocks of buildings.   The famous old
building on the east side of St. Martins-le-Grand, with Ionic
porticoes and clock, erected in 1825–9 on the site of the church of
St. Martin's-le-Grand, was demolished in 1912–13, and the site
is now occupied by fine modern offices.   The extensive block
opposite, erected in 1870–3 (destroyed 1940, partly restored
1945–6), forms the Central Telegraph Office which is the hub
of the telegraph service.   To the north is **Headquarters Building,**
which contains the offices of the Postmaster-General and the
Administrative and Public Relations Departments.   **King
Edward Building,** which contains the headquarters of the London
Postal Region and the London Chief Office, E.C.1, occupies
part of the site of the old Bluecoat School.   Here London E.C.
district and foreign letters are sorted and despatched, and all
the ordinary work of a district post office is carried on.   In addition it is a concentration and distribution centre for mail addressed to London generally.   The *Public Hall* (entrance in King
Edward Street) is open day and night for the sale of stamps,
despatch of telegrams, etc.   *Poste Restante* is on the left.   An
interpreter is in attendance from 9 a.m. to 5 p.m.   In front of
the building appropriately stands a *Statue of Rowland Hill*,
pioneer of the "penny post."

Faraday Building, in Queen Victoria Street (p. 222), and also
Telephone Exchange Building in Wood Street, are used by the
Telephone Department, in constant communication with every
part of the world.   Other huge postal buildings are at Mount
Pleasant, where inland letters and parcels are dealt with; Ken-
sington (Savings Bank); Manor Gardens, Holloway (National
Savings Certificates); and Studd Street, N. (stores).

Post Office "Tube" Railway.   An interesting underground
railway carries letters and parcel mails from the King Edward
Building to Paddington in one direction and Whitechapel in the
other, with six intermediate stations serving District Offices and
Liverpool Street Station.   The trains are electrically driven and
automatically controlled, and thanks to many ingenious loading
devices 37,000 mail-bags are transmitted daily.   It is computed
that the railway relieves street congestion to the extent of
2,400 van miles every day.

Particulars of the London postal, telegraphic and telephonic arrangements will be found on pp. 34-5.

The G.P.O. Headquarters Building partly shuts in a small open space formerly the graveyards of the Church of **St. Botolph Without, Greyfriars,** and **St. Leonards,** but now known as the **Postmen's Park.** By the suggestion of G. F. Watts, R.A., a cloister was erected here, in which are placed from time to time tablets commemorative of acts of heroism, especially in humble life. The great artist is himself commemorated by a small statuette. A tablet on the railings overlooking Aldersgate Street commemorates the evangelical conversion of John and Charles Wesley, which occurred in this neighbourhood in 1738.

In Shaftesbury Place, Aldersgate Street, is the magnificent Hall of the **Ironmongers' Company.**

Disregarding **Newgate Street** (p. 231) for the while, we will turn into **St. Paul's Churchyard,** the north side of which is closed to the passage of vehicles. Here are some noted drapery establishments. We can enter St. Paul's by the North Porch, but it will be better first to pass round to the western end in order to gain a good idea of the exterior.

St. Paul's Cathedral

Plans I and II M. and N. 7 and 8.

Admission.—The Cathedral is open daily from 9 to 5 or 7 in summer, but visitors are, of course, expected to refrain from walking about during service time (*see* below). The nave, choir, transepts and east end can be viewed without charge. Tickets must be obtained (10.45 a.m. to 3.30 p.m. 4.45 to ¾ of an hour before closing) at the office adjoining the South Transept for the Crypt, 6*d.*, and the Whispering Gallery and Stone Gallery, 1*s.*

Services.—*Week-days.*—Holy Communion 8 a.m. in Chapel of St. Dunstan; Matins 10 a.m. (Choral except Wed. and Fri.), in Choir. Weds. and Fri., mid-day service (Choral) 12.30 p.m. Evensong (Choral), 4 p.m.

Sundays.—Litany, in Chapel of St. Dunstan, 7.45 a.m. Holy Communion, in Chapel of St. Dunstan, 8 a.m. Matins, sermon, and Holy Communion (Choral), 10.30. Evensong (Choral) with Sermon, 3.15 p.m. Second Evensong and Sermon 6.30 p.m.

On Christmas Day, Good Friday and Ascension Day the services are as on Sundays, except that there is no second Evensong on Christmas and Ascension Days, and on Good Friday there is 10.30 Matins with Sermon, the Three Hours' service (12–3) is held, Evensong is at 3.15 p.m. and Evening service at 6.30 p.m.

On ordinary Saints' Days and Holy Days there is a sermon at Evensong.

Nearest Stations.—St. Paul's (Central Line), Blackfriars or Mansion House (District), Blackfriars (formerly St. Paul's) (Southern Region).

Many bus routes pass St. Paul's Cathedral.

Principal Dimensions.—Length, including portico but not steps, 515 ft.; interior, 479 ft.; width across transepts from door to door, 250 ft.; nave and aisles only, 102 ft. Height from pavement to top of cross, 365 ft.; height of inner dome, 225 ft.; diameter, 112 ft.; height of western towers, 221 ft. The golden ball is 6 ft. in diameter.

Historical Note.—Opinions are generally agreed that the present Cathedral is at least the third to occupy the site, more probably the fourth or fifth. Tradition even speaks of a Temple of Diana long before the introduction of Christianity. Early in the seventh century, probably A.D. 607, we find Ethelbert, King of Kent, rearing what for those days must have been a stately fane, and endowing it with, among other gifts, the manor of Tillingham in Essex: a manor, it is interesting to note, still in the possession of the Dean and Chapter, constituting probably the most ancient tenure in the country. This structure, after various vicissitudes, was destroyed by fire in 1087, shortly after the Norman Conquest. Its successor, immediately commenced but not completed for upwards of two centuries, is still referred to as **Old St. Paul's.** Colossal as is the present building, Old St. Paul's was even larger, having a length of 586 ft., while the spire, destroyed by fire in 1561, was 489 ft. in height (some authorities say 520 ft.). On the north-east side of the present choir, close to Cheapside, stood until 1643 old **St. Paul's Cross,** so often referred to in the history of the Reformation period. In 1910 a monument was erected close to the spot.

In the gardens on the south side of the Cathedral are exposed some remains of the old Cloisters and of the Chapter House. Others were discovered in 1912 as far distant as the north side of Paternoster Row.

Old St. Paul's fell to somewhat base uses in its later days, the nave becoming a public promenade and a place of assignation for all sorts of doubtful characters, while a theatre was actually erected against the outer walls. Under Charles I extensive restoration, in which Inigo Jones was the leading spirit, took place, but the Commonwealth Parliament appropriated the funds, and Cromwell stabled his troopers' horses in the nave. In 1666 came the Great Fire and Wren's opportunity. He had already, as Assistant-Surveyor-General of His Majesty's Works, submitted a scheme for the repair and adaptation of the old building, but the Fire gave him an almost clear ground to work upon. He was, however, unfortunately hampered throughout by an officious Committee. A model of his favourite design is still preserved in the Cathedral. It is simply marvellous that while engaged on this stupendous undertaking Wren was yet able to build almost simultaneously upwards of thirty other City churches, no two of which are alike in conception or detail, though all bear an exact and harmonious relation to the great central building. The Cathedral was begun in 1675, opened for service in 1697, and completed in 1710, Wren receiving all through the not very princely salary of £200 a year. The necessary funds (estimated at about a million pounds, or ten times that sum in present values) were raised, except for a comparatively small amount, by taxes on coal and wine entering the Port of London. In Wren's old age, we are told, he retired to Hampton, but once every year insisted upon being carried to a spot beneath the dome where he could contemplate the work of his hands. He died in 1723, at the ripe old age of ninety-one. *Lector, si monumentum requiris circumspice*—"Reader, if thou seekest his monument look around," tersely says the tablet over his tombstone.

A restoration was carried out between the two world wars. The task occupied five years and involved the consolidation of the piers with metal rods and with liquid cement injected under pressure; and the encircling of the Dome by an enormous chain of rustless steel, 30 tons in weight and 450 yards long. Not the least notable feature of the work is the manner in which it has secured the safety of the Dome without in the slightest degree altering its appearance.

During the war the Cathedral suffered considerable damage, including the loss of the High Altar, the furnishings of the Sacrarium, most of the glass from the windows, and damage to the Reredos and to the North Transept.

Exterior

The Cathedral is built entirely of Portland Stone, on the plan of a Latin cross, a form which expands easily to the eye of a spectator, and exhibits its beautiful combinations at one view. A modification of the simple cross is made at the western end by projections northward and southward, forming St. Dunstan's Chapel and the Chapel of the Order of St. Michael and St. George. The flanking bell towers serve the purpose of elongating the west front and giving it more importance. Wren would have had a Greek cross (i.e., a cross having four equal arms), with a huge central dome supported by eight pillars, but he was overruled by the Court party, who feared that such a building would be unsuited to the Roman Catholic ritual they hoped to see re-established. In general appearance St. Paul's bears a marked resemblance to St. Peter's at Rome, but is, of course, much smaller. Though in plan a Gothic building, its character is almost entirely masked by Classic details, Wren's openly expressed intention being "to reconcile as near as possible the Gothic to a better manner of architecture." The exterior columns and coupled pilasters consist of two orders, the lower Corinthian, the upper Composite. This upper wall is little more than a screen to hide what in a Gothic church would be the flying buttresses, but it is of sufficient solidity to form an essential part of the system of abutments by which the thrust of the dome is resisted.

The **Western Façade,** looking down Ludgate Hill, has a width of 180 ft., with a double portico, on the pediment of which is a bas-relief by Bird, representing the conversion of St. Paul. On the apex stands a colossal statue of St. Paul, with St. Peter on his right and St. James on his left. In the north tower is a peal of twelve bells, presented by various City Companies and hung in 1878 (the tenor weighs 62 cwt., the note being B flat); in the south, or clock tower, is *Great Paul*, the largest bell in England. It weighs nearly 17 tons, and is over $9\frac{1}{2}$ ft. in diameter. It is rung for five minutes daily at one o'clock and is used as the five-minute service bell on Sundays.   The *Clock* face is 17 ft. in diameter.   The copper hands, especially shaped to resist wind and snow, have lengths of 9 ft. 6 in. and 5 ft. respectively.   The clock strikes on three old bells, the biggest, on which the hours are sounded, weighing 5¼ tons.   This bell (cast *temp.* Edward I, and formerly hung in New Palace Yard, Westminster) is always tolled on the occasion of the death of the Sovereign, the Archbishop of Canterbury, the Bishop of London, the Dean of St. Paul's or the Lord Mayor.   In the first case the tolling continues for two hours, in other cases for one hour.

Facing Ludgate Hill stands a *Statue of Queen Anne.** The well-fed and remarkably tame pigeons here are generally surrounded by an admiring crowd.

At the foot of the twenty-two steps leading up to the doorway may be seen a slab inscribed, "Here Queen Victoria returned thanks to Almighty God for the sixtieth anniversary of her accession, June 22, 1897."

Passing now round to the south porch (Cannon Street side), we see that the double portico of the western front is repeated. The five statues of apostles replaced in 1900 the weather-beaten effigies erected by Bird.   In the pediment will be noted a phœnix, with the motto "Resurgam."   It is said that when Wren was marking out the ground, he sent a mad to bring a stone from a heap of charred remains of the old Cathedral to indicate where the centre of the dome should be.   The stone thus brought happened to be part of an old gravestone with this single word upon it.   Regarding this as a good omen, Wren adopted the word as his motto.

Both externally and internally the great **Dome** is the most imposing feature of the Cathedral, though, as we have said, a distant view is necessary to appreciate its majesty.   Many visitors do not realise that the dome is really double, the true dome (that seen from the inside) being much lower than the outer.   Between the inner dome (brick) and the outer dome (wood covered with lead) is a cone of brickwork supporting the lantern and the ball and cross.

Interior

The amount of internal decoration contemplated by Wren is a point that has been much discussed, but it is hard to believe that he intended these vast spaces to be entirely unadorned, though it is only in our own generation that the work of enrichment has been seriously undertaken.   To the left on entering

* The original statue, by Bird, of which this is a modern copy, provoked the wits of the day, one of whom, taking advantage of the fact that facing it there stood a much-frequented tavern, produced the following couplet, which greatly tickled the popular fancy—

"Brandy Nan, Brandy Nan, you're left in the lurch,
    Your face to the gin shop, your back to the church."

Viewed from the rubble and weeds of the bombed surrounds, St. Paul's Cathedral rises magnificently and presents a picture of great beauty, considerable charm and dignity.

[*J. Allan Cash*]

A view across the river at Blackfriars showing Unilever House in centre background, St. Paul's Cathedral and to the right the rising bulk of Faraday House.

is the **Chapel of All Souls,** or the **Kitchener Memorial Chapel.**
Prominent on the floor is a recumbent effigy of the Field-Marshal,
by *Reid Dick.* On either hand are statues of St. Michael and St.
George, given by the nursing services. A receptacle in the north
wall contains the Roll of Honour of the Royal Engineers. The
two large silver
candlesticks before
the altar were
formed from medals
belonging to men of
the London Rifle
Brigade who lost
their lives in the
war.

Beyond is **St.
Dunstan's Chapel,**
where the early
morning services
are held. It has a
Salviati mosaic,
representing the
Three Marys at the
Sepulchre. In the
opposite (south)
aisle is the **Chapel
of the Order of St.
Michael and St.
George.** The Order
is a Colonial one,
being conferred
only for distin-
guished service be-
yond the seas. At
the western end is
a modern throne, of
oak and lime, in
accordance with the
Grinling Gibbons
work in the Cath-
edral. The central
seat is that of the
Sovereign; on either
side are the stalls of
the Grand Master
and the Chancellor

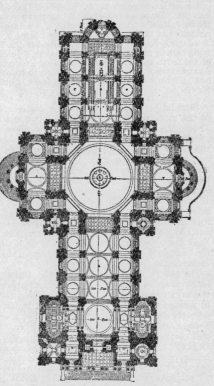

GROUND PLAN OF ST. PAUL'S CATHEDRAL

of the Order. From these diverge the oak stalls of the Knights
Grand Cross of the Order, each overhung by a silk banner
emblazoned with his personal arms.

St. Paul's is second only to Westminster Abbey in the number of its
Monuments to the mighty dead. We can only indicate a few. In

the north aisle are monuments of *Lord Leighton, P.R.A.* (1896), *General Gordon* (killed at Khartoum, 1885). On the adjacent piers a marble bust of *Lord Roberts* (1832–1914). The gallant Field-Marshal rests in the Crypt.   In an arch between nave and aisle is the *Wellington Monument* by Alfred Stevens, the upper portion tardily completed from an unfinished sketch in 1912.   On the inner side of the eastern-most pillars of the nave are G. F. Watts's "Time, Death and Judgment" and his "Peace and Goodwill." Against a pillar in the south aisle is *Holman Hunt's* "Light of the World," a larger replica of the earlier rendering of the same subject in the chapel of Keble College, Oxford. A welcome flash of colour is introduced to the Transept by the banners hung here in connection with the George V Jubilee celebrations in 1935: in the south transept those of the King Emperor, the United Kingdom, Australia and New Zealand.   The north transept is now out of use but formerly contained those of India, Canada, South Africa and Newfoundland.

Standing under the Dome one realises the great dimensions of the structure. The highest part of the inner dome is 218 ft. above the floor; the windows seen through the opening are nearly 300 ft., and are above the outer dome.   The ceiling of the inner **Dome** is adorned with eight paintings by Thornhill, representing scenes from the life of St. Paul. In the niches above the Gallery are statues of the Doctors of the Church, while the spandrels between the great arches are covered by eight large mosaics representing apostles and prophets.   *G. F. Watts* was responsible for St. Matthew and St. John on the north side; St. Mark and St. Luke were designed by *A. Brittan*; the four prophets were the work of *Alfred Stevens*.   In accordance with Wren's intentions, the "quarter domes," at a lower level, have been decorated in mosaic by *Sir William Richmond, R.A.,* the subjects being the Crucifixion, the Entombment, the Resurrection and the Ascension.

On the right of the Choir is the **Pulpit,*** of marble, with a large sounding-board.   The wonderfully rich choir stalls and the organ case were carved by *Grinling Gibbons.*   The **Reredos,** of white Parian marble, and flanked by an open colonnade, was severely damaged during the 1939-45 war, and has been removed; a fresh arrangement of the sanctuary is in preparation, which will bring it into closer agreement with the ideas of Wren.   The **Organ,** one of the finest in the world, is divided, the keyboard being placed on the north side, and the entire instrument is fitted with electric action. It has 5 manuals, 116 stops and 5,055 pipes, and was reconstructed by Willis in 1872, 1900 and 1930.   It still incorporates pipes from the original organ built in 1695 by "Father" Smith.   The splendid gates on either side of the altar are reproductions of older work; those leading to the apse were designed by that great artist *Tijou* and made of Sussex iron.   The apse and the vaulting and walls are decorated with

---

*It is said that the preacher who hopes to be heard in St. Paul's must always look towards the Joshua Reynolds monument across the Dome; but this has to some extent been corrected by microphones.

richly-coloured **Mosaics** by *Sir William Richmond.* The chief panels of the apse represent our Lord enthroned, with recording angels on either side. In the choir the most notable decorations are those of the three "saucer-domes," or cupolas, representing three days of creation, beginning at the west with Beasts, and continuing with Fishes and Birds.

Tickets for the **Crypt** must be obtained at the South Crypt entrance. The Crypt extends beneath the entire church. Here lie the remains of most of those whose monuments appear in the Cathedral. The portion of the Crypt beneath the Choir is known as **Painters' Corner,** and contains either the graves or memorials of *Sir Joshua Reynolds, Sir Benjamin West, Sir Thomas Lawrence, J. M. W. Turner, John Opie, Lord Leighton, Sir John Millais, Holman Hunt, Sir L. Alma-Tadema, Melton Prior, William Blake* and other famous artists. Of even greater interest to many is the plain black marble slab beneath the last window recess of the south aisle, marking the **Grave of Sir Christopher Wren.** Above is the tablet bearing the often-quoted epitaph already referred to (p. 214). The east end forms the **Chapel of St. Faith.** When *old* St. Paul's was built the Church of St. Faith was pulled down to make room for the extension of the Choir and the parishioners were given the Chapel of St. Faith as their parish church, and so it has remained. It contains a few mutilated monuments from the old building. The place of honour immediately under the centre of the dome is occupied by the **Grave of Nelson.** The coffin was made from the mainmast of the French flagship at the Battle of Aboukir, *L'Orient.* The Italian sarcophagus was constructed by order of Cardinal Wolsey for his own interment. The **Tomb of Wellington** consists of a great block of porphyry resting on a granite base. The funeral car (cast from captured cannon) on which the Duke's remains were brought to the Cathedral stands at the extreme west end of the crypt. Close to Wellington's tomb are the graves of *Admiral Earl Jellicoe* (d. 1935) and of *Admiral Earl Beatty* (d. 1936), and a memorial of *Lord Charles Beresford* (d. 1919). In "Field-Marshals' Corner" rest the remains of three other great soldiers, *Field-Marshal Viscount Wolseley* (d. 1913), *Field-Marshal Earl Roberts, K.G.* (d. 1914), and *Field-Marshal Sir Henry Wilson* (assassinated, 1922). Here, too, are mural tablets to *Field-Marshal Sir Evelyn Wood,* to *Florence Nightingale,* and to "*Lawrence of Arabia*" (d. 1935), and a bronze bust of *George Washington,* presented by the Sulgrave Institution of America in 1921.

By the 143 steps of the Library Staircase (*for admission see* p. 213) we reach the triforium, a gallery running above the south aisle to the **Library,** which is immediately over the Chapel of the Order of St. Michael and St. George (p. 217). Here are shown a number of interesting autographs and ancient MSS., portraits, seals, etc. Among them is a promise signed by Charles II, of £1,000 a year towards the rebuilding fund. Needless to say, there is no record of the receipt of the money. Next the visitor will be directed to the **Whispering Gallery,** which runs round the interior of the dome. A slight whisper against the wall on one side is distinctly audible on the other, a distance in a straight line of more than 100 ft. A further dark and narrow flight leads up to the **Stone Gallery,** encircling the foot of the outer dome. From this on a clear day a magnificent view over London is gained. The **Golden Gallery** (for which an extra charge is made) is above the dome and at the foot of the lantern. The height from the pavement to the Cross is 365 ft. The ball and cross were renewed in 1821. Those who succeed in reaching the Stone Gallery have ascended 375 steps, while those who attain the foot of the ball have 627 steps to their credit.

St. Paul's has been the scene of many **Thanksgiving Services** of national importance. Queen Elizabeth rejoiced with her people at the overthrow of the Armada, and in 1702 Queen Anne publicly returned thanks for Marlborough's victories in the Low Countries and for the destruction of the Spanish fleet at Vigo. In 1704 the visit was repeated in gratitude for the victory at Blenheim. In more recent times we may recall the national thanksgiving in 1872 for the recovery from serious illness of King Edward VII, then Prince of Wales. In 1897 Queen Victoria took part in a solemn service at the foot of the steps in gratitude for the completion of a reign of sixty years, an event recorded by an inscription in the pavement. On June 8th, 1902, King Edward VII and Queen Alexandra returned thanks for the restoration of peace in South Africa, and on the following 28th October for the recovery of the former from the sudden illness which delayed his Coronation. The Cathedral was also the scene of several very impressive services of national supplication during the 1914–18 War. On July 6, 1919, King George V and Queen Mary attended a great Peace Thanksgiving service at the close of the hostilities with Germany; their Majesties were here again in June, 1930, at the services celebrating the restoration of the Cathedral, and on May 6, 1935, they came to St. Paul's for the Thanksgiving Service which formed the central act of the Silver Jubilee celebration.

Still more recently have been the State Thanksgiving Services, attended by King George VI, May 13, 1945, for victory in Europe and on August 19, of the same year, for victory in Japan in World War II; and the opening service of the Festival of Britain in 1951.

South-east of the Cathedral is the St. Paul's Garden opened in 1951 as a symbolic and permanent contribution by the City of London to the Festival of Britain.

Dean's Court, in the south-west corner of St. Paul's Churchyard, leads past the **Deanery** to the **Choir House** in Great Carter Lane. **Doctors' Commons,** where marriage licences are issued by the Bishop of London's Registry, survives in name only. In Bell Yard, to the south, was, before its destruction by bombs, a tablet recording the site of "the Bell, Carter Lane," whence Richard Quiney wrote the letter to Shakespeare, dated October

25, 1598, now in the Birthplace Museum at Stratford, the only letter extant addressed to the poet.

Cannon Street, at the south-east corner of the Churchyard, is referred to on p. 223, but at this end formerly stood the **Cordwainers' Hall,** now completely destroyed.   Not everyone is aware that a cordwainer is a shoemaker, the name being indirectly derived from Cordovan, or *cordwain*, leather.

Paternoster Row (Plan I. M. 7), a narrow lane behind the north side of St. Paul's Churchyard, was long known the world over in connection with the book trade.   Now it is a row of memories only, as on the 29th December, 1940, the entire Row was destroyed.   Near at hand are Amer Corner, Ave Maria Lane, Creed Lane, and Godliman Street, all suggestive of the former exclusively ecclesiastical aspect of the locality.*

To the eastern end of Paternoster Row, in **Panyer Alley,** was a tablet claiming:

> "When ye have sought the Citty round,
>   Yet still this is the highest ground.
>   August the 27, 1688."

The tablet, taken to safety, awaits some rebuilding before its return.   Its claim, however, is in some doubt as the honour more rightly belongs to Cornhill.

At the western end of Paternoster Row is **Warwick Lane;** the building on the left, with terra-cotta bas-reliefs by *Tinworth,* is the **Cutlers' Hall.**

A section of **Old London Wall** may be seen by courtesy of the Oxford University Press at their premises in Warwick Square.

Stationers' Hall, near the foot of Paternoster Row, is the hall of the Stationers' and Newspaper Makers' Company, the members of which, unlike members of most City Companies, have generally some actual connection with the trade from which they take their name.   Formerly all books published in Great Britain had to be registered here before copyright proceedings could be taken, but the passing of the Copyright Act of 1911 rendered this unnecessary, mere authorship now securing copyright in the British Empire for a period of fifty years from the author's death.   Among the treasures of the Company are some very early registers—that of 1569 including "a boke intituled Ewclide," then first translated into English—and the composing stick used by Benjamin Franklin when working at a press in London.

---

* Sermon Lane, however, derives its name from the shere-monlers—men who cut the silver discs ready for stamping in a mint which stood near-by and "Godliman" is probably "Godelmynger"—a kind of cordwain.

Ludgate Hill (Plan I. M. 7) rises steeply from Ludgate Circus to St. Paul's. King Lud, after whom the hill is generally believed to be named, is regarded by all modern historians as mythical. A tablet on **St. Martin's Church** (Wren's) marks the site of the Old Lud Gate (*see* p. 70); and outside St. Dunstan's, Fleet Street (*see* p. 200), is a statue of Elizabeth I which at one time stood over the Gate. As will be seen many buildings were destroyed here during the war.

Old Bailey (Plan I. M. 7), of unhappy memories, connects Ludgate Hill with Newgate Street. The name is derived from the situation of the original building in the bailey of the old City wall. Here stood for many years the gloomy Newgate Prison, demolished in 1902–3. Numerous relics of the old prison, such as whipping-blocks, leg-irons, etc., can be seen at the Guildhall (p. 208), and others are in the London Museum (p. 139). On the more northerly part of the site is the **Central Criminal Court,** opened in 1905, an imposing block erected at a cost of a quarter of a million pounds to replace the former inconvenient and dingy Sessions House.

The building was designed by *E. W. Mountford.* On the Old Bailey front the old stone of the prison was utilised as far as possible. Over the main entrance is a sculptured group by F. W. Pomeroy, A.R.A., representing the Recording Angel, supported by Fortitude and Truth. A conspicuous feature of the structure is the copper-covered dome, 195 ft high, surmounted by a large bronzed figure of Justice. The building can be viewed on *Tuesdays and Fridays,* 10 *to* 4 (when the sittings of the Court permit), on application to the Keeper. Tickets of admission to important trials can generally only be obtained from one of the Sheriffs or Aldermen. The public galleries are entered from Newgate Street.

From the south side of Ludgate Hill a labyrinth of lanes would bring us down to Queen Victoria Street and the river. In Blackfriars Lane is the **Apothecaries' Hall,** dating from 1670. A tablet recalls that here stood the monastery of Blackfriars, built in 1278.

Queen Victoria Street (Plan II. M. and N. 8) runs diagonally from Blackfriars Bridge (p. 202) to the Bank, a distance of about two-thirds of a mile. Near its foot is the office of *The Times,* extending back to Printing House Square, in which, during the Stuart period, stood the King's printing-house. The newspaper is produced on the spot where stood the Blackfriars Playhouse, with which Shakespeare was so intimately connected. Almost opposite is **Blackfriars Station** (formerly *St. Paul's*),

(Southern Region), from which, at a lower level than Queen Victoria Street, **Upper Thames Street,** with its wharves and warehouses, follows the north bank of the river to London Bridge. Chaucer first saw the light in Thames Street, close to the present railway arch, in 1340. One of the docks still retains the name of **Castle Baynard,** an important fortress sometimes used as a royal residence and rendered famous by Shakespeare in *Richard III.* Its name is given to one of the City wards. Continuing up Queen Victoria Street, we see on the left the ruined Church of **St. Andrew-by-the-Wardrobe,** still another Wren church that suffered severely during the war. The quaint affix is explained by the fact that the office of the King's Great Wardrobe was formerly in the vicinity. Adjoining is the "Bible House" of the **British and Foreign Bible Society,** with a library containing a unique collection of copies and translations of Holy Scripture in many languages. Opposite is the **London Auction Mart,** the headquarters of London auctioneers. **Faraday Buildings** bear little external evidence of its interest and importance: yet from here, or by means of connections made in this building, one can telephone to practically any part of the world as easily as to another part of London. Then on the left we reach the **Heralds' College,** or College of Arms, incorporated and endowed by Richard III in 1484. The house was rebuilt as it stands after the Great Fire. The office of Earl Marshal and head of the College is hereditary in the person of the Duke of Norfolk. The College comprises the three kings of arms—Garter, Clarenceux and Norroy—six heralds and four pursuivants. In addition to their ceremonial functions, the Heralds regulate the bearing of arms, and preserve and trace pedigrees, genealogies, etc. On the south side of the street is **St. Benet's Church** (Wren's), now used as a Welsh Church; and on the north is **St. Nicholas Cole Abbey,** the first of the City churches rebuilt by Wren. It suffered heavy damage in the war but is to be restored.

At the *Mansion House Station* of the Underground Queen Victoria Street crosses **Cannon Street** (Plan II. N. 8), and thence continues to the Bank. At the corner of Cannon Street and Queen Street is the *London Chamber of Commerce.* A short distance to the east are **Cannon Street Stations** (Southern Region and Underground). A tablet in the church of **St. Michael Royal,** College Hill, commemorates the burial-place of "Sir Richard Whittington, four times Lord Mayor of London, 1396–1419." The building dates only from 1690, the Church known to "Dick" having perished in the Fire of 1666; but the position of the tomb is shown on the south side of the altar, near the organ. Nowadays it is doubted whether the "Sir" was more than a courtesy title (there is no official record of a knighthood); and learned historians even go as far as to contradict the ballad's assurance that Dick was Lord Mayor of London. (*See* also p. 22).

In Dowgate Hill is **Skinners' Hall,** with a fine series of historical paintings by *Frank Brangwyn, R.A.* In the wall of the ruined **St. Swithin's Church,** Cannon Street, may be seen the famous **London Stone,** supposed, though considerable difference of opinion exists on the subject, to have been the *milliarium* of the Roman Forum in London, from which distances along the great highways were reckoned. In **St. Swithin's Lane** is **Founders' Hall** and also **New Court,** the latter the headquarters of the great house of Rothschilds. **St. Mary, Abchurch,** another of Wren's churches, has cupola paintings by Thornhill and carvings by Grinling Gibbons. In **Walbrook,** just behind the Mansion House, is **St. Stephen's Church,** generally considered one of Wren's masterpieces. The most notable feature is the cupola, "a kind of probationary trial previous to the architect's greater dome of St. Paul's." Here, in the family vault, lies Sir John Vanbrugh, the famous architect upon whom was penned the witty epitaph: "Lie heavy on him, earth, for he laid many a heavy load on thee."

We have now regained our starting-point at the **Bank** (p. 205).

ROUTE X.—MOORGATE—CITY ROAD—LONDON WALL—CRIPPLEGATE— THE CHARTERHOUSE — THE MARKETS — CLERKENWELL — SMITH- FIELD—NEWGATE STREET—HOLBORN VIADUCT.

Starting again from the Bank, we walk northward along **Prince's Street,** the whole of the east side of which is occupied by the Bank of England. **Gresham Street** (p. 210) runs off to the left, and to the right is **Lothbury** (p. 237); but we will keep northward along **Moorgate** to the old City boundary, still known as London Wall. Just beyond, with entrance in Moorfields, is the *Moorgate Station* of the Metropolitan Railway, serving also as the terminus of the L.M.R. (Midland) and E.R. (Great Northern) City services, and close at hand is the station on the Northern Line, serving the Finsbury Park area of North London. A tablet on No. 75 Moorgate marks the site of the old gate from which the thoroughfare takes its name.

Were we to follow Moorgate northward we should pass on the right **Finsbury Circus,*** with pleasant gardens forming an ideal

* Finsbury Circus and Square are sometimes confused by strangers with the suburb of Finsbury Park, several miles to the north, where there is an important connection of the Underground Lines with the electrified Eastern Region lines to Barnet, Edgware etc.

setting for the bowling green. On the left of the City Road, just beyond **Finsbury Square,** are the headquarters and drill ground of the **Honourable Artillery Company,** generally known as the H.A.C., the oldest military body in the kingdom. The corps was formed in 1537, under the title of the Guild or Fraternity of St. George, and from it were always selected the officers of the City Trained Bands. It rendered magnificent service during the War, and its ranks furnished a large number of officers for the Regular Army. The "Troop of Colour" is held annually in July. In the museum are many torn and tattered flags, suits of old armour, portraits, etc. The Ancient and Honourable Artillery Company of Boston (Mass.), the oldest corps in America, was founded in 1638 by emigrant members of the H.A.C.

To the north is **Bunhill** (Bonehill, *see* p. 191) **Fields Cemetery,** for more than two centuries the chief burial-place of Nonconformists. A little to the south of the central walk is the **Tomb of John Bunyan,** with recumbent figure erected in 1862; while to the north of the walk is an obelisk in memory of **Daniel Defoe,** subscribed for by youthful readers of *Robinson Crusoe.* Here, too, are buried Isaac Watts, the hymn-writer; the redoubtable Susannah Wesley, mother of John and Charles Wesley; John Owen; Henry Richard and William Cromwell, descendants of the Protector; and William Blake, the poet-artist. In the Friends' Burial-Ground adjoining is the **Grave of George Fox,** the founder of the Society. In **Bunhill Row** Milton wrote the greater part of *Paradise Lost,* and here he died (1674). A warehouse (No. 124) now occupies the site (tablet).

On the east side of the City Road stands **Wesley's Chapel** (Plan I. O. 6), the "Cathedral of Methodism." The first stone was laid by John Wesley in 1777, and here he preached during the later years of his life. He is buried in the graveyard behind. In front is his statue, a centenary memorial, and in the chapel is a tablet in memory of his brother Charles. Adjoining the Chapel is **Wesley's House,** part of which is now used as a Museum (*open week-days* 10–1, 2–4; *admission 6d.*).

At the corner of City Road and Old Street (there is little to justify the name) is St. Luke's Hospital; close by is the famous **Moorfields Ophthalmic Hospital.** Here too is the *Leysian Mission House* (Methodist).

This is a digression, however. We will assume that the visitor, on reaching **London Wall** (Plan I. N. and O. 7), turns left (westward) and follows approximately the course of the old City wall (*see* p. 69), a long section of which is exposed to the view of the passer-by in the disused churchyard of St. Alphage, near the top of Wood Street. The old porch of **St. Alphage** (the church was demolished in 1919), on the south side of London wall, is now but a bombed ruin, though it formerly served as a chapel for private prayer. There are to be seen some memorials removed from the church, including one to Sir Rowland Hayward, Lord Mayor in 1570 and again in 1590, including his two wives and sixteen children. Near the north end of **Wood Street**— formerly a centre of wholesale haberdashery—is the Church of **St. Giles, Cripplegate** (Plan I. N. 7), known the world over as the burial-place of John Milton. The poet was born in the neighbouring ward of Bread Street on the 9th December, 1608 (*see* p. 211). Though fortunate in escaping the great fire which swept this quarter in 1897 and again the greater Fire in 1666, the church succumbed to the intensive bombing of the last war, and only the walls now remain. It is, however, to be rebuilt. A church was built on the site as early as 1090, but the present ruin dates from the end of the fourteenth century.

A bust and bronze **Statue of Milton** were saved from the ruins and are now in store until reconstruction has taken place. Milton died in 1674 at the age of 66 and his place of interment in the church was marked by a stone tablet which unfortunately was destroyed. The parish registers, saved, record at that date: "John Milton, gentleman, Consumption, chancel, 12 (November)." Oliver Cromwell and Elizabeth Boucher were married in this church on August 22, 1620. Other worthies here interred were Foxe, author of the *Book of Martyrs*; Frobisher, the explorer; and Speed, the topographer. In the south-west angle of the Churchyard, at some distance from the passage railing, may be seen another fragment of the old London wall—a circular bastion, dwarfed by the warehouses which tower above it.

In Monkwell Street, now flattened by bombs, is the site of the **Barbers' Hall**, originally the Hall of the Barber-Surgeons, the precursors of the modern Royal College of Surgeons.

In Jewin Street, Milton lived for a while. To the east is all that remains of **Milton Street,** leading from Fore Street to Chiswell Street, and which was considered the "Grub Street" of literary tradition. Its modern name (dating from 1830) was not, as is commonly supposed, a tribute to the poet, but to a builder of the same name, who included the street in his sphere of operations. In Golden Lane, slightly to the north, is the **Cripplegate Institute** and **Library.** Passing along the **Barbican** —another reminder of the old fortified wall—we turn right at **Aldersgate Street** (p. 211), and the first turning on the left, Carthusian Street, leads into Charterhouse Square, on the north side of which stands that mellow institution, the **Charterhouse** (Plan I. M. 6), considered by Sir W. Besant "the most beautiful and most venerable monument of old London."

The name is a corruption of Chartreuse. The original Carthusian Monastery was founded for twenty-four monks in 1371, and after the Dissolution became the property successively of Sir Edward (afterwards Lord) North and the Duke of Norfolk, each of whom built a residence for himself. Queen Elizabeth and James I both resided here for some days. In 1611 the property was purchased by "good old Thomas Sutton," Queen's Master of Ordnance, and endowed as a school of forty poor boys and a hospital for eighty poor men. The foundation for "poor brethren" still exists, though financial depreciation has necessitated a reduction of numbers. Charterhouse sustained terrible damage in 1941, but it is to be rebuilt and it is hoped that the "poor brethren" will return. No one will visit this place without calling to mind Thackeray's dear old Colonel Newcome, who was one of the "poor brethren." The *Gatehouse* dates from the sixteenth century; the upper part was rebuilt about 1700. On the right of the *Entrance Court* is the façade of the house built by the Duke of Norfolk about 1565. The *Great Hall*, in which the brethren as were able dined daily and where the Founder's Day Dinner mentioned by Thackeray in *The Newcomes* was held, was one of the finest Elizabethan rooms in existence. It was built early in the sixteenth century, and added to and improved some sixty years later by the Duke of Norfolk. The roof was burnt in 1941. Fortunately the wood panelling added by the Duke had been removed to safety. The *Brothers' Library*, formerly the Scholars' Hall, was also badly damaged. and most of the Elizabethan buildings were destroyed. The Chapel is reached by way of a *Cloister*, with memorials of Havelock, John Wesley, Roger Williams (the founder of Rhode Island), and other old scholars. The *Chapel* was altered by the monks early in the sixteenth century, and further altered by the Sutton Trustees in 1614. Its most notable feature is the elaborate monument of Thomas Sutton, the founder. The Charterhouse is now in process of rebuilding which will probably take some years, and is closed to visitors for the time being.

The **Charterhouse School**—of which Steele, Addison, Wesley, Havelock, Grote, Leech, Thackeray and other famous men were scholars—was transferred in 1872 to Godalming. Prior to its destruction by fire the Hall had been occupied by the Merchant Taylors' School.

Close at hand is a long range of buildings used as the **Metropolitan Meat Market** (p. 30), west of which are the Poultry, Fish, Fruit and Vegetable Markets, lining Farringdon Street.

It is worth while to turn for a few yards up **St. John Street,** an unattractive thoroughfare running northward from the Meat Market to Islington. Almost immediately we have on the left *St. John's Lane,* spanned by that interesting relic of the old priory of the Knights of St. John of Jerusalem, **St. John's Gate** (Plan I. M. 6), built by Prior Docwra in 1504. The Order was suppressed by Henry VIII, and in the reign of Edward VI Lord Protector Somerset pulled down most of the Priory buildings, and carted away the materials to help in the construction of Somerset House. In the rooms over the Gate the *Gentleman's Magazine* first saw the light. The rooms and the modern hall adjoining are occupied by the Order of St. John in England and by its foundation, that useful society the *St. John Ambulance Association*. To view the rooms it is necessary to write the Secretary of the Order. Permission is usually given for Saturday afternoons. Near the gate stands an old-world smithy; Smithfield's horse-drawn traffic provides plenty of work. In St. John Square, north of the gate, is the site of **St. John's Church**, the Norman crypt of which formed part of the Priory Church. The church was destroyed by fire bombs. A short distance to the west is Clerkenwell Green, with the **Old Sessions House** of the County of London. The densely-populated neighbourhood of **Clerkenwell** is mostly occupied by watchmakers and metal-workers. Towards the northern end of St. John Street is the **Northampton Polytechnic Institute.**

The historic **Sadler's Wells Theatre** was reopened, after re-building, in January, 1931. Drama, opera and ballet are presented at popular prices, in co-ordination with productions at the "Old Vic" (*see* p. 258). The **"Angel,"** a busy tramway and omnibus centre, takes its name from the sign of a tavern which, repeatedly rebuilt, overlooked the cross-roads for centuries. Its modern successor is a restaurant owned by Messrs. Lyons. A short distance along **Upper Street** is the **Agricultural Hall,** the scene of important cattle and dog shows and trade exhibitions. **Islington** may still be "merrie," as in Gilpin's day, but if so it very successfully disguises the fact. Along the Caledonian Road is the site of the former Metropolitan Cattle Market.

At Islington we are in close touch with the busy northern suburb of **Finsbury Park** (not to be confused with Finsbury *Circus* in the City). The Park is much used for cricket, football, etc. A mile or so farther north is **Alexandra Palace.** This great building, finely situated on Muswell Hill, was acquired in 1901 for the public use, and is controlled by a board of Trustees representing various local authorities. The building contains the well-known Roller Skating Rink which is the largest and finest in London. The Grounds, open daily, are nearly 200 acres in extent and command fine views of London and the country to the north, and contain a boating lake, sports ground, miniature railway, golf course, putting green, tennis courts, etc.

Adjoining is the *Alexandra Park Racecourse*. The most interesting modern development, however, is the adoption of part
of the Palace for **Television** transmissions by the B.B.C.

Returning to Charterhouse Street, we cross the **Meat Markets,**
covering an area of nearly ten acres, to the open space still
known as **Smithfield** (Plan I. M. 7), or "smooth field," an
ancient jousting ground outside the City walls.   The name of
Giltspur Street, leading into Newgate Street, is an obvious
reminder of the same picturesque period.   In most minds, however, Smithfield has more sombre associations.   Here, as the
Martyrs' Memorial on the wall of St. Bartholomew's Hospital
records, forty-three Protestants in the reign of Mary suffered
death at the stake.   It was at Smithfield, moreover, that Sir
William Walworth, Lord Mayor, according to the traditional
story, struck down Wat Tyler.   For centuries the annual "Bart-
lemy Fair" was the occasion of popular revels of a far from
dignified description.   On the south side is **St. Bartholomew's
Hospital,** known as "Bart's," the oldest Hospital in the Empire
and the only General Hospital in the City of London.

The Hospital originally formed part of an Augustinian Priory
and was founded in 1123 by Rahere, the minstrel and favourite
of Henry I, and later the first Prior of the Church of St. Bartholomew-the-Great, where his tomb is to be seen.   Rahere on a
pilgrimage to Rome saw St. Bartholomew in a vision who told
him to return and build a Hospital House and Church in a
Smoothfield (Smithfield).   The hospital escaped the Great
Fire though the fire reached Pye Corner just outside.   After
the suppression of the monasteries by Henry VIII., at the
request of Londoners revenues were restored and the Hospital
granted a new charter.   The City Corporation maintain a considerable share in the management of the Hospital.   The Henry
VIII Gateway was built in 1702 and is decorated with the
King's Statue and figures of Sickness and Lameness.   Between
1729 and 1738 the Hospital was almost entirely rebuilt.   In the
Great Hall are portraits of famous physicians and surgeons by
Kneller, Reynolds, Lawrence, Millais and others.   The murals
on the staircase were painted gratuitously by Hogarth.   The
older quadrangle buildings in the Square were erected by Gibbs
in 1730.   The new Nurses' Block was built after the 1914–18 war.
A Surgical block was built in 1930 on the site of the old Christ's
Hospital Building and in 1937 a new Medical block, called the
King George V Wing, was opened.   The fountain in the centre
of the square was erected in 1859.   The names of 112 Bart's men,
who gave their lives in the 1914–18 war, are inscribed on the walls
of the archway under the Great Hall.   In the Second World
War the Hospital was the centre of some of the greatest damage

in the country. Seven bombs fell on it and much damage was suffered. The Clinical Lecture Theatres and the Clerk's House were destroyed and damage done to the Medical Block and to the old Gibbs' East Wing. The Medical College Buildings in Charterhouse Square were partly destroyed. The College is the largest in the country.

Within the Hospital is the Parish Church of St. Bartholomew the Less.

East of the Hospital, in Little Britain, a picturesque Elizabethan half-timbered Gateway marks the entrance to the Church of **St. Bartholomew the Great** (Plan I. M. 7), the oldest church standing in London, if we except the chapel in the Tower. No visitor should miss seeing this fine Norman building (*open free daily from* 9.30 *to dusk. Admission to cloister and crypt,* 6d.). Services, *see* p. 20.

Like the Hospital, the Church was founded by Rahere in 1123, but the edifice we see is merely the choir and a small portion of the nave of the original Priory Church. The Early English nave, destroyed by Henry VIII, occupied the site of the graveyard, as can be seen by the remains. Through the exertions of several enthusiastic Rectors and others the church has been restored in recent years, at a cost of upwards of £60,000, and most of the encroachments which defaced and circumscribed it removed. The *Lady Chapel* at the east end, with its handsome wrought-iron screen, was long used for commercial purposes; in it Benjamin Franklin served a year as a journeyman printer. Its last tenant was a fringe manufacturer. The north transept was actually used as a blacksmith's forge. The best view of the church as a whole is from under the organ gallery looking east. Another pleasing vista is that looking westward through the massive Norman columns of the choir. On the north side of the choir is the *Tomb of Rahere* (d. 1143), with a richly decorated early Perpendicular canopy (*c.* 1405). The body is still above ground, immediately beneath the figure. On either side of the recumbent effigy is an Augustinian canon in his habit, holding an open Bible and pointing to Isaiah li. 3. The passage, beautifully appropriate to Rahere's work in draining the horse market site in Smithfield, and founding a church and hospital on the spot where formerly stood the gallows, runs, "He will comfort all her waste places; and He will make her wilderness like Eden, and her desert like the garden of the Lord." In the triforium opposite is *Prior Bolton's Window* with his rebus, Bolt-in-tun. In the south ambulatory is another fine monument to Sir Walter Mildmay (1589). He was founder of Emmanual College, Cambridge, Chancellor of the Exchequer to Queen Elizabeth, and one of the commissioners who tried Mary, Queen of Scots. The *Crypt*, the vaulting of which has been renewed, was originally a bone crypt. Later it became a wine and coal cellar; it is now

used as a mortuary chapel.   The most recent object of reclama-
tion has been the *Cloister* (Early English), long used as stables.

In the churchyard is observed annually on Good Friday a
curious ceremony in accordance with which twenty-one aged
widows of the City of London pick sixpences from a certain flat
tombstone covering the remains of a lady who many years ago
is said to have left a sum of money for the purpose.

Hogarth was baptized in St. Bartholomew's Church in 1697,
though the record of the fact was made in the wrong book.   He
was born in the adjoining **Bartholomew Close.**

Proceeding in the direction of Newgate Street, we pass between
huge buildings of the **General Post Office** (p. 212), and have on
our right the badly damaged **Christ Church:**

Like nearly all the City churches, it was the work of Wren,
though the lower part contains many traces of the earlier monastery church, notably the marble pavement of the sanctuary.
In one part of the flooring the effect of the Fire on the marble
can be clearly seen.   In the porch are several memorials of
officials and others, removed from Christ's Hospital in 1905 on
the demolition of that building.   Particular attention should be
paid to the marble font, for the carving is believed to be by
Grinling Gibbons.   It is certainly characteristic, and would
appear to be an almost solitary example of his work in stone.
The pulpit and part of the reading-desk were undoubtedly carved
by him.   The richly-decorated organ is a fine mellow instrument
beloved by musicians.   It has responded to the touch of both
Handel and Mendelssohn.   In the chancel are six carved panels,
representing the Apostles and the Last Supper, said to have
been taken from a ship of the Spanish Armada.   Richard Baxter,
the celebrated Nonconformist, and Lawrence Sheriff, the founder
of Rugby School, are buried here.   The "Spital Sermon,"
preached on the second Wednesday after Easter, is attended by
the Lord Mayor in state, in accordance with ancient custom.
It was formerly given at the old Spital Cross, Spitalfields, and
there is record of one discourse which attained such a length
that the civic dignitaries in desperation requested the preacher
to "print the rest."   When published, the sermon filled 230
pages!   Another annual function is the attendance of the Blue-
Coat boys (*see* below) on St. Matthew's Day.   They are afterwards regaled at the Mansion House, each boy receiving a gold
or silver coin according to his standing in the school.   The Blue-
Coat School or **Christ's Hospital,** founded by Edward VI in 1552,
on the site of a monastery of the Grey Friars adjoining Christ
Church, was in 1902 removed to Horsham.

The greater part of the site is now occupied by the King
Edward VII block of the General Post Office (p. 212) the
remainder by the new buildings of St. Bartholomew's Hospital.

Following **Newgate Street** (Plan I. M. 7) westward, we may
take note that at No. 87 Sir Henry Irving served for some time

as a publisher's clerk (tablet).   On the left is the curved façade
of the **Central Criminal Court** (p. 222).   On the right is **St.
Sepulchre's Church,** one of the bells of which was always tolled,
until 1890, on the occasion of an execution at Newgate.   At
an earlier period, when Tyburn (p. 155) was the place of execution, it was the considerate custom at this church to present a
bunch of flowers to each criminal who passed along to his doom.
In a glass case on the north wall is a handbell formerly rung
outside the condemned cell at Newgate, at the midnight preced-
ing execution, to the accompaniment of the rhymed admonish-
ment of which a copy is also shown.   The church was almost
rebuilt in the seventeenth century, the best features being the
fine porch and the heavily pinnacled square tower.   The organ
was built in 1677 by Renatus Harris.   On the south side of the
choir is buried the redoubtable *Captain John Smith,* "sometime
Governour of Virginia and Admirall of New England."   Roger
Ascham (1515–1568), author of the *Schoolmaster,* also lies here.
Below the courtyard of the Post Office, immediately east of St.
Sepulchre's Church, is a well-preserved bastion of the old **Roman
Wall** of London (*see* p. 69).   To view it write for permission to
the Secretary, General Post Office.

Westward of the churchyard begins **Holborn Viaduct** (Plan
I. M. 7), spanning the old Holborn Valley, through which
formerly ran the River Fleet (p. 200).   Before the construction
of the iron bridge over Farringdon Street, the steep Holborn
Hill was one of the most dangerous parts of London.   The
huge **Atlantic House** houses several Government departments.
The Viaduct is much longer than is generally supposed—over a
quarter of a mile—buildings lining the approaches to the bridge
across **Farringdon Street** (p. 202) (reached by steps).   At the
east end is **Holborn Viaduct Station** (Southern Region—S.E.
section).   The **City Temple,** west of Farringdon Street, has now
only its four walls standing.   It has had a number of famous
ministers, including Dr. Parker (d. 1902), for whose ministry
the edifice was erected in 1874, and the Rev. R. J. Campbell.
Close by are the ruins of **St. Andrew's Church,** built by Wren in
1686.   It was burnt out in April 1941.   The Church had many
interesting associations.   The registers, which were saved from
the fire, together with much valuable plate, record the burial of
Thomas Chatterton (August 28, 1770), and the christening on
July 31, 1817, at the age of twelve, of Benjamin Disraeli, afterwards Lord Beaconsfield.   Hazlitt was married here in 1808,
Charles Lamb acting as best man.

Rahere's Tomb in St. Bartholomew's Church. With the
exception of the chapel in the Tower, St. Bartholomew's is the
oldest church standing in London. The original Priory Church
was founded by Rahere in the year 1123.

London (*h**).

" The Cathedral Collegiate Church of St. Saviour and St. Mary Overie," Southwark, where James I of Scotland was married to the niece of Cardinal Beaufort. Chief interest in the Church lies in its great literary associations.

At **Holborn Circus** (Plan I. M. 7), in which stands a poor equestrian *Statue of the Prince Consort*, we reach the eastward limit of Route No. VI (p. 169). Here is the well-known emporium, *Gamage's.* **Hatton Garden,** running northward from the Circus to Clerkenwell Road, and **Ely Place,** a *cut-de-sac* immediately to the east, stand on the site of the famous palace of the Bishops of Ely, where John of Gaunt, father of Henry IV, died in 1399. Says Gloucester in Shakespeare's *Richard III*:

> "My lord of Ely, when I was last in Holborn,
> I saw good strawberries in your garden there;
> I do beseech you send for some of them."

Later the palace was occupied by Sir Christopher Hatton, Lord Keeper to Elizabeth I. Hatton Garden is the centre of the world's diamond trade, and also contains the London offices of many of the leading manufacturers of pottery. The only portion of the palace which escaped the Fire has been restored, and now forms **St. Etheldreda's Church,** Ely Place, the only pre-Reformation church in London that has been restored to the Roman Catholic worship. The building is two-storied, and both the Chapel itself and the Undercroft should be seen. The church is thought by some to date from the Saxon period. The tracery of the east and west windows—the former said to be the largest east window in London, as it is certainly the most beautiful—the oak roof, and the cloister, in which fig-trees still flourish, make this quiet nook, in the heart of the great City, a place of exceptional interest. **Ely Place** is itself of great interest, being private property and exempt from Corporation jurisdiction. A gold-braided porter preserves the dignity and order of the place, and at night, when the gates are closed, he reassures those within with a medieval "Fine night, all's well."

ROUTE XI.—THREADNEEDLE STREET—BISHOPSGATE—BETHNAL GREEN MUSEUM—GEFFRYES' MUSEUM—LIVERPOOL STREET—BROAD STREET —THE STOCK EXCHANGE—LOTHBURY.

From the Bank we turn this time along the quaintly-named **Threadneedle Street,** skirting the northern side of the Royal Exchange. Note the cleverly designed building of the *Eagle Star Insurance Company Limited.* The red granite building in Old Broad Street, on the left, is the **Stock Exchange** (*see* p. 236). On the right of Threadneedle Street, beyond Finch Lane, is **Merchant Taylors' Hall,** the largest of those belonging to the London Livery Companies. The Company, incorporated in 1327, has an income of £50,000 a year. The present hall which dates from 1671, was badly damaged in an air raid on 17th September, 1940, and only the walls, part of reception room and offices survived. **Bishopsgate,** taking its name from the old Bishop's Gate (a tablet marks the site), is a continuation north-ward of Gracechurch Street.

Nearly opposite Threadneedle Street is the *Bank of Scotland,* a corporation only a year younger than the Bank of England.

Bearing left along Bishopsgate, a few yards beyond the Bank of Scotland, on the right is the short thoroughfare known as Great St. Helen's and giving access to **St. Helen's Church** (*open daily* 11.30 *to* 3, *except Saturdays*), unrivalled among City churches for the spaciousness of its interior.

The church occupies part of the site of a very ancient nunnery founded, if tradition is to be believed, in memory of Helena, mother of Constantine. The demolition of buildings in St. Helen's Place in 1922 exposed remains of a building of Saxon date, and another believed to be Roman. There were also revealed some arches of the nunnery. The present church, dating in part from the thirteenth century, and consisting of a nave divided into two aisles by pillars and pointed arches, was judiciously restored by J. L. Pearson in 1893, at the expense of some of the City companies. On account of its many memorials of illustrious Londoners, St. Helen's is frequently termed the "Westminster Abbey of the City." The most notable monu-ments are those of Sir Thomas Gresham, Sir Julius Cæsar (not the invader of Britain, but a Master of the Rolls of James I's time), Sir John Crosby (d. 1475), of Crosby Hall, and his lady, and Sir Wm. Pickering. A memorial window in the northern aisle, or Nun's Choir, was erected in 1884, on the probability that a William Shakespeare assessed for rates in the parish in 1598 was the poet. The church has recently been restored.

Spanning the entrance to St. Helen's Place is a magnificent modern building erected for the Hudson's Bay Company (note the decorative allusions to trading: the building as a whole should be viewed from across the street). In St. Helen's Place is the **Leathersellers' Hall,** a modern building beneath which is the crypt of the old St. Helen's Nunnery. Near at hand is **St. Ethelburga's Church,** one of the oldest and smallest in London, fortunate in escaping the Great Fire. This church was long famous for the shops which masked its front; but these projected into the busy pavement and were demolished in 1933. Windows commemorate Henry Hudson and his companions, who received Holy Communion in the church before setting out in the *Hopeful,* 1607. A tablet on the house at the corner of Camomile Street marks the site of the former *Bishop's Gate,* erected by Bishop Erkenwald in Saxon days. On the left is the Church of **St.**

Botolph Without, where Keats was baptized in 1795, its graveyard now laid out as a garden. Here stands a Memorial Cross,
erected in 1916 and inscribed "In Memoriam. Officers and men
of the Honourable Artillery Company who died in the Great
War." Other sides are inscribed to Lord Kitchener, J. T.
Cornwell (the youthful hero of Jutland), and "Our Brave Dead
of Bishopsgate."

It is curious that **Houndsditch,** leading eastward through an
unmistakably Jewish quarter to Aldgate, has a church of St.
Botolph at each end. The name is a reminder of the old ditch
without the City wall. The Sunday morning "old clo'" sales
in this locality form a curious spectacle of "Living London."

Were we to continue northward up Bishopsgate past **Liverpool Street Station** (*see* p. 236), we should shortly reach **Shoreditch,** passing on the way the **Bishopsgate Institute,** opened in
1894, and partly built by means of the surplus funds of a bequest
left in 1481 to provide flannel petticoats for poor old women.
The library, available to all persons resident or employed in the
eastern part of the City, contains about 45,000 volumes.

Situated in the Bethnal Green Road is the—

Bethnal Green Museum

Plan I. Q. 5.

Access.—*Underground* (Central Line), Bethnal Green Station. *Bus* 106 or *Trolleybus*
653 to Bethnal Green; or *Trolleybus* to Cambridge Heath, 3 minutes' walk.
Rail—From Liverpool Street to Cambridge Heath, 5 minutes' walk.

Admission.—Free. Open daily, 10–6; Sundays, 2.30–6. Closed Good Friday and
Christmas Day.

This branch of the Victoria and Albert Museum was established
in 1872 as a museum for East London. The building is part of
the old iron structure which composed the original South Kensington Museum, and it is thus in direct descent from the Great
Exhibition of 1851.

The collection includes a representative selection of works of
British Art with special reference to local products, e.g. Spitalfields silks and a local collection of topographical prints and
drawings exhibited on the lower floors. A representation of
Art outside the British Isles is housed on the upper floor.

Old Ford Road, to the north of the Museum, leads in half a
mile to **Victoria Park,** the principal playground of East London,
occupying over 200 acres and having a boating lake.

Shoreditch Church (St. Leonard's) is of great interest to
Shakespearians on account of its records and memorials of
James Burbage, Richard Tarleton, Will Somers, Spenser ("slain"
by Ben Jonson), etc. Note also the old stocks and whipping-
post. The name of **Curtain Road,** to the west, recalls the fact

that here stood two of the earliest theatres in London: "The Theatre," which preceded the more famous *Globe* at Southwark as the scene of Shakespearian productions, and the Curtain Theatre. A tablet marks the site of the former. A window (since destroyed) taken from the former St. James's Church (which faced the site of the "Curtain") commemorated the 300th anniversary of Shakespeare's arrival in London.

In Kingsland Road, half a mile or so beyond Shoreditch Church, and easily reached by bus, is the **Geffrye Museum,** a small but most interesting collection of furniture and old wood-work housed in the tree-shaded hospital founded by "Sir Rob. Geffryes, Knt., Alderman and Ironmonger." Formerly known as the Ironmongers' Almshouses, the buildings were bought by the L.C.C. and converted into a museum in 1913. The galleries are panelled and form a series of period rooms consisting of furniture and domestic equipment from 1600 to the present day. Varied educational work is carried out in the Museum, parti-cularly with School parties, and practical activities are provided for children who visit it in their spare time. (Open 10-5 week-days, except Mondays; Sundays, 2-5.)

A great part of the west side of Bishopsgate at its northern end is occupied by **Liverpool Street Station** (Plan I. O. 7), the terminus and headquarters of the Eastern Region of British Railways. Adjoining Liverpool Street Station on the west is **Broad Street Station** (Plan I. O. 7), the terminus of the electrified North London line (London Midland—for Willesden Junction, Richmond, Watford, etc.). Below ground are the Liverpool Street Stations of the Metropolitan and Central Lines. In Eldon Street is the Roman Catholic Church of **St. Mary, Moorfields.**

Neither **New Broad Street** nor **Old Broad Street,** leading south-ward to the Bank, have any apparent right to their name, though the soaring blocks of offices make the thoroughfare appear narrower than it is. In Old Broad Street (No. 19) is the **City of London Club,** frequented principally by bankers and merchants. At the eastern end of **London Wall** (p. 225) is **Carpenters' Hall.** The Church of **All Hallows-on-the-Wall** has its foundations in the old Roman wall, and the vestry perpetuates the outline of a bastion. The present church dates from 1764, but there was a church here before the Conquest. Throgmorton Avenue leads down to **Throgmorton Street,** generally crowded by bare-headed individuals of varying degrees of frivolity, whose presence betrays the whereabouts of that important institution, the **Stock Exchange** (Plan I. O. 7) in Capel Court. Only mem-bers are admitted to the building, but as not a little business is

done "in the street," strangers may derive a certain edification
from observing the solemnity with which matters of high finance
are conducted. "Jobbers" deal in particular securities only;
"brokers" act as intermediaries between jobbers and the public.
Members are not allowed to advertise. Persons who do so are
"outside brokers," not amenable to the stringent rules and regu-
lations of the "House." In Throgmorton Street is the **Drapers'
Hall,** with garden attached, a luxury indeed on such a site. The
hall dates in part from 1667. To the north, in Austin Friars,
rises the new **Dutch Church.** The original church, destroyed in
1941, formed part of an important Augustinian Friary, which
came into the hands of Henry VIII at the Dissolution and was
granted by the boy king, Edward VI, in 1550, "to the Dutch
nation in London, to be their preaching place," a purpose it
ever since served. It is said to have had the largest floor-space
of any City church, St. Paul's Cathedral excepted. The foundation stone for the new church was laid by Princess Irene of the
Netherlands in 1950. **Lothbury,** in which are the offices of some
of the principal financial magnates and the headquarters of the
Westminster Bank, skirts the north side of the Bank of England.
St. Margaret's Church, Lothbury, has a magnificent screen,
while **Bartholomew Lane,** on the east, will bring us back to our
starting-point.

**ROUTE XII.—CORNHILL—GRACECHURCH STREET—LEADENHALL STREET
—ALDGATE—WHITECHAPEL—FENCHURCH STREET—MARK LANE.**

Another "spoke" radiating from the Bank is **Cornhill** (Plan
II. N. and O. 8), having on its south side the headquarters of
Lloyds Bank. At No. 41 (tablet) was born Gray, author of the
famous *Elegy*. Farther east is **St. Michael's Church,** rebuilt
by Wren after the Fire, and restored by Sir G. G. Scott. It has
a fine Gothic tower, modelled on Magdalen Tower, Oxford, and
a pulpit carved by Grinling Gibbons. The organ of **St. Peter's
Church,** almost next door, was several times played by Mendelssohn, and in the vestry his autograph is treasured. The church
was founded, according to an ancient tablet in the vestry, by
"Lucius, the first Christian king of this land then called
Britaine." Many remains of Roman London have been discovered hereabouts, and authorities place here the site of the
Roman forum.

At the intersection **Gracechurch Street** (Plan II. O. 8) leads
southward to London Bridge (p. 243). The peculiar name
recalls a herb or grass market, at one time held in the yard of the

demolished St. Benet's Church, hence known as the "Grass Church." Here Cornhill ceases, and its eastward continuation becomes **Leadenhall Street.** On the right is **Leadenhall Market,** for vegetables, poultry, etc. Until a few years ago dogs, cats, etc., were also shown, the last-named in steady demand for long voyages in rat-haunted ships and for warehouses. It is interesting in the circumstances to recall that the ground on which the market stands was given to the City by Dick Whittington. On this side of Leadenhall Street is the huge headquarters of **Lloyd's,** where obliging "underwriters" will quote a premium for every imaginable form of risk. The institution takes its name from the old Lloyd's Coffee House in Lombard Street, where seventeenth-century shipowners were accustomed to forgather. Lloyd's signal stations are dotted all round our coasts. *Lloyd's Register of British and Foreign Shipping (see* p. 241) is a separate undertaking, mainly concerned with the classification of vessels. The phrase "A1 at Lloyd's" is derived from the sign for wooden vessels of the highest class. The highest class of steel and iron vessels are registered 100 A1.

At the foot of **St. Mary Axe,** over the name of which antiquaries still wrangle, is **St. Andrew Undershaft** (*open daily* 12 *to* 2).

The church derives its name, according to Stow, from a long shaft, or Maypole, higher than the church steeple, which used to be set up opposite the south door. The Puritans declared the inoffensive shaft an idol, and had it "raised from the hooks whereon it had rested for two-and-thirty years, sawn in pieces and burnt." At the end of the north aisle is the alabaster monument of Stow (d. 1605), the chronicler of London, who is shown at his writing-table, with a real pen in hand. The pen is replaced annually by the Lord Mayor of London at the Stow Commemoration Service, the old pen being given to the school which produces the best essay on London, the writer of the essay receiving a copy of Stow's work from the Lord Mayor.

In St. Mary Axe, too, is the **Baltic Mercantile and Shipping Exchange,** the headquarters of merchants, shippers, brokers, etc., trading mainly in grain and similar products. Like Lloyd's, it sprang from a famous old coffee-house.

Continuing along Leadenhall Street, we have on the left the Church of **St. Katherine Cree** (*open daily* 11 *to* 3). rebuilt, except the Gothic tower, it is thought, by Inigo Jones in 1631. In allusion to its dedication, it has a Catherine-wheel window' Holbein, the artist, is thought to have been buried here in 1543. When the body of the church was rebuilt in 1630, one of the old pillars was left *in situ*. It now only shows 3 ft. above ground, the rest of it—15 ft.—being beneath the surface; a silent evidence of how much the ground has risen in the City. The "lion sermon," to commemorate the escape of a Lord Mayor of Charles I's time from the jaws of a lion in Africa, is annually preached in this church. The "flower sermon" instituted in 1853 has been revived and now takes the form of twin services—one in spring and one in autumn.

We are now at **Aldgate** (Plan I. O. 7), the site of a former City portal, Ale-gate, or All-gate (i.e. open to all), having beyond it one of the "without" wards—Portsoken, "the field beyond the gates." A plaque on Aldgate Post Office recalls that Chaucer lived in a house over Aldgate during 1374. Many a facetious debtor has attempted to right himself by a "draught (draft) on Aldgate Pump." Hereabouts, as a glance at shop signs and passing faces betrays, is the principal Jewish quarter of the Metropolis. Turning to the left, we pass close to Duke's Place, in which is the **Great Synagogue,** the Hebrew cathedral of London. At the corner of Houndsditch (p. 235) is the Church of **St. Botolph, Aldgate,** with a spacious open churchyard (among the graves is that of William Symington, one of the pioneers of steam navigation). In the church is preserved, though it is rarely shown, a somewhat ghastly relic—the supposed head of the Duke of Suffolk, beheaded on Tower Hill in 1554. The Minories, on the right, is an unattractive thoroughfare leading southward to the Tower of London. In St. Clare Street was the quaint little Holy Trinity Church, long used as the St. Botolph Institute. It formerly belonged to an abbey of Minoresses, or nuns of St. Clare—hence the name of the main street. The church also sometimes alluded to as "the Mumbling Church," a name which has been explained by reference to the exemption the church enjoyed from episcopal authority in matters ecclesiastical. It claimed the right to marry all comers without banns or licence. Many clandestine marriage ceremonies, therefore, were doubtless mumbled over there. American visitors are interested in the monuments to the Legge family (Earls of Dartmouth), with which George Washington was connected. One contains a representation of the Stars and Stripes. During the rebuilding of Nos. 15 and 16, **America Square,** near the Minories, in 1908, a splendidly preserved section (60 ft.) of the **Roman City Wall** was unearthed. No. 14 was the home, early in the nineteenth century, of Baron Meyer de Rothschild, the founder of the English branch of the great financial house. To the west of the Minories is **Jewry Street,** in which is the **Cass Technical Institute.**

Another massive fragment of the old wall is incorporated in the basement of Roman House at the bottom of this street.

Continuing along Aldgate, we have on the left **Middlesex Street** (formerly *Petticoat Lane*), famed for its open-air market on Sunday mornings.

From here the Underground runs for two miles beneath the Whitechapel and Mile End Roads to form a junction with the Tilbury and Southend Line (L.M.R.) near Bow Road. Following **Whitechapel High Street,** we shortly have on the right **Commercial Road,** leading to Stepney, Limehouse, and the East and West India Docks. Here stands the **Sailors' Palace,** the headquarters of the successful work for seamen carried on in nearly all the ports of the world by the British Sailors' Society (At Home and Abroad) Inc. In Stepney Causeway, a short distance west of Stepney Station, are the administrative headquarters of **Dr. Barnardo's Homes** (Plan II. R. 8), caring for a huge family of destitute children, numbering over 8,000. Vistors desiring further information, or to inspect the various branches, should apply to the General Secretary for a *Guide to Visitors*.

In **Commercial Street,** leading northward from Whitechapel High Street, is **St. Jude's Church,** which has been for many years a centre of sweetness and light in a sordid district. **Toynbee Hall,** adjoining, has long been an important educational centre, where University graduates have grappled at first hand with the problems of poverty and shared the lives of East End dwellers. Close at hand is the **Whitechapel Art Gallery** (Plan I. P. 7). A free Library and Museum adjoin.

In the **Whitechapel Road,** about half a mile beyond the Art Gallery, is the **London Hospital,** with accommodation for nearly 1,000 in-patients and an army of out-patients. The Hospital was founded in 1759. At the back is the large church of **St. Philip, Stepney.** Cambridge Road, on the left, would take us northward to the **Bethnal Green Museum** (p. 235). No. 88, Mile End Road, marked by a tablet, was the residence of that dauntless navigator, Captain Cook. In the rear of the Beth Holim, at 253, Mile End Road, is a secluded little burial ground, granted to the Jewish fraternity in London by Cromwell in 1657. It will be noticed that **Mile End** is just about a mile from the old City wall, a fact to which it doubtless owes its name. **Stepney Green,** on the south side of Mile End Road, leads obliquely to **St. Dunstan's,** the parish church of Stepney, a fine Perpendicular building, with registers dating back to 1568. It contains several tombs of fifteenth- and sixteenth-century worthies, including Sir Henry Colet, father of Dean Colet of St. Paul's.

Another is the well-known "fish and ring" monument to Dame Rebecca Berry, who was long supposed to be the heroine of the ballad called "The Cruel Knight and the Fortunate Farmer's Daughter." According to the story—a curious variant of that of St. Mungo, which gave rise to the "fish and ring" in the Glasgow arms—a knight was passing a cottage when he heard the cries of a woman. His knowledge of the occult sciences warning him that the child then born was destined to be his wife, he attempted unsuccessfully to encompass the death of the child, in order to escape this ignoble alliance. When she had grown to woman's estate he took her to sea with the intention of drowning her. Relenting of his purpose, he cast a ring into the sea and commanded her never to see his face again unless she could produce the ring. The woman became a cook, and, finding the ring in a cod-fish married the knight.

Towards the eastern end of Mile End Road is the **People's Palace** (Plan I. R. and S. 6), the outcome of a suggestion in Sir Walter Besant's *All Sorts and Conditions of Men*. The funds were mainly provided by the trustees of Mr. Barber Beaumont and by the Drapers' Company. Following upon a fire, the Palace has been rebuilt and is now thoroughly well equipped

Next door is Queen Mary College (part of the University of London), and a centre of much useful education.

We have wandered rather far from the City, however, and must beg the reader to put on the magic slippers and return at a bound to **Aldgate** (p. 238). Varying our outward route, we will regain the Bank by way of **Fenchurch Street** (Plan II. O. 8). In Lloyd's Avenue, on the south side, is the fine building of **Lloyd's Shipping Registry,** with beautiful friezes and marbles. **Fenchurch Street Station** is the terminus of the former London, Tilbury and Southend Railway (now part of the London Midland Region), and is also used by the Eastern Region of British Railways.

At the corner of Mark Lane and Fenchurch Street is the site formerly occupied by the old "King's Head," where Queen Elizabeth dined immediately after her release from the Tower in 1554.

Steps in front of the station lead down to Hart Street, where is the shell of **St. Olave's Church.** The dedication refers to St. Olaf of Norway (995-1035). The building dated from the middle of the fifteenth century, and contained many quaint old monuments and brasses.

It is chiefly interesting, however, as "our owne church" of Samuel Pepys, the diarist (1633-1703). He and his wife are buried here. Memorials to them had, happily, been removed and were saved from destruction. His association with the parish arose from the fact that he was Secretary to the Admiralty, the Navy Office at that period being in Crutched Friars. St. Olave's owed its preservation from the Great Fire to Pepys himsefl. it being at his suggestion that men were brought from the dockyards to blow up surrounding houses and thus stay the conflagration. The parents of Joseph Chamberlain were married here in 1835. Every year, on Trinity Monday, the Master and Brethren of Trinity House attended service at St. Olave's. It was also the official church of the Clothworkers' and Ironmongers' Companies.

Crutched Friars is a crooked street deriving its name from a former monastery of the Friars of the Holy Cross. Commercial as is all this quarter now, it is to be remembered that when the Court was in residence at the Tower, the nobility and gentry had mansions hereabouts and the great religious houses gave it an ecclesiastical importance hard indeed to realise to-day.

Mark Lane (a corruption of *Mart Lane*), connecting Fenchurch Street with Great Tower Street, is the distributing centre of the corn trade, the dealers on market days, chiefly Mondays, meeting in the two **Corn Exchanges,** the old building dating from 1827, the new hall from 1881. Mark Lane has been described as "the cradle of the British Navy," the Navy Office, or Admiralty, having been here until 1656, when it was removed to Crutched Friars, and subsequently westward. **Mincing Lane,** running parallel on the west, is the centre of the wholesale tea trade. Mark and Mincing Lanes and the streets thereabouts are also the headquarters of the wine trade, and the whole locality is honeycombed with vaults. In Mincing Lane was the **Clothworkers' Hall,** destroyed in May 1941. One of the Company's most treasured possessions is a loving cup presented by Pepys, who was Master in 1677.

Continuing along Fenchurch Street, we cross Gracechurch Street (p. 237) and enter **Lombard Street** (Plan II. N. and O. 8), generally considered the richest street in the world. On either side massive banks display plates bearing names we would gladly be more familiar with, and some hang out "signs" in the approved medieval style. On the north side is the Church of *St. Edmund King and Martyr*, one of Wren's buildings. The neighbouring fane of *All Hallows* is all but demolished.

In Post Office Court is that useful institution the **Bankers' Clearing House,** where cheques having a face value of thousands of millions change hands every year. The name of the street is an obvious reminder of the old Lombard moneylenders. Pope was born in Plough Court in 1688. At the western end of the street is **St. Mary Woolnoth,** already referred to (p. 207).

ROUTE XIII.—KING WILLIAM STREET—LONDON BRIDGE—THE TOWER— TOWER BRIDGE—THE DOCKS.

Now let us complete our rambles from the Bank by following **King William Street,** named after "our sailor king," in a south-easterly direction to London Bridge, whence we can turn eastward to the Tower and the Docks. A pedestrian **Subway** at the intersection of the roads gives access to *Monument Station* (Underground), and in Fish Street Hill, a few yards to the east, is the **Monument** itself (Plan II. O. 8). London has thousands of monuments, and many of far greater significance than this; but by Londoners the column is invariably referred to as "The Monument." It is a fluted Doric column, 202 ft. high, the loftiest, and also considered to be the finest, isolated stone column in the world, erected by Wren to commemorate the Great Fire of 1666, which broke out in Pudding Lane close by, and destroyed property valued at over ten million pounds (p. 71). Persons desirous of so doing may, on payment of sixpence, ascend (*week-days only*) to the "caged" gallery near the top. The view is sublime, but the steps are 311. The cage is designed to protect would-be suicides from themselves. The gilt urn, like Moses's bush, burns but is not consumed.

London Bridge (Plan II. N. 8) dates from 1831, and was designed by John Rennie. Considerably over 20,000 vehicles and more than 110,000 foot passengers cross it every day.

The Thames at this point narrows to 900 ft., but is much wider both above and below. The bridge is a granite structure of five arches, having a length of 928 ft. and a width of 65 ft. The span of the central arch is 152 ft. Until after the middle of the eighteenth century, London Bridge afforded the only means of crossing the Thames hereabouts except by boat. The predecessor of the present structure was more like a street than a bridge, being lined on both sides with houses and having fortified gates at each end. A model can be seen in the London Museum (p. 139). The gates were more often than not garnished with human heads.

From the east side of the bridge is gained a fine view of the busy **Pool**, so admirably rendered in the pictures of Vicat Cole, W. L. Wyllie, Chas. Dixon and others. *Adelaide House* towers above the bridge on the east. Below the west side is **Fishmongers' Hall.** The Fishmongers, incorporated so long ago as the reign of Edward I, are one of the wealthiest of the great companies. On the staircase is a statue of "Brave Walworth, knight, Lord Mayor," who slew rebellious Tyler; and the actual dagger is also shown, though it is quite erroneous to suppose, as many do, that this is the object which figures in the City arms. As a matter of fact, the heraldic emblem is not a dagger at all, but the blunt-pointed sword of St. Paul, the patron saint of London, and the City authorities so represent it on all official documents.

The northern approach to London Bridge spans **Lower Thames**

Street, a decidedly "fishy" thoroughfare—if a road which is perpetually blocked can be called a thoroughfare—skirting the north bank of the Thames between London Bridge and the Tower. Just below the bridge, at the foot of Fish Street Hill, is the Church of **St. Magnus the Martyr,** rebuilt by Wren after the Fire. Here are buried the remains of Miles Coverdale, author of the first complete translation of the Bible. We are now in the somewhat unsavoury locality of **Billingsgate,** which has been almost from time immemorial the principal fish market of London. To be seen at its best (or worst), the Market should be visited shortly after the opening at 5 a.m. Adjoining is the **Custom House,** the fine river front of which, 488 ft. long, is an imposing feature in the view from London Bridge. Opposite, at the corner of St. Mary-at-Hill, is the **Coal Exchange,** with a tower over 100 ft. high. Among the curiosities shown here are the remains of a Roman bath, and a sword in the City arms made of wood of a mulberry tree said to have been planted by Peter the Great when learning shipbuilding in this country. In Rood Lane, close by, is the interesting church of **St. Margaret Pattens,** rebuilt by Wren in 1687. Its canopied pews are unique in London, and it has some noteworthy pictures. Some pattens in a case hint at the origin of the name. In Idol Lane is the church of **St. Dunstan-in-the-East,** badly damaged in 1940. It was rebuilt in the early part of last century to replace a building designed by Wren, of which the steeple remains, being by common consent the most graceful in London.

We turn now into **Great Tower Street,** the eastward continuation of **Eastcheap.** Nearly opposite *Tower Hill Station* stands the church of **All Hallows, Barking,** so called not because it is in Barking, which is 7 miles distant, but because it was founded by the nuns of Barking Abbey, an effigy of whose first Abbess, St. Ethelburga, may be seen in the porch. The Church, though still in use for occasional services, was reduced to a shell in 1941. All that remains of the famous original carvings by Grinling Gibbons, is the font cover, which was removed to St. Paul's Cathedral. A new font has been specially hewn for the church by a tunnelling company of the Royal Engineers from limestone from Gibraltar. The registers record the baptism of William Penn on October 23, 1644; he was born on the east side of Tower Hill (see below). In 1911 the Pennsylvania Society of New York erected a bronze tablet in the church in commemoration of the fact. Remains of Roman London have been discovered below the church and in the crypt is a model of Roman

London. Not long before the war the undercroft had been rebuilt, and the south-east portion of the church developed as a Mariners' Chapel. The north aisle, known as the Richard Cœur de Lion chapel, is being restored.

All Hallows is the Guild Church of the " Toc H " movement and normally holds the Lamp of Maintenance lit by the Duke of Windsor, when Prince of Wales, in 1922, the sword of Edmund Street, etc. The Altar used by Richard and the Crusaders from the Templar Chapel in Palestine has been secured for the Chapel and is at present in the crypt with the Toc H lamp resting on it. Renovations in 1924 disclosed a stone slab which was thought by some to have covered the "Lion Heart" of Richard I, that monarch having built here a chapel for the reception of his heart. But the relic is generally believed to be at Rouen. As a result of war damage some interesting discoveries were made, among which were a number of stone fragments believed to have been embedded in the pillars for over 800 years.

We have now reached **Tower Hill,** as interesting a spot historically as any in the City. Here is the **Merchant Navy Memorial.** Slightly to the north-west, on the lawn of Trinity Square gardens, is a slab of granite paving with the inscription, "Site of ancient scaffold. Here the Earl of Kilmarnock and Lord Balmerino suffered, 18th August, 1746." These were almost the last persons in England to be beheaded (the honour of being the last belongs to Lord Lovat, 1747).

Were the list to be a full one a stone of enormous dimensions would be required. This was the place of public execution; only a few "privileged" persons were executed in the privacy of the Tower itself (see p. 249). A less dismal association is the fact that "at his father's house on the east side of Tower Hill, up a court adjoining the City Wall," William Penn, the founder of Pennsylvania, was born in 1644; and in 1951 a terrace for public use was built on the site of demolished buildings as part of the Tower Hill Improvement Trust's project to restore to the City its ancient pleasance.

From the foot of the hill a passage leads to the **Tower Pier,** whence pleasure steamers leave on day trips to Southend, Margate, etc. Other steamers and also motor launches ply to and from Greenwich and Westminster. The adjacent stretch of sand is popular with children.

THE TOWER

Plan II. O. 8.

Admission.—The Tower is open daily, except Christmas Day and Good Friday 10–5 summer, 10–4 winter. Open Sundays 2–5 summer only. Visitors are permitted to remain in the Tower one hour after closing time.

Fees.—Entry tickets, 1s. adults, 6d. children (3 to 14), must be purchased at the Ticket Office, West Gate. Jewel House tickets at Jewel House 1s. adults, 6d. children (3 to 14).
Ceremony of the Keys.—A limited number of visitors is permitted to witness this ancient ceremony with no charge. Applications, at least 48 hours in advance, should be addressed to the Constable's Office, Tower of London, E.C.3, stating the night requested with alternative and the number in party. Time of arrival 9.40, depart 10 p.m.
    Admission to the Tower on Saturdays and Bank Holidays is free.
Nearest Station.—Tower Hill (District Line).

The fortress, including the **Moat,** now drained and used as a drill and playground, occupies an irregular pentagon of about 18 acres, the circuit of the outer walls being nearly two-thirds of a mile.

Historical Note.—Tradition has it that a fortress stood here in Roman times. In 1078 William the Conqueror built the great central keep, or White Tower, for the purpose of protecting and overawing the City. His architect was Gundulph, Bishop of Rochester, and the work bears a marked resemblance to that of Rochester Castle. The keep first became known as "La Tour Blanche" in the reign of Edward III, possibly, as some authorities contend, because it was at that time whitewashed. The inner wall, with its thirteen towers, was added during the thirteenth century, the moat by Richard I. Henry III made extensive additions, Edward I surrounded the whole by a second wall with towers commanding the river, and Henry VIII added rounded bastions on the north side.

In viewing the Tower, it must be borne in mind that it has served the three purposes of a fortress, a palace, and a prison. Several of the Norman and Plantagenet kings were glad of its protection. Four foreign kings were detained here: King John the Good of France, after his overthrow by the Black Prince at Poitiers; and three Scots kings, Baliol, David II after the battle of Neville's Cross, and James I of Scotland. The most touching of all Tower memories is, of course, the murder, in 1483, of the young king Edward V and his brother, the Duke of York, traditionally, at the instigation of Gloucester, afterwards Richard III. Some bones, supposed to be theirs, were found beneath an exterior staircase on the south side of the White Tower leading to St. John's Chapel, and were interred, by order of Charles II, in Westminster Abbey. A plate in the wall marks the place where the bones were found, but now that the entrance to the White Tower is made from the north, this spot is no longer shown. The Tudor sovereigns made fairly frequent use of the Tower as a residence, but it can have been little to the taste of Elizabeth I, who spent some few weeks here as a prisoner. James I and Charles II were crowned from here; but the Tower has long ceased to have any special association with royalty, except from the fact that it serves as a place of custody for the Crown jewels. It is significant, however (cf. Temple Bar, p. 196), that the official designation is "Her Majesty's Royal Fortress and Palace of the Tower of London."

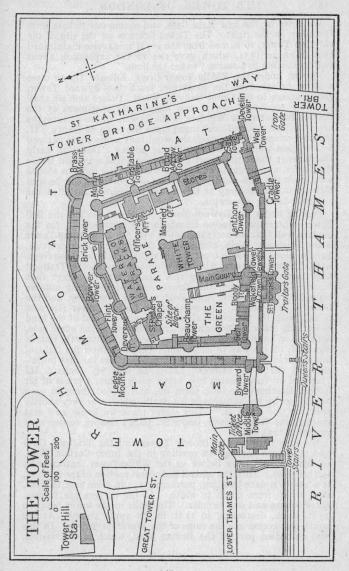

THE TOWER

Scale of Feet

0   100   200

Tower Hill Sta.

ST KATHARINE'S WAY

TOWER BRIDGE APPROACH

TOWER BRI.

MOAT

Brass Mount

Martin Tower

Constable Tower

Broad Arrow Tower

Stores

Develin Tower

Iron Gate

Salt Tower

Well Tower

Brick Tower

Officers' Qrs

Married Qrs

WHITE TOWER

Lanthorn Tower

Cradle Tower

Bowyer Tower

Flint Tower

WATERLOO BARRACKS

PARADE

Main Guard

Develin Tower

Sister Block

Bloody Tr.

Wakefield Tower

Crown Jewels

St Thomas's Tower

St Peter's Chapel

Devereux

Beauchamp Tower

THE GREEN

Bell Tower

Traitors' Gate

Legge Mount

Byward Tower

Queen's Stairs

MOAT

Ticket Office

Middle Tower

Main Gate

TOWER HILL

Tower Stairs

GREAT TOWER ST.

LOWER THAMES ST.

RIVER THAMES

247

We enter by the new **Main Gate**, and obtain our tickets from the office on the right. The Ticket Office is on the site of the old **Lion Tower**, so named from the royal menagerie maintained here down to 1834, which gave rise to the expression about visitors coming to London "to see the lions."

Passing under the **Middle Tower** (*temp*. Edward I), we cross a stone bridge over the Moat and reach the **Byward Tower**, giving access to the Outer Baily or Ward. Before this we shall probably encounter one or two magnificent specimens of the famous **Beefeaters,** or Warders of the Tower, whose picturesque uniform has remained unchanged since the reign of Henry VII. Byward comes from *by-word*, the word that alone could get you by, or pass-word, as we should say to-day. Down to early Plantagenet times the Court of Common Pleas was held inside the Tower, and litigants and others who had the right to attend were given the pass-word. The spikes of a portcullis can be seen high up in the archway of this Tower in which is included the original winding apparatus.

Passing under the Byward Tower, we see on the left the **Bell Tower,** where the Princess Elizabeth was imprisoned. On the western wall that connects this tower with the **Beauchamp Tower** is the Prisoners' Walk, along which the Princess took exercise. Farther along the south front, on the right, overlooking the river, is **St. Thomas's Tower,** with the wide archway of the **Traitors' Gate** beneath it. It was by this gloomy water passage that State prisoners entered the Tower, some of the most notable being Sir Thomas More, Anne Boleyn, Lady Jane Grey, and the Duke of Monmouth. Opposite is the **Bloody Tower** (*see* also p. 250) with its portcullis, almost the only survival of the kind in working order. Through the little window on the north side, Archbishop Laud leaned out to bless Thomas Wentworth, Earl of Strafford, on his way to execution. Below, and on the right of this archway, according to Sir Thomas More, was the first burial-place of the little Princes. Later, he tells us, Richard III "insisted on their resting in a better place, when a priest of Sir Robert Brackenbury took them up, and buried them in such secrecy, as by the occasion of his death, which was very shortly after, no one knew it." This secret place we know now was south of the White Tower, below St. John's Chapel, consecrated ground at that time.

We pass between the Bloody Tower and the Traitors' Gate and then turn through an opening in the Inner Curtain Wall, on the left, and have before us the **White Tower** (entrance on farther side). This, the central and oldest portion of the fortress, is a nearly square building, measuring 118 ft. from east to west, and 107 ft. from north to south. At the corners are turrets, three square and one circular. The walls in the lower part are 15 ft. thick, decreasing to 11 ft. in the upper storey. At the south-east corner are the ruins of the **Wardrobe Tower**. In this was embodied part of the **Roman Wall,** which is still visible.

[*J. Allan Cash*

The Tower of London, which has served the purpose of fortress, palace and prison. Though with an historic past it has now no special association with royalty except that it is a place of custody for the Crown Jewels.

One of London's water-buses that ply between Putney and Greenwich : now a popular mode of transport in the Metropolis.

The Tower Bridge was opened in 1894 and was built by the City Corporation at a cost of a million and a half pounds.

To the right is the **Salt Tower,** with a dismal dungeon in which, for some time, gunpowder and saltpetre were stored—hence, probably, the name.   Prisoners also occupied the dungeon and other parts of the tower and have left inscriptions on the wall. The **Broad Arrow Tower** was also a dreaded prison throughout the troublous times of Elizabeth and Mary.

At the north-east corner of the Inner Ward is the **Martin Tower.**   It consists of two storeys and dates from Henry III's reign, but it has been considerably modernised.   The upper floor is reputed to be a haunt of the ghost of Queen Anne.   Up to 1841 the Crown Jewels were kept in this Tower, but in that year a fire broke out and the regalia were rescued with such hazard that it was considered advisable to remove them to quarters less exposed to danger.   It was from this Tower that Colonel Blood made his famous attempt to steal the Crown Jewels in 1671.

Entering the White Tower by an external stairway, we find ourselves on the lower floor of the **Armouries,** which comprise an extensive and valuable collection founded by Henry VIII. Generally speaking, the earlier arms and armour are on the top floor, while the lower floor contains the later weapons, Indian armour and personal relics, but a strictly chronological arrangement is not possible.   The collection includes very few pieces prior in date to the fifteenth century.   In a vault at the farther end of this floor are exhibited an execution block, headsman's axes, gibbet, etc.   Here were confined Sir Walter Raleigh, after his return from Guiana, Sir William Wallace, Guy Fawkes, and other notabilities.   It will be noted that all this part is actually above ground, and the dungeons in their present state hardly suggest their old-time terrors.   From this floor we ascend a winding staircase in the thickness of the wall to the middle floor, in an angle of which is the **Chapel of St. John,** one of the most perfect specimens of Norman architecture extant. It has lately been restored, and soft candle lighting displays its features to advantage.   When the Kings of England lived in the Tower this was their private Chapel.   Here "Bloody Mary" was married by proxy to Philip of Spain, and here her unfortunate rival, Lady Jane Grey, prayed the night before her execution.   Wat Tyler dragged the Archbishop of Canterbury from the altar of St. John's Chapel to death upon Tower Hill. On a higher floor the King's Council met, and it was here that Richard III said to Lord Hastings: "Dost thou answer me with an if?   By St. George, I will not dine until thy head is cut off." This chamber witnessed, too, the deposition of Richard II, from which, as Shakespeare shows, so many tragedies sprang.

From the Chapel we pass through the Sword room and Banqueting hall to the upper floors of the Armouries and then descend by many steps to the **Vaults.**   Here are exhibited a number of ancient mortars and other curios, including a fine sculpture of the Lion of St. Mark and relics of the *Royal George.*

Leaving the White Tower and turning left, we cross the **Green,** with its ravens, to the Beauchamp Tower. To the north of the path is the **Site of the Scaffold**, paved with granite by order of Queen Victoria. Here were beheaded Lord Hastings (1483), Anne Boleyn (1536), the Countess of Salisbury, the "last of the Plantagenets" (1541), Catharine Howard (1542), Viscountess Rochford (1542), Lady Jane Grey (1554), and the Earl of Essex (1601). Anne Boleyn was beheaded with a sword, the others by axe. All were buried in the gloomy **Chapel of St. Peter ad Vincula,** as were also most of the celebrated persons beheaded on Tower Hill (p. 245). Well does Macaulay say of the chapel cemetery: "In truth, there is no sadder spot on earth than this." The Chapel may be viewed on application to the Yeoman Warder on duty on Tower Green, and the public are admitted to the 11 a.m. Sunday service.

Eastward of the Chapel of St. Peter are the **Waterloo Barracks,** but these and certain portions of the Tower are not shown.

The **Beauchamp Tower,** on the west side of Tower Green, and forming part of the inner wall, is one of the most interesting portions of the fortress. Built by Edward I, it was long a place of confinement for prisoners of rank, and its inner walls are covered with inscriptions left by these unhappy mortals. A large number of the glass-protected inscriptions in the principal room on the first floor have been dexterously transferred from other parts of the building.

On the south side the Green is overlooked by the **Queen's House,** formerly the Lieutenant's lodgings, in the council room of which Guy Fawkes and his fellow-conspirators were examined by torture. This building was the scene of Lord Nithsdale's famous escape in female disguise (1716). Adjoining it is the house of the Gentleman Gaoler, from a window of which Lady Jane Grey saw her husband led to slaughter from the Beauchamp Tower, and his headless body brought to the Chapel, while the scaffold was even then being prepared for her own death.

A doorway in the south-east corner of the green leads to the first floor of the Bloody Tower (*see* also p. 248). On the right, immediately on entering, will be observed the apparatus for raising and lowering the ancient portcullis. In this tower Sir Walter Raleigh spent the first years of his second imprisonment, that lasted twelve years, and here began his *History of the World*. The walls bear carvings by prisoners. Cranmer and Ridley were confined here, also Judge Jeffreys, who drank himself to death within these walls. Ascending to the room on the second floor, reputed to be the scene of the murder of the Princes, we pass out to the Prisoners' Walk, wherefrom Sir Walter Raleigh would acknowledge cheers from passing vessels.

Leaving the Bloody Tower, we descend the steps in front to the **Inner Baily,** and turn rightward to the **Wakefield Tower,** which was built by Henry III and was originally called the Record Tower, sometimes the Hall Tower. Its present name is derived from the battle of Wakefield, as a result of which it was crowded with Yorkist prisoners. With equal propriety it might be renamed the Culloden Tower, having been crowded with rebels of '45. Henry VI is said to have been stabbed by the orders of Richard Crookback in its little eastern chapel. But for many the chief interest of this tower is as the repository of the **Crown Jewels.** The large circular apartment has in the centre a double case of steel. The blazing crowns, sceptres, swords, etc., are all labelled and can be plainly seen when the crowd is not great. Among them is the Imperial State Crown. It contains 2,783 diamonds, 277 pearls (one of which is from the River Conway in Wales), 17 sapphires including the Edward and Stuart sapphires, 11 emeralds and 5 rubies including the celebrated Black Prince's Ruby which came into the Royal Regalia in 1367 and was worn by Henry V at the Battle of Agincourt. On the band of this Crown is the second star of Africa cut from the Cullinan diamond; it was presented to Edward VII by the Transvaal in 1908. This diamond is oblong in shape and weighs 317 carats. "The Great Star of Africa" (egg-shaped) is even larger, weighing 530 carats, and is, in fact, the largest cut-diamond in the world. It is set in the Sovereign's sceptre but, like the sister jewel, can be removed and worn as a pendant. The case also contains the Imperial Crown worn by King George V as King-Emperor at Delhi in December, 1911; St. Edward's Crown, worn by King George VI at his Coronation in 1937; the State Crown worn by his Queen on the same occasion; and the orb, anointing spoon, state sword, and other Coronation regalia. The massive "saltcellars" are a remarkable feature of the collection. In the recesses are cases containing insignia of the various knightly orders, state trumpets, etc.

Between the Moat and the river is a broad **Gun Wharf,** with seats, affording a pleasant and interesting outlook. For the **Tower Pier** *see* p. 245.

The **Tower Bridge** (Plan II. O. 9), opened 1894, was built by the City Corporation at a cost of a million and a half pounds. The bridge has several novel features, one being the raised footway, 142 ft. above high water, reached by stairs in the Gothic towers, though this footway is generally closed; the other, the twin bascules, or leaves, which are raised to allow the passage of large vessels. A bell is rung when the "elevation" is about to take place, which happens about fourteen times daily. The central span is 200 ft. long; those on either side, with chain suspension, 270 ft. each. The designers were Sir Horace Jones and Sir J. Wolfe Barry. Over 10,000 vehicles and more than twice that number of pedestrians use the bridge daily. An interesting survival of the early days of the Bridge is the neighbouring tug, riding at anchor but with steam up and ready to go to the assistance of any vessel in difficulties and threatening the bridge. The maintenance of the tug (which annually costs (£5,500) was one of the conditions under which sanction was given for the erection of the bridge.

The northern approach road to the Tower Bridge passes close to that interesting national institution, the **Royal Mint** (Plan II. P. 8). For permission to view, it is necessary to apply by letter not less than four weeks in advance to the Deputy-Master, stating number of party (maximum, six), date of intended visit, etc. (*No admission on Saturdays, Sundays or Bank Holidays.*) Machinery for coinage purposes is of a most interesting character and is employed at the Royal Mint for the production of United Kingdom, Commonwealth and Foreign coins of silver, cupro-nickel, nickel-brass and bronze. An average of 400 million coins are struck annually. There are branches of the Royal Mint at Melbourne and Perth, Australia.

In Trinity Place, on the eastern side of Tower Hill, is a splendid section of the **Roman City Wall,** and beside it, in the wall of an electric sub-station, a reproduction of a Roman memorial stone discovered on the site in 1936.

To the north of the Tower, in Trinity Square, stands the shell of **Trinity House,** burnt out by enemy action in December 1940. The Corporation of Trinity House is the General Lighthouse Authority for England and Wales and the premier Pilotage Authority in the U.K. The Corporation was already a body of importance when Henry VIII granted its first charter in 1514 under the style of "The Guild or Fraternity of the most Glorious and Undividable Trinity and of St. Clement in the Parish Church of Deptford Strond." It consists of a Master, Deputy-Master, about 20 Elder Brethren, and a number of Younger Brethren. Its duties are being carried on in temporary accommodation (Ocean House, Great Tower Street) pending rebuilding of its headquarters. The magnificent block opposite is the headquarters of the **Port of London Authority,** designed by Sir Edwin Cooper, A.R.A. Externally, the predominant feature is the massive tower, rising above a fine portico of Corinthian columns.

The Docks

To a multitude of people who daily pass over the Thames river bridges to and from the City, the Port of London means possibly nothing more than a short stretch of river and a few riverside wharves, jetties and warehouses. Actually, the Port of London comprises 69 miles of the tidal Thames with a wide and deep navigable channel from the sea to the City, the hundreds of wharves, factories, warehouses, etc., on either bank, some small docks and the five great dock systems. The latter have an aggregate area of nearly 3,000 acres of which over 700 acres are water, with nearly 37 miles of deep water quayside. The docks extend from Tower Bridge to Tilbury. Hidden from general view of the river behind the banks and surrounded by Custom Fences, a glimpse of some of these docks and an idea of the extent and importance of the Port can be obtained by taking a launch down river from the Westminster Pier. Return may be made by water, bus, or rail.

The Port of London is administered by the Port of London Authority, a corporate body, established under the Port of London Act, 1908, consisting of a governing board of 28 members, partly elected and partly appointed, with power to elect a chairman and vice-chairman from outside their number. The members are representatives of all interests in the Port.

Since the P.L.A. came into being vast schemes for the improvement of the Port have been carried out, including the construction of new docks, entrance locks, dry docks, etc. Recent improvements include new quayside warehouses and transit sheds, two and three storeys high, the upper floors being used for "working" operations and storage, and the ground floors affording sorting and immediate delivery facilities for imported goods and the collection before shipment of goods for export. The docks are equipped with the latest mechanical labour-aiding equipment, including fleets of electric trucks, quay cranes, mobile and floating cranes, the largest of which has a lifting capacity up to 150 tons.

Next to the River Thames, the Port's most valuable possession is its five dock systems.

Proceeding down river from Tower Bridge, the first dock system is the **London** and **St. Katharine Docks** on the north side. With a land area of 81 acres and a water area of 44 acres (Plan II. P and Q. 8 and 9) the London and St. Katharine Docks afford the main warehousing accommodation for wine, wool, ivory, spices, skins, etc. To the north of the London Docks lies the Highway, a modern name which hardly disguises the former notorious Ratcliff Highway.

From Wapping Station the **Thames Tunnel** (Plan II. Q. 9), 1,200 ft. long, the first of the tunnels to be constructed beneath the river, connects with Rotherhithe on the south bank, and is part of the Underground Railway system. Other river tunnels provide connections for vehicles and pedestrians between the north and south of the river; one is the **Rotherhithe Tunnel,** constructed by the L.C.C. at a cost of upwards of two million pounds and opened in 1908, the northern approach road beginning near Stepney Station and the southern approach at Lower Road, near to the Rotherhithe Station. The tunnel and its approaches are about a mile and a quarter in length.

The **Surrey Commercial Docks** and the **Surrey Canal** at Rotherhithe occupy a combined land and water area of 455 acres in the curved peninsular flanked by the Lower Pool and the Limehouse Reach. These docks are principally used for softwood timber discharge and storage.

About midway between the London and St. Katherine Docks and the West India Docks on the north side is the **Regents Canal Dock** at Limehouse, the inlet to the Regents Canal, a commercial waterway which makes a circuit of North London (we have already seen it at the Zoo) and, as the Grand Union Canal traverses the Midlands and eventually unites the Thames with the Mersey at Liverpool, though few cargoes make the entire journey.   In Limehouse is the area known as " **Chinatown** " where little knots of Chinese nationals foregather, and the lodging-houses and eating-places bear signs of which few Britishers know the meaning.   The **India** and **Millwall Docks** (Plan II. T and U. 9 and 10) occupy the northern portion of the **Isle of Dogs,** a tongue of land which here causes the river to make a wide detour southward to Greenwich, and then northward again to Blackwall. At the Millwall Docks is a huge Granary with a capacity of 24,000 tons. For **Greenwich** see p. 265.   Here is the Greenwich Subway for foot passengers only.   At Blackwall is the **East India Dock** which is comparatively small.   The old East India Export Dock has been drained and is the site of a new electricity power station now under construction.

Hereabouts is the **Blackwall Tunnel** (Plan II. V. 9) providing free communication for pedestrians and vehicles between Blackwall and East Greenwich.   The existing tunnel is 6,200 ft. long, but only about a fifth of it is actually under the bed of the river.   (To facilitate traffic the L.C.C. has undertaken the duplication of the tunnel).   Immediately to the east of the East India Docks is Bow Creek, where the *River Lea* finds an outlet to the Thames.   Below the entrance to Bow Creek and in the areas of Silvertown, West Ham, East Ham and North Woolwich are the **Royal Victoria, Royal Albert** and **King George V. Docks,** extending parallel with the river for three miles, and having a combined water area of 237 acres with 11 miles of quays for ocean-going liners. Together these three docks form the largest impounded docks in the world.   The water is maintained by a powerful electrical pumping installation at a depth from 28 to 42 ft.   Here are great warehouses for tobacco and Cold Stores for frozen meat from Australia and New Zealand.   The largest Cold Stores, situated in the Royal Albert Dock, is capable of storing over 300,000 carcases.

To provide accommodation for the largest modern cargo and passenger liners the King George V. Dock was constructed by the P.L.A. in 1921, south of the Royal Albert Dock.   This is 4,500 ft. long and 700 ft. wide; it has a water area of nearly 65 acres and a quayage of approx. 3 miles.   There is also a large dry dock 750 ft. in length and 100 ft. wide.

Some sixteen miles farther down the river are the extensive **Tilbury Docks,** with a land area of 620½ acres and a water area of 104½ acres. Many vessels belonging to some of the best known shipping companies trading with India and the Far East use these docks.

In the river at **Tilbury** the P.L.A. have provided a rail-connected jetty especially designed to provide accommodation for large ships entering the Port to load or discharge part only of their cargoes.   For passengers a river landing-stage 1,142 ft. long and 80 ft. wide is provided, which can accommodate liners at any stage of the tide.

More than a hundred shipping companies normally operate regular direct services from the Port of London to over 300 ports throughout the world and between 700/800 ships on regular services leave London every month bound for these distributing destinations.   The Port deals with over one-sixth, representing over 53 million net register tonnage, of the total volume of shipping using all ports of the United Kingdom.

SOUTH LONDON

ROUTE XIV.—THE BOROUGH—ST. SAVIOUR'S CATHEDRAL—IMPERIAL WAR MUSEUM—LAMBETH PALACE—BATTERSEA PARK—DULWICH GALLERY.

COMPARED with London north of the Thames, the south, or Surrey side, has little to interest the visitor. The districts adjoining the river are almost entirely industrial; while the outer regions like Camberwell, Clapham, Brixton, etc., though by no means without their amenities, are little more than dormitories for people employed in the City.

One part of South London that no visitor who has read his Dickens, or has any regard for historical associations, will care to overlook, is that known as the **Borough.**

Crossing London Bridge (p. 243), we have on our left the approach road to the **London Bridge Stations** (Plan II. O. 9); and on the right the broad stone steps which give access to—

Southwark Cathedral, (St. Saviour's)

(Plan II. N. 9. Services, see p. 20.)

Though restored in recent years, the building is one of the oldest and most interesting in London. Portions of the Norman nave, dating from the early part of the twelfth century, were incorporated by Blomfield in the new nave, erected 1891-7. The choir and Lady Chapel were built by Peter de Rupibus about 1207. In 1937 a new constitution was granted to the Cathedral under the title of "The Cathedral Collegiate Church of St. Saviour and St. Mary Overie."

James I of Scotland was here wedded to the niece of Cardinal Beaufort. But the chief interest of the church lies in its literary associations, some of the most notable names in English literature having been connected with the parish of Southwark. John Gower, the friend of Chaucer, Edmund Shakespeare, brother of the poet, and Massinger and Fletcher, the dramatists, were buried here; as was also Lawrence Fletcher, joint lessee with Shakespeare and Burbage of the Globe Theatre, Bankside. John Harvard, founder of the famous University in the States, was baptized here on the 29th November, 1607, his father being then a churchwarden. To mark the tercentenary of his birth, the Chapel of St. John, north of the chancel, was in 1907 restored by "sons and friends of Harvard University," and a memorial window inserted. This and many other similar memorial windows were lost during the war. Also commemorated are the

Protestant martyrs who, during Mary's reign, were tried in the Lady Chapel (which—a kitchen in Elizabethan times—has been restored). There is a fine *Memorial of William Shakespeare*, whose theatre, the Globe stood close, at hand.

Adjoining the church is the **Borough Market,** for fruit and vegetables; westward is **Southwark Bridge,** rebuilt 1921. The northern end is dominated by **Vintners' Hall,** a fine modern building. On the south side of Park Street, near the Bridge, a memorial marks the site of the **Globe Playhouse** of Shakespeare's time.

On the opposite side of the Borough High Street, St. Thomas Street leads to **Guy's Hospital** (Plan II. N. 9), founded in 1721 by the miserly bookseller, Thomas Guy.

Continuing down the Borough High Street, we pass the site of the *Talbot* or *Tabard Inn*, from which the Canterbury Pilgrims were accustomed to set out, as described by Chaucer. The old *Tabard* was burnt down in 1873. Lower down is the successor to the *White Hart*, where Mr. Pickwick first encountered the jovial Sam Weller. Between Nos. 75 and 77 the *George Inn*, with its dormer roofs and its quaint inner courtyard and galleries, still reminds us of these old-world hostelries. It is now the property of the National Trust. In the graveyard of the damaged **St. George's Church,** at the corner of Great Dover Street, are the graves of many generations of debtors confined in the now demolished *Marshalsea Gaol*, immortalised in *Little Dorrit* and commemorated by a tablet in the churchyard. In Lant Street, 50 yards beyond the Church, the irrepressible Bob Sawyer lodged with Mrs. Raddle while acquiring the status of a "saw-bones" at Guy's.

The southward continuation of Borough High Street is **Newington Causeway,** at the end of which is the **Elephant and Castle.** Six important thoroughfares meet here, and it is one of the busiest of London's tram, bus and tube centres. A few yards to the south, in Newington Butts, are the remains of the **Metropolitan Tabernacle,** which was successor to a larger structure built to accommodate the immense congregations attracted by the preaching of Charles Haddon Spurgeon.

St. George's Road, close by, will bring us to the former **Bethlem Hospital,** or **Bedlam,** built in 1812–15 to replace the famous "Old Bedlam" in Moorfields, founded so long ago as 1247, the oldest institution for the treatment of the insane in the world. The hospital is now in Kent, having outgrown its site, and the buildings house—

The Imperial War Museum

Plan II. M. 10.

Access.—Nearest Tube station—*Lambeth North; Waterloo* and *Elephant and Castle* are also close at hand. Westminster is about 10 minutes' walk from the Museum. Buses, etc., crossing Westminster Bridge nearly all pass the Museum; and most of the buses crossing Blackfriars, London and Lambeth Bridges are also useful—in the former case alight at St. George's Circus and walk along Lambeth Road; at Elephant and Castle and walk along St. George's Road; or at the Lambeth Baths and walk along Lambeth Road.

Open free daily, except Good Friday and Christmas Day, from 10 a.m. to 6 p.m. on week-days, and from 2 p.m. on Sundays.

The formation of a National War Museum was approved by the War Cabinet in 1917 and the Imperial War Museum was established by Act of Parliament in 1920. It commemorates the effort and sacrifice of the men and women of the Empire in the two World Wars and provides a record of all aspects, military, social, political and economic, of those two periods of national history.

The Museum is a Government Department administered by a Board of Trustees, of which H.R.H. the Duke of Gloucester is President.

The Exhibition Galleries contain naval, military and air service relics and souvenirs, models, weapons, uniforms and medals illustrating the war services of the fighting and civil defence services, and the war effort and experiences of the home front. The Picture Galleries contain a collection of paintings, drawings, and sculpture, unique in forming the record of eye-witnesses, who are also among the leading British artists working in the two periods of the World Wars, officially employed by the Government in the different theatres of war and on the home front. The variety of subjects and styles results in an extremely diversified exhibition which includes portraits, war scenes at home and overseas, and the many aspects of a subject that has affected so greatly the lives of all.

The Reference Library contains books, pamphlets and literature dealing with all aspects of the two wars throughout the world. Other Reference Sections deal with the cinematograph films of the World Wars, air photographs, maps, posters, war currency and stamps, and commemorative medals.

The Photographic Department contains all the official war photographs of both periods, many private collections, and official photographs from Allied and enemy sources. Prints of these can be ordered and reproductions arranged.

Postcards of pictures and exhibits in the Museum's collection, illustrated booklets relating to the three services of 1914–18, and many official publications relating to the 1939–45 war, are on sale at the Museum.

At the junction of St. George's Road with the Westminster Bridge Road stands **St. George's Roman Catholic Cathedral** (Plan II. M. 10), designed by Pugin, and opened in 1848, but still wanting its central tower. The building has been severely damaged but fortunately can be restored. Here Cardinal Wiseman was enthroned as first Archbishop of Westminster. A few yards to the west, at the corner of Westminster Bridge Road and Kennington Road, is **Christ Church**, built to replace the old Surrey Chapel, rendered famous by the preaching of Rowland Hill. The tower and spire were built with American contributions as a memorial of Lincoln, the stonework being appropriately ornamented with the stars and stripes.

At **St. George's Circus** (Plan II. M. 10) the roads from Blackfriars, Waterloo, Westminster and Lambeth Bridges all meet.

The Waterloo Road would bring us in a few minutes to **Waterloo** (Plan II. L. 9, *see* p. 60), the terminus of the South-Western section of the Southern Region. The fine entrance archway is a memorial of railwaymen fallen in the Great War. Opposite the station is the **Union Jack Club,** for soldiers and sailors, founded as a memorial of men of both services who lost their lives in the South African and Chinese Wars. At the corner of New Cut is the " Old Vic " wherein opera (in English) and Shakespeare are played to such enthusiastic audiences.

From St. George's Circus a bus or tram will take us to **Lambeth Palace** (Plan II. L. 10), near Lambeth Bridge.

By arrangement individuals and parties can be shown the historic parts of Lambeth Palace; applications should be addressed to The Secretary, Lambeth Palace, S.E.1.

This mellow pile entered by a Tudor Gateway has been for nearly seven centuries the London residence of the Archbishops of Canterbury. The part actually occupied by the Archbishop was rebuilt by Archbishop Howley in 1834. Considerable damage was suffered during air raids in the Second World War. Among the most interesting portions of the older building are the *Gatehouse* built by Cardinal Morton in 1490; the *Lollards' Tower*, erected by Archbishop Chicheley about 1436; and the *Guard Room*, with portraits of archbishops by Holbein, Van Dyck, Reynolds, Lawrence, Herkomer, and others. The *Chapel* built by Archbishop Boniface in 1245 was almost completely destroyed and the *Great Hall*, used as the Library, the work of Archbishop Juxon, also badly damaged; but the latter has now been repaired. The books at present in the **Library** number between 30,000 and 40,000 in addition to some 2,000 MSS. Upwards of 8,000 volumes were damaged in the raids, with about half that number probably completely lost. Students have access on three days per week, for further information apply to the Assistant Librarian. In the gardens are some luxuriant fig-trees, said to have been brought from Spain, and planted by Cardinal Pole, Legate to the court of Queen Mary, and Archbishop of Canterbury.

Ten acres of the grounds are maintained for public use under the name of the **Archbishop's Park**. Adjoining the south gateway of the Palace is **St. Mary's Church,** containing the graves of six archbishops. It has a fine Perpendicular tower.

One of the windows shattered in the war showed a representation of a pedlar and his dog, commemorating the bequest to the church of a piece of land by a pedlar who had been sheltered by the priest. The receipts from the land amounted at first to 2s. 8d. per year, but when the London County Council found it necessary to acquire the "Pedlar's Acre" in connection with their new County Hall, they had to pay the handsome sum of £81,000.

Opposite the Palace the river is crossed by the rebuilt **Lambeth Bridge,** at the far end of which are **Thames House** and the headquarters of *Imperial Chemical Industries*. Behind Thames House, in St. John's Gardens, is the **Westminster Hospital,** opened by King George VI in 1939. There are over 400 beds, a large outpatients' department and training schools for doctors and nurses. Across the river the headquarters of the **London Fire Service** (*see* p. 26) are among the finest in the world. We can either cross the river by the bridge, or follow the **Albert Embankment** (p. 78) to Westminster Bridge, passing the series of detached and badly damaged buildings serving as **St. Thomas's Hospital** (Plan II. L. 9 and 10). Or from Lambeth Bridge we could continue westward in the direction of Battersea Park. As we approach Vauxhall Bridge the **Tate Gallery** (*see* p. 117) is well seen across the water. The road bridge beneath **Vauxhall Station** (Southern Region: S.W. section) leads to **Kennington Oval,** the headquarters of the Surrey C.C. and the scene of many county matches. Beyond, bordering the main road to Clapham is **Kennington Park,** formerly Kennington Common, the scene of the Chartist assembly in 1848.

Battersea Park, one of the largest and most attractive of South London pleasure grounds, adjoins the south bank of the river, almost opposite Chelsea Hospital. It is 198 acres in extent, and includes a large expanse of water and a well-kept *Subtropical Garden*. Some 37 acres of the section fronting the river were set out as Festival Gardens in connection with the Festival of Britain 1951. Near the east end of the Park the river is crossed by the **Chelsea Suspension Bridge** (rebuilt 1935–7), and at the west end by the **Albert Suspension Bridge.**

For **Chelsea** and its many interesting associations, *see* p. 182.

One or two other features of South London not included in the above route demand mention. The most important is the **Dulwich College Picture Gallery,** about half a mile from North-

Dulwich Station (Southern Region, S.E. section, or by bus by way of Red Post Hill). Entrance in Gallery Road. Most of these important and valuable works of art (originally bought as the nucleus of a projected National Gallery of Poland) were bequeathed to the College in 1811 by Sir Francis Bourgeois, R.A. It contains two well-known works by *Murillo*, and is strong in Dutch and Flemish masters, including *Cuyp, Wouverman, Rembrandt, Van Dyck*, and the two *Teniers*. There are also examples of *Gainsborough, Reynolds*, and other British masters. (*The Gallery suffered considerable damage during the war but has now been restored. Intending visitors should apply to the Clerk to the Governors for particulars of hours, etc.*) Dulwich College was founded in 1619 by Edward Alleyn, the actor, and is a large and flourishing institution.

An interesting survival in this locality is the *Toll Gate* across the road near Dulwich College.

Hardly more than a mile farther south is the site of the Crystal Palace, that monument of the Great Exhibition of 1851 and of the skill of Sir Joseph Paxton. The Palace, alas, was destroyed by fire in December, 1936, but the grounds are still used for a variety of purposes.

Popular open spaces in this locality are Dulwich Park (72 acres), famous for its spring show of rhododendrons and its rock garden, Peckham Rye (115 acres) and Brockwell Park (127 acres). In Nunhead Lane, Peckham Rye, is the "Nun's Head," an ancient inn, said to have been licenced in the reign of Henry VII. At 100, London Road, is the Horniman Museum and Library (*open daily, except Tuesdays and Christmas Day, from* 10.30 a.m. to 6 p.m., Sundays from 2). Contents include series devoted to "Man and his tools", "art," "magic and religion" and musical instruments. The zoological series also include collections of insects, and aquaria. The public reference library contains some 20,000 volumes on Ethnology, Archaeology and Zoology.

Next to the Museum are the grounds of the Horniman Gardens, a very lovely and popular park.

Clapham Common is an open space of 220 acres. Tooting Common, to the south-east, contains nearly 150 acres. Tooting Bec is so called as having been a dependency of the famous Abbey of Bec, in Normandy.

John Ruskin spent the earlier part of his life at Denmark Hill and Herne Hill, a fact which is commemorated by the name of Ruskin Park, on the west side of Denmark Hill. Adjoining is King's College Hospital.

TRIPS FROM TOWN

THE nearer suburbs encircling London will not, as a rule, arouse enthusiasm; but once the stranger has passed this middle belt, no matter whether he goes north, south, east or west, he will find within the compass of an easy excursion innumerable places of beauty and historic interest. In recent years considerable success has attended the commendable efforts of local authorities to preserve for the public, as opportunity arises, many pleasant stretches in what is known as the *Green Belt* that would otherwise be built upon. All we can do, in the limited space at our command, is to set out in alphabetical order a few particulars of the places most likely to attract, together with the facilities for reaching them. Several of the large tourist firms arrange day and half-day tours from London, combining rail, coach or steamer, etc., as well as luncheon and tea, at inclusive rates (*see* also p. 31). The country services of the buses and the Green Line coaches are also useful in this connection. Strangers desirous of spending an evening in beautiful surroundings without incurring a long journey should not overlook the easy access provided by the tube and electric railways to such spots as Hampstead Heath and Ken Wood, Richmond and Kew, etc. On certain days in each week during the summer the railways issue day and half-day excursion tickets at reduced fares to most of the places mentioned below. The trips are usually advertised in the newspapers.

For the benefit of motorists we add a note of the road routes to the more distant resorts.

Ashridge Park.

Admission.—The Gardens are open to the public 2–7 on Sundays and public holidays from Whitsun to September 30th. Admission 1s. and 9d. Teas may be obtained at the tea pavilion, 2s.

Rail to Berkhamsted station from Euston; thence walk over Berkhamsted Common, or by bus (about 3½ miles).

Road *via* Edgware and the Watford by-pass to Berkhamsted. Or *via* St. Albans and Hemel Hempstead.

Motor Coach to Berkhamsted from Victoria, Hyde Park Corner or Marble Arch.

Ashridge Park, formerly the seat of Lord Brownlow, was, with some 150 acres of charming grounds, in 1928 presented by the late Mr. Urban Broughton to Trustees (The Bonar Law

Trust), as a memorial to his lifelong friend Andrew Bonar Law. The donor's intentions were set out in the Trust Deed: 1. To honour the memory of a great statesman; 2. To preserve a beautiful and historic building; 3. To use the House and Gardens as a centre for instruction in Citizenship.

A further 300 acres of the Park is owned by the National Trust, making, with **Berkhamsted Common** (lovely with gorse and bracken and beech woods) and **Ivinghoe Beacon** (with fine views), a total open space of more than 3,000 acres under its care.

Barnet.

Train (Eastern Region) from King's Cross or Finsbury Park Stations to *New* Barnet. Or by bus. Alternatively *High* Barnet on Northern Line.
Road Route *via* Finchley and Great North Road (13 miles) to Station Road, *New* Barnet. Green Line coaches from Victoria, Marble Arch, King's Cross, etc.

To Londoners Barnet is known as a pleasant northern suburb; historians know it on account of the Battle of Barnet (1471) where Warwick was slain. Recently the place has acquired new interest in the **Abbey Art Centre and Museum** at Park Road, New Barnet. The former Abbey is now housing an artist's colony. The only parts at present open to the public are the thirteenth-century tithebarn Church and the Museum and an Ethnological section. (Admission, 6d. Open Sat. and Sun. afternoons, other times by appointment.)

An excursion to Barnet may well be combined with a visit to Hatfield or St. Albans.

Brighton.

Electric trains from London Bridge or Victoria (Southern Region) 51 miles. The faster trains do the journey in an hour.
Road Route, *via* Westminster Bridge, Brixton, Streatham, Croydon by-pass, Red Hill, Crawley and Pyecombe (51¼ miles). There are several alternative routes, slightly longer but less crowded.
Motor Coaches run from and to London daily throughout the year. See announcements in newspapers.

With its five miles of sea front, its magnificent hotels and shops, and many facilities for amusement, Brighton is never likely to lose its hold on the affections of Londoners. The principal features are the fine promenades, the Piers, the Pavilion (built by the Prince Regent, afterwards George IV), the Aquarium and the great Sports Stadium; but Brighton is less interesting in itself than as a background against which to view the extraordinary and diversified crowds which flock there, especially at week-ends and on Bank Holidays. A favourite excursion is that to the Devil's Dyke, high up on the spacious South Down range. Our *Guide to Brighton* should be consulted for fuller information.

Burnham Beeches (Bucks).

Rail (Western Region) from Paddington (21 miles). Or by Eastern Region (Marylebone) to Beaconsfield.
    In connection with certain trains buses run between Slough and Beaconsfield, *via* Stoke Poges and Farnham Royal, through tickets being issued to cover motor and the rail journey to and from London. In summer there are also

conveyances from Slough Station to Burnham Beeches. As Burnham Beeches Station is a mile and a half from the woods, and there is no public conveyance, it is usually more convenient to book to Slough. Burnham Beeches are included with Maidenhead and other Thames resorts in many circular trips from Town.

Buses.—The service from Hounslow to Windsor passes through Slough.

Coaches.—Green Line coaches in summer direct to Burnham Beeches from Trafalgar Square and Hyde Park Corner.

Road Route, *via* Chiswick, the Great West Road and the Colnbrook by-pass to Slough; or *via* Acton, Hanwell, Uxbridge and Farnham.

Londoners are indebted to the City Corporation for the preservation and maintenance of this magnificent pleasure-ground, comprising over 400 acres of the finest sylvan scenery in England. In autumn especially, when the trees are all "in russet mantle clad," the place is one of great beauty. The pollard beeches are generally considered the finest in the world. In 1921 the late Viscount Burnham presented an additional 65 acres as a memorial of his father, the first Lord Burnham, whose work for journalism is commemorated in the name Fleet Wood. About midway between Slough and Burnham Beeches (say two miles from either) is **Stoke Poges,** the scene of Gray's famous *Elegy*. The red-brick tomb of the poet's mother, in which he was himself interred, will be seen close to the south wall of the church.

Chalfont St. Giles (Bucks).

Rail (Metropolitan) from Baker Street, or from Marylebone, to Chalfont and Latimer station, from which the village is about 3 miles distant. Or from Marylebone or Paddington to Seer Green, Gerrard's Cross (whence buses run to Chalfont St. Giles) or Beaconsfield.

Road Route, *via* Harrow, Pinner and Rickmansworth, or *via* Uxbridge. Green Line coaches from Oxford Circus and Baker St. Station to Chalfont.

This prettily placed village is visited on account of **Milton's Cottage,** where *Paradise Lost* was finished and *Paradise Regained* commenced. It stands at the end of the village, on the left. (*Admission 6d. Museum open daily except Tuesday and Sunday mornings April–Sept.* 10–1 2.15–6; *closes at dusk Oct.–March.*) Altered little since the poet's time and beautifully situated among beech trees about two miles to the south, and most conveniently reached by bus from Beaconsfield station (W.R.), is **Jordans,** the charming old Meeting House in the grounds of which rest the remains of William Penn, the founder of Pennsylvania, and his wife and children. A little above the Meeting House is the *Hostel*, with a barn containing timbers from the *Mayflower*.

London Airport, Heathrow.

Underground to Hounslow West, thence by bus or Green Line coach direct. Passengers by air services arriving at or departing from the Airport are conveyed to and from the West End by special motor coaches.

Heathrow is the main terminal for principal air services in Britain, with huge air-liners of various nationalities constantly arriving and departing. Visitors are admitted (6d.) to an enclosure (car park, 1s.) from whence the busy scene may be witnessed. The excursion is well worth making. (*See* p. 17.)

Epping Forest.

Rail from Liverpool Street. Chingford is the most popular approach, but the stations at Loughton and Theydon Bois are also in touch with some of the most charming parts of the Forest.

Buses and Trolleybuses.—Several routes bring the Forest within easy reach of the central parts of London. Green Line coaches from Baker Street Station and Liverpool Street.

Epping Forest, comprising 5,604 acres, is merely a "remainder" of the Great Forest of Waltham, which until a century or so ago reached almost to London. When successive encroachments bade fair in a short while entirely to obliterate the Forest, the Corporation of London intervened, and after expensive litigation succeeded in securing all the unenclosed portion for the use and enjoyment of the public for ever. The one-day visitor will be well advised not to lose touch with the central high road that runs right through the Forest, from Woodford, through Buckhurst Hill, to Epping, a distance from south to north of over ten miles. The finest part is generally considered to be *High Beach*, a little to the west of the point where the road to Loughton crosses the highway just referred to at the *Robin Hood Inn*. Tennyson resided here when he wrote *Locksley Hall*. The elevated spire of High Beach Church is the most serviceable of Forest landmarks. Near at hand is the *King's Oak Hotel*, a favourite resort of picnic parties. The most common trees are the oak, hornbeam, beech, and birch. **Gilwell Park,** in the words of the Chief Scout, is "the home and Mecca of the Boy Scout Movement."

About two miles south-east of Chigwell is **Hainault Forest.** Owing to nineteenth-century disafforestation only about a third of the 1,100 acres is woodland. Two public golf courses (18 holes) are maintained by the London County Council, where anyone may play for 1s. 6d. a round. Needless to say, the courses are besieged by players, especially during week-ends and holidays.

Epsom (Surrey)

Rail from Waterloo (14¼ m.), or from Victoria and London Bridge to *Epsom* Station (2 m. from Racecourse), 15¾ m. Or by Southern Region (Brighton section) to *Epsom Downs* Station (16 m.).

The nearest station to the Racecourse is **Tattenham Corner,** reached from Charing Cross, Cannon Street and London Bridge Stations.

Road Route (14¼ m.) *via* Clapham, Balham, Tooting, Merton and Ewell.

Bus services from Morden Station. Green Line coaches from Victoria.

Epsom, with its delightful surroundings, is well worth a visit. The famous Racecourse is on Epsom Downs, about 500 ft. above sea-level, and the scene of the **Derby** and the Oaks, normally run towards the end of May or beginning of June.

Gravesend

Gravesend, reached either by Southern Region, or from Fenchurch Street or St. Pancras *via* Tilbury, is the entrance to the Port of London and the home of most of the Thames pilots. Pilotage in the London district is compulsory, with few exceptions, for vessels exceeding 60 tons burden engaged in the foreign trade. Gravesend men are generally considered the most skilful river boatmen in the world. With its opposite neighbour, **Tilbury** (p. 254), Gravesend is a favourite yachting station. Visitors from the United States will certainly find their way to the *Parish Church of Saint George*, to see the register containing the entry of the burial of the famous Indian Princess, Pocahontas, who did so much to befriend the early settlers of Virginia, and died at Gravesend in 1616 during a visit to this country. She is commemorated by two stained-glass windows, the gift of the Virginia Society of Colonial Dames of America.

Greenwich.

Steamers and Motor Launches provide the most pleasant and interesting way of travelling to and from Greenwich. The vessels start from and return to *Westminster Pier*, in the shadow of Big Ben. Fare, 3s. return. Many of the boats call also at Tower Pier (*see* p. 245).

Rail by Southern Region (6¼ m.), from Charing Cross to *Maze Hill*, a few minutes' walk from National Maritime Museum, by way of Park Place and Park Row.

Trams and buses from Blackfriars, Westminster Bridge or Waterloo.

Greenwich is of peculiar interest to visitors from Britain overseas, for under the old constitutional theory all the colonies were reckoned as part of the Royal manor of Greenwich. During the War of Independence it was gravely argued in the House of Commons that Americans could not reasonably complain of "taxation without representation," seeing that they were represented in Parliament by the Kent members.

The Royal Naval College, a long range of buildings with an imposing frontage to the river, occupies the site of an old royal palace used as a residence by successive sovereigns from the early part of the fifteenth century to the time of the Commonwealth. Henry VIII and his daughters Elizabeth and Mary were born here; and here the youthful Edward VI passed away. Charles II commenced to rebuild the palace, but completed only part of the west, or King Charles, wing, overlooking the river. Building was resumed by King William at the request of Queen Mary for conversion into a hospital for superannuated seamen. It no longer serves this purpose. The Hospital was closed by Act of Parliament in 1869 and in 1873 the buildings were taken over by the Admiralty and converted into the Royal Naval College for the higher education of Naval Officers.

The buildings of the College comprise four blocks. In the south-eastern block, under one of the twin domes, is the **Chapel**, rebuilt by James Stuart following Wren's external design, and beneath the other dome is the **Painted Hall**, built by Wren and decorated with paintings by Thornhill. These are open to the public daily 2.30 to 5 except Thursdays and Sundays. Chapel is open for Divine Service on Sunday mornings.

National Maritime Museum

Access.—*See* above.

Admission.—Free. Open week-days, 10 to 6; Sundays, 2.30 to 6. Closed on Good Friday, Christmas Eve and Christmas Day.

Entrance at junction of Park Row and Park Place.

Refreshment Room and Tea Garden, opening from the Navigation Room.

This Museum was founded by Act of Parliament in 1934 and comprises the Queen's House and the buildings erected at the beginning of the nineteenth century for the accommodation of the Royal Hospital School, which migrated to Suffolk in 1933.

The **Queen's House,** the oldest Italianate house in England, was begun in 1618 by Inigo Jones for Anne of Denmark, Queen Consort of James I, and completed in 1635 for Henrietta Maria, the Queen of Charles I. It is unique in that it was built over the road between Deptford and Woolwich. On the south of the House is a loggia, overlooking the Park and the Observatory.

In the Queen's House are collected the portraits, battle-pieces and models illustrating sea affairs from Tudor times until the accession of Queen Anne.

In the *Caird Galleries* note the marble Rotunda, designed by Sir Edwin Lutyens and Sir William Reid Dick, which commemorates Sir James Caird, to whom the Museum is indebted for the cost of its construction as well as for more than half of the exhibits. Beyond the Caird Rotunda is the *Library*, containing a unique collection of books and manuscripts, atlases and charts. On either side of the Rotunda are the Medal Room and the Seal Room.

A staircase constructed from the timbers of H.M. ships *Defence, Defiance, Ganges* and *Arethusa* leads to the Caird Galleries, with paintings, models and relics associated with Anson, Hawke, Cook, Howe, Duncan, St. Vincent and Nelson and their stirring times. It is quite impossible in the space at our disposal even to attempt to describe the contents of these rooms, which provide a wonderful illustration of the evolution of the British Royal and Merchant Navies.

In Church Street, close to Greenwich Park station, is the **Church of St. Alfege,** containing the tombs of General Wolfe (d. 1759) and Thomas Tallis, the sixteenth-century church musician.

South of the College is **Greenwich Park,** a royal domain of 185 acres, laid out by Charles II and commanding magnificent views Londonwards. Crowning a hill in the centre is the **Royal Observatory,** to which interested visitors are occasionally admitted on making written application to the Director. The time-ball descends precisely at 1 p.m. and the correct time is then telegraphed to all the most important towns. Visitors generally seek out the line marking the *Greenwich Meridian,* which crosses the path a few yards north of the Observatory gates. Greenwich Observatory originated in a desire to provide seamen with satisfactory data for determining their positions at sea and thus the Greenwich meridian became and remains of world-wide importance. Opposite the gates of the Observatory is a fine statue of *General Wolfe,* by Professor Tait Mackenzie. It was presented to this country by the Canadian People.

Adjoining Greenwich Park on the south is **Blackheath** (267 acres), where Wat Tyler and Jack Cade marshalled their hosts, and where many a pretty highway robbery has taken place. Here, too, golf was introduced by James I.

Hampstead Heath.

Nearest Stations.—Hampstead for south side, Golder's Green for north, both on the Northern Line; Hampstead Heath (London Midland).
Bus or Trolleybus from Holborn, King's Cross, Hampstead Road, etc.

Hampstead Heath, with its broken heights, its grassy glades and furze-covered expanses, and its far-reaching views, is without exception the best of London's open spaces. The Heath proper comprises only 240 acres, but adjoining common lands increase the public area to 804 acres. A magnificent view is gained from the *Flagstaff* on the Heath (440 ft. above sea-level). On the north are the **Golder's Hill Estate** (36 acres), and **Waterlow Park** (29 acres), while to the east is **Parliament Hill** (267 acres). Also to the north is **Kenwood,** known as the Iveagh Bequest. The mansion is a fine example of the work of Robert Adam, and the pictures include an outstanding self-portrait by Rembrandt, and many works of the British School. Open free every day (except Wednesdays and Fridays when 1s. is charged), from 10–6 week-days and 2.30–6 Sundays, summer. Closes at dusk in winter. Close at hand also are the beautiful **Highgate Woods** (69 acres), maintained by the City Corporation.

Well Walk, close to the High Street, takes its name from the famous spa so extensively patronised by "the quality" in the seventeenth and eighteenth centuries. John Keats lodged here in 1817–18, and later lived at *Wentworth Place* at the foot of John Street (now known as Keats Grove). *Wentworth Place* (in 1838 the name was changed to *Lawn Cottage* and later to *Lawn Bank*, but the original name has now been revived), in the garden of which the *Ode to the Nightingale* was written, is now maintained as a Keats Memorial and Museum. *The Keats House is open (free) each week-day from* 10 *to* 6 *p.m. (October to March* 10 *to* 4 *p.m.). The Museum adjoining, containing a unique collection of relics of Keats and his contemporaries, is open each week-day from* 10 *to* 7 *p.m. Both House and Museum are closed on Sundays.*

In the graveyard of Hampstead Church are buried Sir J. Macintosh, the historian; Joanna Baillie; John Constable, some of whose most famous pictures were inspired by the locality; G. du Maurier (1896); and Sir W. Besant (1901). In the neighbourhood of the Finchley Road is the **Everyman Theatre.**

In Hoop Lane, off the Finchley Road, on the northern borders of Hampstead Heath, is the **Golder's Green Crematorium.**

Close at hand is the extensive **Hampstead Garden Suburb.**

Hampton Court Gardens and Palace

Rail from Waterloo (Southern Region) to Hampton Court Station, 15 m. Or from London Midland and Underground Stations *via* Richmond, to Teddington.
Buses from Putney, Highgate, etc.

Rail and Trolleybus.—To Hammersmith, by Underground, thence by trolleybus *via* Twickenham. Or by tram to Wimbledon, changing there to the trolleybus for Kingston and Hampton Court.

Coaches (Green Line) from Victoria and Hyde Park Corner.

Steamers run during the summer months (see announcements in newspapers) from Westminster Bridge to Hampton Court.

Admission.—The Gardens are open daily until dusk. Portions of the Palace are open daily 10 to 4, 5 or 6, Sundays from 2. To view the State Apartments, Chapel, Haunted Gallery and Great Hall a charge of 1s. is made on week-days. (Saturdays, 6d.; Bank Holidays and Sundays free; children half-price.) Lecture tours at 11 and 3 on Tuesdays to Fridays, and 11 on Saturdays during summer. No extra charge. The Great Kitchen and Cellars (3d.) and the Orangery (3d.) are open at the same hours as the State Apartments. Admission to Great Vine, 2d.; Maze, 3d.; Tudor Tennis Court, 3d., 2–6 p.m., Sundays, Wednesdays, Saturdays; Banqueting House, 1s., children, 6d., Mondays, Tuesdays, Thursdays, Fridays from 2 p.m.

No visitor to London, however pressed for time, should fail to see the beautiful and stately palace built by Cardinal Wolsey for his own delight, and afterwards "presented"—not very willingly, we must believe—to his royal master, Henry VIII. It is the largest and in many respects the finest of all the royal palaces of England, though it has not been occupied by the sovereign since the time of George II. It contains about a

PLAN OF HAMPTON COURT MAZE

thousand rooms, of which four-fifths are occupied by royal pensioners and other privileged persons; but the magnificent State Apartments, with their fine pictures, the Courts, and the charming gardens are open to all. In recent years several parts not formerly visible have been opened to the public, including the old moat and a fine battlemented bridge, built by Henry VIII for his "owne darling," Anne Boleyn; the famous "Haunted Gallery"; and "My Lord Cardinall's Lodgynges." The "ghost" of the Haunted Gallery is supposed to be that of Catherine Howard, another of Henry's unfortunate "darlings."

The Palace is of red brick, now delightfully mellowed by time. Perhaps the finest portions of the original building are the **Great Gatehouse** and the **Clock Court.** In the latter is the famous astronomical clock constructed for Henry VIII. The **Great Hall,** with its magnificent tapestries and wonderful timber roof (recently restored), was built by the same monarch. The **State**

Rooms, surrounding the Fountain Court, were added for William III by Sir Christopher Wren. The Palace was used as a residence by Henry VIII, Cromwell, the Stuart kings, William III, George I and George II. The paintings are part of the Royal Collection. The celebrated "Hampton Court Beauties," by *Kneller*; and the "Windsor Beauties," of the Court of Charles II by *Lely*, should be seen. The finest tapestries are the eight pieces in the Great Hall, illustrating the life of Abraham, and the copies of the famous Raphael cartoons, presented by Baron D'Erlanger.

The **Great Kitchen** and the **Tilt Yard** are open to the public.

Notable features of the beautiful **Gardens** are the *Great Vine,** (*2d.*), planted in 1768; and the *Maze* (*3d.*), adjoining the Lion Gates, the intricacies of which can easily be threaded by one who bears in mind always to follow the hedge on the *right* when going in and the *left* hedge when coming out. In the Wren **Orangery** (*admission 3d.*) are nine large tempera paintings by Andrea Mantegna, representing the triumph of Julius Cæsar. Opposite the eastern façade of the Palace is the **Long Water** (nearly ¾ of a mile long), constructed by Charles II. The **Home Park** (600 acres) is bounded on all but the western side by the Thames. It is open to the public.

Opposite the **Lion Gates** is the principal entrance to **Bushy Park,** a royal demesne of over 1,000 acres, noted for its tame deer. The famous *Chestnut Avenue,* the flowering of which during May lures crowds of sightseers, stretches right across the Park to Teddington, the vista broken only by the *Diana Fountain.* Many of the trees are over 200 years old.

Harrow-on-the-Hill

Rail from Baker Street (Met.) or Marylebone, 9½ m. Other routes are by Bakerloo Tube, joining the L.M.R. line at Queen's Park, or by Underground and Piccadilly Lines to *South Harrow Station.* Also from Euston or Broad Street.
Road Route *via* Maida Vale, Cricklewood, Hendon and Kenton. Green Line coaches from Victoria and Marble Arch.

Harrow is chiefly visited for the famous **School,** founded in 1571 by John Lyon, a yeoman of the parish. It rivals Eton in the affections of the aristocracy. Among distinguished scholars may be mentioned Lord Byron, Sheridan, Sir Robert Peel, Palmerston and Cardinal Manning. The view from the churchyard terrace (400 ft. high), from the Peachey tomb (now protected by an iron casing), on which Byron used to lie outstretched, is very extensive. The finely-placed *Church,* consecrated in 1094, with its Norman tower, is also of great interest (*open all day*).

Hatfield (Herts)

Rail from King's Cross, 17¾ m.
Road Route *via* Highgate, Finchley, Barnet and Potter's Bar or the Barnet by-pass. Green Line coaches from Hyde Park Corner, Marble Arch and Baker Street Station (Routes 716 and 717).

* An offshoot of this vine in the Royal Gardens at Windsor, planted in 1775, has long since outgrown its parent.

Admission.—Hatfield House is shown to visitors daily except Sundays between Easter week and the end of September, from 10 a.m. to 5 p.m. on payment of a fee. Picnics in the park are not allowed. The entrance to Hatfield Park is immediately opposite the station and bus stop. A statue of the third Marquis of Salisbury, the great Victorian statesman, stands in front of the gates.

Hatfield House the historic home of the Cecils, was built in 1611 by the first Earl of Salisbury, who had exchanged Theobald's Park with James I for Hatfield Park. It is a lovely Jacobean building of mellow red brick, containing many works of art and historical relics. Adjoining the gardens is a portion of the Old Palace of the Bishops of Ely, where Queen Elizabeth, as princess, was imprisoned during the reign of her sister, Mary Tudor. The *Church,* just outside the Park, is in the Decorated style. The *Salisbury Chapel* contains memorials to the Cecil family.

Henley

Rail from Paddington 35¾ m.
   Also by Messrs. Salter Bros.' Saloon **Steamers** from Kingston (p. 273).
Road Route *via* Hammersmith, Chiswick, the Great West Road, Slough and Maidenhead; or *via* Uxbridge, Beaconsfield, Bourne End and Marlow.

This pleasant little town is one of the most popular centres for river scenery. During **Regatta Week** (beginning of **July**) accommodation is at a premium. See our *Guide to the Thames.*

Kew Gardens

Rail to either Kew Bridge (L.M.R. and S.R.) or Kew Gardens (from Broad Street) Stations. Kew Gardens Station is also served by District Line trains. The former station is ten minutes' walk from the principal, or northern, entrance; from the latter it is five minutes' walk to the Victoria Gate.
Steamers during summer from Westminster Bridge (see announcements).
Buses from Hammersmith, Kensington, etc., pass three entrances.
Trolleybuses from Hammersmith, Shepherd's Bush, etc., to Kew Bridge.
Admission.—The Gardens are open daily from 10 a.m. to 8 p.m. or dusk. Closed on Christmas Day, The Hot-houses open at 1 p.m.
Fee, threepence.
Photography and Sketching is permitted out of doors on any day, and on Friday afternoons within the Houses. (Special permission for the latter is required.)
Refreshments (teas and light luncheons) are served, in summer, at the Pavilion near the Temperate House.
Cars may be parked near the main entrance, Kew Green.

The prime function of the **Royal Botanic Gardens** is the correct identification of plants. For this purpose the scientific staff have at their disposal a *Herbarium* containing over 6,000,000 sheets of dried specimens. In the Gardens themselves between 45,000 and 50,000 different kinds of plants are cultivated, supplementary to the dried collection. The visitor may wander at will through what is practically a lordly park, of nearly 300 acres, with every species of tree, shrub and flower plainly labelled for his edification. The grounds comprise stately avenues and sequestered walks, lakes and ponds, palm-houses and conservatories, gorgeous flower-beds, rockeries, museums and classic temples, and a large herbaceous ground. The most important features are large *Palm House,* kept always at a temperature of 80°, *Temperate House,* four *Museums,* and the *North Gallery.* Other houses are devoted to Australian plants, tropical aroids, tropical ferns, filmy ferns, succulents, begonias, orchids, water-lilies, alpine plants, etc. Always delightful, Kew should be seen also at such seasons as "bluebell time," or when the masses of rhododendrons or daffodils are in bloom.

Among other works of universal importance carried out at Kew was the raising from seeds specially brought from Brazil

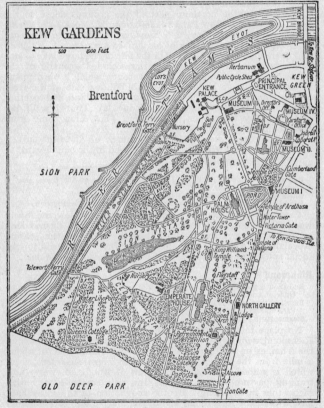

—at that time the world's sole source of rubber supply—of the 1,000 plants with which the rubber industry was introduced into the Malay Peninsula and Ceylon. Kew was also instrumental in introducing the almost indispensable quinine plan from South America into India.

A touch of quaintness is given to the southern end of the Gardens by the **Chinese Pagoda,** 163 ft. high, and its neighbour, a **Japanese Gateway** which is a small-scale model of the gate of the great Buddhist Temple of Nishi Hongwanji. A notable addition to the Gardens is a **Flagpole** of Douglas fir from Vancouver island, presented by the Government of British Columbia. Said to be the tallest in the world, it is 214 ft. in height and weighs 18½ tons. In the northern part of the grounds, close to the main entrance, is **Kew Palace** (*admission, 6d.; open daily during Summer,* 10–6 *week-days,* 2–6 *Sundays*); a favourite residence of George III; many relics of his family may be seen. Queen Charlotte died here in 1818. On the left of the large lake as one proceeds towards the river are the secluded grounds of the Queen's Cottage, an enclosed path through which is open to the public. The large building on the Middlesex side of the river is *Syon House,* a seat of the Duke of Northumberland and together with part of the grounds is open Wednesday, Thursday, Friday and Saturday afternoons in summer. (The Lion came from Northumberland Avenue—*see* p. 76.)

On **Kew Green** stands the brick church of *St. Anne* (1714). Gainsborough, the artist (d. 1788) is buried in the churchyard.

Maidenhead

Rail from Paddington (W.R.), 24½ m. *Taplow* station on the Bucks side, is equally near the river.
Buses connect Maidenhead with Windsor and with Henley.
Road Route (28 m.) *via* Hammersmith, the Great West Road and Slough.

Charming river scenery, especially the reach below the lovely wooded grounds of **Cliveden. Boulter's Lock,** the busiest lock on the Thames, provides an interesting sight in the season, especially on a fine Sunday in June or July, though its former social splendour has departed. See our *Guide to the Thames.*

Richmond

Rail (Southern—S.W.) from Waterloo (9¾ m.); or from Broad Street. Also by Underground.
Buses.—There are several services. Green Line coaches from Victoria and Hyde Park Corner.
Steamboats in summer and motor launches (see announcements).

No place in the environs of London is more attractive than Richmond, delightfully situated on the slope of a hill overlooking the Thames on the Surrey side. It is an uphill walk of about a mile from the station to the beautiful *Terrace Gardens,* from which is gained that matchless **View** of woodland, water and tranquil pasture-land that poets and painters have vied with each other in depicting. By the acquisition of the Petersham meadows in the foreground and of the Marble Hill estate across the river at Twickenham, this view is now secured to the public for all time. Occupying the site and perpetuating the name of the historic hotel is the *Star and Garter Home* for Disabled Soldiers and Sailors, a beautiful building forming the Women's Memorial of the Great War. **Richmond Park,** 2,358 acres in extent and between ten and eleven miles in circumference, was first enclosed by Charles I. The Park is one of the most popular resorts of Londoners, and during week-ends and on public holidays the stream of cars on the principal thoroughfares is unending. Several convenient parking places are provided. Large herds of fallow and red deer roam the Park. The public *Golf Courses* are exceedingly popular. Nearly in the middle are the *Pen Ponds*, covering 18 acres, a favourite resort of skaters. The *White Lodge* was the residence before her marriage of Queen Mary, and was in 1894 the birthplace of King Edward VIII. The house figures, like Richmond Hill, in Scott's *Heart of Midlothian*. *Pembroke Lodge* was the seat of Lord John Russell.

The Richmond "Maids of Honour," it may be well to explain, are a kind of sweet cheese-cake.

South of Richmond, and reached from it by a pleasant walk either along the picturesque tow-path or through the Park, is the Royal Borough of **Kingston,** with Hampton Court Palace on the opposite bank of the river. At Kingston may be seen, enclosed by railings, the *Coronation Stone*, on which Athelstan and other Saxon kings were crowned. The stretch of river between Richmond and Kingston is very popular with boating parties. Kingston is the starting-point of Messrs. Salter Bros.' steamers to Henley and Oxford. See our *Guide to the Thames*.

St. Albans (Herts)

Rail from St. Pancras or King's Cross; or from Euston or Broad Street, *via* Watford (London Midland Region).
Bus Service from Golder's Green.
Road Route (20 m.) *via* Marble Arch, Cricklewood, Hendon, Edgware and Elstree; or (21 m.) *via* Great North Road to Barnet. Green Line Coaches from Victoria, Hyde Park Corner, Marble Arch and Judd Street (727).

This ancient city, the *Verulamium* of the Romans, and the burial-place of the great Francis Bacon, Viscount St. Albans, is well worth a pilgrimage from London. The **Cathedral** boasts one of the longest naves in England (275 ft.), and is a mixture of the Norman, Early English and Decorated styles, not too happily restored by the late Lord Grimthorpe. Bacon's monument is in *St. Michael's Church*, parts of which are even older than the Abbey. Excavations have revealed the *theatre* site of the Roman Verulamium (*admission*, 6d.) and Roman City Wall (*free*). Some of the most interesting of other "finds" can be viewed in the adjoining *Museum* (6d. covers also the hypocaust). The quaint round tavern known as *The Fighting Cocks* proudly claims to be the oldest inhabited house in England.

Southend and Westcliff

Rail from Fenchurch Street (35¾ m.), from Liverpool Street (41½ m.) and St. Pancras (42 m.).
Steamer from London Bridge during summer; *see* newspapers.
Road Route (about 45 m.) *via* Tottenham or Leyton to Woodford, where begins the Southend Road, affording a clear run right to Southend.

Southend shares with Brighton the advantage of being sufficiently near to London to be available as a place of residence for

City men and combines the usual "seaside" attractions with many peculiar to the River, including a constant procession of shipping to and from the busy Pool of London. The tide recedes so far that the Pier has a length of a mile and a half.

The Surrey Hills

Access.—Southern Region cheap tickets issued to the principal centres, available for return from a different station from that at which the rail is left on the outward journey; in many cases the available stations lie on either side of very beautiful tracts. Buses and the Green Line Coaches also run to the hills, but as much of the journey is through suburban highways crowded with vehicular traffic this is not recommended as a means of approach if a good train service is available. There are also day or half-day Motor Coach Tours.

The choicest features of the country immediately south of London are comprised in the chalk range running east and west some 10 to 15 miles from Town. On the northern edge the chief starting-points for exploration are Epsom (*see* p. 264), Leatherhead, Banstead and Purley. Along or near the southern edge of the range are such famous beauty-spots as Guildford, Box Hill (Dorking) and Leith Hill (965 ft.), the two latter with wonderful views across the Sussex Weald. Box Hill has been acquired for the nation and placed under the National Trust.

The Thames

Many Londoners still find their principal recreation on the Upper Thames, the river of pleasure *par excellence*. To quote the late Sydney Crossley:

"In point of real beauty, one questions whether the surroundings of the Thames are surpassed in the world. Grander scenery than that offered by Mapledurham, Cliveden, Marlow, Sonning, or the woods of Wytham is, of course, to be found in many places. But where is the simple rustic beauty of the Thames to be found elsewhere? Certain spots, occasional reaches, there may be on other rivers which rival certain reaches on it, but one knows of no single stream which presents such an endless variety of changing beauties as does the Thames. And there is something exceptionally English about it all. There is no single spot on the Thames that could be situated anywhere but in England."

To the average Londoner, the lower reaches by Richmond, Kingston, Molesey and Windsor are more familiar than the parts more particularly referred to above, but the Western Region line renders the whole stream up to and even beyond Henley available for a day, or even a half-day's boating or fishing. Those who merely wish to see the river in leisurely and pleasant fashion cannot do better than avail themselves of the excellent steam launches run daily in summer by Messrs. Salter Bros. between Kingston and Oxford. Two days are required for the entire trip, but passengers can board or leave the boats at any lock or stopping place. Motor-Coach Trips embrace some of the choicest scenery of the Thames Valley, and many allow time for a short boating excursion.

For a full description of the Thames and its many beauty spots, and for details as to excursions, see the *Guide to the Thames* in this series, containing specially-drawn charts of the river.

Waltham Abbey

Rail from Liverpool Street (12¾ m.) to Waltham Cross station.
Buses to Waltham Cross, connecting with a local service to Waltham Abbey. Green Line Coaches from Oxford Circus.
Trolleybus from Finsbury Park and Stamford Hill.

This ancient Abbey, situated on the Lea, about three miles from the western border of Epping Forest, was founded by the Saxon Harold, and here he knelt to pray before setting out for the fatal field of Hastings. The nave has been restored, and is now used as the parish church. **Waltham Cross,** a mile west of the Abbey, was erected by Edward I, like Charing Cross and others, to mark the places where the body of Queen Eleanor rested on its way from Grantham to London.

Whipsnade

Access.—Rail from St. Pancras (L.M.R.) to Luton, completing the journey by bus. It is well to inquire as to services before leaving London. Motor coaches, etc., from London.
Admission daily, including Sundays, from 10 a.m. to 7.30 p.m.or sunset if earlier. Adults, 2s., children, 1s.
Refreshments can be obtained at several pavilions in the extensive grounds.

The "Country Zoo" belonging to the Zoological Society and organised in connection with the Zoological Gardens in Regent's Park (p. 152) provides one of the most popular trips from Town. It is an area of 500 acres on the Chiltern Hills and the general purpose is to use it "as a park in which wild animals have more space and freedom than in London, and as a sanctuary for British wild birds and plants." Strangers should bear in mind that the animals here are not caged, but roam in large enclosures; field glasses are therefore sometimes useful.

Windsor and Eton

Rail (W.R.) from Paddington (21¼ m.), or from Waterloo (25¾ m.).
Buses from Hounslow. Green Line Coaches from Trafalgar Square.
Road Route (22½ m.) *via* Hammersmith, Chiswick, the Great West Road, Staines and Old Windsor (there are many alternative routes).

Windsor Castle

Admission.—When shown during the absence of the Court (*see* newspapers), the *State Apartments* and the *Queen's Doll's House* (entrance on North Terrace) are open to the public daily, except Sundays, from 11 to 3, Nov. 1 to March 31; until 4, April 1 to May 31 and during October; 11 to 5, June 1 to September 30. Adults are charged 1s.. children 6d. For the Queen's Doll's House the fee is 6d. The *Old Master Drawings* can be seen at the same times as the State Apartments, admission 6d. The *Albert Memorial Chapel* and the *Round Tower* are open on the same days and at the same hours as the State Apartments; the Round Tower is open only from April to September 30. The *Curfew Tower* (admission 6d.) can be seen any day on application to the keeper at the Tower at the back of the Horseshoe Cloister. *St. George's Chapel* may be viewed any week-day between 11 a.m. and 3.45 p.m.,

Sundays 2.30 to 4 p.m., admission 1s. except for services. The Chapel is usually closed during January. Guides are available to conduct visitors round the *Precincts* any week-day, 10–5 in summer; 10–4 winter. Apply at Henry VIII's Gateway.

Gratuities to guides and wardens of the Castle are forbidden.

Cars are allowed only on the metalled roadway running southward through the Park to Ascot and the speed limit must be strictly observed. Parking is usually permitted on the grass verge of one side of this roadway. No picnicking.

Windsor Castle, famous the world over as the residence of the British Sovereign, was founded by William the Conqueror, and has been extended and altered by nearly every succeeding monarch. Under Queen Victoria no less a sum than £900,000 was expended in this way, and King Edward VII carried out an extensive rearrangement and embellishment of the interior.

Even when the State Apartments are not accessible (*see above*) the visitor will find plenty to occupy and interest him. The Castle comprises two main portions, the **Lower Ward,** in which are St. George's Chapel, the Albert Memorial Chapel, the Horse Shoe Cloisters, and the residences of the Knights of Windsor and others; and the **Upper Ward,** in which are the State Apartments, the Queen's Private Apartments (scarcely ever shown), and the south wing, in which the royal guests and visitors are accommodated. Between the two portions is the massive **Round Tower,** which should be ascended for the sake of the extensive view over the Thames Valley. The Castle is nearly a mile in circumference.

Passing under **Henry VIII's Gateway,** we have before us **St. George's Chapel,** a beautiful example of the Perpendicular style, begun by Edward IV and completed by Henry VIII. In the richly-decorated Choir, with its fan-vaulting, are the stalls of the Knights of the Garter. A subterranean passage leads to the Tomb House, constructed by order of George III, below the Albert Memorial Chapel. Here lie the bodies of George III, George IV, William IV, George V and George VI.

The **Albert Memorial Chapel,** originally intended by Henry VIII for his own mausoleum, and afterwards presented to Cardinal Wolsey, was restored and sumptuously decorated by Queen Victoria in memory of the Prince Consort. The Chapel can only be seen from the barrier.

The **State Apartments,** in which foreign sovereigns visiting Her Majesty are accommodated, are entered from the North Terrace. They are beautifully furnished, and are hung with priceless pictures by Rubens, Rembrandt, Van Dyck, and others. Much of the carving was done by Grinling Gibbons. The **Waterloo Chamber,** used for banquets and theatrical performances, is entirely hung with portraits of persons associated with the close of Napoleon's military career.

Adjoining the entrance to the State Apartments is that to the **Queen's Doll's House,** a wonderfully exact model of a twentieth-century house, the building, furniture and equipment being on the scale of one-twelfth.

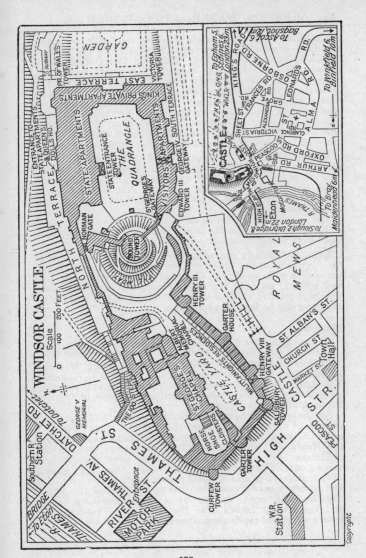

WINDSOR CASTLE

Scale

0   100   200 FEET

N

GARDEN

EAST TERRACE

KINGS PRIVATE APARTMENTS

PR. OF WALES TOWER
VICTORIA TOWER
SUBWAY

ENTRANCE TO
STATE APARTMENTS
& QUEEN'S
STATE APARTMENTS
(STATE APARTMENTS
& QUEEN'S DOLLS HO.)

NORTH TERRACE

STATE ENTRANCE TOWER

THE QUADRANGLE

STATE APARTMENTS

NORMAN GATE

ST. GEORGE'S GATE

VISITORS' APARTMENTS

SOUTH TERRACE

EDWARD III TOWER

GEORGE IV. GATEWAY

ROUND TOWER

HENRY III TOWER

GARTER HOUSE

GEORGE V. MEMORIAL

THE 100 STEPS

DATCHET RD.
To Datchet 2½m.

Southern R.
Station

ALBERT MEMORIAL CHAPEL

ST. GEORGE'S CHAPEL

MILIT KNIGHTS' RESIDENCES

CASTLE HILL

ROYAL MEWS

ST. ALBAN'S ST.

CHURCH ST.

HENRY VIII GATEWAY

MARKET ST.

Town Hall

HIGH

STR.

PEASCOD ST.

HORSE SHOE CLOISTERS

SALISBURY TOWER

GARTER TOWER

CURFEW TOWER

THAMES ST.

THAMES AV.

Entrance
RIVER ST.

MOTOR PARK

BRIDGE

To Eton 1m.
R. THAMES

W.R. Station

CASTLE ST.

Copyright

KING'S ROAD

To Ascot 6.
To Bagshot 11m.
To Ascot 6.
Binfield 10m.
To Winkfield 6.

R.D.

OSBORNE RD.

THE LONG WALK 3m. To London 23m.
To Egham 5.
To Egham 5. Staines 6.

GROVE RD.
FRANCES RD.
ST. LEONARDS RD.

ALMA RD.

SHEET ST.
VICTORIA ST.
CLARENCE RD.

OXFORD RD.

ARTHUR RD.
PEASCOD ST.

CASTLE

HIGH ST.

To Slough 2. Uxbridge 8.
London 22m.

To Bray.
Maidenhead 6m.

To Eton
R. THAMES

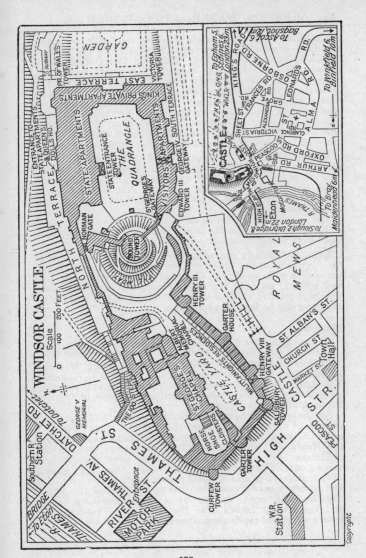

277

The **Home Park,** immediately adjoining the Castle, comprises about 400 acres, and is bordered on three sides by the Thames. Notable features are the *Long Walk* and *Queen Anne's Ride* (grass). Close to Frogmore House is the **Royal Mausoleum,** where rest the bodies of Queen Victoria and the Prince Consort (*open free to the public on one day only a year, on Whit-Mondays from 11 to 4. No ticket required*). **Windsor Great Park** stretches southward from the Castle for upwards of five miles, and comprises 18,000 acres. There are few restrictions for pedestrians. One of the finest views in England is that of the Castle from Snow Hill, at the southern end of the **Long Walk.**

Virginia Water is at the southern end of the Great Park, and may be directly reached from London by Southern Region to Virginia Water station (about 1½ miles distant). Coaches and buses also run from Windsor and from Staines and London. The route from London is by the Great West Road, Staines, and Egham by-pass.

The *Lake* (artificial) covers an area of about 150 acres, and is rather more than two miles long. The *Ruins*—genuine antiquities—were brought from Tripoli and re-erected in 1825.

Eton, immediately opposite Windsor, on the Bucks side of the river, is gained by crossing the bridge. The famous **College,** founded in 1440 by Henry VI, includes among its pupils, past and present, many of the greatest names in English history. The boys number about a thousand. Both School and Chapel can generally be seen on application.

Woolwich

Rail from Charing Cross, Cannon Street and London Bridge to Woolwich Arsenal station (10 m.). Trams and buses from Westminster and Blackfriars Bridge.

Visitors of British nationality desirous of seeing **Woolwich Arsenal** must obtain an order from the War Office, Whitehall. The Arsenal covers 600 acres, and employs several thousand men. Some of the operations, particularly those in the Gun Factory, are of great interest.

Southward is **Eltham,** with the banqueting hall and other remains of a Palace of Plantagenet and Tudor kings. Henry V spent Christmas at Eltham Palace after his victory at Agincourt, and Henry VIII and Elizabeth I passed several years of their childhood here. Extensive restorations have recently been carried out. The Great Hall (*open free on Thursdays; summer 11–7, winter 11–4*) has a fine hammer-beam timber roof, that was formerly only rivalled by that in the Hall of the Middle Temple. The moat, crossed by a fifteenth-century bridge, and the ancient houses close by, combine to make Eltham Palace a scene of captivating interest and beauty.

INDEX

Where more than one reference is given, the first is the principal. For Banks, Bridges, Churches, Clubs, Docks, Hospitals, Libraries, Music Halls, Monuments, Parks, Railway Stations, Railways, Theatres, *see* lists under those headings.

iii